*

AMERICAN WRITERS SERIES
*
HARRY HAYDEN CLARK
General Editor

*

*

AMERICAN WRITERS SERIES

Volumes of representative selections, prepared by American scholars under the general editorship of Harry H. Clark, University of Wisconsin

*

WILLIAM CULLEN BRYANT, *Tremaine McDowell, University of Minnesota*

JAMES FENIMORE COOPER, *Robert E. Spiller, Swarthmore College*

JONATHAN EDWARDS, *Clarence H. Faust, University of Chicago, and Thomas H. Johnson, Hackley School*

RALPH WALDO EMERSON, *Frederic I. Carpenter, Harvard University*

BENJAMIN FRANKLIN, *Frank L. Mott and Chester E. Jorgenson, University of Iowa*

ALEXANDER HAMILTON AND THOMAS JEFFERSON, *Frederick C. Prescott, Cornell University*

NATHANIEL HAWTHORNE, *Austin Warren, Boston University*

OLIVER WENDELL HOLMES, *Robert Shafer, University of Cincinnati*

WASHINGTON IRVING, *Henry A. Pochmann, Mississippi State College*

HENRY WADSWORTH LONGFELLOW, *Odell Shepard, Trinity College*

JAMES RUSSELL LOWELL, *Norman Foerster, University of Iowa and Harry H. Clark, University of Wisconsin*

HERMAN MELVILLE, *Willard Thorp, Princeton University*

THOMAS PAINE, *Harry H. Clark, University of Wisconsin*

EDGAR ALLAN POE, *Margaret Alterton, University of Iowa, and Hardin Craig, Stanford University*

SOUTHERN POETS, *Edd W. Parks, Cumberland University*

HENRY DAVID THOREAU, *Bartholow Crawford, University of Iowa*

MARK TWAIN, *Fred Lewis Pattee, Rollins College*

WALT WHITMAN, *Floyd Stovall, University of Texas*

JOHN GREENLEAF WHITTIER, *Harry H. Clark, University of Wisconsin*

*Pen drawing by Kerr Eby, after
a drawing by S. W. Cheney*

WILLIAM CULLEN BRYANT

ÆT. 51

William Cullen Bryant

REPRESENTATIVE SELECTIONS, WITH
INTRODUCTION, BIBLIOGRAPHY, AND NOTES

BY

TREMAINE McDOWELL

Associate Professor of English
University of Minnesota

AMERICAN BOOK COMPANY

New York · Cincinnati · Chicago
Boston · Atlanta

PREFACE

A century ago, Bryant was the greatest of American poets—although few of his contemporaries recognized his pre-eminence. Then, after a few years of unacknowledged supremacy in the early 1830's, he was surpassed by Poe and the New England group. But for several decades, his priority among native poets and his reputation as an editor brought him general recognition as a major American author. After his death, his reputation gradually declined, until today he has become a lesser figure in our literature. The present volume is not designed to re-establish him as a great poet. Rather, Bryant is here accepted for what he was: a poet of minor rank when judged by absolute standards, but a significant early Romanticist and a distinguished liberal when examined historically. And this liberalism is undoubtedly his most notable characteristic—because in the work of any transitional author such as Bryant, novel and forward-looking aspects are obviously more significant than are obligations to the past.

Bryant, returning from abroad at the age of fifty-eight, wore for the first time a beard, which he described as "the growth of my chin while wandering in the East." Thus disguised, he was not recognized at the dock by a representative of his own newspaper, the *Post;* and at Roslyn, he was mistaken for an Arabian sheik. But today we know the man Bryant only as an austere and bearded patriarch, while we know the poet Bryant only as the youthful author of "Thanatopsis." Students of literature, however, should know both poet and man in youth, in early manhood, and particularly in full maturity. To present the authentic Bryant in historical perspective, the introduction to this volume describes his inherited conservatism, traces the stages whereby his pen and his mind were emancipated, outlines his mature beliefs concerning politics, religion, and literature, and finally records the partial mediation of his late years. The selections from Bryant which follow are chosen to illustrate these steps in his development. Because prose is as important as poetry in such a study, his literary criticism, his travel letters, his tales, and his editorial utterances are all represented. (Bryant's prose is so little known, so rarely available to students, and so extensive that in the present volume it is given a disproportionately large amount of space as compared with his poetry, which, although obviously superior to his prose as literature, is so concise that it can be adequately sampled in relatively small compass.) Read and interpreted as a whole, his poetry and prose take on new meaning; and from them emerges a Bryant unfamiliar to the casual reader.

The poems are arranged in order of composition, an arrangement made possible by the work of Bryant himself, who dated many poems in manuscript, of Parke Godwin, who dated others, and of the present editor, who has corrected and augmented the findings of his predecessors. The prose is likewise arranged in order of composition, save that editorials from the *Post* are printed in one group. Each selection, unless statement to the contrary is made in the notes, is printed in the final form authorized by the author, the revisions of his literary executor, Parke Godwin, being ignored. Where no source for the text of individual poems is specifically indicated in the notes, the text is that of the *Poetical Works* of 1876, the last edition which passed through the poet's hands.

Three appendices are provided. The first is made up of uncollected or unpublished verse, chosen to illustrate Bryant's early interest in public affairs, nature, death, and love, and his later concern with Gothic terror. Of small literary merit, this verse is nevertheless of historical and biographical interest. The second appendix lists Bryant's literary essays and addresses, for the convenience of students who wish to investigate his long neglected but highly significant work as a pioneer in American criticism. The last appendix presents extracts from contemporary reviews of and essays on Bryant over a span of fifty-six years, from brief comment on *The Embargo* in 1808 to uncritical eulogy of *Thirty Poems* in 1864. These extracts serve two purposes: they chart the poet's reputation throughout his lifetime, and they record the simple merits and the obvious defects of his poetry.

All collected poems and prose included in this volume are used by special arrangement with D. Appleton-Century Company, the authorized publishers. Unpublished verse is printed with the generous consent of the Minna G. Goddard Estate and of Mr. Conrad G. Goddard.

Thanks are due to Mr. C. A. Moore, Mr. C. W. Nichols, and Mr. Stanley T. Williams, who have been so kind as to read the following introduction, and to the general editor of this series, Mr. Harry H. Clark, who has made helpful suggestions concerning the entire volume.

T. McD.

CONTENTS

WILLIAM CULLEN BRYANT

I. EARLY CONSERVATISM

Cullen Bryant was by all odds the most distinguished pupil at the exhibition which in 1808 brought to an end the school term in Cummington township, Hampshire County, Massachusetts. Thirteen years of age, he was already known in the county as a poet, he had published a pamphlet of verse in Boston, and he had been noticed by the most influential magazine in New England. Now he stood for the last time before the men who had shaped his early years—his schoolmaster, his pastor, his father, and his grandfather. And they, listening to Cullen's part in the exhibition, might well smile benignantly, for they had stamped on his receptive mind their major beliefs and prejudices.

The gentlemen now seated on the rough-hewn benches of the Cummington schoolhouse were of the same political party—all were Federalists. And such, of course, was Cullen Bryant. Frail in body and unskilled in physical combat, he early learned to use his pen as a weapon against his mates.[1] Encouraged by triumphs over his contemporaries and excited by the turmoil which followed the Embargo of 1807, he versified current Federalistic criticisms and libels of Thomas Jefferson and the Democrats. In his poem, "The Embargo," young Bryant voiced negative aspects of Federalism, attacking personal defects of the President, the stupidity of Democrats, and the vileness of "French intrigue." At the moment, Democracy was in his mind exemplified by a mob of blockheads "with gaping mouth,

[1] Bryant's boyish lampoons have disappeared; but crude doggerel replies from his victims survive. See Tremaine McDowell, "The Juvenile Verse of William Cullen Bryant," *Studies in Philology*, XXVI, 99–101 (Jan., 1929).

and stupid stare"—easy dupes of demagogues who ranted of liberty and equality and an easy millennium in which

> Spontaneous banquets shall succeed to want,
> No tax shall vex you, and no sheriff haunt.[2]

The citizens of Cummington were, in the main, rigidly orthodox in theology, even inclining toward extreme varieties of Calvinism. Cullen Bryant, promptly responding to this religionism all about him, versified the first chapter of Job at the age of ten. Then came a paraphrase of one of the Psalms and doggerel lines on the eclipse of 1806 and on the Judgment Day.[3] But better known were the solemn verses which he recited at the close of the school year, later to be printed in the *Hampshire Gazette*[4] and repeated by Massachusetts school children for some years thereafter. Here the boy ignored the incipient Unitarianism of that day and definitely accepted the orthodox creed of his community:

> Then let us tread, as lowly Jesus trod,
> The path that leads the sinner to his God;
> Keep Heaven's bright mansions ever in our eyes,
> Press tow'rds the mark and seize the glorious prize.

None of the guides who directed the early years of Cullen Bryant instilled in him the love of nature; rather, his affection for the world about him was intuitive and spontaneous. But, because he found no symbols to express this affection except the formalities of neo-classical pastoralism, his disquisitions on "contented ploughmen," droughts, and the Connecticut River were stiff with artifice and convention; and his stanzas were

---

[2] *The Embargo; . . . and Other Poems.* Boston: 1809, p. 14. The poems published in this volume are not included in Bryant's collected works. That students may know at what point in Bryant's career each of his utterances falls, the place and date of original publication of each item will be given in these footnotes when the item is first cited.

[3] See *Studies in Philology*, XXVI, 96–99.

[4] March 18, 1807. This poem is not included in Bryant's collected works.

filled with embowering woods and "celebrious streams," lovely flowerets and cultur'd gardens, spire-crown'd churches and humbler clustering spires, all breathed upon by fragrant zephyrs and the music of the spheres.[5]

Of the company now assembled in the small brown schoolhouse, those who concerned themselves with polite letters were disciples of neo-classicism. Therefore, when Cullen Bryant prayed that he "might receive the gift of poetic genius, and write verses that might endure,"[6] he was petitioning the Deity to make of him a small Augustan. Devotedly he studied "Johnson deep" and "Addison refined," but most ardently he pored over the pages where shone "Pope's celestial fire." Inevitably, the schoolboy's first lines were heroic couplets; and his early vocabulary was dominated by the commonplaces of poetic diction. And when "The Embargo" appeared, that satire was a patchwork of adaptations, imitations, and borrowings —conscious and unconscious—from the eighteenth-century wits. Thus at thirteen the boy, ignorant of the Romantic revolution already under way in England, still worshipped at empty shrines and dutifully sought to write

> With classic purity, unstudied ease,
> To sense instructive, pleasing to the ear,
> Correct, yet flowing, elegant and clear.[7]

In short, these early masters who listened to Cullen's valedictory had made of him a son of the eighteenth century, as devout as he was belated. And now, his years in the Cummington schoolhouse at an end, he went forth a Federalist, a Calvinist, and a Classicist. The stages whereby Bryant the youth and the man moved steadily away from this acquired

---

[5] *The Embargo; . . . and Other Poems*, pp. 27–29, 33–35.

[6] Autobiographical fragment by Bryant in Parke Godwin, *A Biography of William Cullen Bryant.* New York: 1883, I, 26.

[7] "The Reward of Literary Merit," *The Embargo; . . . and Other Poems*, p. 30.

conservatism toward Democracy, Unitarianism, and Romanticism form the chapters in the history of his mind and of his art.

II. POLITICAL IDEALISM

Partisan politics rarely occupied Cullen Bryant's mind in the years immediately following his departure from the Cummington school. But when he embarked upon the study of law, he naturally gave increased attention to contemporary events.[8] While the second war with England ran its course and New England became more outspoken in its opposition to the conflict, hot sectionalism rapidly undermined his hereditary Federalism. Soon he whipped himself into a frenzy of devotion to Massachusetts and proposed to enlist in the army which, he anticipated, would soon be raised to repulse federal usurpation. Before the future barrister could get himself into a uniform or fire a shot to make Massachusetts "an independent empire," peace was declared—an event which, he bemoaned, "has blown my military projects to the moon."[9]

After Bryant was established as a practising lawyer in Great Barrington, the Federal party gradually disintegrated and party alignments grew indistinct; Monroe was elected President without serious opposition; and "the era of good feeling" was inaugurated. During these auspicious years, Bryant was concerned more with the advancement of humanity than of party. Now his lifelong devotion to world peace found expression in his Phi Beta Kappa poem, "The Ages," where he viewed the past merely as a prelude to that happy time when man shall lay away the sword and enjoy

[8] Representative of Bryant's political verse of this period are three uncollected odes for the Fourth of July, printed in the *Hampshire Gazette*, July 15, 1812; *idem*, July 6, 1814; and the *Columbian Centinel*, July 8, 1815.

[9] Letter to Judge Samuel Howe, March 19, 1815, in Godwin, I, 137. Bryant expounded his secessionist views in detail in two letters, one to his father, Oct. 15, 1814, and the other to his brother Austin, Feb. 5, 1815, both published in Godwin, I, 128–130, 134–136.

the peace that yet shall be
When o'er earth's continents, and isles between,
The noise of war shall cease from sea to sea.[10]

But dearer to him than peace was the emancipation of mankind; and the Massachusetts lawyer ever welcomed shedding of blood in the name of liberty. He cursed the "degenerate Spaniards" who put their necks again within the yoke once broken by their patriot ancestors;[11] he eulogized the Greeks in their struggle for freedom;[12] and through the years he followed the fortunes of liberty on the Italian peninsula, eagerly awaiting the day when "Italy shall be free!"[13]

Meanwhile Bryant was giving thought to international trade. He had come to know the Sedgwick brothers of nearby Stockbridge—all distinguished liberals and all advocates of free trade. Influenced by these friends and by his reading in such economists as David Ricardo, Jean Baptiste Say, Adam Smith, and Henry Thornton, he became in Great Barrington a confirmed freetrader.[14] And when at last the Federalist party disappeared and when, because of devotion to protective tariffs, the majority of New Englanders became National-Republicans, the young lawyer's faith in free trade made of him a Democratic-Republican.[15]

When in 1826 Bryant began his half-century of service on the *New York Evening Post*, his political liberalism had assumed its final form—he was a democrat. Although he moved thereafter from party to party in the pursuit of his ideals, he actually

[10] "After a Tempest," *United States Literary Gazette*, I, 190 (Oct. 1, 1824).

[11] "Spain," written in 1822; and "Romero," *New-York Review*, II, 236 (Feb., 1829).

[12] "Song of the Greek Amazon," *United States Literary Gazette*, I, 253 (Dec. 1, 1824); and "The Greek Partisan," *idem*, II, 142–3 (May 10, 1825).

[13] "Italy," *New York Ledger*, Oct. 20, 1860.

[14] The works of these economists were available to Bryant in American editions during the 1820's. The exact details of his conversion to free trade are not known; for a general statement, see Godwin, I, 184.

[15] *Idem*, I, 185.

followed no new prophets and discovered no new gospels. Furthermore, he rarely analyzed his beliefs, nor did he attempt to discover their rational foundations, to defend them, or to organize them—to the mature Bryant, the truths on which he relied were self-evident. Because he found the reading public likewise unconcerned with theory but interested in persons and events, he rarely discussed his principles in the *Post*. Thus, since he undertook no elaborate exposition of his theories, they must be deduced from his concrete comments on men and issues.

Illuminating, for example, are Bryant's opinions of the men upon whom, as candidates for the presidency of the United States, he from time to time passed judgment. A romantic liking for hunters of the West[16] predisposed him to favor such a man as Andrew Jackson, and made it easy for the New York editor to discover in Old Hickory "simplicity and frankness, . . . incorruptible honesty, . . . [a] strong sense of justice, . . . [and] fearless directness."[17] But this prejudice for heroic frontiersmen at no point contravened his general liberalism. Rather, each ideal reinforced the other; and both combined to make him an ally of "the old hero" in his campaigns against high tariffs, the United States bank, paper money, and speculation.[18] But neither coonskin cap nor long rifle was alone sufficient to win the support of the *Post*. When General William Harrison's log-cabin, hard-cider campaign got under way, its fraudulent character at once disgusted Bryant, who turned against it the weapons of his ridicule and satire.[19] Nor was friendship with the editor in itself assurance that a candidate could rely on the aid of the *Post*. When Samuel J. Tilden, a friend of many years and an ancient comrade in anti-slavery battles, was nominated by the Democrats, Bryant had already

16 For Bryant's treatment of the frontier, see pp. xlvii–xlix below.
17 Quoted in Godwin, I, 242.
18 *Idem*, I, 242, 291, 324–5.   19 *Idem*, I, 381.

concluded that democracy was no longer served by the party which bore its name. He therefore refused to run as a presidential elector for Tilden or to support him editorially.[20] It is evident, then, that even though prejudice occasionally coincided with principle when Bryant evaluated public men, personalities were at no point allowed to interfere with the operation of his democratic faith.

Bryant's political idealism was further revealed in his editorial campaigns for more intelligent legislation on such matters as crime and punishment,[21] currency and banking,[22] and particularly free contract and free speech. Notable was his declaration in 1836 when the right of labor to make wage agreements was denied: "The idea that arrangements and combinations for certain rates of wages are injurious to trade and commerce, is as absurd as the idea that the current prices of the markets, which are always the result of understandings and combinations, are injurious."[23] Later he protested: "Can any thing be imagined more abhorrent to every sentiment of generosity or justice, than the law which arms the rich with the legal right to fix, by assize, the wages of the poor? If this is not SLAVERY, we have forgotten its definition."[24] Equally liberal was his attitude toward free speech:

The right to discuss freely and openly, by speech, by the pen, by the press, all political questions, and to examine and animadvert on all political institutions, is a right so clear and certain, so interwoven with our other liberties, so necessary, in

[20] *Idem*, II, 375–9.

[21] The *Post* aided in reshaping prison discipline in New York and in abolishing capital punishment in that state (*idem*, II, 261–2; Allan Nevins, *The Evening Post*. New York: 1922, p. 132).

[22] Bryant urged that the national currency be maintained on a sound basis, that lotteries be outlawed, that adequate bankruptcy laws be enacted, and that a sub-treasury system be established (*idem*, pp. 132, 351).

[23] *Post*, May 31, 1836. It was not to be expected that Bryant as a liberal of the 1830's should favor the use of violence to enforce picketing and to prevent laborers from working where they chose.

[24] *Idem*, June 13, 1836.

fact, to their existence, that without it we must fall at once
into despotism or anarchy. To say that he who holds unpopular opinions must hold them at the peril of his life, and that, if
he expresses them in public, he has only himself to blame if
they who disagree with him should rise and put him to death,
is to strike at all rights, all liberties, all protection of law,
and to justify or extenuate all crimes.[25]

Naturally the controversy over negro slavery brought from
Bryant his most persistent defense of human freedom. Having
as a Massachusetts lawyer announced his opposition to slavery,[26]
the editor of the *Post* was inclined to sympathize with the first
abolition societies when they appeared in the early 1830's.
Soon his paper was damned by Democratic leaders for its
sympathy with "those miscreants," the abolitionists.[27] When
the annexation of Texas as a slave state was proposed, the
Post denounced the scheme, although Bryant was too nationalistic to oppose, as did Lowell and Thoreau, the war with
Mexico. In 1848, he bolted the Democratic party and supported
the radical "Barnburners." When their Free Soil party col-
lapsed, he returned temporarily to the Democratic fold, where
he attacked with equal vigor his fellow partisan Clay and his
party opponent, Webster. His arraignment of the latter was
as severe as Whittier's:[28]

Mr. Webster [declared Bryant] stands before the public as a
man who has deserted the cause which he lately defended, deserted it under circumstances which force upon him the imputation of a sordid motive, deserted it when his apostasy was desired by the Administration, and immediately after an office

[25] *Idem*, Nov. 18, 1837. See also the *Post*, August 8, 1836.
[26] *An Oration. Delivered in Stockbridge. July 4, 1820.* Stockbridge:
1820, p. 10. This little-known address is not included in Bryant's collected
works.
[27] Nevins, pp. 145–8.
[28] Compare Bryant's utterance with Whittier's "Ichabod" and his later
poem, "The Lost Occasion," which is a modification but not a retraction
of his early condemnation of Webster.

had been conferred upon his son, to say nothing of what has been done by the Administration for his other relatives.[29]

At last, completely alienated by the Kansas-Nebraska bill, Bryant left the Democrats to become an early member of the Republican party. On the editorial page, he now characterized the Fugitive Slave Law as "the most ruffianly act ever authorized by a deliberative assembly;"[30] the cause of the Free-Soil men in Kansas as "a great and righteous cause;"[31] the Dred Scott decision as a "disgrace," a mere "trick of interpretation;"[32] and John Brown as one of the "martyrs and heroes" of history.[33] And when secession was proposed in the South, he abandoned his youthful arguments for states' rights and flatly announced: "If a State secedes, it is in rebellion, and the seceders are traitors."[34]

It remained for the Civil War to bring to white heat his passion for liberty. Prose was no longer an adequate vehicle for his emotion; the poet came to the aid of the editor:

> Oh country, marvel of the earth!
> O realm to sudden greatness grown!
> The age that gloried in thy birth,
> Shall it behold thee overthrown?
> Shall traitors lay that greatness low?
> No, land of Hope and Blessing, No![35]

Throughout the war, Bryant was an extremist, demanding in the *Post* that all thought of compromise with the South be abandoned, that no concessions be made to the border states or to Northern Democrats, and that every weapon be employed against the rebels: a complete blockade of their harbors, the use of ironclads against their forts, the emancipation of their slaves, and the confiscation of their property.[36] In the military

[29] Quoted in Nevins, p. 246
[30] Quoted in *idem*, p. 250.
[31] *Ibid.*
[32] *Idem*, p. 254-5.
[33] *Idem*, p. 258.
[34] *Post*, Nov. 12, 1860.
[35] "Not Yet," *New York Ledger*, August 17, 1861.
[36] Nevins, p. 286.

operations of Northern generals, he found incompetence and overcaution. His motto was: "We must have action."[37] Persistently he urged speed: "Promptness in filling up the ranks already thinned by the war, promptness in organizing and sending forward new regiments, promptness in moving on the enemy."[38] In the main, he was a supporter of Lincoln,[39] but for his caution Bryant had no patience. The *Post* frankly charged Lincoln with "languor," "slumbers," "want of earnestness," and indecision.[40] Only during the last year of the war did Bryant's strictures become less severe, when he admitted that the President had "gained wisdom with experience."[41] The coming of peace and the death of Lincoln again so moved the editor that he turned to poetry for full expression of his exaltation and his grief.[42] And thus at last the fiery Bryant paid just tribute to the moderation and the sanity of the Great Emancipator:

> Oh, slow to smite and swift to spare,
> Gentle and merciful and just!

These lucid pronouncements on men and events were for a half-century animated by the same central belief, namely, Bryant's simple faith that liberty for the individual is an infallible panacea for all political ills. To him, the only function of the state is to assure to every man full freedom. The duty of government is "to maintain the conditions of universal liberty or the equilibrium and harmony of the social forces so that the energies of the individual may the most freely act and expand, according

---

[37] *Post*, July 3, 1862.   [38] *Idem*, August 19, 1862.
[39] Bryant first saw Lincoln in 1832, when the former, riding alone across the Illinois prairie, met a troop of volunteers raised for the Black Hawk War and led by a "tall, awkward, uncouth lad, . . . whose conversation delighted him by its raciness and originality" (Godwin, I, 283). When next the two met, Bryant presided while Lincoln spoke in Cooper Union, New York. The editor now concluded that the Black Hawk volunteer was ready for the presidency; and the *Post* campaigned for Lincoln in 1860.
[40] *Post*, July 7 and 23, 1862.   [41] *Idem*, Sept. 20, 1864.
[42] "The Death of Slavery," *Atlantic Monthly*, XVIII, 120–1 (July, 1866); and "The Death of Lincoln," *Post*, April 20, 1865.

to his own judgment, his own capacities, his own views of the duties and destinies of man here upon earth. It must not undertake directly any enterprises of its own—religious, intellectual, artistic, or economical—but it must secure a perfectly safe and open field to every kind of enterprise and to every one of its members."[43] Bryant was a Utopian—a Utopian who frequently sought to remake society as a whole, through local and national reforms, but who was even more concerned with reaching the perfect state through the emancipation and the perfecting of individuals. Back of this rigorous individualism lay a moral passion for justice and a high ethical devotion to truth. Back of this simple political creed lay a deep reservoir of emotion, not often allowed expression in personal conduct but frequently pouring out on the editorial page. Thus reason and emotion combined to make of Bryant an altruistic and a vehement defender of "free soil, free labor, and free men"—one of the great political liberals of nineteenth-century America.

III. RELIGIOUS LIBERALISM

A gentleman, Bryant remarked late in life, does not publicly discuss his religion. Therefore, even though the poet is now frequently condemned as excessively didactic, he in fact made relatively few definite statements concerning his religious faith. However, these few utterances, together with the events of his life, reveal that he early abandoned the Calvinism of his boyhood.

During the years subsequent to Cullen's graduation from the Cummington school, no unorthodox ideas entered his head, be-

[43] Summary of Bryant's views by Parke Godwin, his fellow editor and son-in-law, Godwin, I, 254. Details of Bryant's utterances and actions concerning public affairs may be found in Godwin, I, 251–62, 291–2, 304–6, 312–64, 379–90, 405–23; II, 29–44, 55–6, 62–4, 73–93, 120–205, 221–32, 269–70, 339, 374–9, 402–4; in John Bigelow, *William Cullen Bryant*. Boston: 1890, pp. 70–116, 200–57; and in Nevins, pp. 121–38, 166–206, 242–405.

cause he was preparing for college under the personal supervision of devout clergymen.[44] But while he was a student at Williams College, the piety of its faculty and the rigidity of its laws could not insulate him from new and heterodox influences. One group of his contemporaries undoubtedly shook his faith in the conventions of religion when they stole and finally burned the chapel Bible and even, in a drunken carousal, performed a mock celebration of the sacrament. A second group, led by the most mature member of his class, a man of twenty-four, exposed the young Calvinist to Deism. A few years earlier, French philosophy had flooded the campuses of New England; and the doctrines of Volney still lingered in Williamstown—doctrines readily comprehensible by a mind as eager and receptive as young Bryant's.[45] A further liberalizing influence came from ancient classical poetry. The library of Williams College, he discovered, surpassed his father's private collection only in this one field; and here he read with particular eagerness, opening his mind to the influence of paganism in general and of Stoicism in particular.[46] But chief of the solvents operating on his Calvinism was his father's liberalism. Doctor Peter Bryant knew the early Unitarians of Boston, he subscribed to the journals of the new movement, and in the Cummington meetinghouse he dramatized his nonconformity by remaining seated during the singing of the trinitarian doxology.[47] The sober journals and the rational arguments of New England Unitarianism doubtless repelled many youths of that day; but the records of Cullen Bryant's reading prove that he was now genuinely interested in and capable of understanding the abstractions of metaphysics

[44] Tremaine McDowell, "Cullen Bryant Prepares for College," *South Atlantic Quarterly*, XXX, 125–33 (April, 1931).

[45] Tremaine McDowell, "Cullen Bryant at Williams College," *New England Quarterly*, I, 443–66 (Oct., 1928).

[46] *Idem*, I, 459–61.

[47] *Life and Poetry of John Howard Bryant*. [n.p.: 1894?], pp. 7–8; Godwin, I, 56.

and theology.[48] At sixteen, then, he was ready to break with the orthodoxy of Cummington.

This break was announced in "Thanatopsis." Written in the autumn of 1811 shortly before Bryant reached his seventeenth birthday, the poem voiced the youth's own reply to the question raised by Robert Blair, by Beilby Porteus, by Henry Kirke White: How shall a man face death?[49] Bryant knew well the answer of orthodox Cummington: Let a man accept the doctrines of historical Christianity and then joyously approach the grave as the gateway to a new and more beauteous existence in Paradise. Of all this, no word appeared either in the first version of "Thanatopsis" or in later revisions.[50] Although exponents of orthodoxy have read their own beliefs into the poem, the impartial observer finds in this discussion of death no reliance on the doctrines of election or conversion, on the delights of a future life or the joys of heaven, on Calvin or Christ.[51] Any citizen of Cum-

---

[48] For example, Bryant in 1809 and 1810 read Thomas Reid, *An Inquiry into the Human Mind* and Dugald Stewart, *Elements of the Philosophy of the Human Mind* (James Grant Wilson, *Bryant and His Friends*. New York: 1885, p. 430, footnote).

[49] Bryant in his last years could not recall exactly when the first draft of "Thanatopsis" was written. The evidence shows, however, that it was composed in September or October of 1811, when Bryant was still sixteen (see pp. 389–90 below).

[50] Although Bryant in 1821 added to "Thanatopsis" an introduction (putting into the mouth of Nature the lines which on first publication formed the entire poem) and a conclusion, and although he made slight revisions in the form of the poem during later years, it is highly significant that he nowhere altered its thought.

[51] It should be remembered that the "still voice" which speaks in the final version of "Thanatopsis" (line 17) is the voice of Nature, not of Cummington's God. Likewise, "that mysterious realm" (line 75) is not the Heaven of Calvinists but "the pale realms of death" (text of 1821). And finally, the "unfaltering trust" of the closing lines is the serene confidence which comes to any man who accepts with full confidence his own particular philosophy or religion—be it Stoic or Brahmin, Deistic or Confucian, Congregational or Presbyterian. Bryant in later years repeatedly consoled himself with the thought of rejoining loved ones in paradise, but from the writing of "Thanatopsis" in 1811 to the composition of "To a Waterfowl" in 1815, he did not turn for personal solace to the delights of a future life. Rather, he was now momentarily convinced that death brings only a "night of solid gloom" filled with "dreamless slumber" (see

mington who, after more than a decade of nurture in its severe orthodoxy, could omit from "Thanatopsis" all mention of these fundamental beliefs was either a madman or a rebel. And Bryant the youthful rebel was something of a Stoic and more of a Deist. During the four years which followed, he maintained this same non-Christian attitude. In the numerous poems of the period which dealt extensively or exclusively with death, he never accepted for himself the consolations of orthodox religion. For the moment he defied the grave, armed with the Stoic faith that death brings release from the miseries of human existence and the Deistic belief that the grave brings, not further individual existence, but final union with the insensate physical universe.[52]

When Bryant came of age, he opened a law office in the hamlet of Plainfield, and for the first time faced the world alone, without father or tutor to counsel or support him. The experience apparently had a sobering effect on him. Thereafter, Christian elements appeared more and more frequently in his poetry; and Bryant turned often to the God who guides the waterfowl "from zone to zone" in "certain flight," confident that He,

> In the long way that I must tread alone
> Will lead my steps aright.[53]

But he was never again a Calvinist; he turned, not to the orthodoxy of Cummington, but to the Unitarianism of Boston. Re-

---

the following uncollected poems: "A Chorus of Ghosts," "The Night Has Reached Its Solemn Noon," "Death's Messenger," and "Oh, Thou Whom the World Dreadeth," all published in Godwin, I, 115–17, 132; and "Not That from Life," *North American Review*, V, 338–9, Sept., 1817). It is therefore unwarranted to assume that this "unfaltering trust" is faith in the joys of immortality.

[52] The obvious Deism of the poem has been noted by Howard Mumford Jones (*America and French Culture, 1750–1848*. Chapel Hill: 1927, p. 317), who describes "Thanatopsis" as the emotional equivalent of Volney's prose (*idem*, p. 406).

[53] "To a Waterfowl," *North American Review*, VI, 383–4 (March, 1818). This return from youthful explorations of paganism to Christianity may be attributed to Bryant's early religious training, as well as to the sobriety and earnestness which became evident once the adolescent student of love and law had become a practicing attorney.

moving to Great Barrington, he found there no Unitarian society. Like all other reputable citizens, he became a pewholder in one of the orthodox churches (where he was "terribly prone to pick the sermons all to pieces"), but he became a member of none.[54] Addressing the local Bible Society, the young lawyer discreetly avoided controversial topics, but he suggested his own position by alluding to Christ merely as "the first Great Teacher of the Gospel." [55] By 1820, his liberalism had become so well known that he was asked to contribute to a new Unitarian hymnal. When the collection was published, it contained numerous tributes to the second member of the Trinity; but no such passages appeared in the hymns from Bryant's pen.[56]

The poet's religious beliefs had now assumed their mature form. Sometimes phrased in the diction of the older orthodoxy, these beliefs have often been mistaken for extreme conservatism. They were, however, for that day essentially liberal. For example, he employed familiar religious imagery which portrays God as a personal deity, with the attributes of humanity. But in reality, God was to him a spirit, transcending the anthropomorphic deity worshipped by the devout citizens of Cummington. The poet at times presented an active, almost human creator, but Bryant obviously employed the personal aspects of God metaphorically when he alluded to a deity who holds in his complacent arms, the earth, the air, the deep, and who shapes the universe into his own "boundless visible smile." [57] Nor can a personal God ever be identified with such an abstraction as

---

[54] D. D. Field, *History of the County of Berkshire.* Pittsfield: 1829, p. 141; Robert C. Waterston, *Tribute to William Cullen Bryant.* Boston: 1878, p. 9.

[55] "Address on the Bible," *Berkshire Star*, Jan. 29, 1818. This item is not included among Bryant's collected works.

[56] Bryant wrote Numbers 29, 73, 129, 157, and 373 in *A Collection of Psalms and Hymns, for Social and Private Worship.* New York: 1820. For an account of Bryant's later revision of his hymns, in which he alluded to Christ, see pp. lxvi f. and 396 below.

[57] "Song of the Stars," *United States Literary Gazette*, I, 349 (March 1, 1825).

"eternal change"[58] or defined as the "Flight of Time" or the "Great First Cause."[59] Not consciously committed to the faith of the Pantheists, Bryant nevertheless worshipped a deity closer to theirs than to that of his New England forebears.

Bryant's God in his severity bore a further superficial resemblance to the deity of Cummington. Actually, however, Bryant's deity in his destructive moods is not angered because mankind has affronted his dignity, disobeyed his mandates, or broken tribal laws. Rather, he is motivated by the poet's own undying passion for liberty and social justice. It is the lawless "conqueror of nations" and the assassin of human freedom who particularly are singled out for destruction by the divine "Scourge of Wrong." God's great agent, Death, whose function it is to "free the oppressed and crush the oppressor,"[60] smites the murderers of patriot Greeks and the persecutors of just Waldenses.[61] The wrath of God is, to Bryant's mind, more frequently constructive than punitive, and its chief purpose is to "proclaim liberty throughout the land" and

> To banish, from the groaning earth,
> All forms of tyranny and wrong.[62]

Bryant's deity, then, was not as much a God of anger as a champion of justice and liberty and truth—"the truth that made our fathers free."

Most devoutly of all, Bryant worshipped the God of love. Repeatedly the poet characterized him as "Bestower of health," "Giver of sunshine," and "Teacher of hopes"—"patient, . . . slow to avenge, and kind to spare." God's brow, although

---

[58] "The Flood of Years," *Scribner's Monthly*, XII, 562 (July, 1876).
[59] "An Evening Reverie," *Knickerbocker Magazine*, XVII, 68 (Jan., 1841); "Lectures on Poetry" (delivered in 1826), *Prose Writings*, I, 18.
[60] "The Massacre at Scio."
[61] *Ibid.* and "Hymn of the Waldenses," *United States Literary Gazette*, I, 156–7 (Sept. 1, 1824).
[62] "Proclaim Liberty throughout the Land," *Hymns*. New York: 1864, pp. 35–6.

"dread and dazzling," had never yet been forsaken by love.[63] This divine love, Bryant declared, bears

> Meekly with hate, and scorn and wrong
> And loads itself with generous cares,
> And toils, and hopes, and watches long.[64]

Of all the attributes of God, the poet emphasized most frequently his loving-kindness.

Often Bryant dealt with the physical world and its phenomena in the diction of conventional religion. But, contrary to the theology of his youth, he did not in maturity view the creation of the universe as a completed fact. True, God's creative activity in the past was perfect and in that sense, finished; but "the perpetual work" of creation nevertheless is "renewed forever." [65] This perpetual renewal Bryant interpreted in terms of flux and "the motions of eternal change." [66] In the "grand march of seasons, days and hours," [67] he sees God's hand still actively molding nature, ever creating and recreating through "the vast cycle of being." From "The Ages" of 1821 to "The Flood of Years" of 1876, Bryant celebrated that "eternal change which is the life of Nature" [68] and ever "waits on growth," [69] characterizing his God as the "great Movement of the Universe." Here Bryant followed, not Darwin, but eighteenth-century exponents of perfectibility.[70]

[63] "The Loving-kindness of Our God" and "Imploring the Divine Compassion," *A Collection of Psalms and Hymns*, nos. 29 and 73 [no page numbers].

[64] "Except the Lord Build the House," *Hymns*, pp. 22–3.

[65] "A Forest Hymn," *United States Literary Gazette*, II, 29 (April 1, 1825).

[66] "The Fountain," *Democratic Review*, V, 408 (April, 1839) and "An Evening Revery." In the latter poem, Bryant alludes to "the circle of eternal change."

[67] "The Life That Is," *Thirty Poems*. New York: 1864, p. 50.

[68] "The Evening Wind," *The Talisman for 1830*. New York: 1829, p. 6.

[69] "The Flood of Years."

[70] For Bryant's mature rejection of Darwin, see his remarks on "Darwin's Theory," delivered in 1871 (*Prose Writings*, II, 291–3).

Finally, Bryant's conception of mankind was externally colored, like all his religious thought, by ancient beliefs. Thus his frequent references to the fall of man as recorded in Genesis, to human "sorrows, crimes, and cares," and to a world "full of guilt and misery" clearly echo the theology of his ancestors. But Bryant in maturity never accepted the belief that man is by nature utterly evil or that the race is destined for destruction. Rather, he believed that "boundless goodness and infinite power . . . pervades and upholds" all men.[71] He concluded that in the long conflict between this goodness and the evil which is also manifest in humanity, goodness will eventually triumph and man will eventually be perfected. In "The Ages" he proposed that thoughtful observers should "sit at the feet of History" and learn from her of the progress already made by humanity. In the past, such evils as cruel neglect of the sick and the diseased, open murder, and savage warfare for conquest had been publicly countenanced; now such inhumanity is outlawed; and

> a thousand cheerful omens give
> Hope of yet happier days, whose dawn is nigh.

The agent for the perfecting of man is the same power which ever shapes nature—"the motions of eternal change." When man shall at length reach his full perfection, then shall progress make his earth a heaven, for

> He who has tamed the elements, shall not live
> The slave of his own passions; he whose eye
> Unwinds the eternal dances of the sky,
> And in the abyss of brightness dares to span

---

[71] "Lectures on Poetry," *loc. cit.*, I, 18. Here Bryant is discussing human goodness or "the power that is our own," rather than "the power that is above" (*ibid.*). Forty years later, Bryant in "Among the Trees" (*Putnam's Magazine*, N.S., III, 15, January, 1869) was still hopefully looking toward
> An age when, in the eternal strife between
> Evil and Good, the Power of Good shall win
> A grander mastery.

The sun's broad circle, rising yet more high,
  In God's magnificent works his will shall scan—
And love and peace shall make their paradise with man.[72]

This Christianity of Bryant's middle years is accurately described by no tag or label. He was ever ethical, but he was no dogmatist. He neither formulated nor accepted theological creeds. Eclectic in his beliefs, he was equally catholic in worship. Finding the groves God's true temples, he worshipped there; when it was inconvenient to pray beneath the sky, one meetinghouse was as acceptable as another—in Great Barrington he sat among the Congregationalists; in Roslyn, among the Presbyterians; in New York, among the Unitarians. But devout in worship, virtuous in conduct, and didactic in spirit as Bryant was, strictly orthodox according to the theology of his own generation he was not. The continued influence of his early Deism combined with his later Unitarianism to make him definitely heterodox. And, as one who could not accept the doctrine of the trinity, he was little better than an infidel in the eyes of conservatives. For was not his aging contemporary, James Fenimore Cooper, roundly denouncing Unitarianism as a godless abomination, shamelessly pushing onward "with the goal of infidelity in open view"?[73]

IV. NATURE

"I was always," declared Bryant, "from my earliest years a delighted observer of external nature—the splendors of a winter daybreak over the wide wastes of snow seen from our windows, the glories of the autumnal woods, the gloomy approaches of the thunderstorm, and its departure amid sunshine and rainbows,

[72] "The Ages," *Poems.* Cambridge: 1821, pp. 7–21. Although Bryant never became as unreserved a believer in natural goodness as had been Thomas Paine or Philip Freneau, he never abandoned his optimistic faith in human perfectibility. Thus at the age of seventy-four, he reiterated this ideal in "Among the Trees."
[73] *The Redskins.* New York: 1846, II, 129–30.

the return of spring, with its flowers, and the first snowfall of winter."[74] A tiny boy, he slipped away to the brook near the homestead to gather blossoms. Then followed longer excursions over the Hampshire hillsides, until at length he came to know every stream and every tree for miles about. The sunshine and the clouds became his friends; when he escaped to nature, he was in the presence of a spirit

> With whom I early grew familiar, one
> Who never had a frown for me, whose voice
> Never rebuked me for the hours I stole
> From cares I loved not.[75]

Then came to Bryant ecstatic moments, when

'Mong the high and hoar fells that for ages have listened
  To the rush of the pebble-paved river between,
Where the king-fisher screamed, and gray precipice glistened,
  All breathless with awe have I gazed on the scene.

Now thrilled his young veins and throbbed his young bosom, while

> Each gaze at the glories of earth, sky, and ocean
>   To my kindled emotions was wind over fire.[76]

Just at the point where the youthful Bryant was reaching out for fit Romantic symbols to express this passionate delight in the physical universe, he left behind him Cummington and its beloved hills. For several years thereafter, his communion with nature was broken and fragmentary. Returning occasionally to the homestead, he again found himself for brief moments at one with nature and was moved to write "The Yellow Violet" and

[74] Quoted in Godwin, I, 25.

[75] "A Winter Piece," *The Idle Man*, Vol. II, no. 4, p. 6 (1822). For a discussion of Wordsworth's influence on Bryant, clearly evident in these lines, see pp. xlii–xlv below.

[76] "Stanzas," *New-York Review*, I, 200 (Feb., 1826), later revised under the title, "I Cannot Forget with What Fervid Devotion."

such unpublished lyrics as "This Grassy Slope, This Ancient Tree." [77] But even these precious experiences became rare, for he now passed into a period of youthful despair. As a student of law, Bryant speculated concerning and innocently experimented with life until, to his own heated fancy, his spirit was soiled and his soul was wearied. Then, revisiting the scenes of his early ecstasies, he imagined himself rejected by nature, and he sadly exclaimed:

> I have mixed with the world, and its follies have stained me,
> No longer your pure rural worshipper now. [78]

Settled at Great Barrington in 1816, his wanderings and uncertainties at an end, Bryant slowly became intimate with the streams and mountains of western Massachusetts. Within a few years, he came to know the varied charms of Green River, of the winds of the Berkshires, and of walks among their valleys. Eventually his communion with nature became as close, if not as ecstatic, as it had been among the Cummington hills; and his heart was completely won by the beauty of the western counties. Often and ever delightedly he climbed their peaks, and entranced he gazed down upon the

> glorious realm outspread—
> Yon stretching valleys, green and gay,
> And yon free hill-tops, o'er whose head
> The loose white clouds are borne away. [79]

His joy in river and forest persisted amid the rigors of the various seasons for, with remarkable persistence, he pursued nature through the calendar, from windy March to May and June, through the droughts and thundershowers of midsummer, on into mellow October and November, and back again to the

[77] For this poem, see Appendix I, p. 352.
[78] "Stanzas." For a discussion of the influence of Byron on Bryant during these years, see pp. xl–xlii below.
[79] "The West Wind," *The Idle Man*, Vol. II, no. 1, p. 155 (1822).

harsh storms of January. Thus, long before Whittier recounted
the joys of winter at a New England fireside, Bryant knew the
more virile pleasures of winter walks and winter woods. Conditions were at last propitious. Bryant's ear was attuned to the
voice of the western Berkshires. He was familiar with the poetry
of Wordsworth. He was stimulated by commendation from the
editors of the *North American Review* and their friends.[80] He
had in 1821 fathered a slender volume of verse. Now came a request for regular contributions to the *United States Literary
Gazette*. He responded in 1824 and 1825 with a rich series of
poems which established him as the first distinguished Romantic
poet of nature in America.[81] In these poems he revealed his
mature conception of the natural world, a conception not to be
altered during the half-century which followed.

The poetry of nature written by Bryant had, first of all, a most
substantial basis. Doctor Peter Bryant made his own drugs and
he early instructed his sons in botany. Cullen continued its
study through his youth, and in young manhood assembled a
modest but useful scientific library of his own. A "passionate
botanist" himself, he taught his family and his friends to botan-
ize, even inveigling the latter into scientific expeditions which
kept them from their regular duties for an entire day.[82] In this
manner, the poet came to know "the name of every tree, flower,
and spire of grass" in the Berkshires.[83] Specific references to
plants and flowers in his poetry are therefore to be accepted as

[80] Tremaine McDowell, "Bryant and *The North American Review*,"
American Literature, I, 14–26 (March, 1929).

[81] Representative of Bryant's contributions to the *Gazette* are "The
Rivulet," "March," "Summer Wind," "After a Tempest," "Autumn
Woods," "November," "To a Cloud," and "Hymn to the North Star."

[82] *The Bryant Record.* Princeton: 1898, p. 98; Charles J. Taylor, *Western Massachusetts.* New York: 1926, II, 585. For evidence of Bryant's
later interest in botany, see his address, "Our Native Fruits and Flowers,"
Prose Writings, II, 194–202, and his editorials in the *Post* urging a central park in New York City.

[83] Recollection of Bryant's friend, Colonel Taylor, quoted in Godwin,
I, 203.

authentic, despite an ill-informed attempt by John Burroughs to convict the poet of error.[84] A tabulation by a student of American letters has revealed that Bryant's allusions to natural objects are as varied and extensive as they are accurate. His birds and mammals are sufficient to stock a zoological garden; his trees are nearly thirty in number; and, of all the flowers known to him, some forty-five were mentioned in his poetry.[85]

That this adherence to American themes was conscious is made clear by a letter from Bryant to his brother:

I saw some lines by you to the skylark. Did you ever see such a bird? Let me counsel you to draw your own images, in describing Nature, from what you observe around you. . . . The skylark is an English bird, and an American who has never visited Europe has no right to be in raptures about it.[86]

Therefore, because Bryant's reporting was not only accurate but considered, to him belongs all honor as a pioneer recorder of New England scenes. "It is his proper praise," said Emerson, "that he first and he only made known to mankind our northern landscape." [87] And, because the flora and fauna of other sections of the United States had heretofore been merely catalogued and tabulated in verse, Bryant was the first notable painter of landscapes among American poets.

The relation between nature and its Deity was never exactly

[84] John Burroughs in *Pepacton* (Boston: 1888, pp. 105–111) fallaciously based his criticism of Bryant on his own knowledge of other regions. That Bryant is accurate in recording data of the flora of his own peculiar upland region is proved beyond contention by a contemporary "Table of Plants" published in 1829 by Field (*History of the County of Berkshire*, pp. 61–7).

[85] Norman Foerster, *Nature in American Literature*. New York: 1923, p. 10. For a notable discussion of several aspects of Bryant's treatment of nature, see Foerster's entire essay (*idem*, pp. 7–19). The use of nature by early American authors is examined in Mary E. Woolley, "The Development of the Love of Romantic Scenery in America," *American Historical Review*, III, 56–66 (Oct., 1897) and Selden L. Whitcomb, "Nature in Early American Literature," *Sewanee Review*, II, 159–79 (Feb., 1894).

[86] Quoted in Godwin, I, 281–2.

[87] *The Bryant Festival at "The Century."* New York: 1865, p. 17.

defined by Bryant. In his early Romantic poems of nature, he weighed the possibility that the universe might be an emanation of God. The wind was his breath; the stars became his "visible smile"; and "the barky trunks," the "fresh moist ground" [88] were "all instinct" with him. And when Bryant characterized a delicate forest flower as "an emanation of the dwelling life," he fell for an instant into Pantheism. Immediately, however, his conception of the Creator and of his Creation shifted; nature was reduced to a mere "token" of God; and his momentary Pantheism vanished.[89] In later years this occasional brightness faded and the poet no longer attempted actually to fuse God and the universe.

The relation between nature and Bryant was most notable for its joyousness. Inevitably he found in the heart of the universe emotions other than gladness—melancholy days often fill his autumn woods with sadness and, on occasion, all the earth mourns with man, uplifting "a general cry for guilt and wrong." [90] But to no other American poet has nature seemed more joyous than to the supposedly somber Bryant. For him, as for Wordsworth, the rocks breathed tranquillity and the trees shed contentment; the sky radiated joy and the clouds played gaily in space. In his presence, flowers smiled and rivulets laughed continually; squirrels chirped in merriment and birds sported in wantonness of spirit; leaves and shadows danced; and even insects experienced their "daily gladness." [91] This appreciation of "Dame Nature's laughter," early announced in his poetry, grew steadily as he became more sharply disillusioned concerning mankind, particularly concerning "the sons of strife" and "the jostling crowd" who filled public life.[92] This gladness persisted

---

[88] "A Forest Hymn."   [89] *Ibid.*
[90] "Earth," *New-York Mirror*, XII, 307 (March 28, 1835).
[91] "Inscription for the Entrance to a Wood," *North American Review*, V, 340 (Sept., 1817); "Life," *The Fountain and Other Poems*. New York: 1842, pp. 35-40.
[92] "Green River."

in Bryant's universe even during his sober later years, when at
sixty he could write the lilting lines of "Robert of Lincoln." [93]
That the joyousness of nature was actually the poet's emotion
projected into the universe did not lessen, for him, the poig-
nancy of these ecstatic experiences. Thus when nature met
Bryant in optimistic mood, joy communed with gladness.

Of the many aspects of external nature which brought delight
to Bryant, he wooed most persistently the wind, the rain, and
the tempest. Bryant's mother, like most eighteenth-century
diarists, made in her journal daily records of the wind; and her
son was equally faithful but vastly more romantic in observing
the weather. Breezes blow almost constantly through his poems.
Particularly charming was the wind of his Hampshire hills
which, he declared,

> shall come to thee,
> Like one that loves thee nor will let thee pass
> Ungreeted, and shall give its light embrace.[94]

Not only was the breeze a lover; but Bryant was its suitor:

> For me, I lie
> Languidly in the shade, where the thick turf,
> Yet virgin from the kisses of the sun,
> Retains some freshness, and I woo the wind.[95]

Thus embracing the wind and embraced by it, he decorously
took his place among the Romantic generation who clasped
rocks to their hearts and bestowed kisses on the universe. As for
the rain and the storm, they delighted Bryant by their pleasing
darkness and their agreeable terror. The rain "sheds a nameless
horror round" [96] while it shrouds upland steeps and hollow vales,

[93] *Putnam's Monthly*, XXX, 576–7 (June, 1855).
[94] These lines were added to "Inscription for the Entrance to a Wood"
in 1821.
[95] "Summer Wind," *United States Literary Gazette*, I, 107 (July 15,
1824).
[96] "The Hurricane," *The Talisman for 1828*. New York: 1827, pp.
114–5.

drives squirrel and butterfly to cover, and blots out the very sun. Then

> slowly falls the dull blank night, and still
> All through the starless hours, the mighty Rain
> Smites with perpetual sound the forest-leaves,
> And beats the matted grass.[97]

With even keener joy, he welcomed violent storm and tempest. While the poet waits "with a thrill in every vein," the hurricane approaches—"silent, and slow, and terribly strong." And when it strikes, the poet shouts:

> He is come! he is come! do ye not behold
> His ample robes on the wind unrolled?
> Giant of air! we bid thee hail![98]

The austerity of bearing evident in Bryant the New York editor has long led historians to assume that he was incapable of writing ecstatically on any theme; but the emotional and at times sensuous elements in his treatment of wind, storm, and rain clearly demonstrate that he was essentially a Romantic.[99]

In nature Bryant found much besides joy and pleasing terror. Here was education for youth: companionship, counsel, revery, and ecstasy for the boy Cullen;[100] culture for the girl who eventually became his wife;[101] and nurture for their small

[97] "A Rain-Dream," *Crayon*, I, 25 (Jan. 10, 1855).

[98] "The Hurricane." Similar delight in the tempest is expressed in "A Hymn of the Sea" (*Christian Examiner*, XXXIII, 95–6, Sept., 1842) and in certain stanzas of "The Winds" (*Knickerbocker Magazine*, XIV, 162, August, 1839), of which the following is representative:

> What change is this! Ye take the cataract's sound;
> Ye take the whirlpool's fury and its might;
> The mountain shudders as ye sweep the ground;
> The valley woods lie prone beneath your flight.

[99] The sensuous nature of Bryant's allusions to the breeze was excellently discussed in 1923 by Foerster in *Nature in American Literature*, p. 11.

[100] The doctrine of education by nature is clearly implicit in such poems as "The Rivulet," "A Winter Piece," and "I Cannot Forget the High Spell that Enchanted."

[101] The influence of nature on Frances Fairchild is recorded in that obviously Wordsworthian poem, "Oh Fairest of the Rural Maids" (*Poems*. New York: 1832, p. 125), and in the hitherto unpublished verses entitled "Housatonic" (see Appendix I, p. 354).

daughter, solicitously introduced to nature by the poet himself:

> For I have taught her, with delighted eye,
>   To gaze upon the mountains—to behold,
> With deep affection, the pure ample sky
>   And clouds along its blue abysses rolled,
> To love the song of waters, and to hear
> The melody of winds with charmèd ear.[102]

Here Bryant himself found, again in Wordsworthian fashion, a healing balm for his sick heart, borne by a spirit that spoke to him and soothed him.[103]

>   The calm shade
>   Shall bring a kindred calm, and the sweet breeze
>   That makes the green leaves dance, shall waft a balm
>   To thy sick heart.[104]

And here too was remembrance. Mankind, during Bryant's middle age and his last years, lost "the coloring of romance" which it once wore. But nature, changing not, retained its earlier radiance. Thus the man returned to tree and stream that they might remind him of the splendor and the dignity which in his youth had clothed all humanity. Often and persistently, therefore, he sought in the physical universe reality or God, joy or terror, wisdom or peace. And it was in his poetry of nature that Bryant's Romantic instincts and his poetic genius both came to fullest, most memorable expression.

V. LITERARY ROMANTICISM

While Bryant thus voiced his passionate delight in nature, he was at the same time writing on other Romantic themes, experi-

[102] "Lines on Revisiting the Country," *New-York Review*, I, 246 (August, 1825).
[103] "A Winter Piece."
[104] These lines were added to "Inscription for the Entrance to a Wood" in 1821.

menting in new and varied verse-forms, and defending the critical tenets of the Romantic movement.

His youthful transition from the Augustans was guided by Blair, White, Cowper, and Thomson. Particularly to the work of this last author, Bryant in old age paid high tribute.[105] That in 1811 the young poet was conscious of the revolutionary elements in the poetry of Thomson and his contemporaries is inconceivable; but their influence on the first version of "Thanatopsis" is clearly evident.

Of the poets of the Romantic generation proper, Lord Byron was the first whom the young American imitated. As a student of law, he thought much and wrote often of love, producing a group of some twenty-five poems,[106] centering about either an imaginary affair with a nymph created by his own fancy or an actual affection for a "beautiful and accomplished" young lady from Rhode Island, a visitor at the Bryant homestead.[107] Although the earlier effusions in this series are idyllic in tone, others are touched with melancholy. Typical are these sentimental lines, hitherto unpublished:

[105] Bryant in 1871 said: "Before the time of Burns there was a long period in which the poets of Great Britain 'looked at nature through the spectacles of books'—a period during which, as remarked by Wordsworth, scarce a single new image from nature found its way into their verses. They contented themselves with ringing the changes on those which the authors before them had made familiar. Then arose a Scottish poet, James Thomson, who flung these spectacles to the ground, crushing them under his remorseless heel, and looking at nature with his own unassisted and clear sighted eyes, crowded his poem of the seasons with images as new, fresh, and bright as Nature herself. He it was who, in the time of Pope, when the poetry in vogue was the poetry of the drawing-room, started boldly away from the common track, and, to the wonder and delight of his readers, gave them the poetry of the woods and fields, and, in part of his poem, the poetry of the household" ("Speech at the Burns Anniversary, January 25, 1871," *Prose Writings*, II, 321).

[106] Bryant, revealing excellent critical judgment, published none of these love poems. More than a dozen are printed in part or in whole in Godwin, I, 108–117. An additional dozen are preserved in manuscript.

[107] Godwin, I, 107. According to Bryant's brother Arthur, the two lovers "maintained an earnest correspondence." Godwin deduces that the affair "did not run smoothly, and the end proved very painful." It has been impossible to identify the young lady.

> Nymph of the darkly glancing eye
>> And soul-expressive face
> Say whence that frequent deep drawn sigh
>> That air of pensive grace
> Say what can plant the thorns of care
>> Beneath that breast of snow
> A form so bright and mind so fair
> A pang should never know [108]

Then the lover's gentle sorrow deepened into black despair until, to the supposed sorrow of friends and family, he fell into the sere and yellow leaf, "withered," he soberly insisted, "withered before a woman's eye." [109] Whenever he returned to Cummington, he felt the guilt and sin of life had so polluted his youthful innocence that the whole universe shrank "from the signet of care" on his brow.[110] This signet of care obviously came not as much from his own harmless philandering as from the poetry of Byron. The young student of law was in fact so ardent an

[108] Published from the original manuscript with the consent of the Minna G. Goddard Estate and Mr. Conrad G. Goddard. Bryant rarely punctuated his poems until he prepared a final draft for publication.

[109] Three stanzas will illustrate the lad's real or fancied despair (Godwin, I, 110):

> "Yet, sometimes there dejected strays
> The genius of my better days;
> And I am troubled when I trace
> The darkened grandeur of his face,
> While thus he breathes his warnings high,
> Betwixt rebuke and prophecy.
>
> " 'When riper years this dream dispel,
> Thy heart shall rue its folly well;
> And thou with bitter tears shall gaze
> On the blank train of wasted days;
> And curse the withering spell at length,
> That broke thy early spirit's strength.
>
> " 'There were, in early life, of thee
> Who augured high and happily;
> Who loved and watched the opening shoot,
> And propped the stem and looked for fruit;
> And they shall see its blossoms die,
> Withered before a woman's eye.' "

[110] "Inscription for the Entrance to a Wood."

admirer of Childe Harold that he refused to accept *Lara* as actually a production of the master himself:

It possesses some merit, but I think it cannot be written by Lord Byron. The flow of this poet's versification is admirably copied, but it seems to me to want his energy of expression, his exuberance of thought, the peculiar vein of melancholy which imparts its tinge to everything he writes; in short, all the stronger features of his genius. Conrad, ... who makes his appearance in this tale as a Spanish peer, under the name of "Lara," is degenerated into a lurking assassin, a midnight murderer. ... May it not be the effort of some American genius? [111]

But after the young poet had passed out of his period of adolescent love, Byron was no longer his master; and only distant echoes of Childe Harold remained.[112]

Bryant recalled concerning his first reading of *Lyrical Ballads:* "A thousand springs seemed to gush up at once into my heart and the face of Nature, of a sudden, to change into a strange freshness and life." [113] He apparently met the poetry of

[111] To William Baylies, Dec., 1815, quoted in Godwin, I, 133.

[112] After Byron no longer influenced Bryant's verse, he still exercised a personal fascination over the American, because in 1824 the latter, his eyes moist, rebuked a flippant reference to the author of *Don Juan* with the command: "Silence, sir! poor Byron is now no more" (Godwin, I, 205). It is said, however, that in old age Bryant no longer respected Byron the man (John Bigelow, quoted in *The Bryant Festival at "The Century,"* pp. 57–8). His final verdict on Byron the poet ("Introduction," *A Library of Poetry and Song*. New York: 1871, p. xxix) was as follows: "The genius of Byron was of a more vigorous mould than that of Keats; but notwithstanding his great popularity and the number of his imitators at one time, he made a less permanent impression on the character of English poetry. His misanthropy and gloom, his scoffing vein, and the fierceness of his animosities, after the first glow of admiration was over, had a repellent effect upon readers, and made them turn to more cheerful strains." For a general account of Byron's reputation and vogue in the United States, see W. E. Leonard, *Byron and Byronism in America* (Boston: 1905), where it is suggested that Byron influenced Bryant's "The Ages" and "A Meditation on Rhode Island Coal."

[113] Statement of Bryant to Richard Henry Dana, reported by the latter in *Poems and Prose Writings*. Boston: 1833, p. 148. It has been suggested that Dana's own enthusiasm for Wordsworth may have colored his recollection of Bryant's original statement.

Wordsworth, the second and last of his masters among the English Romanticists, while studying law at Worthington, presumably during the winter of 1811-12.[114] But the young student, more concerned with love than with nature, was now following Byron as his model. By 1815, Wordsworthian undertones appeared in "The Yellow Violet" and "Inscription for the Entrance to a Wood."[115] Not until Bryant had become intimately acquainted with the streams and mountains of Berkshire did the influence of *Lyrical Ballads* become fully evident in his verse. Then his treatment of nature, in the familiar opening of "Thanatopsis" (added in 1821), in "A Walk at Sunset," in "The Rivulet," and in the hitherto unpublished poem, "The Early Anemone,"[116] became distinctly Wordsworthian. In certain lines of "Summer Wind," "A Forest Hymn," and "The Conjunction of Jupiter and Venus," not only the thought but also the versification is reminiscent of the English poet.[117] Feeble as is his imitation of Wordsworth's verse in "Monument Mountain," Bryant in "A Winter Piece" wrote lines which the author of "The Prelude" might have acknowledged without shame as his own:

[114] Godwin, I, 104.

[115] "The Yellow Violet" (*Poems*. Cambridge: 1821, pp. 33–4) bears a resemblance to Wordsworth's first poem "To a Daisy" (but not as definite a resemblance as Wordsworth's poem bears to the familiar lines of Burns on the same flower); and the "Inscription" announces Bryant's belief in the curative power of nature, a doctrine popularized but certainly not originated by Wordsworth.

[116] "The Early Anemone" appears in Appendix I, p. 355.

[117] Wordsworth clearly influenced both the substance and the style of Bryant's discussion of impulse in "The Conjunction of Jupiter and Venus" (*United States Literary Gazette*, IV, 451, Sept., 1826). Having declared that he would not always follow reason, Bryant goes on to say:

> the spirit needs
> Impulses from a deeper source than hers,
> And there are motions, in the mind of man,
> That she must look upon with awe. I bow
> Reverently to her dictates, but not less
> Hold to the fair illusions of old time—
> Illusions that shed brightness over life,
> And glory over Nature.

> The swelling hills,
> The quiet dells retiring far between,
> With gentle invitation to explore
> Their windings, were a calm society
> That talked with me and soothed me.

Particularly interesting is a group of personal poems in which Bryant, although writing in Wordsworthian fashion, actually recorded impressions of and relations with members of his own family. The rural philosopher, for example, who appeared in "The Old Man's Counsel," might easily be mistaken for an English farmer of the Lake Country:

> a white-haired man,
> Pithy of speech, and merry when he would;
> A genial optimist, who daily drew
> From what he saw his quaint moralities.[118]

He was, however, the poet's grandfather, Deacon Ebenezer Snell. The fairest of all rural maids, to whom Bryant addressed his familiar lyric, might well be Wordsworth's Lucy, particularly the Lucy described in "Three Years She Grew in Sun and Shower." But the rural maid was in reality Frances Fairchild. And when a child in her "fourth bright year" was taught to gaze "with delighted eye" on hill and vale,[119] her education resembled that of little Dora Wordsworth; yet she was in actuality Bryant's daughter Fanny. It is obvious that in such poems the American employed the English poet's symbols to express his own emotions. The resemblances between the two poets, it is now evident, fall into two groups—similarities in style and similarities in thought. During the 1820's, Wordsworth's poetry clearly exercised a formative influence on the diction and the versification of the American. Particularly profitable was the enrichment of poetic vocabulary—words, turns of phrase, images—which came to

---

[118] *Democratic Review*, VII, 112 (Feb., 1840).
[119] "Lines on Revisiting the Country."

him through a loving perusal of *Lyrical Ballads*. Then, in later years, these borrowed elements were assimilated and Bryant's style became his own. It cannot be demonstrated, on the other hand, that he ever derived any novel ideas from Wordsworth. Apparently the author of "Thanatopsis" discovered for himself that nature can stimulate and delight, soothe and heal; these discoveries the English poet confirmed. Furthermore, the central ideas of both differed at many points. To dismiss Bryant as merely imitative and derivative is, therefore, undiscriminating and uncritical.[120]

Of the Romantic themes favored by Bryant, one of the earliest to emerge in his verse was the noble savage.[121] Occasionally he portrayed Indians as barbarians, either "roaming hunter tribes, warlike and fierce," or warrior clans who laid up glory "for many an age to last."[122] Such was the bloodthirsty savage

[120] Bryant's final estimate of Wordsworth ("Introduction," *A Library of Poetry and Song*, pp. xxviii–xxix) was sober and judicial, untouched by the ecstasy of his first encounter: "Wordsworth is generally spoken of as one who gave to our literature that impulse which brought the poets back from the capricious forms of expression in vogue before his time to a certain fearless simplicity . . . Yet the poetry of Wordsworth was but the consummation of a tendency already existing and active. Cowper had already felt it in writing his *Task*, and in his longer rhymed poems . . . Percy's *Reliques* had accustomed English readers to perceive the extreme beauty of the old ballads in their absolute simplicity. . . . Burns's inimitable Scottish poems . . . had taught the same lesson. We may infer that the genius of Wordsworth was in a great degree influenced by these, just as he in his turn contributed to form the taste of those who wrote after him. It was long, however, before he reached the eminence which he now holds in the estimation of the literary world. . . . Yet his fame has slowly climbed from stage to stage until now his influence is perceived in all the English poetry of the day. If this were the place to criticize his poetry, I should say, of his more stately poems in blank verse, that they often lack compression,—that the thought suffers by too great expansion. . . . Yet I must own that even his most diffuse amplifications have in them a certain grandeur that fills the mind." This emphasis on Wordsworth's debt to his predecessors suggests that Bryant considered himself a successor to the English poet, rather than his imitator.

[121] At seventeen, Bryant composed a spirited "Indian War Song" (Godwin, I, 90) and not long thereafter planned an elaborate poem on the red man.

[122] "The Prairies," *Knickerbocker*, II, 410–13 (Dec., 1833); "A Walk at Sunset," *The Idle Man*, Vol. I, no. 3, pp. 74–6 (1821).

who spread terror through Bryant's prose tale, "The Indian Spring." [123] More frequently he envisioned red heroes gifted with unsurpassed endurance and valor, "a noble race!" An Indian of this generous mould was ever master of the elements and ruler of forest and stream:

> In many a flood to madness tossed,
>   In many a storm has been his path;
> He hid him not from heat or frost,
>   But met them, and defied their wrath.
>
> Then they were kind—the forests here,
>   Rivers, and stiller waters, paid
> A tribute to the net and spear
>   Of the red ruler of the shade.

This superiority of the savage lay, Bryant believed with the Primitivists, in his lack of artificial culture and his nearness to the Creator:

> For he was fresher from the hand
>   That formed of earth the human face,
> And to the elements did stand
>   In nearer kindred than our race. [124]

The poet believed also that red men experienced delight in the presence of these same elements:

> They who here roamed, of yore, the forest wide,
>   Felt, by such charm, their simple bosoms won. [125]

To his savages, he attempted to give verisimilitude by referring to "broidered mocsen," bow and arrows, and "wampum-belts" and by alluding to their customs, particularly in the burial of the dead. His supposed aborigines were, however, merely the con-

---

[123] *The Talisman for 1830*, pp. 7–26.
[124] "The Disinterred Warrior," *Poems*. New York: 1832, p. 173.
[125] "A Walk at Sunset."

ventional heroes and heroines of romance, employed not to reveal Indian character but to act in familiar tragic episodes dear
to all sentimentalists: a damsel mourns the death of her lover,[126]
a husband rescues his abducted wife,[127] a maiden commits sui-
cide because she cannot marry her beloved.[128] That this concern
with the noble savage was not localized became evident when
the poet wrote of a beauteous brown fairy of the South Seas who
became the bride of a white man,[129] and of a gallant Eskimo who
sang to his Arctic sweetheart of seafowl and bear.[130] It is clear
that Bryant dealt, not with realities of Indian atrocities or the
squalor of aboriginal life, but with creations of romantic fancy.[131]

The prairie and its pioneers likewise had for Bryant a lasting
fascination. Early and sentimentally he rhymed of hunters of the
West who go "in depths of woods to seek the deer" and who
serenade their loved ones with songs of swans and night-spar-
rows, mistletoe, and "jessamine."[132] In his prose fiction, written
apparently in emulation of Cooper, he portrayed more virile
and yet picturesque frontiersmen, of whom Le Moire is representative: a dark-faced and long-haired hunter, clad in a "blue
frock-coat trimmed with yellow fringe and bound by a sash at

---

[126] "An Indian Girl's Lament," *New-York Review*, II, 159–60 (Jan., 1826).

[127] "An Indian Story," *United States Literary Gazette*, I, 92 (July 1, 1824).

[128] "Monument Mountain," *idem*, I, 173–4 (Sept. 15, 1824).

[129] "A Song of Pitcairn's Island," *New-York Review*, I, 78–9 (June, 1825).

[130] "The Arctic Lover," *Knickerbocker*, I, 28–9 (Jan., 1833).

[131] Essentially sentimental are the Indian episodes in Bryant's uncol-
lected sketch entitled "The Cascade of Melsingah" (*The Talisman for
1828*, pp. 198–227). Sentimental also is his unqualified approval of Fitz-
Greene Halleck's Romantic portrait of an Indian in the latter's poem,
"Red Jacket," first expressed in 1836 ("The Writings of Fitz-Greene
Halleck," *New-York Mirror*, XIV, 97, Sept. 24, 1836) and repeated in
1869 ("Notices of the Life and Writings of Fitz-Greene Halleck," *Prose
Writings*, I, 386). For a general survey of the subject, see Albert Keiser,
The Indian in American Literature. New York: 1933.

[132] "The Hunter of the West" and "The Hunter's Serenade," *The
Talisman for 1829*, pp. 307–9.

the waist," deerskin pantaloons, and deerskin moccasins.[133] After Bryant came face to face with authentic plainsmen and their families,[134] in his prose he no longer romanticized the frock-coated pioneer. Rather, he recorded the actualities of his dreary life: his wretched dwelling, its single room half filled with beds and cribs on which lay a sick man and several children all brown with dirt; his sweaty wife and daughter who cooked greasy meals in a huge fireplace; and the stifling air, the whimperings and whinings, and the offensive odors of the place, which prevented Bryant from sleeping.[135] This realistic treatment persisted in his later travel-letters written in Illinois and Michigan.[136] But in verse he was still capable of sentimentalizing western hunters, creating a heroic pioneer who through a long day on horseback thinks Bryant's own thoughts, listens to "the aged past," beholds the "boundless future," and at last rides back at evening to the "kind voice" and the "glad eyes" of his loved one.[137] Likewise, Bryant's final attitude toward westerners was idealistic:

> What cordial welcomes greet the guest
> By thy lone rivers of the West;
> How faith is kept, and truth revered,
> And man is loved, and God is feared.[138]

[133] "The Skeleton's Cave," *Tales of the Glauber Spa.* New York: 1832, I, 196. Frontier or pioneer characters appear also in "Story of the Island of Cuba," *The Talisman for 1829.* New York: 1828, pp. 163–220, and "The Marriage Blunder," *The Talisman for 1830,* pp. 255–99.

[134] Bryant in 1832 crossed the Allegheny Mountains by stage, went down the Ohio River to St. Louis by steamboat, and traveled over Illinois by wagon and on horseback (Godwin, I, 283).

[135] Letter to Mrs. W. C. Bryant, Jacksonville, Ill., June 19, 1832; published in *Prose Writings,* II, 18–19.

[136] *Letters of a Traveller.* New York: 1850, Letters VII, VIII, XXXI–XXXVII.

[137] "The Hunter of the Prairies," *New-York Mirror,* XII, 353 (May 9, 1835). For additional Romantic hunters, see "The Maiden's Sorrow" (*Graham's Lady's and Gentleman's Magazine,* XXI, 64, August, 1842) and "The White-Footed Deer" (*The White-Footed Deer and Other Poems.* New York: 1844, pp. 1–4).

[138] "Oh Mother of a Mighty Race," *Graham's Lady's and Gentleman's Magazine,* XXX, 20 (Jan., 1847).

Concerning the plains themselves, the poet was never disillusioned. On first beholding them he found prose inadequate to express his delight and awe: "What I have thought and felt amid these boundless wastes and awful solitudes I shall reserve for the only form of expression in which it can properly be uttered."[139] Thus inspired, he glorified the western landscape in verse:

> Ay, this is freedom!—these pure skies
> Were never stained with village smoke:
> The fragrant wind, that through them flies,
> Is breathed from wastes by plough unbroke. . . .
>
> For here the fair savannas know
> No barriers in the bloomy grass;
> Wherever breeze of heaven may blow,
> Or beam of heaven may glance, I pass.[140]

Repeated visits to his brothers in Illinois kept western scenes fresh in his mind; and his later prose descriptions of the prairies remained eloquently appreciative.[141]

Bryant's concern with the past was often unromantic, particularly when he wrote in didactic mood. His treatment of the history and the legends of his own country, however, was commonly both nationalistic and emotional. His commemoration of Indian and pioneer has already been discussed. To the Pilgrims he paid high tribute[142] and likewise to the heroes of the American Revolution.[143] Particularly Romantic was his treatment of the past in a group of little-known tales and sketches, not to be found in his collected works: "A Pennsylvania Legend,"[144] "A

---

[139] Letter to Mrs. W. C. Bryant, *Prose Writings*, II, 20.
[140] "The Hunter of the Prairies." See also "The Prairies."
[141] *Letters of a Traveller*, Letters VII, VIII.
[142] "The Twenty-second of December," *Poems* (1832), p. 238.
[143] "Song of Marion's Men," *New-York Mirror*, IX, 153 (Nov. 5, 1831); "Seventy-Six," *idem*, XII, 368 (May 23, 1835); and "The Green Mountain Boys," *idem*, XIV, 156 (Nov. 12, 1836).
[144] *New-York Review*, II, 49–64 (Dec., 1825).

Border Tradition,"[145] "The Cascade of Melsingah,"[146] "The Legend of the Devil's Pulpit,"[147] two series of "Reminiscences of New-York,"[148] and "Medfield."[149] Here, perhaps stimulated by the vogue of Irving's stories, Bryant soberly recorded picturesque anecdotes and supernatural legends. Attempting to give his narratives suitable atmosphere, he half seriously professed to take great pleasure in superstition and old wives' tales:

As long . . . as there are aged crones to talk, and children to listen, the labours of philosophy cannot be crowned with perfect success. A dread of supernatural visitations, awakened in our tender years, keeps possession of the mind like an instinct, and bids defiance to the attempts of reason to dislodge it. For my part, I look upon myself as a debtor to the old nurses and servant maids, who kept me from my sleep with tales of goblins and apparitions, for one of the highest pleasures I enjoy. It is owing to them, I believe, that I read, with a deep sense of delight, narratives which seem to inspire many of my enlightened and reasoning acquaintances with no feeling but that of disgust. Yet I cannot but notice a remarkable scarcity of well attested incidents of this sort in modern years. The incredulity of the age has caused the supernatural interpositions, that were once so frequent, to be withdrawn; portents and prodigies are not shown to mockers, and spectres will not walk abroad to be made the subjects of philosophical analysis.[150]

This passage introduces one of Bryant's typical legends, that of a poor hunchback who, having become rich and handsome through the aid of a friendly dryad, eventually brings ugliness and poverty back upon himself by destroying the tree in which

---

[145] *The United States Review and Literary Gazette*, I, 40–53 (Oct., 1826).
[146] *The Talisman for 1828*, pp. 198–227.
[147] *Idem*, pp. 229–88. Bryant wrote only "parts" of this tale (Godwin, I, 241, footnote).
[148] *The Talisman for 1829*, pp. 310–42; *The Talisman for 1830*, pp. 337–58. Bryant wrote only "parts" of these sketches (Godwin, I, 241, footnote).
[149] *Tales of the Glauber Spa*, I, 243–76.
[150] "A Pennsylvania Legend," *op. cit.*, II, 49–50.

lives his wood-sprite. But Bryant's touch was too heavy for such fanciful narratives; they became dull and diffuse in his hands.

With tradition and superstition, he often associated grotesque horror. When discussing death in relation to members of his family or to himself, he found its claims too serious to be romanticized.[151] But when he wrote ballads on the tragic fate of Indians and hunters, travellers and robbers, the element of terror appeared. Versifying the details of a murder among the Berkshires, he fancied that when the dreadful deed was done,

> The mountain wolf and wild-cat stole
> To banquet on the dead.[152]

Recounting a melodramatic robbery by a gloomy bandit, he raised a hurricane to foil the villain, whereupon

> Rider and steed and robber whirled
>   O'er precipices vast,
> 'Mong trunks, and boughs, and shattered crags,
>   Mangled and crushed are cast.
> The catamount and eagle made,
>   At morn, a grim repast. [153]

Bryant's first visit to Germany further encouraged him to dabble in blood. There, for example, he wrote seriously and with no thought of burlesque his remarkable tale of handsome Albert, led into the forest by a dark-haired enchantress.

Next day, within a mossy glen, 'mid mouldering trunks were found

---

[151] For example, the contention that "Thanatopsis" is an imaginative youth's fanciful commentary on death as a distant and therefore attractive theme (William Lyon Phelps, *Howells, James, Bryant and Other Essays.* New York: 1924, pp. 15–16) is unsound in view of Bryant's lifelong fear of the grave. For a moving expression of this fear, see the hitherto unpublished poem, "They Taught Me, and It Was a Fearful Creed," in Appendix I, p. 353.

[152] "The Murdered Traveller," *United States Literary Gazette*, I, 286 (Jan. 1, 1825).

[153] "The Robber," *New-York Mirror*, XI, 4 (July 6, 1833). This poem was not collected by Bryant.

The fragments of a human form upon the bloody ground;
White bones from which the flesh was torn, and locks of glossy
    hair;
They laid them in the place of graves, yet wist not whose they
    were.

And whether famished evening wolves had mangled Albert so,
Or that strange dame so gay and fair were some mysterious foe,
Or whether to that forest-lodge, beyond the mountain blue,
He went to dwell with her, the friends who mourned him never
    knew.[154]

Returning to America, he versified a tragic German legend[155] and translated Romantic poems by Uhland, Müller, and Chamisso.[156] Meanwhile, he was writing prose tales of terror: "An Adventure in the East Indies,"[157] "Story of the Island of Cuba,"[158] "The Indian Spring," and "The Skeleton's Cave." In the last story, he permitted himself one particularly grotesque touch: three characters, entombed with a mouldering skeleton, are so

[154] "The Strange Lady," *New-York Mirror*, XIII, 364 (May 14, 1836). See also a second tragic poem written in Germany, "The Hunter's Vision," *idem*, XIII, 145 (Nov. 7, 1835).

[155] "A Presentiment," *idem*, XIV, 322 (April 15, 1837). This is the tale of the child and the Erl-King used by Goethe.

[156] "The Count of Griers," *idem*, XIII, 236 (Jan. 23, 1836); "A Northern Legend," *Graham's Lady's and Gentleman's Magazine*, XXII, 52 (Jan., 1843); "The Paradise of Tears," *idem*, XXVI, 202 (Nov., 1844). Bryant later translated "I Think of Thee" from Goethe; "The Saw-Mill" from Kerner; "The Words of the Koran" from Zedlitz; and "The Poet's First Song" from Houwald. See A. H. Herrick, "William Cullen Bryants Beziehungen zur Deutschen Dichtung," *Modern Language Notes*, XXXII, 344–51 (June, 1917).

[157] *The Talisman for 1828*, pp. 10–23. The adventure recorded in this uncollected tale is a tiger-hunt.

[158] In this tale, Bryant records such bloody deeds by a trio of savages as the following: "The brother presented himself with a musket, but was struck to the floor before he could fire, and the murderers passed into the house over his dead body. Shrieks and howls of agony and supplication burst from the building, and through the open door the wife and her children were seen clinging to the knees of the savages, and butchered in the midst of their cries for mercy. The bodies of the two negro boys, bleeding from deep wounds, were then tossed out; and the mother, rushing forth to make her escape, was overtaken and pinned with one of their huge lances to the ground" (*op. cit.*, pp. 186–7).

hard pressed by starvation that one of the group finally suggests that his companions devour him. "Look at my veins," he begs, "they are full yet, and the muscles have not shrunk away from my limbs; would you not both live the longer, if I were to die?"[159]

Bryant's Romantic liking for the languages and literatures of France, Italy, and particularly Spain developed during his early years in New York City. Here a family of French Catholics caught his interest and apparently led him to improve his knowledge of the French language. Then, in the midst of his heavy toil as a magazine editor, he learned to read Italian, Spanish, and Portuguese.[160] The first result of this activity was a review of a sixteenth-century work on the Provençal poets, in which Bryant recounted sentimental legends and rhapsodized over the golden age of the troubadours:

The very air of that country breathed the infection of poetry. Illustrious and learned strangers visited the courts of its princes and nobles, and went away poets. Grave jurisconsults opened their mouths in verse; gloomy astrologers, laborious mathematicians, and fierce warriors addressed songs to high-born and beautiful ladies. Probably in no age of the world, were men of letters so highly honored, or so liberally rewarded.[161]

Then followed another review;[162] a tale of Spanish life in Cuba[163] and one of French life in North America;[164] and essays, enlivened by colorful anecdotes, on Spanish customs, Moorish ballads, and female troubadours.[165] Even more notable was Bryant's delight in the physical beauty of Granada and all southern Spain,

[159] *Op. cit.*, I, 230. Gothic terror in American literature has never been adequately discussed. For preliminary surveys, see Oral S. Coad, "The Gothic Element in American Literature before 1835," *Journal of English and Germanic Philology*, XXIV, 72–93 (Jan., 1925), and Edith Birkhead, *The Tale of Terror*. London: 1921, pp. 197–220.

[160] Godwin, I, 214, 220.

[161] *New-York Review*, I, 108–9 (July, 1825).

[162] Bryant reviewed Robert Benson's *Sketches of Corsica*, in *New-York Review*, II, 348–63 (April, 1826).

[163] "Story of the Island of Cuba." [164] "The Marriage Blunder."

[165] *The Talisman for 1829*, pp. 43–51; *The Talisman for 1830*, pp. 227–37, 238–54.

revealed before Irving had published his Spanish sketches and
before Bryant had visited Europe.[166] Most notable of all were
the verse translations from European poets which he made during these years—translations from the Provençal of Bernard
Rascas [167] and Peire Vidal,[168] from the Portuguese of Belchior
Manuel Curvo Semedo,[169] from the Spanish of anonymous bal-
ladists and song writers,[170] of Leonardo de Argensola,[171] Fer-
nand Ruiz de Villegas,[172] Louis Ponce de Leon,[173] Pedro de
Castro y Añaya,[174] and José Iglesias de la Casa.[175] Writing before Longfellow had left college or Lowell had left dame school,
Bryant was a pioneer interpreter of Romance literatures to
America.[176]

On these varied subjects and, above all, on external nature,
Bryant wrote his Romantic prose and verse. But American
poetry in the early nineteenth century was in need not only of
fresh subjects but of new verse-forms. Until the youthful Bryant began to rhyme, only Philip Freneau had with complete
success broken away from the heroic couplet and only he had
revealed ingenuity and intelligence in handling the technical

[166] *The Talisman for 1829*, pp. 43–9.
[167] "The Love of God." It is now impossible to learn where certain
of these translations were first printed. The majority appeared between
1825 and 1830; others, made late in Bryant's life, were not published
until after his death.
[168] "Love in the Age of Chivalry."   [169] "Sonnet."
[170] "Fatima and Raduan," "The Alcayde of Molina," "The Death of
Aliatar," "Diamante Falso," "Eve," "The Siesta," "The Serenade."
[171] "Mary Magdalen."   [172] "'Tis Sweet, in the Green Spring."
[173] "The Life of the Blessed."   [174] "Stay, Rivulet, nor Haste to Leave."
[175] "Song."
[176] This interest continued throughout Bryant's life. As soon as it became financially possible for him to travel abroad, he was a regular voyager
to Europe, making his first crossing at the age of thirty-nine and his sixth
return at seventy-three. His observations were set down at once in his
notebooks, then published in the *Post*, and finally collected in two series
of *Letters of a Traveller*. To the last, Spain remained his favored country;
and during his last years, Bryant continued to translate Spanish poetry:
"To the Nightingale" of Pedro de Castro y Añaya, "The Ascension" of
Louis Ponce de Leon, "The Lost Bird" of Carolina Coronado, "The
Ruins of Italica" of Francisco de Rioja, and several "Fables" of the
Mexican poet, José Rosas.

problems of versification. Even before the boy Cullen turned
from Augustan themes and Augustan rhyme, he began experi-
menting with blank verse[177] and with the quatrain.[178] Thus at
sixteen he was prepared to abandon the heroic couplet. In his
first published blank verse, there was such ease and power that
Richard Henry Dana warned an editor of the *North American
Review*: "Ah! Phillips, you have been imposed upon; no one on
this side of the Atlantic is capable of writing such verses."[179]
And indeed no American poet of that day save young Bryant
could have composed the sonorous lines of "Thanatopsis."
During the years which followed, he continued to work in un-
rhymed pentameters[180] until he came to his highest proficiency
in the second version of "Thanatopsis" and "A Forest Hymn."
Meanwhile Bryant was perfecting himself in the use of the quatrain, which eventually became his favorite stanza. Most frequently he used conventional tetrameters rhyming *a b a b*, but he
soon learned to alternate trimeters with tetrameters,[181] to rhyme
four tetrameters *a a b b*,[182] to intersperse anapests among iambics,[183]
to alternate trimeters with pentameters,[184] and to combine a
trimeter, two pentameters, and a final trimeter, unexpectedly
rhyming *a b a b*.[185] His few heroic couplets were conventional;

[177] A blank-verse paraphrase of David's lament over Jonathan, written
about 1804-5, is published in Godwin, I, 76, footnote.
[178] "Drought," written in 1807, and "The Contented Ploughman,"
written in 1808, *The Embargo; . . . and Other Poems*, pp. 33-5; "The
Genius of Columbia," written in 1810 and printed in Godwin, I, 80-1,
footnote.
[179] Quoted in *idem*, I, 150.
[180] "Inscription for the Entrance to a Wood"; "The Burial Place,"
The Idle Man, Vol. II, no. 2, 192-4 (1821); "Hymn to Death," *New-
York Review*, I, 388-92 (Oct., 1825); and "A Winter Piece."
[181] "Let No Rude Sound Be Uttered Nigh," written in 1821 and published in Godwin, I, 108-9.
[182] "Oh Fairest of the Rural Maids"; "To the Fringed Gentian," *Poems*
(1832), p. 204; and others.
[183] "I Cannot Forget with What Fervid Devotion."
[184] "The Past," *The Talisman for 1829*, pp. 73-5.
[185] "To a Waterfowl" and "Autumn Woods," *United States Literary
Gazette*, I, 203 (Oct. 15, 1824).

but he employed free tetrameter couplets[186] with a fluency and an ease unknown to the Connecticut Wits. He early began to explore the possibilities of the six-line measure,[187] until at Great Barrington he was employing six varieties of this stanza.[188] As early as 1813 he wrote in the Spenserian measure,[189] a form which had rarely been used in America. He was a pioneer also in the use of the sonnet, writing in the 1820's examples of the English type[190] and in later years a hybrid form. When Bryant's use of five-, eight-, and ten-line stanzas and of irregular measures is also taken into consideration, the unusual range of his technical resources becomes evident. These achievements, simple and unpretentious as they now appear, were in that day notable triumphs in the modernization of American prosody. Bryant therefore commands high respect as an early and a competent craftsman in verse.

In a period when Americans still revered the Augustans and were slow to approve Wordsworth and Coleridge,[191] Bryant be-

---

[186] "Green River," *The Idle Man*, Vol. I, no. 2, pp. 61–3 (1821); "The Rivulet," *United States Literary Gazette*, I, 44–5 (May 15, 1824); and others.

[187] "Yes, I Have Listened All Too Long," written in 1812 and published in Godwin I, 109–10; "Ode for the 4th of July, 1814," *Hampshire Gazette*, July 6, 1814.

[188] See "Spain"; "The Indian Girl's Lament"; "The Old Man's Funeral"; "Hymn to the North Star," *United States Literary Gazette*, I, 298 (Jan. 15, 1825); "I Broke the Spell That Held Me Long"; and "Hymn of the Waldenses."

[189] "To a Friend on His Marriage," in Jacob Porter, *To the Memory of Mrs. Betsey Porter.* Cambridge: 1813, pp. 5–6. Later poems in Spenserian stanza are "The Ages" and "After a Tempest."

[190] "Aye, Thou Art for the Grave," *United States Literary Gazette*, I, 75 (June 15, 1824); "Mutation," *idem*, I, 237 (Nov. 15, 1824); "November," *ibid.* Bryant's versification is discussed in detail in Gay W. Allen, *American Prosody.* New York: 1935, pp. 31–52.

[191] Bryant in his last years recalled that Wordsworth and Coleridge's *Lyrical Ballads* "were at first little read, and of those who liked them there were few who were not afraid to express their admiration" ("Introduction," *A Library of Poetry and Song*, pp. xxviii–xxix). Unfortunately there is in Annabel Newton, *Wordsworth in Early American Criticism* (Chicago: [1928]), no adequate discussion of this early prejudice against Wordsworth in New England.

gan his career as literary critic with a memorable protest against Augustan regularity.[192] His demand that poets be allowed to introduce trisyllabic feet freely in iambic measures is, of course, no longer revolutionary; but when it was written, the proposal was audacious. "The liberty for which I have been contending," he remarked, "has often been censured and ridiculed. The utmost favour which it has, at any time, to my knowledge, received from the critics, is to have been silently allowed—no one has openly defended it." [193] In his second piece of critical writing, a review of Solyman Brown, *An Essay on American Poetry*, Bryant continued to attack eighteenth-century formality which, he believed, "allows just as much play and freedom to the faculties of the writer as a pair of stilts allows the body." The imagination must at all costs be freed from this well-trodden circle, where it is "doomed to the chains of a perpetual mannerism, and condemned to tinkle the same eternal tune with its fetters."[194] Specifically, he criticized Timothy Dwight for the "unbroken monotony" of his verse, Joel Barlow for dullness, and Robert Treat Paine for a bewildered attempt to express in the epigrammatic style of Pope ideas which he himself did not understand.[195] Thus, while freely granting certain merits to the Augustans, he conclusively rejected their formality and rigidity.

[192] Although "On the Use of Trisyllabic Feet in Iambic Verse" was the second of Bryant's critical articles to be published, it was the first to be written. According to Godwin (*Prose Writings*, I, 56, footnote), Bryant began the essay "as early as 1811."

[193] *North American Review*, IX, 431 (Sept., 1819). Godwin prints this essay from a revised manuscript (*Prose Writings*, I, 57–67), to which references to Byron, Moore, and other Romanticists have been added. (In the original, only Moore is quoted.) While Bryant was thus defending the use of trisyllabic feet in iambic measure, he was putting the theory into practice in "Thanatopsis."

[194] *North American Review*, VII, 204 (July, 1818). This review was written in 1818.

[195] *Idem*, VII, 201–3, 205–6. Bryant's early lack of sympathy with the radicalism of Freneau, as revealed in this review, is explained by the fact that in 1818 the former was still a Federalist. Had the essay been written later, after Bryant was committed to democracy, his treatment of Freneau might well have been favorable.

The doctrines which Bryant substituted for the rejected tenets of the eighteenth century were, in the main, Romantic. Only at one point did morality and didacticism overwhelm him, namely, when he discussed the uses of literature. An author, Bryant believed, serves only an inferior end when he amuses; his chief aim should be to perfect the moral character of his readers. It is poetry rather than prose which best accomplishes this sober aim:

It cherishes patriotism, the incitement to vigorous toils endured for the welfare of communities. It luxuriates among the natural affections, the springs of all the gentle charities of domestic life. It has so refined and transformed and hallowed the love of the sexes that piety itself has sometimes taken the language of that passion to clothe its most fervent aspirations. . . . All moral lessons which are uninteresting and unimpressive, and, therefore, worthless, it leaves to prose; but all those which touch the heart, and are, therefore, important and effectual, are its own.[196]

It was this same moralistic Bryant who condemned Lord Byron for "indecency and blasphemy" in his treatment of biblical subjects,[197] and who in compiling his *Selections from the American Poets* invariably omitted all "amatory poems and drinking songs" as "not proper for a book designed . . . to be read by very young persons."[198] To his credit, he also insisted that poetry must not be "merely didactic," nor can it "concern itself with abstract reasonings, nor with any course of investigation that fatigues the mind."[199] Recalling the extent to which Wordsworth and his contemporaries indulged in didacticism, the literary historian cannot deny that Bryant belonged to the Romantic generation merely because he believed that poetry should teach "lessons of wisdom."

196 "Lectures on Poetry," *Prose Writings*, I, 17–18.
197 Review of James A. Hillhouse, *Hadad*, in *New-York Review*, I, 3 (June, 1825).
198 "To the Reader," *Selections from the American Poets*. New York: 1840, p. iii.
199 "Lectures on Poetry," *op. cit.*, I, 11.

The Romantic faith in originality, rationally interpreted, became a major plank in Bryant's critical platform. The idea that poetry is, like painting and sculpture, essentially an imitative art, he sharply denied. Likewise, he believed that when all the energy of poets is "employed in servilely copying the works of their predecessors, it is not only impossible that any great work should be produced among them, but the period of a literary reformation . . . is postponed to a distant futurity." [200] On the other hand, he decried frantic attempts at originality which result in "puerile conceits, . . . extravagant vagaries of imagination, . . . overstrained exaggerations of passion, . . . mawkish and childish simplicity." [201] But, were he forced to choose between an age marked by "too great carefulness of imitation" and an age "remarkable for an excessive ambition of originality," he would decide in favor of the latter.[202] Sanely, he did not break utterly with the past, because art develops not only out of experiment but out of a continuous series of experiments.[203] The poet, therefore, first familiarizes himself with the achievements of his predecessors; then, if he is truly creative, he goes on in his own fashion to delight us "with new modes of sublimity, of beauty, and of human emotion." [204]

That the artist deals primarily with the imagination and the emotions was a belief equally fundamental in Bryant's creed. Of all artists, it is the poet who appeals most frequently and most successfully to the imagination. "To this restless faculty— which is . . . ever wandering from the combination of ideas

[200] *Idem*, I, 44.

[201] *Idem*, I, 36. Specifically, Bryant disapproved of the "grandiloquous nonsense of euphuism," the "laborious wit of the metaphysical poets," the "puling effeminacy of the cockney school" (*ibid.*), and the "almost mock-heroic swell" which sometimes appears in Scott (review of Walter Scott's *Lives of the Novelists* in *New-York Review*, I, 414, April, 1825).

[202] "Lectures on Poetry," *op. cit.*, I, 43.

[203] *Idem*, I, 36. Bryant again emphasized the continuity of the creative process in his introduction to *A Library of Poetry and Song*, pp. xxiii–xxiv.

[204] "Lectures on Poetry," *op. cit.*, I, 40.

directly presented to it to other considerations of its own—it is
the office of poetry to furnish the exercise in which it delights." [205]
Thus the imagination of each reader, stimulated by a poem,
reacts in individual fashion and supplies in its own way the details necessary to interpret the poet's suggestions and symbols.
Even a cold imagination, according to Bryant, will, on meeting
Milton's concise description of Eve among her flowers, supply
her with "the finest forms, attitudes, and movements of female
loveliness and dignity, which, after all, are not described, but
only hinted at by the poet." [206] But with critics who find in the
exercise of the imagination the sole province of poetry, Bryant
disagreed. Poetry is not merely a collection of vivid images; its
"great spring" is emotion and its true office is to "touch the
heart." Bryant anticipated the critical position of Poe when he
declared: "The most beautiful poetry is that which takes the
strongest hold of the feelings, and, if it is really the most beautiful, then it is poetry in the highest sense." Not only must the
poet appeal to the human heart, but he himself must be moved
by high emotion. Absence of feeling in the poet results in bad
poetry; attempting to treat a subject which does not interest
him, he drops into one of two extremes: extravagance or tameness. Profound emotion, on the other hand, "is always a sure
guide. It rarely offends against good taste, because it instinctively chooses the most effectual means of communicating itself
. . . It may sometimes transgress arbitrary rules, . . . but it speaks

---

[205] *Idem*, I, 6.

[206] *Idem*, I, 7. Bryant was at the same time praising the heated fancy of
that extravagant Romantic, James Gates Percival: "To us there is something exceedingly delightful in the reckless intoxication with which this
author surrenders himself to the enchantments of that multitude of glorious
and beautiful images that come crowding upon his mind. . . . The writings
of no poet seem to be more the involuntary overflowings of his mind. . . .
That in some of the poems of Percival, this very abundance of poetic
wealth should be somewhat oppressive to readers of colder imagination,
is not at all extraordinary" (review of Percival, *Poem. Delivered . . .
September 13, 1825*, in *New-York Review*, II, 245–6, March, 1826). This
review is not found in Bryant's collected works.

a language which reaches the heart."[207] Although Bryant announced, "I would not always reason,"[208] he also announced, with his usual caution, that emotion should never pass beyond the bounds of the rational and that imagination should ever be guided by intellect. And at last, after more than a half-century of versifying, he supplemented these early pronouncements on emotion with an impassioned warning that the writing of poetry cannot be considered "the pastime of a drowsy summer day":

> But gather all thy powers,
> And wreak them on the verse that thou dost weave.

No cold rhymer laying a smooth array of phrase upon the page can waken the listless public:

> The secret wouldst thou know
>   To touch the heart or fire the blood at will?
> Let thine own eyes o'erflow;
>   Let thy lips quiver with the passionate thrill;
> Seize the great thought, ere yet its power be past,
> And bind, in words, the fleet emotion fast.[209]

Bryant's failure to move readers of the present century is to be attributed not only to the shift in literary fashions which has outmoded his didacticism, but also to the shift in emotional patterns which has antiquated those scenes and ideas which, a century ago, made Bryant's "lips quiver," and his "eyes o'erflow."

One method of assuring originality and emotional appeal, Bryant more than once insisted, lay in the use of native themes. Contrary to the view, widely accepted by early nineteenth-century observers, that America offered no suitable materials for the novelist or the poet,[210] he found high promise in "the

---

[207] "Lectures on Poetry," *op. cit.*, I, 8, 10.
[208] "The Conjunction of Jupiter and Venus."
[209] "The Poet," *Thirty Poems.* New York: 1864, p. 208.
[210] Typical was the contention of John Bristed that in America neither the white population, placed on "a dead level of equality" by democratic institutions, nor those "miserable barbarians," the red men, could be made attractive by the novelist (*America and Its Resources.* London:

fertility of our country, and its history, in the materials of romance." On the one hand, he pointed out that the envied trappings of European aristocracy were not requisite to the production of prose fiction and, on the other hand, that democratic equality had produced in the United States a varied people, widely diversified through political, religious, geographical, and racial differences—rich matter for the novelist.[211] To the poet, also, American life offers "the elements of beauty and grandeur, intellectual greatness and moral truth, the stormy and the gentle passions, the casualties and the changes of life, and the light shed upon man's nature by the story of past times and the knowledge of foreign manners."[212] For the encouragement of authors who celebrate native themes, Bryant declared that subservience to British opinion must cease, that the reading public must become sanely patriotic, and that American books must be sought out and commended.[213] This Romantic insistence on nationalism,

---

1818, pp. 355–6). Even after the triumph of *The Spy*, *The Pioneers*, and *The Last of the Mohicans*, Cooper remained equally blind to the resources of American society, announcing in 1836: "This country probably presents as barren a field to the writer of fiction . . . as any other on earth; we are not certain we might not say the most barren" ("Preface," *Home as Found*. Philadelphia: 1836, I, iv).

[211] *North American Review*, XX, 248, 251–6 (April, 1825).

[212] "Lectures on Poetry," *op. cit.*, I, 34.

[213] In 1826 Bryant made the following spirited attack on the timidity of American taste: "We do not like to praise a thing, till we see the seal of transatlantic approbation upon it. We are like those singers at a church, who do very well while sustained by a few skilful and powerful voices, but feel excessively awkward at being obliged to sing alone. We are greatly distressed, and are apt to be wonderfully feeble and faint in our applauses, when we are obliged to utter them without the chorus of the British literati to keep us in countenance. One would be apt to suppose, that as the meritorious productions of our native literature are by no means numerous, they would be sought after with great avidity, and that no well educated man among us would be willing to acknowledge himself unacquainted with their contents. Such, however, is unfortunately not the case. Fashion has almost as much to do in directing what books shall be read, as what dresses shall be worn; and a large class of people look into none but such as her dictates make it necessary to read. It is the fashion throughout the United States, to read the tolerable English works of the day—but fashion has not made it indispensable to read American works of the same degree of merit" (*New-York Review*, II, 251, March, 1826).

however, did not blind Bryant to the dangers of insularity. The writings of an American, he warned, "are not to be applauded merely because they are written by an American, and are not decidedly bad"; rather, "he must produce some more satisfactory evidence of his claim to celebrity than an extract from the parish register."[214] Furthermore, Bryant's concern with the elemental and the universal saved him from provincialism. This sanity and restraint, evident not only when Bryant argued the cause of nationalism but whenever he defended any tenet of Romanticism, made him one of the most convincing critics to be found in the early history of American letters.[215]

Such were the origins, the major themes, and the chief doctrines of Bryant's literary Romanticism. This Romanticism brought upon Bryant the severest criticism which he suffered during his entire career—a savage arraignment on the charge of imitating those "perverters of literature," the Lake School of English poets.[216] Paralleled and at various points stimulated by the idealism of his politics and the liberalism of his religion, this Romanticism dominated his tales, motivated his literary criticism, and shaped much of his poetry. This Romanticism came to fullest expression from 1824 to 1838 when he was most prolific as an author. Stimulated during this period by the demand for and favorable reception of his work in the *United States Literary Gazette*, *The Talisman*, and the *New-York Mir-*

[214] *North American Review*, VII, 199 (July, 1818). For general surveys of nationalism in American letters, see H. H. Clark, "Nationalism in American Literature," *University of Toronto Quarterly*, II, 492–519 (July, 1933); and E. K. Brown, "The National Idea in American Criticism," *Dalhousie Review*, XIV, 133–47 (July, 1934).

[215] Students of criticism will find a list of Bryant's literary articles and addresses in Appendix II, p. 359.

[216] James McHenry, "American Lake Poetry," *American Quarterly Review*, XI, 171–4 (March, 1832). In contrast, Bryant's friend Willard Phillips had earlier insisted that the poet belonged to no school (*North American Review*, XIII, 380–1, Oct., 1821) and Alvan Lamson had defended him against any imputation of "lawless fanaticism and wildness" (*idem*, XXII, 432–4, April, 1826). For extracts from these reviews, see Appendix III, pp. 363 ff., 366 ff., 372 ff.

ror, he then wrote all his tales, the greater part of his criticism, and nearly one-half of his published poems. And it is clear that, viewed relatively, the Romantic elements in his work during the less productive decades which followed was only slightly less extensive. His richest creative years, therefore, were the years during which Bryant, in his own sober and dignified manner, was most thoroughly Romantic.

VI. FINAL MEDIATION

Bryant was by all odds the most patriarchal of American public figures when, in the early summer of 1878, he appeared before a great crowd in New York's Central Park. His contemporary, Cooper had been in the grave for nearly three decades and Irving, for nearly two; of the next literary generation, Poe and Hawthorne were long since dead and their fellows were all but silent; among the third generation, Mark Twain and Henry James and Howells had already made themselves heard. Bryant, who seventy years earlier had graduated from the Cummington school, was now a figure from the past. To the assembled audience, his solemn dignity suggested that this one-time liberal had perhaps become a conservative. The fires of his spirit, long checked and regimented, were obviously burning low. But had they actually expired? Did there remain no traces of the young and virile Bryant?

Heavy-browed and white-bearded, severe and aloof, this "first citizen of New York" now seemed emotionless and impassive. His audience could not know that the lad Cullen had been notorious for his "torrid temper,"[217] that the youthful poet had at times given himself over to emotionalism, that the Massachusetts lawyer had been impatient and pugnacious.[218] But certain of them recalled the morning when Bryant the editor had horse-

---

[217] *Bryant Centennial. Cummington, August the Sixteenth, 1894.* Springfield: 1894, p. 34.
[218] *Berkshire Eagle*, June 20, 1878; Godwin, I, 204.

whipped Stone of *The Commercial Advertiser* on the streets of
New York[219] and the days when his pen had castigated Greeley
of the *Tribune* with equal violence in the columns of the *Post*.[220]
Even yet, behind the mask into which his features had shaped
themselves, flames occasionally gleamed; and on this, his last
public appearance, he was to speak out once more with his earlier fire.

Fresh in all minds was Bryant's return to the beloved classics
of his boyhood,[221] with widely publicized translations of *The Iliad*
and *The Odyssey*.[222] But this emulation of Pope, still a favored
poet with Bryant, is not to be interpreted as a complete reversion
to Augustanism. In reality, the aged poet clung tenaciously to
the Romantic themes which had made him famous. At seventy-
five, his affection for nature set him to dreaming that the trees
might indeed be sentient:

> Nay, doubt we not that under the rough rind,
> In the green veins of these fair growths of earth,
> There dwells a nature that receives delight
> From all the gentle processes of life,
> And shrinks from loss of being.[223]

At seventy-eight, he recorded Indian burial customs[224] and a
Delaware legend.[225] During his last decades, he found for his

---

[219] Philip Hone, *Diary*. New York: 1927, p. 40.

[220] Nevins, pp. 395–400.

[221] Bryant as a lad seized with "eager curiosity" a translation of the *Iliad*,
ran through it with "avidity," and "laid it down with a feeling of disap-
pointment" (Preface, *The Iliad of Homer*. Boston: 1870, p. viii). For
Bryant's early classical translations, see "The Juvenile Verse of William
Cullen Bryant," *op. cit.*, XXVI, 111–13.

[222] Bryant revealed his final attitude toward Homer in this characteriza-
tion of the *Iliad*: "a work of an inexhaustible imagination, with characters vigorously drawn and finely discriminated, and incidents . . . infinitely
diversified,—everywhere a noble simplicity, mellifluous numbers, and
images of beauty and grandeur" (Preface, *The Iliad of Homer*, p. ix).

[223] "Among the Trees."

[224] "Tree-Burial," *New York Ledger*, August 17, 1872.

[225] "A Legend of the Delawares," *idem*, Nov. 9, 1872.

interest in tradition and supernaturalism a new outlet in versified fairy tales and fantasies of cloudland: "Sella,"[226] "The Little People of the Snow,"[227] "A Tale of Cloudland,"[228] "Castles in the Air."[229] In the field of prosody, he likewise continued to experiment, employing even in old age new and intricate stanzaic forms.[230]

Many who listened to Bryant in Central Park knew that this distinguished apostate from the theology of Calvin and Cummington had finally submitted himself to the Christian rite of baptism and had become a member of an organized church. A few knew also what every Protestant hymnal reveals today—that the poet in old age altered his early and rigidly anti-trinitarian hymns to include reverent tributes to Christ whom he now described as "Him who died to save mankind"[231] and even "the Anointed Son of God."[232] But these concessions to conservativism must not be mistaken for a complete return to orthodoxy. The clergyman who baptized the white-haired Bryant was a Unitarian; the church which this son of Cummington joined was likewise Unitarian;[233] and his final references to the second member of the Trinity, emphatic and reverent as they became, did not conclusively admit that Christ is God. "No one," declared John Bigelow concerning his associate on the

[226] *Thirty Poems*, pp. 118–49.

[227] *Idem*, pp. 184–206.

[228] *Poetical Works*, II, 312–20.

[229] *Atlantic Monthly*, XVII, 11–13 (Jan., 1866).

[230] See "The May Sun Sheds an Amber Light," "The Voice of Autumn," "The Conqueror's Grave," "The Planting of the Apple-Tree," "The Snow-Shower," and "Robert of Lincoln."

[231] "Oh God, Whose Dread and Dazzling Brow," *Hymns*, pp. 16–17. Bryant's final attitude toward Christ appears in "The Cloud on the Way," *New York Ledger*, Feb. 10, 1860.

[232] "Deem Not That They Are Blest Alone," *Hymns*, pp. 12–13.

[233] Much moved by the severe illness of his wife, Bryant requested a Unitarian minister, the Rev. R. C. Waterston, to baptize him. (How this rite had been neglected in the Cummington of his infancy, it is difficult to imagine.) The ceremony was performed at Naples on April 25, 1858 (Godwin, II, 108–9). After returning to America, Bryant joined the Unitarian congregation of the Rev. Henry W. Bellows of New York.

Post, "ever recognized more completely or more devoutly the divinity of Christ;"[234] but nowhere can an orthodox theologian discover that Bryant accepted "Christ's absolute deity."[235] Less liberal in religion he undoubtedly became but never, even in the last years, did he become strictly orthodox.

During the last presidential campaign, the *Post* had appeared to modify its radical stand in politics by supporting a presidential candidate backed by the moneyed interests—Rutherford B. Hayes. But for Hayes, Bryant himself had no enthusiasm; he was not supporting the man, but the party which he had helped to build.[236] He had not become a political reactionary; to the end he continued to evaluate every issue in the terms of democracy. And now, as a statue of Mazzini was unveiled in Central Park, Bryant made his final plea for human liberty. Weakly at first but with increasing power, "the grand old man of the *Post*" reiterated his faith in freedom and concluded his public career with an eloquent apostrophe to the great Italian patriot:

Image of the illustrious champion of civil and religious liberty, cast in enduring bronze to typify the imperishable renown of thy original, remain for ages yet to come where we place thee, in this resort of millions; remain till the day shall dawn—far distant though it may be—when the rights and duties of human brotherhood shall be acknowledged by all the races of mankind![237]

[234] Bigelow, p. 275. Bigelow added (p. 280) "I do not remember to have heard of his defining his creed upon any of the differentiating questions of theology, or of avowing a single dogma; neither do I believe that such an utterance can be found in any of his writings."

[235] A. H. Strong, *American Poets and Their Theology.* Philadelphia: 1916, p. 36. E. J. Bailey (*Religious Thought in the Greater American Poets.* Boston: 1922, pp. 10-32) also concludes that Bryant was heterodox concerning the second member of the trinity. Bryant's final comments on religion are found in his preface to Joseph Alden, *Thoughts on the Religious Life.* New York: 1879. Here he eulogizes Christ but does not deify him. It is possible that uncritical readers find Bryant more conservative than he actually was, because they themselves fail to distinguish between the divinity and the deity of Christ.

[236] Nevins, pp. 403-5.   [237] *Prose Writings,* II, 346.

Bryant in old age did not capitulate to conservatism; he achieved mediation. But while he was thus moderating his views, a half-century was rapidly antiquating them. His attitudes toward letters, the state, and the church which had been courageous and even prophetic in the 1820's were outmoded in the 1870's. Misled by these changes in American life, by Bryant's own final mediation, and even by such superficial considerations as his patriarchal appearance and august manner,[238] literary historians have often failed to view him in true perspective. Rather, they have read the moderation of these last years into his entire career and have wrongly attributed to him, from first to last, a cold heart and an illiberal brain. The authentic Bryant, viewed historically in his own generation, was not only a sober moralist but an impassioned defender of democracy, an enlightened religious liberal, an early American exponent of Romantic theory, and a discoverer and an exploiter of Romantic themes. Of all these achievements, most ecstatic and therefore most memorable was his discovery of external nature. As passing generations ignore and then forget many aspects of Bryant's work, they remember and ever will remember that he was the poet of Hampshire hills and Berkshire streams, "pulsing," in Whitman's phrase, "the first interior verse throbs of a mighty world—bard of the river and of the wood, ever conveying a taste of open air."[239]

[238] Edgar Allan Poe justly remarked of Bryant: "The peculiarly melancholy expression of his countenance has caused him to be accused of harshness, or coldness of heart. Never was there a greater mistake" (*Godey's Magazine and Lady's Book*, XXXII, 186, April, 1846). For Poe's reviews of Bryant, see Appendix III, pp. 382–6.

[239] *Specimen Days*. Philadelphia: 1883, p. 181. After the publication of *Leaves of Grass*, Bryant crossed on the Brooklyn ferry to Long Island, to talk and walk with Whitman. Although Bryant could not give Whitman his full approval, each poet respected the other as a democrat and a lover of nature.

A BRYANT CHRONOLOGY

1794. Born Nov. 3 at Cummington, Hampshire Co., Mass.

1803-4. Began to make rhymes.

1807. A school poem published in the *Hampshire Gazette* of Northampton.

1808. *The Embargo, or Sketches of the Times; a Satire* published in Boston.

1808-9. Prepared for college with an uncle, Rev. Thomas Snell, at North Brookfield.

1809. *The Embargo; . . . and Other Poems* published in Boston.

1809-10. Studied at home and with Rev. Moses Hallock at Plainfield.

1810-11. Spent one year at Williams College, as a sophomore.

1811. Withdrew from Williams College and wrote first draft of "Thanatopsis" (Sept. or Oct.).

1811-14. Studied law at Worthington with Samuel Howe and wrote love poems.

1814-15. Studied law at Bridgewater with William Baylies and wrote Byronic verse. Admitted to the bar (1815).

1815-16. Practised law in Plainfield. Commissioned adjutant in Massachusetts militia (1816).

1816-25. Lawyer in Great Barrington, Berkshire Co., Mass., arguing civil cases in local, county, and state courts. Hog reeve, town clerk, clerk of the school district, justice of the peace.

1821. Married Frances Fairchild, delivered Phi Beta Kappa poem ("The Ages") at Harvard, and published *Poems* at Cambridge.

1824-25. Contributed numerous poems to the *United States Literary Gazette* of Boston.

1825. Left Great Barrington and the law for New York and joint editorship of the *New-York Review*.

1826-27. Joint editor of the *United States Review and Literary Gazette*. Lectured on poetry before Athenaeum Society and on mythology before the American Academy of Art.

1827-28. Assistant editor of the *New York Evening Post*.

1829-78. Editor-in-chief and part owner of the *Evening Post*. Advocated free trade, abolition, free speech, and other liberal causes. Assisted by John Bigelow and by Parke Godwin. Profits from the *Post*, wisely invested, made Bryant a fortune, at his death popularly estimated at nearly a million dollars.

1832. Published *Poems* in New York (copyright 1831) and in London (ed. Washington Irving), visited his brothers in Illinois, and contributed to *Tales of the Glauber Spa*.

1834-36. First voyage to Europe. Contributed poems to the *New-York Mirror*.

1842. *The Fountain and Other Poems*.

1843. Purchased property at Roslyn, Long Island, where he maintained a residence for the remainder of his life.

1845. Second voyage to Europe.

1846. *The White-Footed Deer and Other Poems*.

1849. Third voyage to Europe.

1850. *Letters of a Traveller*.

1852. Eulogy on James Fenimore Cooper.

1852-53. Fourth voyage to Europe and tour of the Near East.

1855. Assisted in organizing the Republican party.

1857-58. Fifth voyage to Europe. Baptized in Naples (1858).

1859. Presided at Lincoln's address in Cooper Union, New York. *Letters of a Traveller. Second Series*.

1860. Memorial address on Washington Irving.

1861-65. Vigorously supported the Union cause during the Civil War.

1864. *Thirty Poems* (copyright 1863) and *Hymns* (privately published). Bryant's seventieth birthday celebrated by the Century Club.

1866. Frances Fairchild Bryant died.

1866-67. Sixth voyage to Europe.

1867-73. Delivered numerous addresses on the arts and public affairs.

1869. Memorial address on Fitz-Greene Halleck. *Letters from the East.*

1870. *The Iliad of Homer. Translated into English Blank Verse.*

1871-72. *The Odyssey of Homer.* Edited *A Library of Poetry and Song* (copyright 1870).

1874. Eightieth birthday celebrated.

1878. Delivered last public address, on unveiling statue of Mazzini in Central Park. Died June 12.

SELECTED BIBLIOGRAPHY

I. TEXT

Letters of a Traveller. New York: 1850; *Letters of a Traveller. Second Series.* New York: 1859; and *Letters from the East.* New York: 1869. (Only brief extracts from these books are included in Bryant's *Prose Writings*.)

The Iliad of Homer. Translated into English Blank Verse. Boston: 1870. 2 vols.; and *The Odyssey of Homer.* Boston: 1871–2. 2 vols. (Only the fifth book of *The Odyssey* is included in Bryant's *Poetical Works*.)

The Poetical Works of William Cullen Bryant. New York: 1876. (This edition, the last which passed through Bryant's hands, provides the final text for all poems included therein.)

The Poetical Works of William Cullen Bryant. New York: 1883. 2 vols. (Issued as vols. 3-4 of *The Life and Writings of William Cullen Bryant.* To the material included in earlier editions are added hymns, translations, and unpublished poems. The editor, Parke Godwin, makes slight textual changes and supplies useful notes.)

Prose Writings of William Cullen Bryant. New York: 1884. 2 vols. (Issued as vols. 5-6 of *The Life and Writings.* Essays, tales, addresses, travel-letters, literary criticism, and editorials collected and slightly revised by Parke Godwin.)

The Early Poems of William Cullen Bryant. New York: [1893]. (All poems in this volume were printed in Parke Godwin, *A Biography of William Cullen Bryant,* or in the collected works.)

The Poetical Works of William Cullen Bryant. New York: 1903. Roslyn Edition. (The most inclusive one-volume edition. Godwin's notes are omitted; but an inaccurate "Memoir of Bryant" by R. H. Stoddard and "Chronologies of Bryant's Life and Works" compiled by H. C. Sturges—see "Bibliographies" below—are added.)

Numerous poems, a few prose tales, several reviews, and a large number of editorials are still either unpublished or uncollected. Such items occasionally find their way into print, as "Musings," in *Unpublished Poems by Bryant and Thoreau* (Boston: 1907), and twelve uncollected pieces of prose, four uncollected poems, and seven unpublished poems included in the present volume.

II. BIOGRAPHY

Adkins, N. F., *Fitz-Greene Halleck*. New Haven: 1930. (Numerous references to Bryant.)

Bellows, H. W. *In Memoriam, William Cullen Bryant*. New York: [1878]. (Funeral oration by Bryant's pastor.)

Bigelow, John. *William Cullen Bryant*. American Men of Letters Series. Boston: 1890. (Valuable for personal recollections of Bryant the editor and the public figure; by an associate on the *Post*.)

Brenner, Rica. "William Cullen Bryant," in *Twelve American Poets before 1900*. New York: 1933, pp. 23–47. (A sympathetic sketch of Bryant's life.)

Bryant Centennial. Cummington, August the Sixteenth, 1894. Springfield: [1894?]. (Reminiscences and tributes.)

Curtis, G. W. *The Life, Character, and Writings of William Cullen Bryant*. New York: [1879]. (Memorial address by an acquaintance, delivered before the New York Historical Society.)

Hill, D. J. *William Cullen Bryant*. New York: 1879. (An early sketch, acceptable in its day but long since antiquated.)

Godwin, Parke. *A Biography of William Cullen Bryant, with Extracts from His Private Correspondence*. New York: 1883. 2 vols. (Issued as vols. 1-2 of *The Life and Writings*. The standard biography, by Bryant's son-in-law and associate on the *Post*. In the main, a formal, uncritical, and soberly adulatory narrative. Occasionally, however, Godwin reveals a shrewd understanding of his subject. Rich in previously unpublished poems and letters.)

Hatfield, Julia. *The Bryant Homestead Book*. New York: 1870. (Gossipy and unreliable. Endorsed by the aged Bryant but eventually withdrawn from publication as unauthorized.)

Kirkland, Caroline. "William Cullen Bryant," in *Homes of American Authors*. New York: 1853, pp. 65-81; and in *Little Journeys to the Homes of American Authors*. New York, 1896, pp. 47-74. (By a female novelist whom Bryant had praised.)

Laurence, Arthur. "Bryant and the Berkshire Hills," *Century Magazine*, N.S. XXVIII, 368-75 (July, 1895). (Pleasant account of Bryant in western Massachusetts, with illustrations.)

McDowell, Tremaine. "The Ancestry of William Cullen Bryant," *Americana*, XXII, 408-20 (Oct., 1928).

McDowell, Tremaine. "Cullen Bryant Prepares for College," *South Atlantic Quarterly*, XXX, 125-33 (April, 1931).

McDowell, Tremaine. "Cullen Bryant at Williams College," *New England Quarterly*, I, 443-66 (Oct., 1928).

McDowell, Tremaine. "William Cullen Bryant and Yale," *idem*, III, 706-16 (Oct., 1930). (Early letters, previously unpublished.)

McDowell, Tremaine. "Bryant and *The North American Review*," *American Literature*, I, 14-26 (March, 1929). (Details of publication of poetry and prose, including "Thanatopsis.")

Mathews, Amanda. "The Diary of a Poet's Mother," *Magazine of History*, II, 206-9 (Sept., 1905). (Extracts from the diaries of Sarah Snell Bryant.)

Nahmer, Henrietta. "Bryant's New England Home," *New England Magazine*, VI, 65-80 (March, 1892). (Inaccurate but colorful; well illustrated.)

Symington, A. J. *William Cullen Bryant; a Biographical Sketch*. New York: 1880. (Pietistic and inaccurate; now entirely antiquated.)

Waterston, R. C. *Tribute to William Cullen Bryant*. Boston: 1878. (Address before the Massachusetts Historical Society by a personal friend.)

Wilson, J. G. "William Cullen Bryant," in *Bryant and His Friends*. New York: 1886, pp. 11-127 and *passim*. (Anecdotes not published elsewhere and apparently not entirely reliable, collected by a third-rate Boswell.)

III. CRITICISM

Just critical estimates and scholarly studies of Bryant are not numerous. In the following bibliography are therefore included not only authoritative evaluations but representative contemporary estimates, intrinsically of slight value but historically useful as indications of the poet's reputation.

Allen, Gay W. "William Cullen Bryant," in *American Prosody*. New York: 1935, pp. 27-55. (Useful discussion of the mechanics of Bryant's poetry.)

Bailey, E. J. "Bryant," in *Religious Thought in the Greater American Poets*, Boston: 1922, pp. 10-32. (Verbose; finds Bryant heterodox concerning the Second and the Third Person of the Trinity.)

Bartlett, D. W. "Bryant," in *Modern Agitators*. New York: 1855, pp. 183-92. (Recognition of Bryant's humanitarianism.)

Bradley, W. A. *William Cullen Bryant*. English Men of Letters Series. New York and London: 1905. (Excellent comments on individual poems. Final estimate of Bryant unduly simplified through insistence on his "Puritanism" to neglect of other aspects. No new biographical material.)

The Bryant Festival at "The Century." New York: 1865. (Tributes from contemporary authors.)

Cairns, W. B. *British Criticisms of American Writings, 1815-1833*. Madison: 1922, pp. 158-64 and *passim*. (Useful summary of early criticism in English periodicals.)

Chadwick, J. H. "The Origin of a Great Poem," *Harper's New Monthly Magazine*, LXXXIX, 630-5 (Sept., 1894). (Presents no new facts concerning "Thanatopsis.")

Collins, J. C. "Poetry and Poets of America," in *Studies in Poetry*. London: 1905, pp. 21-7. (Praises Bryant for originality and for delicate appreciation of nature.)

Foerster, Norman. "Nature in Bryant's Poetry," *South Atlantic Quarterly*, XVII, 10-17 (Jan., 1918), and in *Nature in American Literature*. Boston: 1923, pp. 7-19. (Excellent demonstration of the range and the sensuousness of Bryant's nature poetry; extreme insistence on his "Puritanism.")

Glicksberg, C. I. "William Cullen Bryant, A Reinterpretation," *Revue Anglo-Américaine*, XI, 495-504 (August, 1934). (Stresses Bryant's greatness as a poet, the compulsions which forced him into journalism, and the liberalism of his political faith.)

Glicksberg, C. I. "William Cullen Bryant and Communism," *Modern Monthly*, VIII, 353-9 (July, 1934). (Bryant was "a true liberal in every sense of the term," but no communist.)

Glicksberg, C. I. "Bryant and the *United States Review*," *New England Quarterly*, VII, 687-701 (December, 1934). (Bryant's co-editorship of and contributions to a literary monthly.)

Glicksberg, C. I. "William Cullen Bryant and Fanny Wright," *American Literature*, VI, 427-32 (Jan., 1935).

Gourmont, Rémy de. *Deux Poètes de la Nature: Bryant et Emerson*. Paris: 1925, pp. 25-50. (Approval for Bryant's preoccupation with death, particularly as a necessary stage in the continual remaking of the universe.)

Herrick, A. H. "William Cullen Bryants Beziehungen zur Deutschen Dichtung," *Modern Language Notes*, XXXII, 344-51 (June, 1917). (Useful tabulation of German material in Bryant's writings.)

Hervey, J. L. "Bryant and 'The New Poetry,'" *Dial*, LIX, 92-3 (Aug. 15, 1915); "A Few Facts about Bryant," 361-3 (Oct. 28, 1915); and "Some Further Remarks about Bryant," 555-7 (Dec. 9, 1915). (Violent defense of Bryant against the strictures of Miss Harriet Monroe—see below.)

Irving, Washington. Preface to *Poems* (London: 1832), pp. iii-vi. (Highly complimentary.[1])

Johnson, W. F. "Thanatopsis, Old and New," *North American Review*, CCXXIV, 556-72 (Nov., 1927). (Examination of the revisions of "Thanatopsis.")

[1] For extracts from this essay see Appendix III.

Kreymborg, Alfred. "Forefather Bryant," in *Our Singing Strength*. New York: 1929, pp. 27-40. (Trite; stresses Bryant's limitations.)

[Legaré, H. S.] Review of *Poems* (New York: 1832), *Southern Review*, VIII, 443-62 (Feb., 1832). (Approval touched with condescension.[1])

Leonard, W. E. "Bryant," in *Cambridge History of American Literature*. New York: 1917. I, 260-78. (Sympathetic yet not uncritical; a fine exposition and appreciation of Bryant's mind and of his merits as a poet.)

[Lewis, C. T.] "Mr. Bryant's Translation of The Iliad," *North American Review*, CXII, 328-70 (April, 1871). (Compared with earlier translations, Bryant's shows "a vast superiority over all others.")

McDowell, Tremaine. "The Juvenile Verse of William Cullen Bryant," *Studies in Philology*, XXVI, 96-116 (Jan., 1929). (Contains previously unpublished verse.)

[McHenry, James.] "American Lake Poetry," *American Quarterly Review*, XI, 154-74 (March, 1832). (Sharp arraignment of Bryant as a follower of Wordsworth.[1])

Monroe, Harriet. "Aere Perennius," *Poetry*, VI, 197-200 (July, 1915). (Condemns Bryant as a man who "preferred to lead a comfortable life" and therefore "sold out.")

Monroe, Harriet. "Bryant and the New Poetry," *Dial*, LIX, 314-5 (Oct. 14, 1915); "William Cullen Bryant Again," 479-80 (Nov. 25, 1915). (Replies to Mr. J. L. Hervey—see above.)

Moore, C. L. "Our Pioneer American Poet," *Dial*, XXXVIII, 223-6 (April 1, 1905). (Revaluation of Bryant from the standpoint of the early twentieth century.)

Nadal, E. S. "William Cullen Bryant," *Macmillan's Magazine*, XXXVIII, 369-75 (Sept., 1878). (Rational explanation of Bryant's limited acceptance in England and of his great vogue in the United States.)

[Neal, John.] "William Cullen Bryant," in "American Writers," *Blackwood's Edinburgh Magazine*, XVI, 304-11 (Sept.,

[1] For extracts from this essay see Appendix III.

1824). (An eruption by an eccentric American Romanticist.[1])

Nevins, Allan. *The Evening Post: A Century of Journalism.* New York: 1922. (A well-informed narrative of Bryant's career as newspaper editor, clearly revealing his political liberalism.)

Otto, Walther. *William Cullen Bryants Poetische Werke und Übersetzungen.* Leipzig: 1903. (Perfunctory; emphasizes Bryant's relations with European literature.)

Palmer, Ray. "William Cullen Bryant and His Writings," *International Review*, I, 433-57 (July, 1874), and in *Men of Mark* (ed. E. P. Whipple). New York: 1877, pp. 102-26. (Adulation such as filled Bryant's last years.)

Parrington, Vernon L. "William Cullen Bryant, Puritan Liberal," in *The Romantic Revolution in America.* New York: 1927, pp. 238-46 (Appreciative summary of Bryant's liberal ideas.)

Pattee, F. L. "The Centenary of Bryant's Poetry," in *Side-Lights on American Literature.* New York: 1922, pp. 293-326. (A shrewd review of Bryant's life and work, designed to prove that he was of the eighteenth, not the nineteenth century.)

Phelps, W. L. "William Cullen Bryant, Father of American Poetry," *Ladies' Home Journal*, XL, 14 ff. (June, 1923), and in *Howells, James, Bryant and Other Essays.* New York: 1924, pp. 1-30. (A brisk essay.)

[Phillips, Willard.] Review of *Poems* (Cambridge: 1821), *North American Review*, XIII, 380-1 (Oct., 1821). (Praise by a personal friend.[1])

Poe, E. A. Review of *Poems* (New York: 1836), *Southern Literary Messenger*, III, 41-9 (Jan., 1837), and in *Complete Works of Edgar Allan Poe.* New York: 1902. Monticello Edition, IX, 268-305. (Notable approval for Bryant's work as a whole, a discussion of his metrics, and detailed analyses of numerous poems.[1])

[1] For extracts from this essay see Appendix III.

Poe, E. A. "A Notice of William Cullen Bryant," *Burton's Gentleman's Magazine*, VI, 203-5 (May, 1840), and in *The Complete Works of Edgar Allan Poe*. New York: 1902. Monticello Edition, X, 85-91. (Defends Bryant as a correct and elevated artist.)

Poe, E. A. Review of *Complete Poetical Works* (New York: 1846), *Godey's Magazine and Lady's Book*, XXXII, 182-6 (April, 1846), and in *The Complete Works of Edgar Allan Poe*. New York: 1902. Monticello Edition, XIII, 125-41. (Explains why Bryant is not a poet of the first or perhaps even of the second rank; praises various poems.[1])

Powell, Thomas. "William Cullen Bryant," in *The Living Authors of America*. New York: 1850, pp. 189-221. (Examination of Bryant as a reflective poet.)

Review of *Poems* (London: 1832), *Foreign Quarterly Review*, X, 121-38 (August, 1832). (Representative of the earlier English attitude toward Bryant—tolerant but unenthusiastic.[1])

Review of *Thirty Poems* (New York: 1864), *Independent*, XVI, 2 (Jan. 21, 1864), and *Littell's Living Age*, LXXX, 307-10 (Feb. 13, 1864). (Representative of the mid-century American attitude—uncritical and reverent.[1])

Russell, J. A. "The Romantic Indian in Bryant's Poetry," *Education*, XLVIII, 642-9 (June, 1928). (Superficial.)

Schick, J. S. "William Cullen Bryant and Théophile Gautier," *Modern Language Journal*, XVII, 260-7 (Jan., 1933). (Bryant's "The Poet" at certain points resembles Gautier's "L'Art.")

Sedgwick, H. J., Jr. "Bryant's Permanent Contribution to Literature," *Atlantic Monthly*, LXXIX, 539-49 (April, 1897). (Disillusioned exposition of Bryant's serenity, simplicity, and lack of force.)

Smith, Frank. "Schoolcraft, Bryant, and Poetic Fame," *American Literature*, V, 170-2 (May, 1933). (A letter on fame and fashions in poetry.)

[1] For extracts from this essay see Appendix III.

[Snelling, W. J.] Review of *Poems* (New York: 1832), *North American Review*, XXXIV, 502-14 (March, 1832). (Vigorous comments by a contemporary versifier.[1])

Stedman, E. C. "Mr. Bryant's 'Thirty Poems,'" *The Round Table*, I, 73-4 (Jan. 16, 1864), and in *Genius and Other Essays*. New York: 1911, pp. 111-24. (A competent review.)

Stedman, E. C. "William Cullen Bryant," in *Poets of America*. Boston: 1885, pp. 62-94. (A sober but appreciative statement of Victorian opinion, emphasizing "the elemental" in Bryant.)

Strong, A. H. "William Cullen Bryant," in *American Poets and Their Theology*. Philadelphia: 1916, pp. 3-48. (Demonstrates that Bryant was thoroughly ethical but never a sound Trinitarian.)

Taylor, Bayard. "Mr. Bryant's Translation of the Iliad," *New York Tribune*, Feb. 10, 1870, and in *Critical Essays and Literary Notes*. New York: 1880, pp. 258-75. (Comment by a poet and translator.)

Thayer, W. R. "Bryant's Centennial," *Review of Reviews*, X, 401-6 (Oct., 1894), and in *Throne-Makers*. Boston: 1899, pp. 309-29. (Rational observations.)

Tuckerman, H. T. "The Poetry of Bryant," *Democratic Review*, XVI, 185-91 (Feb., 1845), and in *Thoughts on the Poets*. New York: 1846, pp. 303-8. (Unqualified praise for the inspired poet of nature, recording "emotions recollected in tranquillity.")

Van Doren, Carl. "The Growth of Thanatopsis," *Nation*, CI, 432-3 (Oct. 7, 1915). (Keen analysis of poem as a pagan reply to Henry Kirke White's "Who will hear of Henry?")

Whipple, E. P. "Bryant," in *Literature and Life*. Boston, 1871, pp. 303-21. (Extreme example of uncritical adulation.)

Wilson, John. "American Poetry. William Cullen Bryant," *Blackwood's Edinburgh Magazine*, XXXI, 646-64 (April, 1832), and in *Essays, Critical and Imaginative*. Edinburgh: 1856, II, 191-223. (Sanely appreciative, stressing Bryant's Americanism.[1])

[1] For extracts from this essay see Appendix III.

IV. BIBLIOGRAPHY

Sturges, H. C. *Chronologies of the Life and Writings of William Cullen Bryant, with a Bibliography of His Works in Prose and Verse.* New York: 1903, and in *Poetical Works.* New York: 1903, Roslyn Edition. (Lists Bryant's individual poems in supposed order of composition, principal editions, and separate publications both in prose and in verse. Useful but inaccurate and incomplete. Various errors in Sturges are corrected and new bibliographical facts are recorded in the footnotes and notes to the present volume.)

The Cambridge History of American Literature. New York: 1917. I, 517-21. (The most recent item here cited was published in 1911.)

Herrick, A. H. "Chronology of a Group of Poems by W. C. Bryant," *Modern Language Notes*, XXXII, 180-2 (March, 1917). (Points out errors in the dating by Godwin and by Sturges of seven poems.)

For material published since 1923 see the annual "American Bibliography" of *P M L A*, and since 1929 the bibliographies published in *American Literature.*

*

Selections from
WILLIAM CULLEN BRYANT

*

POEMS

THANATOPSIS

To him who in the love of Nature holds
Communion with her visible forms, she speaks
A various language; for his gayer hours
She has a voice of gladness, and a smile
And eloquence of beauty, and she glides
Into his darker musings, with a mild
And healing sympathy, that steals away
Their sharpness, ere he is aware. When thoughts
Of the last bitter hour come like a blight
Over thy spirit, and sad images   10
Of the stern agony, and shroud, and pall,
And breathless darkness, and the narrow house,
Make thee to shudder, and grow sick at heart;—
Go forth, under the open sky, and list
To Nature's teachings, while from all around—
Earth and her waters, and the depths of air—
Comes a still voice—Yet a few days, and thee
The all-beholding sun shall see no more
In all his course; nor yet in the cold ground,
Where thy pale form was laid, with many tears,   20
Nor in the embrace of ocean, shall exist
Thy image. Earth, that nourished thee, shall claim
Thy growth, to be resolved to earth again,
And, lost each human trace, surrendering up
Thine individual being, shalt thou go
To mix for ever with the elements,
To be a brother to the insensible rock
And to the sluggish clod, which the rude swain
Turns with his share, and treads upon. The oak
Shall send his roots abroad, and pierce thy mould.   30

Yet not to thine eternal resting-place
Shalt thou retire alone, nor couldst thou wish
Couch more magnificent. Thou shalt lie down
With patriarchs of the infant world—with kings,
The powerful of the earth—the wise, the good,
Fair forms, and hoary seers of ages past,
All in one mighty sepulchre. The hills
Rock-ribbed and ancient as the sun,—the vales
Stretching in pensive quietness between;
The venerable woods—rivers that move   40
In majesty, and the complaining brooks
That make the meadows green; and, poured round all,
Old Ocean's gray and melancholy waste,—
Are but the solemn decorations all
Of the great tomb of man. The golden sun,
The planets, all the infinite host of heaven,
Are shining on the sad abodes of death,
Through the still lapse of ages. All that tread
The globe are but a handful to the tribes
That slumber in its bosom.—Take the wings   50
Of morning, pierce the Barcan wilderness,
Or lose thyself in the continuous woods
Where rolls the Oregon, and hears no sound,
Save his own dashings—yet the dead are there:
And millions in those solitudes, since first
The flight of years began, have laid them down
In their last sleep—the dead reign there alone.
So shalt thou rest, and what if thou withdraw
In silence from the living, and no friend
Take note of thy departure? All that breathe   60
Will share thy destiny. The gay will laugh
When thou art gone, the solemn brood of care
Plod on, and each one as before will chase
His favorite phantom; yet all these shall leave
Their mirth and their employments, and shall come
And make their bed with thee. As the long train
Of ages glide away, the sons of men,

The youth in life's green spring, and he who goes
In the full strength of years, matron and maid,
The speechless babe, and the gray-headed man— 70
Shall one by one be gathered to thy side,
By those, who in their turn shall follow them.

So live, that when thy summons comes to join
The innumerable caravan, which moves
To that mysterious realm, where each shall take
His chamber in the silent halls of death,
Thou go not, like the quarry-slave at night,
Scourged to his dungeon, but, sustained and soothed
By an unfaltering trust, approach thy grave,
Like one who wraps the drapery of his couch 80
About him, and lies down to pleasant dreams.

1811   1817, 1821

THE YELLOW VIOLET

When beechen buds begin to swell,
   And woods the blue-bird's warble know,
The yellow violet's modest bell
   Peeps from the last year's leaves below.

Ere russet fields their green resume,
   Sweet flower, I love, in forest bare,
To meet thee, when thy faint perfume
   Alone is in the virgin air.

Of all her train, the hands of Spring
   First plant thee in the watery mould, 10
And I have seen thee blossoming
   Beside the snow-bank's edges cold.

Thy parent sun, who bade thee view
   Pale skies, and chilling moisture sip,
Has bathed thee in his own bright hue,
   And streaked with jet thy glowing lip.

Yet slight thy form, and low thy seat,
    And earthward bent thy gentle eye,
Unapt the passing view to meet
    When loftier flowers are flaunting nigh.   20

Oft, in the sunless April day,
    Thy early smile has stayed my walk;
But midst the gorgeous blooms of May,
    I passed thee on thy humble stalk.

So they, who climb to wealth, forget
    The friends in darker fortunes tried.
I copied them—but I regret
    That I should ape the ways of pride.

And when again the genial hour
    Awakes the painted tribes of light,   30
I'll not o'erlook the modest flower
    That made the woods of April bright.

1814   1821

INSCRIPTION FOR THE ENTRANCE TO A WOOD

Stranger, if thou hast learned a truth which needs
No school of long experience, that the world
Is full of guilt and misery, and hast seen
Enough of all its sorrows, crimes, and cares,
To tire thee of it, enter this wild wood
And view the haunts of Nature. The calm shade
Shall bring a kindred calm, and the sweet breeze
That makes the green leaves dance, shall waft a balm
To thy sick heart. Thou wilt find nothing here
Of all that pained thee in the haunts of men,   10
And made thee loathe thy life. The primal curse
Fell, it is true, upon the unsinning earth,
But not in vengeance. God hath yoked to guilt
Her pale tormentor, misery. Hence, these shades

Are still the abodes of gladness; the thick roof
Of green and stirring branches is alive
And musical with birds, that sing and sport
In wantonness of spirit; while below
The squirrel, with raised paws and form erect,
Chirps merrily. Throngs of insects in the shade   20
Try their thin wings and dance in the warm beam
That waked them into life. Even the green trees
Partake the deep contentment; as they bend
To the soft winds, the sun from the blue sky
Looks in and sheds a blessing on the scene.
Scarce less the cleft-born wild-flower seems to enjoy
Existence, than the wingèd plunderer
That sucks its sweets. The mossy rocks themselves,
And the old and ponderous trunks of prostrate trees
That lead from knoll to knoll a causey rude   30
Or bridge the sunken brook, and their dark roots,
With all their earth upon them, twisting high,
Breathe fixed tranquillity. The rivulet
Sends forth glad sounds, and tripping o'er its bed
Of pebbly sands, or leaping down the rocks,
Seems, with continuous laughter, to rejoice
In its own being. Softly tread the marge,
Lest from her midway perch thou scare the wren
That dips her bill in water. The cool wind,
That stirs the stream in play, shall come to thee,   40
Like one that loves thee nor will let thee pass
Ungreeted, and shall give its light embrace.
1815   1817

"I CANNOT FORGET WITH WHAT FERVID DEVOTION"

I cannot forget with what fervid devotion
   I worshipped the visions of verse and of fame;
Each gaze at the glories of earth, sky, and ocean,
   To my kindled emotions, was wind over flame.

And deep were my musings in life's early blossom,
  'Mid the twilight of mountain-groves wandering long;
How thrilled my young veins, and how throbbed my full bosom,
  When o'er me descended the spirit of song!

'Mong the deep-cloven fells that for ages had listened
  To the rush of the pebble-paved river between,   10
Where the kingfisher screamed and gray precipice glistened,
  All breathless with awe have I gazed on the scene;

Till I felt the dark power o'er my reveries stealing,
  From the gloom of the thickets that over me hung,
And the thoughts that awoke, in that rapture of feeling,
  Were formed into verse as they rose to my tongue.

Bright visions! I mixed with the world, and ye faded,
  No longer your pure rural worshipper now;
In the haunts your continual presence pervaded,
  Ye shrink from the signet of care on my brow.   20

In the old mossy groves on the breast of the mountain,
  In deep lonely glens where the waters complain,
By the shade of the rock, by the gush of the fountain,
  I seek your loved footsteps, but seek them in vain.

Oh, leave not forlorn and forever forsaken,
  Your pupil and victim to life and its tears!
But sometimes return, and in mercy awaken
  The glories ye showed to his earlier years.
1815   1826

THE HUNTER OF THE WEST. A SONG

  Soon as the glazed and gleaming snow
    Reflects the day-dawn cold and clear,
  The hunter of the West must go,
    In depths of woods to seek the deer.

His rifle on his shoulder placed,
　　His stores of death arranged with skill,
His moccasins and snow-shoes laced—
　　Why lingers he beside the hill?

Far, in the dim and doubtful light,
　　Where woody slopes a valley leave,　　　　10
He sees what none but lover might,
　　The dwelling of his Genevieve.

And oft he turns his truant eye,
　　And pauses oft, and lingers near;
But when he marks the reddening sky,
　　He bounds away to hunt the deer.

1815　　　　　　　　　　　　　　　　　1847

TO A WATERFOWL

Whither, midst falling dew,
While glow the heavens with the last steps of day,
Far, through their rosy depths, dost thou pursue
　　Thy solitary way?

Vainly the fowler's eye
Might mark thy distant flight to do thee wrong,
As, darkly seen against the crimson sky,
　　Thy figure floats along.

Seek'st thou the plashy brink
Of weedy lake, or marge of river wide,　　　　10
Or where the rocking billows rise and sink
　　On the chafed ocean-side?

There is a Power whose care
Teaches thy way along that pathless coast—
The desert and illimitable air—
　　Lone wandering, but not lost.

    All day thy wings have fanned,
At that far height, the cold, thin atmosphere,
Yet stoop not, weary, to the welcome land,
    Though the dark night is near.   20

    And soon that toil shall end;
Soon shalt thou find a summer home, and rest,
And scream among thy fellows; reeds shall bend,
    Soon, o'er thy sheltered nest.

    Thou'rt gone, the abyss of heaven
Hath swallowed up thy form; yet, on my heart
Deeply has sunk the lesson thou hast given,
    And shall not soon depart.

    He who, from zone to zone,
Guides through the boundless sky thy certain flight,
In the long way that I must tread alone,   31
    Will lead my steps aright.

1815   1818

THE BURIAL-PLACE

A FRAGMENT

    Erewhile, on England's pleasant shores, our sires
Left not their churchyards unadorned with shades
Or blossoms, but indulgent to the strong
And natural dread of man's last home, the grave,
Its frost and silence—they disposed around,
To soothe the melancholy spirit that dwelt
Too sadly on life's close, the forms and hues
Of vegetable beauty. There the yew,
Green even amid the snows of winter, told
Of immortality, and gracefully   10
The willow, a perpetual mourner, drooped;
And there the gadding woodbine crept about,
And there the ancient ivy. From the spot

Where the sweet maiden, in her blossoming years
Cut off, was laid with streaming eyes, and hands
That trembled as they placed her there, the rose
Sprung modest, on bowed stalk, and better spoke
Her graces, than the proudest monument.
There children set about their playmate's grave
The pansy. On the infant's little bed,   20
Wet at its planting with maternal tears,
Emblem of early sweetness, early death,
Nestled the lowly primrose. 'Childless dames,
And maids that would not raise the reddened eye—
Orphans, from whose young lids the light of joy
Fled early—silent lovers, who had given
All that they lived for to the arms of earth,
Came often, o'er the recent graves to strew
Their offerings, rue, and rosemary, and flowers.

The pilgrim bands who passed the sea to keep   30
Their Sabbaths in the eye of God alone,
In his wide temple of the wilderness,
Brought not these simple customs of the heart
With them. It might be, while they laid their dead
By the vast solemn skirts of the old groves,
And the fresh virgin soil poured forth strange flowers
About their graves; and the familiar shades
Of their own native isle, and wonted blooms,
And herbs were wanting, which the pious hand
Might plant or scatter there, these gentle rites   40
Passed out of use. Now they are scarcely known,
And rarely in our borders may you meet
The tall larch, sighing in the burial-place,
Or willow, trailing low its boughs to hide
The gleaming marble. Naked rows of graves
And melancholy ranks of monuments
Are seen instead, where the coarse grass, between,
Shoots up its dull green spikes, and in the wind
Hisses, and the neglected bramble nigh,

Offers its berries to the schoolboy's hand,   50
In vain—they grow too near the dead.   Yet here,
Nature, rebuking the neglect of man,
Plants often, by the ancient mossy stone,
The brier-rose, and upon the broken turf
That clothes the fresher grave, the strawberry plant
Sprinkles its swell with blossoms, and lays forth
Her ruddy, pouting fruit. . . . . . .

1818   1821

GREEN RIVER

When breezes are soft and skies are fair,
I steal an hour from study and care,
And hie me away to the woodland scene,
Where wanders the stream with waters of green,
As if the bright fringe of herbs on its brink
Had given their stain to the wave they drink;
And they, whose meadows it murmurs through,
Have named the stream from its own fair hue.

Yet pure its waters—its shallows are bright
With colored pebbles and sparkles of light,   10
And clear the depths where its eddies play,
And dimples deepen and whirl away,
And the plane-tree's speckled arms o'ershoot
The swifter current that mines its root,
Through whose shifting leaves, as you walk the hill,
The quivering glimmer of sun and rill
With a sudden flash on the eye is thrown,
Like the ray that streams from the diamond-stone.
Oh, loveliest there the spring days come,
With blossoms, and birds, and wild-bees' hum;   20
The flowers of summer are fairest there,
And freshest the breath of the summer air;
And sweetest the golden autumn day
In silence and sunshine glides away.

Yet, fair as thou art, thou shunnest to glide,
Beautiful stream! by the village side;
But windest away from haunts of men,
To quiet valley and shaded glen;
And forest, and meadow, and slope of hill,
Around thee, are lonely, lovely, and still,   30
Lonely—save when, by thy rippling tides,
From thicket to thicket the angler glides;
Or the simpler comes, with basket and book
For herbs of power on thy banks to look;
Or haply, some idle dreamer, like me,
To wander, and muse, and gaze on thee,
Still—save the chirp of birds that feed
On the river cherry and seedy reed,
And thy own wild music gushing out
With mellow murmur of fairy shout,   40
From dawn to the blush of another day,
Like traveller singing along his way.

That fairy music I never hear,
Nor gaze on those waters so green and clear,
And mark them winding away from sight,
Darkened with shade or flashing with light,
While o'er them the vine to its thicket clings,
And the zephyr stoops to freshen his wings,
But I wish that fate had left me free
To wander these quiet haunts with thee,   50
Till the eating cares of earth should depart,
And the peace of the scene pass into my heart;
And I envy thy stream, as it glides along
Through its beautiful banks in a trance of song.

Though forced to drudge for the dregs of men,
And scrawl strange words with the barbarous pen,
And mingle among the jostling crowd,
Where the sons of strife are subtle and loud—
I often come to this quiet place,

To breathe the airs that ruffle thy face,   60
And gaze upon thee in silent dream,
For in thy lonely and lovely stream
An image of that calm life appears
That won my heart in my greener years.

1818   1821

"OH FAIREST OF THE RURAL MAIDS"

Oh fairest of the rural maids!
Thy birth was in the forest shades;
Green boughs, and glimpses of the sky,
Were all that met thine infant eye.

Thy sports, thy wanderings, when a child,
Were ever in the sylvan wild;
And all the beauty of the place
Is in thy heart and on thy face.

The twilight of the trees and rocks
Is in the light shade of thy locks;   10
Thy step is as the wind, that weaves
Its playful way among the leaves.

Thine eyes are springs, in whose serene
And silent waters heaven is seen;
Their lashes are the herbs that look
On their young figures in the brook.

The forest depths, by foot unpressed,
Are not more sinless than thy breast;
The holy peace, that fills the air
Of those calm solitudes, is there.   20

1820   1832

"OH GOD! WHOSE DREAD AND DAZZLING BROW"

Oh God! whose dread and dazzling brow
  Love never yet forsook;
On those who seek thy presence now
  In deep compassion look.

For many a frail and erring heart
  Is in thy holy sight,
And feet too willing to depart
  From the plain way of right.

Yet, pleased the humble prayer to hear,
  And kind to all that live,   10
Thou, when thou see'st the contrite tear,
  Art ready to forgive.

Lord, aid us with thy heavenly grace
  Our truest bliss to find;
Nor sternly judge our erring race,
  So feeble and so blind.

1820   1820

HYMN TO DEATH

Oh! could I hope the wise and pure in heart
Might hear my song without a frown, nor deem
My voice unworthy of the theme it tries,—
I would take up the hymn to Death, and say
To the grim power, The world hath slandered thee
And mocked thee. On thy dim and shadowy brow
They place an iron crown, and call thee king
Of terrors, and the spoiler of the world,
Deadly assassin, that strik'st down the fair,
The loved, the good—that breathest on the lights   10
Of virtue set along the vale of life,
And they go out in darkness. I am come,

Not with reproaches, not with cries and prayers,
Such as have stormed thy stern, insensible ear
From the beginning; I am come to speak
Thy praises. True it is, that I have wept
Thy conquests, and may weep them yet again,
And thou from some I love will take a life
Dear to me as my own. Yet while the spell
Is on my spirit, and I talk with thee   20
In sight of all thy trophies, face to face,
Meet is it that my voice should utter forth
Thy nobler triumphs; I will teach the world
To thank thee. Who are thine accusers?—Who?
The living!—they who never felt thy power,
And know thee not. The curses of the wretch
Whose crimes are ripe, his sufferings when thy hand
Is on him, and the hour he dreads is come,
Are writ among thy praises. But the good—
Does he whom thy kind hand dismissed to peace,   30
Upbraid the gentle violence that took off
His fetters, and unbarred his prison-cell?

Raise then the hymn to Death. Deliverer!
God hath anointed thee to free the oppressed
And crush the oppressor. When the armed chief,
The conqueror of nations, walks the world,
And it is changed beneath his feet, and all
Its kingdoms melt into one mighty realm—
Thou, while his head is loftiest and his heart
Blasphemes, imagining his own right hand   40
Almighty, thou dost set thy sudden grasp
Upon him, and the links of that strong chain
Which bound mankind are crumbled; thou dost break
Sceptre and crown, and beat his throne to dust.
Then the earth shouts with gladness, and her tribes
Gather within their ancient bounds again.
Else had the mighty of the olden time,
Nimrod, Sesostris, or the youth who feigned

His birth from Libyan Ammon, smitten yet
The nations with a rod of iron, and driven 50
Their chariot o'er our necks. Thou dost avenge,
In thy good time, the wrongs of those who know
No other friend. Nor dost thou interpose
Only to lay the sufferer asleep,
Where he who made him wretched troubles not
His rest—thou dost strike down his tyrant too.
Oh, there is joy when hands that held the scourge
Drop lifeless, and the pitiless heart is cold.
Thou too dost purge from earth its horrible
And old idolatries;—from the proud fanes 60
Each to his grave their priests go out, till none
Is left to teach their worship; then the fires
Of sacrifice are chilled, and the green moss
O'ercreeps their altars; the fallen images
Cumber the weedy courts, and for loud hymns,
Chanted by kneeling multitudes, the wind
Shrieks in the solitary aisles. When he
Who gives his life to guilt, and laughs at all
The laws that God or man has made, and round
Hedges his seat with power, and shines in wealth,— 70
Lifts up his atheist front to scoff at Heaven,
And celebrates his shame in open day,
Thou, in the pride of all his crimes, cutt'st off
The horrible example. Touched by thine,
The extortioner's hard hand foregoes the gold
Wrung from the o'er-worn poor. The perjurer,
Whose tongue was lithe, e'en now, and voluble
Against his neighbor's life, and he who laughed
And leaped for joy to see a spotless fame
Blasted before his own foul calumnies, 80
Are smit with deadly silence. He, who sold
His conscience to preserve a worthless life,
Even while he hugs himself on his escape,
Trembles, as, doubly terrible, at length,
Thy steps o'ertake him, and there is no time

For parley, nor will bribes unclench thy grasp.
Oft, too, dost thou reform thy victim, long
Ere his last hour. And when the reveller,
Mad in the chase of pleasure, stretches on,
And strains each nerve, and clears the path of life   90
Like wind, thou point'st him to the dreadful goal,
And shak'st thy hour-glass in his reeling eye,
And check'st him in mid course. Thy skeleton hand
Shows to the faint of spirit the right path,
And he is warned, and fears to step aside.
Thou sett'st between the ruffian and his crime
Thy ghastly countenance, and his slack hand
Drops the drawn knife. But, oh, most fearfully
Dost thou show forth Heaven's justice, when thy shafts
Drink up the ebbing spirit—then the hard   100
Of heart and violent of hand restores
The treasure to the friendless wretch he wronged.
Then from the writhing bosom thou dost pluck
The guilty secret; lips, for ages sealed,
Are faithless to their dreadful trust at length,
And give it up; the felon's latest breath
Absolves the innocent man who bears his crime;
The slanderer, horror-smitten, and in tears,
Recalls the deadly obloquy he forged
To work his brother's ruin. Thou dost make   110
Thy penitent victim utter to the air
The dark conspiracy that strikes at life,
And aims to whelm the laws; ere yet the hour
Is come, and the dread sign of murder given.

Thus, from the first of time, hast thou been found
On virtue's side; the wicked, but for thee,
Had been too strong for the good; the great of earth
Had crushed the weak for ever. Schooled in guile
For ages, while each passing year had brought
Its baneful lesson, they had filled the world   120
With their abominations; while its tribes,

Trodden to earth, imbruted, and despoiled,
Had knelt to them in worship; sacrifice
Had smoked on many an altar, temple-roofs
Had echoed with the blasphemous prayer and hymn:
But thou, the great reformer of the world,
Tak'st off the sons of violence and fraud
In their green pupilage, their lore half learned—
Ere guilt had quite o'errun the simple heart
God gave them at their birth, and blotted out   130
His image. Thou dost mark them flushed with hope,
As on the threshold of their vast designs
Doubtful and loose they stand, and strik'st them down.

.   .   .   .

Alas! I little thought that the stern power,
Whose fearful praise I sang, would try me thus
Before the strain was ended. It must cease—
For he is in his grave who taught my youth
The art of verse, and in the bud of life
Offered me to the Muses. Oh, cut off
Untimely! when thy reason in its strength,   140
Ripened by years of toil and studious search,
And watch of Nature's silent lessons, taught
Thy hand to practise best the lenient art
To which thou gavest thy laborious days,
And, last, thy life. And, therefore, when the earth
Received thee, tears were in unyielding eyes
And on hard cheeks, and they who deemed thy skill
Delayed their death-hour, shuddered and turned pale
When thou wert gone. This faltering verse, which thou
Shalt not, as wont, o'erlook, is all I have   150
To offer at thy grave—this—and the hope
To copy thy example, and to leave
A name of which the wretched shall not think
As of an enemy's, whom they forgive
As all forgive the dead. Rest, therefore, thou
Whose early guidance trained my infant steps—

Rest, in the bosom of God, till the brief sleep
Of death is over, and a happier life
Shall dawn to waken thine insensible dust.

    Now thou art not—and yet the men whose guilt   160
Has wearied Heaven for vengeance—he who bears
False witness—he who takes the orphan's bread,
And robs the widow—he who spreads abroad
Polluted hands in mockery of prayer,
Are left to cumber earth. Shuddering I look
On what is written, yet I blot not out
The desultory numbers; let them stand,
The record of an idle revery.

1820   1825

A WINTER PIECE

    The time has been that these wild solitudes,
Yet beautiful as wild, were trod by me
Oftener than now; and when the ills of life
Had chafed my spirit—when the unsteady pulse
Beat with strange flutterings—I would wander forth
And seek the woods. The sunshine on my path
Was to me as a friend. The swelling hills,
The quiet dells retiring far between,
With gentle invitation to explore
Their windings, were a calm society   10
That talked with me and soothed me. Then the chant
Of birds, and chime of brooks, and soft caress
Of the fresh sylvan air, made me forget
The thoughts that broke my peace, and I began
To gather simples by the fountain's brink,
And lose myself in day-dreams. While I stood
In Nature's loneliness, I was with one
With whom I early grew familiar, one
Who never had a frown for me, whose voice

Never rebuked me for the hours I stole   20
From cares I loved not, but of which the world
Deems highest, to converse with her. When shrieked
The bleak November winds, and smote the woods,
And the brown fields were herbless, and the shades,
That met above the merry rivulet,
Were spoiled, I sought, I loved them still; they seemed
Like old companions in adversity.
Still there was beauty in my walks; the brook,
Bordered with sparkling frost-work, was as gay
As with its fringe of summer flowers. Afar,   30
The village with its spires, the path of streams
And dim receding valleys, hid before
By interposing trees, lay visible
Through the bare grove, and my familiar haunts
Seemed new to me. Nor was I slow to come
Among them, when the clouds, from their still skirts,
Had shaken down on earth the feathery snow,
And all was white. The pure keen air abroad,
Albeit it breathed no scent of herb, nor heard
Love-call of bird nor merry hum of bee,   40
Was not the air of death. Bright mosses crept
Over the spotted trunks, and the close buds,
That lay along the boughs, instinct with life,
Patient, and waiting the soft breath of Spring,
Feared not the piercing spirit of the North.
The snow-bird twittered on the beechen bough,
And 'neath the hemlock, whose thick branches bent
Beneath its bright cold burden, and kept dry
A circle, on the earth, of withered leaves,
The partridge found a shelter. Through the snow   50
The rabbit sprang away. The lighter track
Of fox, and the raccoon's broad path, were there,
Crossing each other. From his hollow tree
The squirrel was abroad, gathering the nuts
Just fallen, that asked the winter cold and sway
Of winter blast, to shake them from their hold.

But Winter has yet brighter scenes—he boasts
Splendors beyond what gorgeous Summer knows;
Or Autumn with his many fruits, and woods
All flushed with many hues. Come when the rains   60
Have glazed the snow and clothed the trees with ice,
While the slant sun of February pours
Into the bowers a flood of light. Approach!
The incrusted surface shall upbear thy steps,
And the broad arching portals of the grove
Welcome thy entering. Look! the massy trunks
Are cased in the pure crystal; each light spray,
Nodding and tinkling in the breath of heaven,
Is studded with its trembling water-drops,
That glimmer with an amethystine light.   70
But round the parent-stem the long low boughs
Bend, in a glittering ring, and arbors hide
The glassy floor. Oh! you might deem the spot
The spacious cavern of some virgin mine,
Deep in the womb of earth—where the gems grow,
And diamonds put forth radiant rods and bud
With amethyst and topaz—and the place
Lit up, most royally, with the pure beam
That dwells in them. Or haply the vast hall
Of fairy palace, that outlasts the night,   80
And fades not in the glory of the sun;—
Where crystal columns send forth slender shafts
And crossing arches; and fantastic aisles
Wind from the sight in brightness, and are lost
Among the crowded pillars. Raise thine eye;
Thou seest no cavern roof, no palace vault;
There the blue sky and the white drifting cloud
Look in. Again the wildered fancy dreams
Of spouting fountains, frozen as they rose,
And fixed, with all their branching jets, in air,   90
And all their sluices sealed. All, all is light;
Light without shade. But all shall pass away
With the next sun. From numberless vast trunks

Loosened, the crashing ice shall make a sound
Like the far roar of rivers, and the eve
Shall close o'er the brown woods as it was wont.

And it is pleasant, when the noisy streams
Are just set free, and milder suns melt off
The plashy snow, save only the firm drift
In the deep glen or the close shade of pines— 100
'Tis pleasant to behold the wreaths of smoke
Roll up among the maples of the hill,
Where the shrill sound of youthful voices wakes
The shriller echo, as the clear pure lymph,
That from the wounded trees, in twinkling drops,
Falls, mid the golden brightness of the morn,
Is gathered in with brimming pails, and oft,
Wielded by sturdy hands, the stroke of axe
Makes the woods ring. Along the quiet air,
Come and float calmly off the soft light clouds, 110
Such as you see in summer, and the winds
Scarce stir the branches. Lodged in sunny cleft,
Where the cold breezes come not, blooms alone
The little wind-flower, whose just opened eye
Is blue as the spring heaven it gazes at—
Startling the loiterer in the naked groves
With unexpected beauty, for the time
Of blossoms and green leaves is yet afar.
And ere it comes, the encountering winds shall oft
Muster their wrath again, and rapid clouds 120
Shade heaven, and bounding on the frozen earth
Shall fall their volleyed stores, rounded like hail
And white like snow, and the loud North again
Shall buffet the vexed forest in his rage.

1820   1825

THE WEST WIND

Beneath the forest's skirt I rest,
 Whose branching pines rise dark and high,
And hear the breezes of the West
 Among the thread-like foliage sigh.

Sweet Zephyr! why that sound of woe?
 Is not thy home among the flowers?
Do not the bright June roses blow,
 To meet thy kiss at morning hours?

And lo! thy glorious realm outspread—
 Yon stretching valleys, green and gay, 10
And yon free hill-tops, o'er whose head
 The loose white clouds are borne away.

And there the full broad river runs,
 And many a fount wells fresh and sweet,
To cool thee when the mid-day suns
 Have made thee faint beneath their heat.

Thou wind of joy, and youth, and love;
 Spirit of the new-wakened year!
The sun in his blue realm above
 Smooths a bright path when thou art here. 20

In lawns the murmuring bee is heard,
 The wooing ring-dove in the shade;
On thy soft breath, the new-fledged bird
 Takes wing, half happy, half afraid.

Ah! thou art like our wayward race;—
 When not a shade of pain or ill
Dims the bright smile of Nature's face,
 Thou lov'st to sigh and murmur still.

1821   1822

A WALK AT SUNSET

When insect wings are glistening in the beam
　　Of the low sun, and mountain-tops are bright,
Oh, let me, by the crystal valley-stream,
　　Wander amid the mild and yellow light;
And while the wood-thrush pipes his evening lay,
Give me one lonely hour to hymn the setting day.

Oh, sun! that o'er the western mountains now
　　Go'st down in glory! ever beautiful
And blessed is thy radiance, whether thou
　　Colorest the eastern heaven and night-mist cool,　10
Till the bright day-star vanish, or on high
Climbest and streamest thy white splendors from mid-sky.

Yet, loveliest are thy setting smiles, and fair,
　　Fairest of all that earth beholds, the hues
That live among the clouds, and flush the air,
　　Lingering and deepening at the hour of dews.
Then softest gales are breathed, and softest heard
The plaining voice of streams, and pensive note of bird.

They who here roamed, of yore, the forest wide,
　　Felt, by such charm, their simple bosoms won;　20
They deemed their quivered warrior, when he died,
　　Went to bright isles beneath the setting sun;
Where winds are aye at peace, and skies are fair,
And purple-skirted clouds curtain the crimson air.

So, with the glories of the dying day,
　　Its thousand trembling lights and changing hues,
The memory of the brave who passed away
　　Tenderly mingled;—fitting hour to muse
On such grave theme, and sweet the dream that shed
Brightness and beauty round the destiny of the dead.　30

For ages, on the silent forests here,
    Thy beams did fall before the red man came
To dwell beneath them; in their shade the deer
    Fed, and feared not the arrow's deadly aim.
Nor tree was felled, in all that world of woods,
Save by the beaver's tooth, or winds, or rush of floods.

Then came the hunter tribes, and thou didst look,
    For ages, on their deeds in the hard chase,
And well-fought wars; green sod and silver brook
    Took the first stain of blood; before thy face   40
The warrior generations came and passed,
And glory was laid up for many an age to last.

Now they are gone, gone as thy setting blaze
    Goes down the west, while night is pressing on,
And with them the old tale of better days,
    And trophies of remembered power, are gone.
Yon field that gives the harvest, where the plough
Strikes the white bone, is all that tells their story now.

I stand upon their ashes in thy beam,
    The offspring of another race, I stand,   50
Beside a stream they loved, this valley-stream;
    And where the night-fire of the quivered band
Showed the gray oak by fits, and war-song rung,
I teach the quiet shades the strains of this new tongue.

Farewell! but thou shalt come again—thy light
    Must shine on other changes, and behold
The place of the thronged city still as night—
    States fallen—new empires built upon the old—
But never shalt thou see these realms again   59
Darkened by boundless groves, and roamed by savage men.

1821   1821

SPAIN

Aye, wear the chain—ye who for once have known
The sweets of freedom—yet could crouch again
In blind and trembling worship of a throne;
Aye wear—for ye are worthy—wear the chain
And bow, till ye are weary, to the yoke
      Your patriot fathers broke.

Degenerate Spaniards! let the priestly band
Possess your realm again; and let them wake
The fires of pious murder in your land,
And drag your best and bravest to the stake,   10
And tread down truth, and in the dungeon bind
      The dreaded strength of mind.

Give up the promise of bright days that cast
A glory on your nation from afar;
Call back the darkness of the ages past
To quench that holy dawn's new-risen star;
Let only tyrants and their slaves be found
      Alive on Spanish ground.

Yet mark! ye cast the gift of heaven away,
And your best blood for this shall yet be shed;   20
The fire shall waste your borders, and the way
Be covered with its heaps of festering dead,
And vultures of the cliff on every plain
      Feast high upon the slain.

The spirit that of yore had slept so long,
Then woke, and drove the Moors to Afric's shore,
Lives, and repressed, shall rise one day more strong—
Rise and redeem your shackled race once more,
And crush, mid showers of blood and shrieks and groans,
      Mitres and stars and thrones.   30

1822   1823

THE INDIAN GIRL'S LAMENT

An Indian girl was sitting where
  Her lover, slain in battle, slept;
Her maiden veil, her own black hair,
  Came down o'er eyes that wept;
And wildly, in her woodland tongue,
This sad and simple lay she sung;

"I've pulled away the shrubs that grew
  Too close above thy sleeping head,
And broke the forest-boughs that threw
  Their shadows o'er thy bed,   10
That, shining from the sweet southwest,
The sunbeams might rejoice thy rest.

"It was a weary, weary road
  That led thee to the pleasant coast,
Where thou, in his serene abode,
  Hast met thy father's ghost;
Where everlasting autumn lies
On yellow woods and sunny skies.

"'Twas I the broidered mocsen made,
  That shod thee for that distant land;   20
'Twas I thy bow and arrows laid
  Beside thy still cold hand;
Thy bow in many a battle bent,
Thy arrows never vainly sent.

"With wampum-belts I crossed thy breast,
  And wrapped thee in the bison's hide,
And laid the food that pleased thee best,
  In plenty, by thy side,
And decked thee bravely, as became
A warrior of illustrious name.   30

"Thou'rt happy now, for thou hast passed
　　The long dark journey of the grave,
And in the land of light, at last,
　　Hast joined the good and brave;
Amid the flushed and balmy air,
The bravest and the loveliest there.

"Yet, oft to thine own Indian maid
　　Even there thy thoughts will earthward stray—
To her who sits where thou wert laid,
　　And weeps the hours away,   40
Yet almost can her grief forget,
To think that thou dost love her yet.

"And thou, by one of those still lakes
　　That in a shining cluster lie,
On which the south wind scarcely breaks
　　The image of the sky,
A bower for thee and me hast made
Beneath the many-colored shade.

"And thou dost wait and watch to meet
　　My spirit sent to join the blessed,   50
And, wondering what detains my feet
　　From that bright land of rest,
Dost seem, in every sound, to hear
The rustling of my footsteps near."

1823   1826

THE RIVULET

This little rill, that from the springs
Of yonder grove its current brings,
Plays on the slope awhile, and then
Goes prattling into groves again,
Oft to its warbling waters drew
My little feet, when life was new.

When woods in early green were dressed,
And from the chambers of the west
The warm breezes, travelling out,
Breathed the new scent of flowers about,   10
My truant steps from home would stray,
Upon its grassy side to play,
List the brown thrasher's vernal hymn,
And crop the violet on its brim,
With blooming cheek and open brow,
As young and gay, sweet rill, as thou.

    And when the days of boyhood came,
And I had grown in love with fame,
Duly I sought thy banks, and tried
My first rude numbers by thy side.   20
Words cannot tell how bright and gay
The scenes of life before me lay.
Then glorious hopes, that now to speak
Would bring the blood into my cheek,
Passed o'er me; and I wrote, on high,
A name I deemed should never die.

    Years change thee not. Upon yon hill
The tall old maples, verdant still,
Yet tell, in grandeur of decay,
How swift the years have passed away   30
Since first, a child, and half afraid,
I wandered in the forest shade.
Thou, ever-joyous rivulet,
Dost dimple, leap, and prattle yet;
And sporting with the sands that pave
The windings of thy silver wave,
And dancing to thy own wild chime,
Thou laughest at the lapse of time.
The same sweet sounds are in my ear
My early childhood loved to hear;   40
As pure thy limpid waters run;

As bright they sparkle to the sun;
As fresh and thick the bending ranks
Of herbs that line thy oozy banks;
The violet there, in soft May dew,
Comes up, as modest and as blue;
As green amid thy current's stress,
Floats the scarce-rooted watercress;
And the brown ground-bird, in thy glen,
Still chirps as merrily as then. 50

Thou changest not—but I am changed
Since first thy pleasant banks I ranged;
And the grave stranger, come to see
The play-place of his infancy,
Has scarce a single trace of him
Who sported once upon thy brim.
The visions of my youth are past—
Too bright, too beautiful to last.
I've tried the world—it wears no more
The coloring of romance it wore. 60
Yet well has Nature kept the truth
She promised in my earliest youth.
The radiant beauty shed abroad
On all the glorious works of God,
Shows freshly, to my sobered eye,
Each charm it wore in days gone by.

Yet a few years shall pass away,
And I, all trembling, weak, and gray,
Bowed to the earth, which waits to fold
My ashes in the embracing mould, 70
(If haply the dark will of Fate
Indulge my life so long a date),
May come for the last time to look
Upon my childhood's favorite brook.
Then dimly on my eye shall gleam
The sparkle of thy dancing stream;

And faintly on my ear shall fall
Thy prattling current's merry call;
Yet shalt thou flow as glad and bright
As when thou met'st my infant sight.   80

And I shall sleep—and on thy side,
As ages after ages glide,
Children their early sports shall try,
And pass to hoary age and die.
But thou, unchanged from year to year,
Gayly shalt play and glitter here;
Amid young flowers and tender grass
Thy endless infancy shall pass;
And, singing down thy narrow glen,
Shalt mock the fading race of men.   90

1823   1824

THE MASSACRE AT SCIO

Weep not for Scio's children slain;
    Their blood, by Turkish falchions shed,
Sends not its cry to Heaven in vain
    For vengeance on the murderer's head.

Though high the warm red torrent ran
    Between the flames that lit the sky,
Yet, for each drop, an armèd man
    Shall rise, to free the land, or die.

And for each corpse, that in the sea
    Was thrown, to feast the scaly herds,   10
A hundred of the foe shall be
    A banquet for the mountain-birds.

Stern rites and sad shall Greece ordain
    To keep that day along her shore,
Till the last link of slavery's chain
    Is shattered, to be worn no more.

1824   1824

MARCH

The stormy March is come at last,
  With wind, and cloud, and changing skies;
I hear the rushing of the blast,
  That through the snowy valley flies.

Ah, passing few are they who speak,
  Wild, stormy month! in praise of thee;
Yet, though thy winds are loud and bleak,
  Thou art a welcome month to me.

For thou, to northern lands, again
  The glad and glorious sun dost bring,   10
And thou hast joined the gentle train
  And wear'st the gentle name of Spring.

And, in thy reign of blast and storm,
  Smiles many a long, bright, sunny day,
When the changed winds are soft and warm,
  And heaven puts on the blue of May.

Then sing aloud the gushing rills
  In joy that they again are free,
And, brightly leaping down the hills,
  Renew their journey to the sea.   20

The year's departing beauty hides
  Of wintry storms the sullen threat;
But in thy sternest frown abides
  A look of kindly promise yet.

Thou bring'st the hope of those calm skies,
  And that soft time of sunny showers,
When the wide bloom, on earth that lies,
  Seems of a brighter world than ours.

1824   1824

CONSUMPTION

Ay, thou art for the grave; thy glances shine
    Too brightly to shine long; another Spring
Shall deck her for men's eyes—but not for thine—
    Sealed in a sleep which knows no wakening.
The fields for thee have no medicinal leaf,
    And the vexed ore no mineral of power;
And they who love thee wait in anxious grief
    Till the slow plague shall bring the fatal hour.
Glide softly to thy rest, then; Death should come
    Gently, to one of gentle mould like thee,   10
As light winds wandering through groves of bloom
    Detach the delicate blossom from the tree.
Close thy sweet eyes, calmly, and without pain:
And we will trust in God to see thee yet again.

1824   1824

SUMMER WIND

    It is a sultry day; the sun has drunk
The dew that lay upon the morning grass;
There is no rustling in the lofty elm
That canopies my dwelling, and its shade
Scarce cools me. All is silent, save the faint
And interrupted murmur of the bee,
Settling on the sick flowers, and then again
Instantly on the wing. The plants around
Feel the too potent fervors: the tall maize
Rolls up its long green leaves; the clover droops   10
Its tender foliage, and declines its blooms.
But far in the fierce sunshine tower the hills,
With all their growth of woods, silent and stern,
As if the scorching heat and dazzling light
Were but an element they loved. Bright clouds,
Motionless pillars of the brazen heaven—
Their bases on the mountains—their white tops

Shining in the far ether—fire the air
With a reflected radiance, and make turn
The gazer's eye away. For me, I lie 20
Languidly in the shade, where the thick turf,
Yet virgin from the kisses of the sun,
Retains some freshness, and I woo the wind
That still delays his coming. Why so slow,
Gentle and voluble spirit of the air?
Oh, come and breathe upon the fainting earth
Coolness and life! Is it that in his caves
He hears me? See, on yonder woody ridge,
The pine is bending his proud top, and now
Among the nearer groves, chestnut and oak 30
Are tossing their green boughs about. He comes;
Lo, where the grassy meadow runs in waves!
The deep distressful silence of the scene
Breaks up with mingling of unnumbered sounds
And universal motion. He is come,
Shaking a shower of blossoms from the shrubs,
And bearing on their fragrance; and he brings
Music of birds, and rustling of young boughs,
And sound of swaying branches, and the voice
Of distant waterfalls. All the green herbs 40
Are stirring in his breath; a thousand flowers,
By the road-side and the borders of the brook,
Nod gayly to each other; glossy leaves
Are twinkling in the sun, as if the dew
Were on them yet, and silver waters break
Into small waves and sparkle as he comes.

1824   1824

LOVE'S SEASONS. A SONG

Dost thou idly ask to hear
    At what gentle seasons
Nymphs relent, when lovers near
    Press the tenderest reasons?

Ah, they give their faith too oft
   To the careless wooer;
Maidens' hearts are always soft:
   Would that men's were truer!

Woo the fair one when around
   Early birds are singing;   10
When, o'er all the fragrant ground,
   ·Early herbs are springing;
When the brookside, bank, and grove,
   All with blossoms laden,
Shine with beauty, breathe of love,—
   Woo the timid maiden.

Woo her when, with rosy blush,
   Summer eve is sinking;
When, on rills that softly gush,
   Stars are softly winking;   20
When through boughs that knit the bower
   Moonlight gleams are stealing;
Woo her, till the gentle hour
   Wake a gentler feeling.

Woo her, when autumnal dyes
   Tinge the woody mountain;
When the dropping foliage lies
   In the weedy fountain;
Let the scene, that tells how fast
   Youth is passing over,   30
Warn her, ere her bloom is past,
   To secure her lover.

Woo her when the north winds call
   At the lattice nightly;
When, within the cheerful hall,
   Blaze the fagots brightly;
While the wintry tempest round

Sweeps the landscape hoary,
Sweeter in her ear shall sound
Love's delightful story.   40

1824   1824

"I BROKE THE SPELL THAT HELD ME LONG"

I broke the spell that held me long,
The dear, dear witchery of song.
I said, the poet's idle lore
Shall waste my prime of years no more,
For Poetry, though heavenly born,
Consorts with poverty and scorn.

I broke the spell—nor deemed its power
Could fetter me another hour.
Ah, thoughtless! how could I forget
Its causes were around me yet?   10
For wheresoe'er I looked, the while,
Was Nature's everlasting smile.

Still came and lingered on my sight
Of flowers and streams the bloom and light,
And glory of the stars and sun;
And these and poetry are one.
They, ere the world had held me long,
Recalled me to the love of song.

1824   1824

HYMN OF THE WALDENSES

Hear, Father, hear thy faint afflicted flock
Cry to thee, from the desert and the rock;
While those, who seek to slay thy children, hold
Blasphemous worship under roofs of gold;
And the broad goodly lands, with pleasant airs
That nurse the grape and wave the grain, are theirs.

Yet better were this mountain wilderness,
And this wild life of danger and distress—
Watchings by night and perilous flight by day,
And meetings in the depths of earth to pray—   10
Better, far better, than to kneel with them,
And pay the impious rite thy laws condemn.

Thou, Lord, dost hold the thunder; the firm land
Tosses in billows when it feels thy hand;
Thou dashest nation against nation, then
Stillest the angry world to peace again.
Oh, touch their stony hearts who hunt thy sons—
The murderers of our wives and little ones.

Yet, mighty God, yet shall thy frown look forth
Unveiled, and terribly shall shake the earth.   20
Then the foul power of priestly sin and all
Its long-upheld idolatries shall fall.
Thou shalt raise up the trampled and oppressed,
And thy delivered saints shall dwell in rest.

1824   1824

MONUMENT MOUNTAIN

Thou who wouldst see the lovely and the wild
Mingled in harmony on Nature's face,
Ascend our rocky mountains. Let thy foot
Fail not with weariness, for on their tops
The beauty and the majesty of earth,
Spread wide beneath, shall make thee to forget
The steep and toilsome way. There, as thou stand'st,
The haunts of men below thee, and around
The mountain-summits, thy expanding heart
Shall feel a kindred with that loftier world   10
To which thou art translated, and partake
The enlargement of thy vision. Thou shalt look
Upon the green and rolling forest-tops,
And down into the secrets of the glens,

And streams that with their bordering thickets strive
To hide their windings. Thou shalt gaze, at once,
Here on white villages, and tilth, and herds,
And swarming roads, and there on solitudes
That only hear the torrent, and the wind,
And eagle's shriek. There is a precipice   20
That seems a fragment of some mighty wall,
Built by the hand that fashioned the old world,
To separate its nations, and thrown down
When the flood drowned them. To the north, a path
Conducts you up the narrow battlement.
Steep is the western side, shaggy and wild
With mossy trees, and pinnacles of flint,
And many a hanging crag. But, to the east,
Sheer to the vale go down the bare old cliffs—
Huge pillars, that in middle heaven upbear   30
Their weather-beaten capitals, here dark
With moss, the growth of centuries, and there
Of chalky whiteness where the thunderbolt
Has splintered them. It is a fearful thing
To stand upon the beetling verge, and see
Where storm and lightning, from that huge gray wall,
Have tumbled down vast blocks, and at the base
Dashed them in fragments, and to lay thine ear
Over the dizzy depth, and hear the sound
Of winds, that struggle with the woods below,   40
Come up like ocean murmurs. But the scene
Is lovely round; a beautiful river there
Wanders amid the fresh and fertile meads,
The paradise he made unto himself,
Mining the soil for ages. On each side
The fields swell upward to the hills; beyond,
Above the hills, in the blue distance, rise
The mountain-columns with which earth props heaven.

There is a tale about these reverend rocks,
A sad tradition of unhappy love,   50

And sorrows borne and ended, long ago,
When over these fair vales the savage sought
His game in the thick woods.   There was a maid,
The fairest of the Indian maids, bright-eyed,
With wealth of raven tresses, a light form,
And a gay heart.   About her cabin-door
The wide old woods resounded with her song
And fairy laughter all the summer day.
She loved her cousin; such a love was deemed,
By the morality of those stern tribes,   60
Incestuous, and she struggled hard and long
Against her love, and reasoned with her heart,
As simple Indian maiden might.   In vain.
Then her eye lost its lustre, and her step
Its lightness, and the gray-haired men that passed
Her dwelling, wondered that they heard no more
The accustomed song and laugh of her, whose looks
Were like the cheerful smile of Spring, they said,
Upon the Winter of their age.   She went
To weep where no eye saw, and was not found .   70
When all the merry girls were met to dance,
And all the hunters of the tribe were out;
Nor when they gathered from the rustling husk
The shining ear; nor when, by the river's side,
They pulled the grape and startled the wild shades
With sounds of mirth.   The keen-eyed Indian dames
Would whisper to each other, as they saw
Her wasting form, and say, *The girl will die.*

     One day into the bosom of a friend,
A playmate of her young and innocent years,   80
She poured her griefs.   "Thou know'st, and thou alone,"
She said, "for I have told thee, all my love,
And guilt, and sorrow.   I am sick of life.
All night I weep in darkness, and the morn
Glares on me, as upon a thing accursed,
That has no business on the earth.   I hate

The pastimes and the pleasant toils that once
I loved; the cheerful voices of my friends
Sound in my ear like mockings, and, at night,
In dreams, my mother, from the land of souls,   90
Calls me and chides me. All that look on me
Do seem to know my shame; I cannot bear
Their eyes; I cannot from my heart root out
The love that wrings it so, and I must die."

     It was a summer morning, and they went
To this old precipice. About the cliffs
Lay garlands, ears of maize, and shaggy skins
Of wolf and bear, the offerings of the tribe
Here made to the Great Spirit, for they deemed,
Like worshippers of the elder time, that God   100
Doth walk on the high places and affect
The earth-o'erlooking mountains. She had on
The ornaments with which her father loved
To deck the beauty of his bright-eyed girl,
And bade her wear when stranger warriors came
To be his guests. Here the friends sat them down,
And sang, all day, old songs of love and death,
And decked the poor wan victim's hair with flowers,
And prayed that safe and swift might be her way
To the calm world of sunshine, where no grief   110
Makes the heart heavy and the eyelids red.
Beautiful lay the region of her tribe
Below her—waters resting in the embrace
Of the wide forest, and maize-planted glades
Opening amid the leafy wilderness.
She gazed upon it long, and at the sight
Of her own village peeping through the trees,
And her own dwelling, and the cabin-roof
Of him she loved with an unlawful love,
And came to die for, a warm gush of tears   120
Ran from her eyes. But when the sun grew low
And the hill shadows long, she threw herself

From the steep rock and perished. There was scooped,
Upon the mountain's southern slope, a grave;
And there they laid her, in the very garb
With which the maiden decked herself for death,
With the same withering wild-flowers in her hair.
And o'er the mould that covered her, the tribe
Built up a simple monument, a cone
Of small loose stones. Thenceforward all who passed, 130
Hunter, and dame, and virgin, laid a stone
In silence on the pile. It stands there yet.
And Indians from the distant West, who come
To visit where their fathers' bones are laid,
Yet tell the sorrowful tale, and to this day
The mountain where the hapless maiden died
Is called the Mountain of the Monument.

1824   1824

AFTER A TEMPEST

The day had been a day of wind and storm,
The wind was laid, the storm was overpast,
And stooping from the zenith, bright and warm,
Shone the great sun on the wide earth at last.
I stood upon the upland slope, and cast
Mine eye upon a broad and beauteous scene,
Where the vast plain lay girt by mountains vast,
And hills o'er hills lifted their heads of green,
With pleasant vales scooped out and villages between.

The rain-drops glistened on the trees around,   10
Whose shadows on the tall grass were not stirred,
Save when a shower of diamonds, to the ground,
Was shaken by the flight of startled bird;
For birds were warbling round, and bees were heard
About the flowers; the cheerful rivulet sung
And gossiped, as he hastened oceanward;
To the gray oak the squirrel, chiding, clung,
And chirping from the ground the grasshopper upsprung.

And from beneath the leaves that kept them dry
Flew many a glittering insect here and there,   20
And darted up and down the butterfly,
That seemed a living blossom of the air,
The flocks came scattering from the thicket, where
The violent rain had pent them; in the way
Strolled groups of damsels frolicsome and fair;
The farmer swung the scythe or turned the hay,
And 'twixt the heavy swaths his children were at play.

It was a scene of peace—and, like a spell,
Did that serene and golden sunlight fall
Upon the motionless wood that clothed the fell,   30
And precipice upspringing like a wall,
And glassy river and white waterfall,
And happy living things that trod the bright
And beauteous scene; while far beyond them all,
On many a lovely valley, out of sight,
Was poured from the blue heavens the same soft golden light.

I looked, and thought the quiet of the scene
An emblem of the peace that yet shall be,
When o'er earth's continents, and isles between,
The noise of war shall cease from sea to sea,   40
And married nations dwell in harmony;
When millions, crouching in the dust to one,
No more shall beg their lives on bended knee,
Nor the black stake be dressed, nor in the sun
The o'erlabored captive toil, and wish his life were done.

Too long, at clash of arms amid her bowers
And pools of blood, the earth has stood aghast,
The fair earth, that should only blush with flowers
And ruddy fruits; but not for aye can last
The storm, and sweet the sunshine when 'tis past.   50
Lo, the clouds roll away—they break—they fly,

And, like the glorious light of summer, cast
O'er the wide landscape from the embracing sky,
On all the peaceful world the smile of heaven shall lie.

1824   1824

AUTUMN WOODS

Ere, in the northern gale,
The summer tresses of the trees are gone,
The woods of Autumn, all around our vale,
    Have put their glory on.

The mountains that infold,
In their wide sweep, the colored landscape round,
Seem groups of giant kings, in purple and gold,
    That guard the enchanted ground.

I roam the woods that crown
The uplands, where the mingled splendors glow,   10
Where the gay company of trees look down
    On the green fields below.

My steps are not alone
In these bright walks; the sweet southwest, at play,
Flies, rustling, where the painted leaves are strown
    Along the winding way.

And far in heaven, the while,
The sun, that sends that gale to wander here,
Pours out on the fair earth his quiet smile—
    The sweetest of the year.   20

Where now the solemn shade,
Verdure and gloom where many branches meet;
So grateful, when the noon of summer made
    The valleys sick with heat?

Let in through all the trees
Come the strange rays; the forest depths are bright;
Their sunny colored foliage, in the breeze,
    Twinkles, like beams of light.

    The rivulet, late unseen,
Where bickering through the shrubs its waters run,   30
Shines with the image of its golden screen,
    And glimmerings of the sun.

    But 'neath yon crimson tree,
Lover to listening maid might breathe his flame,
Nor mark, within its roseate canopy,
    Her blush of maiden shame.

    O Autumn! why so soon
Depart the hues that make thy forests glad,
Thy gentle wind and thy fair sunny noon,
    And leave thee wild and sad!   40

    Ah! 'twere a lot too blest
Forever in thy colored shades to stray;
Amid the kisses of the soft southwest
    To roam and dream for aye;

    And leave the vain low strife
That makes men mad—the tug for wealth and power—
The passions and the cares that wither life,
    And waste its little hour.

1824   1824

MUTATION

They talk of short-lived pleasure—be it so—
    Pain dies as quickly: stern, hard-featured Pain
Expires, and lets her weary prisoner go.
    The fiercest agonies have shortest reign;
    And after dreams of horror, comes again

The welcome morning with its rays of peace.
    Oblivion, softly wiping out the stain,
Makes the strong secret pangs of shame to cease:
Remorse is virtue's root; its fair increase
    Are fruits of innocence and blessedness: 10
Thus joy, o'erborne and bound, doth still release
    His young limbs from the chains that round him press.
Weep not that the world changes—did it keep
A stable, changeless state, 'twere cause indeed to weep.

1824   1824

NOVEMBER

Yet one smile more, departing, distant sun!
    One mellow smile through the soft vapory air,
Ere, o'er the frozen earth, the loud winds run,
    Or snows are sifted o'er the meadows bare.
One smile on the brown hills and naked trees,
    And the dark rocks whose summer wreaths are cast,
And the blue gentian-flower, that, in the breeze,
    Nods lonely, of her beauteous race the last.
Yet a few sunny days, in which the bee
    Shall murmur by the hedge that skirts the way,   10
The cricket chirp upon the russet lea,
    And man delight to linger in thy ray.
Yet one rich smile, and we will try to bear
The piercing winter frost, and winds, and darkened air.

1824   1824

TO A CLOUD

Beautiful cloud! with folds so soft and fair,
    Swimming in the pure quiet air!
Thy fleeces bathed in sunlight, while below
    Thy shadow o'er the vale moves slow;
Where, midst their labor, pause the reaper train,
    As cool it comes along the grain.

Beautiful cloud! I would I were with thee
   In thy calm way o'er land and sea;
To rest on thy unrolling skirts, and look
   On Earth as on an open book;   10
On streams that tie her realms with silver bands,
   And the long ways that seam her lands;
And hear her humming cities, and the sound
   Of the great ocean breaking round.
Ay—I would sail, upon thy air-borne car,
   To blooming regions distant far,
To where the sun of Andalusia shines
   On his own olive-groves and vines,
Or the soft lights of Italy's clear sky
   In smiles upon her ruins lie.   20

But I would woo the winds to let us rest
   O'er Greece, long fettered and oppressed,
Whose sons at length have heard the call that comes
   From the old battle-fields and tombs,
And risen, and drawn the sword, and on the foe
   Have dealt the swift and desperate blow,
And the Othman power is cloven, and the stroke
   Has touched its chains, and they are broke.
Ay, we would linger, till the sunset there
   Should come, to purple all the air,   30
And thou reflect upon the sacred ground
   The ruddy radiance streaming round.

Bright meteor! for the summer noontide made!
   Thy peerless beauty yet shall fade.
The sun, that fills with light each glistening fold,
   Shall set, and leave thee dark and cold:
The blast shall rend thy skirts, or thou mayst frown
   In the dark heaven when storms come down;
And weep in rain, till man's inquiring eye
   Miss thee, forever, from the sky.   40

1824   1824

SONG OF THE STARS

When the radiant morn of creation broke,
And the world in the smile of God awoke,
And the empty realms of darkness and death
Were moved through their depths by his mighty breath,
And orbs of beauty and spheres of flame
From the void abyss by myriads came—
In the joy of youth as they darted away,
Through the widening wastes of space to play,
Their silver voices in chorus rang,
And this was the song the bright ones sang: 10

"Away, away, through the wide, wide sky,
The fair blue fields that before us lie—
Each sun with the worlds that round him roll,
Each planet, poised on her turning pole;
With her isles of green, and her clouds of white,
And her waters that lie like fluid light.

"For the source of glory uncovers his face,
And the brightness o'erflows unbounded space,
And we drink as we go the luminous tides
In our ruddy air and our blooming sides: 20
Lo, yonder the living splendors play;
Away, on our joyous path, away!

"Look, look, through our glittering ranks afar,
In the infinite azure, star after star,
How they brighten and bloom as they swiftly pass!
How the verdure runs o'er each rolling mass!
And the path of the gentle winds is seen,
Where the small waves dance, and the young woods lean.

"And see, where the brighter day-beams pour,
How the rainbows hang in the sunny shower;   30
And the morn and eve, with their pomp of hues,

Shift o'er the bright planets and shed their dews;
And 'twixt them both, o'er the teeming ground,
With her shadowy cone the night goes round!

"Away, away! in our blossoming bowers,
In the soft air wrapping these spheres of ours,
In the seas and fountains that shine with morn,
See, Love is brooding, and Life is born,
And breathing myriads are breaking from night,
To rejoice, like us, in motion and light.   4c

"Glide on in your beauty, ye youthful spheres,
To weave the dance that measures the years;
Glide on, in the glory and gladness sent
To the farthest wall of the firmament—
The boundless visible smile of Him
To the veil of whose brow your lamps are dim."

1825   1825

A FOREST HYMN

The groves were God's first temples.   Ere man learned
To hew the shaft, and lay the architrave,
And spread the roof above them—ere he framed
The lofty vault, to gather and roll back
The sound of anthems; in the darkling wood,
Amid the cool and silence, he knelt down,
And offered to the Mightiest solemn thanks
And supplication.   For his simple heart
Might not resist the sacred influences
Which, from the stilly twilight of the place,   10
And from the gray old trunks that high in heaven
Mingled their mossy boughs, and from the sound
Of the invisible breath that swayed at once
All their green tops, stole over him, and bowed
His spirit with the thought of boundless power
And inaccessible majesty.   Ah, why

Should we, in the world's riper years, neglect
God's ancient sanctuaries, and adore
Only among the crowd, and under roofs
That our frail hands have raised? Let me, at least,   20
Here, in the shadow of this aged wood,
Offer one hymn—thrice happy, if it find
Acceptance in His ear.

                              Father, thy hand
Hath reared these venerable columns, thou
Didst weave this verdant roof. Thou didst look down
Upon the naked earth, and, forthwith, rose
All these fair ranks of trees. They, in thy sun,
Budded, and shook their green leaves in thy breeze,
And shot toward heaven. The century-living crow
Whose birth was in their tops, grew old and died   30
Among their branches, till, at last, they stood,
As now they stand, massy, and tall, and dark,
Fit shrine for humble worshipper to hold
Communion with his Maker. These dim vaults,
These winding aisles, of human pomp or pride
Report not. No fantastic carvings show
The boast of our vain race to change the form
Of thy fair works. But thou art here—thou fill'st
The solitude. Thou art in the soft winds
That run along the summit of these trees   40
In music; thou art in the cooler breath
That from the inmost darkness of the place
Comes, scarcely felt; the barky trunks, the ground,
The fresh moist ground, are all instinct with thee.
Here is continual worship;—Nature, here,
In the tranquillity that thou dost love,
Enjoys thy presence. Noiselessly, around,
From perch to perch, the solitary bird
Passes; and yon clear spring, that, midst its herbs,
Wells softly forth and wandering steeps the roots   50
Of half the mighty forest, tells no tale

Of all the good it does. Thou hast not left
Thyself without a witness, in these shades,
Of thy perfections. Grandeur, strength, and grace
Are here to speak of thee. This mighty oak—
By whose immovable stem I stand and seem
Almost annihilated—not a prince,
In all that proud old world beyond the deep,
E'er wore his crown as loftily as he
Wears the green coronal of leaves with which   60
Thy hand has graced him. Nestled at his root
Is beauty, such as blooms not in the glare
Of the broad sun. That delicate forest flower,
With scented breath and look so like a smile,
Seems, as it issues from the shapeless mould,
An emanation of the indwelling Life,
A visible token of the upholding Love,
That are the soul of this great universe.

My heart is awed within me when I think
Of the great miracle that still goes on,   70
In silence, round me—the perpetual work
Of thy creation, finished, yet renewed
Forever. Written on thy works I read
The lesson of thy own eternity.
Lo! all grow old and die—but see again,
How on the faltering footsteps of decay
Youth presses—ever-gay and beautiful youth
In all its beautiful forms. These lofty trees
Wave not less proudly that their ancestors
Moulder beneath them. Oh, there is not lost   80
One of earth's charms: upon her bosom yet,
After the flight of untold centuries,
The freshness of her far beginning lies
And yet shall lie. Life mocks the idle hate
Of his arch-enemy Death—yea, seats himself
Upon the tyrant's throne—the sepulchre,
And of the triumphs of his ghastly foe

Makes his own nourishment. For he came forth
From thine own bosom, and shall have no end.

There have been holy men who hid themselves   90
Deep in the woody wilderness, and gave
Their lives to thought and prayer, till they outlived
The generation born with them, nor seemed
Less aged than the hoary trees and rocks
Around them;—and there have been holy men
Who deemed it were not well to pass life thus.
But let me often to these solitudes
Retire, and in thy presence reassure
My feeble virtue. Here its enemies,
The passions, at thy plainer footsteps shrink   100
And tremble and are still. O God! when thou
Dost scare the world with tempests, set on fire
The heavens with falling thunderbolts, or fill,
With all the waters of the firmament,
The swift dark whirlwind that uproots the woods
And drowns the villages; when, at thy call,
Uprises the great deep and throws himself
Upon the continent, and overwhelms
Its cities—who forgets not, at the sight
Of these tremendous tokens of thy power,   110
His pride, and lays his strifes and follies by?
Oh, from these sterner aspects of thy face
Spare me and mine, nor let us need the wrath
Of the mad, unchained elements to teach
Who rules them. Be it ours to meditate,
In these calm shades, thy milder majesty,
And to the beautiful order of thy works
Learn to conform the order of our lives.

1825   1825

JUNE

I gazed upon the glorious sky
    And the green mountains round,
And thought that when I came to lie
    At rest within the ground,
'Twere pleasant, that in flowery June,
When brooks send up a cheerful tune,
    And groves a joyous sound,
The sexton's hand, my grave to make,
The rich, green mountain-turf should break.

A cell within the frozen mould,
    A coffin borne through sleet,
And icy clods above it rolled,
    While fierce the tempests beat—
Away!—I will not think of these—
Blue be the sky and soft the breeze,
    Earth green beneath the feet,
And be the damp mould gently pressed
Into my narrow place of rest.

There through the long, long summer hours,
    The golden light should lie,
And thick young herbs and groups of flowers
    Stand in their beauty by.
The oriole should build and tell
His love-tale close beside my cell;
    The idle butterfly
Should rest him there, and there be heard
The housewife bee and humming-bird.

And what if cheerful shouts at noon
    Come, from the village sent,
Or song of maids, beneath the moon
    With fairy laughter blent?
And what if, in the evening light,

Betrothèd lovers walk in sight
    Of my low monument?
I would the lovely scene around
Might know no sadder sight nor sound.

I know that I no more should see
    The season's glorious show,
Nor would its brightness shine for me,
    Nor its wild music flow;   40
But if, around my place of sleep,
The friends I love should come to weep,
    They might not haste to go.
Soft airs, and song, and light, and bloom
Should keep them lingering by my tomb.

These to their softened hearts should bear
    The thought of what has been,
And speak of one who cannot share
    The gladness of the scene;
Whose part, in all the pomp that fills   50
The circuit of the summer hills,
    Is that his grave is green;
And deeply would their hearts rejoice
To hear again his living voice.

1825   1826

LINES ON REVISITING THE COUNTRY

I stand upon my native hills again,
    Broad, round, and green, that in the summer sky
With garniture of waving grass and grain,
    Orchards, and beechen forests, basking lie,
While deep the sunless glens are scooped between,
Where brawl o'er shallow beds the streams unseen.

A lisping voice and glancing eyes are near,
    And ever-restless feet of one, who, now,

Gathers the blossoms of her fourth bright year;
   There plays a gladness o'er her fair young brow   10
As breaks the varied scene upon her sight,
Upheaved and spread in verdure and in light.

For I have taught her, with delighted eye,
   To gaze upon the mountains—to behold,
With deep affection, the pure ample sky
   And clouds along its blue abysses rolled,
To love the song of waters, and to hear
The melody of winds with charmèd ear.

Here have I 'scaped the city's stifling heat,
   Its horrid sounds, and its polluted air,   20
And, where the season's milder fervors beat,
   And gales, that sweep the forest borders, bear
The song of bird and sound of running stream,
Am come awhile to wander and to dream.

Ay, flame thy fiercest, sun! thou canst not wake,
   In this pure air, the plague that walks unseen.
The maize-leaf and the maple-bough but take,
   From thy strong heats, a deeper, glossier green.
The mountain wind, that faints not in thy ray,
Sweeps the blue steams of pestilence away.   30

The mountain wind! most spiritual thing of all
   The wide earth knows; when, in the sultry time,
He stoops him from his vast cerulean hall,
   He seems the breath of a celestial clime!
As if from heaven's wide-open gates did flow
Health and refreshment on the world below.

1825   1825

THE AFRICAN CHIEF

Chained in the market-place he stood,
    A man of giant frame,
Amid the gathering multitude
    That shrunk to hear his name—
All stern of look and strong of limb,
    His dark eye on the ground:—
And silently they gazed on him
    As on a lion bound.

Vainly, but well, that chief had fought,
    He was a captive now,   10
Yet pride, that fortune humbles not,
    Was written on his brow.
The scars his dark broad bosom wore
    Showed warrior true and brave;
A prince among his tribe before,
    He could not be a slave.

Then to his conqueror he spake:
    "My brother is a king;
Undo this necklace from my neck,
    And take this bracelet ring,   20
And send me where my brother reigns,
    And I will fill thy hands
With store of ivory from the plains,
    And gold-dust from the sands."

"Not for thy ivory nor thy gold
    Will I unbind thy chain;
That bloody hand shall never hold
    The battle-spear again.
A price thy nation never gave
    Shall yet be paid for thee;   30
For thou shalt be the Christian's slave,
    In lands beyond the sea,"

Then wept the warrior chief, and bade
    To shred his locks away;
And one by one, each heavy braid
    Before the victor lay.
Thick were the platted locks, and long,
    And closely hidden there
Shone many a wedge of gold among
    The dark and crispèd hair.   40

"Look, feast thy greedy eye with gold
    Long kept for sorest need:
Take it—thou askest sums untold—
    And say that I am freed.
Take it—my wife, the long, long day,
    Weeps by the cocoa-tree,
And my young children leave their play,
    And ask in vain for me."

"I take thy gold, but I have made
    Thy fetters fast and strong,   50
And ween that by the cocoa-shade
    Thy wife will wait thee long."
Strong was the agony that shook
    The captive's frame to hear,
And the proud meaning of his look
    Was changed to mortal fear.

His heart was broken—crazed his brain:
    At once his eye grew wild;
He struggled fiercely with his chain,
    Whispered, and wept, and smiled;   60
Yet wore not long those fatal bands,
    And once, at shut of day,
They drew him forth upon the sands,
    The foul hyena's prey.

1825   1826

TO A MOSQUITO

Fair insect! that, with threadlike legs spread out,
 And blood-extracting bill and filmy wing,
Dost murmur, as thou slowly sail'st about,
 In pitiless ears full many a plaintive thing,
And tell how little our large veins would bleed,
Would we but yield them to thy bitter need.

Unwillingly, I own, and, what is worse,
 Full angrily men hearken to thy plaint;
Thou gettest many a brush, and many a curse,
 For saying thou art gaunt, and starved, and faint; 10
Even the old beggar, while he asks for food,
Would kill thee, hapless stranger, if he could.

I call thee stranger, for the town, I ween,
 Has not the honor of so proud a birth—
Thou com'st from Jersey meadows, fresh and green,
 The offspring of the gods, though born on earth;
For Titan was thy sire, and fair was she,
The ocean-nymph that nursed thy infancy.

Beneath the rushes was thy cradle swung,
 And when at length thy gauzy wings grew strong, 20
Abroad to gentle airs their folds were flung,
 Rose in the sky and bore thee soft along;
The south wind breathed to waft thee on thy way,
And danced and shone beneath the billowy bay.

Calm rose afar the city spires, and thence
 Came the deep murmur of its throng of men,
And as its grateful odors met thy sense,
 They seemed the perfumes of thy native fen.
Fair lay its crowded streets, and at the sight
Thy tiny song grew shriller with delight. 30

At length thy pinions fluttered in Broadway—
   Ah! there were fairy steps, and white necks kissed
By wanton airs, and eyes whose killing ray
   Shone through the snowy veils like stars through mist;
And fresh as morn, on many a cheek and chin,
Bloomed the bright blood through the transparent skin.

Sure these were sights to touch an anchorite!
   What! do I hear thy slender voice complain?
Thou wailest when I talk of beauty's light,
   As if it brought the memory of pain;   40
Thou art a wayward being—well—come near,
And pour thy tale of sorrow in my ear.

What sayest thou—slanderer!—rouge makes thee sick?
   And China bloom at best is sorry food?
And Rowland's Kalydor, if laid on thick,
   Poisons the thirsty wretch that bores for blood?
Go! 'twas a just reward that met thy crime—
But shun the sacrilege another time.

That bloom was made to look at, not to touch;
   To worship, not approach, that radiant white;   50
And well might sudden vengeance light on such
   As dared, like thee, most impiously to bite.
Thou shouldst have gazed at distance and admired,
Murmured thy adoration, and retired.

Thou'rt welcome to the town; but why come here
   To bleed a brother poet, gaunt like thee?
Alas! the little blood I have is dear,
   And thin will be the banquet drawn from me.
Look round—the pale-eyed sisters in my cell,
Thy old acquaintance, Song and Famine, dwell.   60

Try some plump alderman, and suck the blood
   Enriched by generous wine and costly meat;

On well-filled skins, sleek as thy native mud,
    Fix thy light pump and press thy freckled feet.
Go to the men for whom, in ocean's halls,
The oyster breeds, and the green turtle sprawls.

There corks are drawn, and the red vintage flows
    To fill the swelling veins for thee, and now
The ruddy cheek and now the ruddier nose
    Shall tempt thee, as thou flittest round the brow.   70
And when the hour of sleep its quiet brings,
No angry hands shall rise to brush thy wings.

1825   1825

THE DEATH OF THE FLOWERS

The melancholy days have come, the saddest of the year,
Of wailing winds, and naked woods, and meadows brown and
    sere;
Heaped in the hollows of the grove, the autumn leaves lie dead;
They rustle to the eddying gust, and to the rabbit's tread;
The robin and the wren are flown, and from the shrubs the jay,
And from the wood-top calls the crow through all the gloomy
    day.

Where are the flowers, the fair young flowers, that lately sprang
    and stood
In brighter light and softer airs, a beauteous sisterhood?
Alas! they all are in their graves, the gentle race of flowers
Are lying in their lowly beds, with the fair and good of ours. 10
The rain is falling where they lie, but the cold November rain
Calls not from out the gloomy earth the lovely ones again.

The wind-flower and the violet, they perished long ago,
And the brier-rose and the orchis died amid the summer glow;
But on the hill the golden-rod, and the aster in the wood,
And the yellow sunflower by the brook in autumn beauty stood,

Till fell the frost from the clear cold heaven, as falls the plague
on men,
And the brightness of their smile was gone, from upland, glade,
and glen.

And now, when comes the calm mild day, as still such days will
come,
To call the squirrel and the bee from out their winter home; 20
When the sound of dropping nuts is heard, though all the trees
are still,
And twinkle in the smoky light the waters of the rill,
The south wind searches for the flowers whose fragrance late
he bore,
And sighs to find them in the wood and by the stream no more.

And then I think of one who in her youthful beauty died,
The fair meek blossom that grew up and faded by my side.
In the cold moist earth we laid her, when the forests cast the
leaf,
And we wept that one so lovely should have a life so brief:
Yet not unmeet it was that one, like that young friend of ours,
So gentle and so beautiful, should perish with the flowers. 30
1825   1825

THE GLADNESS OF NATURE

Is this a time to be cloudy and sad,
    When our mother Nature laughs around;
When even the deep blue heavens look glad,
    And gladness breathes from the blossoming ground?

There are notes of joy from the hang-bird and wren,
    And the gossip of swallows through all the sky;
The ground-squirrel gayly chirps by his den,
    And the wilding bee hums merrily by.

The clouds are at play in the azure space,
    And their shadows at play on the bright-green vale, 10

And here they stretch to the frolic chase,
    And there they roll on the easy gale.

There's a dance of leaves in that aspen bower,
    There's a titter of winds in that beechen tree,
There's a smile on the fruit, and a smile on the flower,
    And a laugh from the brook that runs to the sea.

And look at the broad-faced sun, how he smiles
    On the dewy earth that smiles in his ray,
On the leaping waters and gay young isles;
    Ay, look, and he'll smile thy gloom away.   20

1826   1826

A SUMMER RAMBLE

The quiet August noon has come;
    A slumberous silence fills the sky,
The fields are still, the woods are dumb,
    In glassy sleep the waters lie.

And mark yon soft white clouds that rest
    Above our vale, a moveless throng;
The cattle on the mountain's breast
    Enjoy the grateful shadow long.

Oh, how unlike those merry hours,
    In early June, when Earth laughs out,   10
When the fresh winds make love to flowers,
    And woodlands sing and waters shout—

When in the grass sweet voices talk,
    And strains of tiny music swell
From every moss-cup of the rock,
    From every nameless blossom's bell!

But now a joy too deep for sound,
    A peace no other season knows,

Hushes the heavens and wraps the ground,
   The blessing of supreme repose.   20

Away! I will not be, to-day,
   The only slave of toil and care;
Away from desk and dust! away!
   I'll be as idle as the air.

Beneath the open sky abroad,
   Among the plants and breathing things,
The sinless, peaceful works of God,
   I'll share the calm the season brings.

Come, thou, in whose soft eyes I see
   The gentle meanings of thy heart,   30
One day amid the woods with me,
   From men and all their cares apart.

And where, upon the meadow's breast,
   The shadow of the thicket lies,
The blue wild-flowers thou gatherest
   Shall glow yet deeper near thine eyes.

Come, and when mid the calm profound,
   I turn, those gentle eyes to seek,
They, like the lovely landscape round,
   Of innocence and peace shall speak.   40

Rest here, beneath the unmoving shade,
   And on the silent valleys gaze,
Winding and widening, till they fade
   In yon soft ring of summer haze.

The village trees their summits rear
   Still as its spire, and yonder flock
At rest in those calm fields appear
   As chiselled from the lifeless rock.

One tranquil mount the scene o'erlooks—
    There the hushed winds their sabbath keep, 50
While a near hum from bees and brooks
    Comes faintly like the breath of sleep.

Well may the gazer deem that when,
    Worn with the struggle and the strife,
And heart-sick at the wrongs of men,
    The good forsakes the scene of life;

Like this deep quiet that, awhile,
    Lingers the lovely landscape o'er,
Shall be the peace whose holy smile
    Welcomes him to a happier shore. 60

1826   1826

THE HURRICANE

Lord of the winds! I feel thee nigh,
I know thy breath in the burning sky!
And I wait, with a thrill in every vein,
For the coming of the hurricane!

And lo! on the wing of the heavy gales,
Through the boundless arch of heaven he sails;
Silent and slow, and terribly strong,
The mighty shadow is borne along,
Like the dark eternity to come;
While the world below, dismayed and dumb, 10
Through the calm of the thick hot atmosphere,
Looks up at its gloomy folds with fear.

They darken fast; and the golden blaze
Of the sun is quenched in the lurid haze,
And he sends through the shade a funeral ray—
A glare that is neither night nor day,
A beam that touches, with hues of death,

The clouds above and the earth beneath.
To its covert glides the silent bird,
While the hurricane's distant voice is heard   20
Uplifted among the mountains round,
And the forests hear and answer the sound.

He is come! he is come! do ye not behold
His ample robes on the wind unrolled?
Giant of air! we bid thee hail!—
How his gray skirts toss in the whirling gale;
How his huge and writhing arms are bent
To clasp the zone of the firmament,
And fold at length, in their dark embrace,
From mountain to mountain the visible space!   30

Darker—still darker! the whirlwinds bear
The dust of the plains to the middle air:
And hark to the crashing, long and loud,
Of the chariot of God in the thunder-cloud!
You may trace its path by the flashes that start
From the rapid wheels where'er they dart,
As the fire-bolts leap to the world below,
And flood the skies with a lurid glow.

What roar is that?—'tis the rain that breaks
In torrents away from the airy lakes,   40
Heavily poured on the shuddering ground,
And shedding a nameless horror round.
Ah! well-known woods, and mountains, and skies,
With the very clouds!—ye are lost to my eyes.
I seek ye vainly, and see in your place
The shadowy tempest that sweeps through space,
A whirling ocean that fills the wall
Of the crystal heaven, and buries all.
And I, cut off from the world, remain
Alone with the terrible hurricane.   50

1827   1827

THE PAST

Thou unrelenting Past!
Strong are the barriers round thy dark domain,
    And fetters, sure and fast,
Hold all that enter thy unbreathing reign.

    Far in thy realm withdrawn
Old empires sit in sullenness and gloom,
    And glorious ages gone
Lie deep within the shadow of thy womb.

    Childhood, with all its mirth,
Youth, Manhood, Age that draws us to the ground,   10
    And last, Man's Life on earth,
Glide to thy dim dominions, and are bound.

    Thou hast my better years;
Thou hast my earlier friends, the good, the kind,
    Yielded to thee with tears—
The venerable form, the exalted mind.

    My spirit yearns to bring
The lost ones back—yearns with desire intense,
    And struggles hard to wring
Thy bolts apart, and pluck thy captives thence.   20

    In vain; thy gates deny
All passage save to those who hence depart;
    Nor to the streaming eye
Thou giv'st them back—nor to the broken heart.

    In thy abysses hide
Beauty and excellence unknown; to thee
    Earth's wonder and her pride
Are gathered, as the waters to the sea;

Labors of good to man,
Unpublished charity, unbroken faith, 30
Love, that midst grief began,
And grew with years, and faltered not in death.

Full many a mighty name
Lurks in thy depths, unuttered, unrevered;
With thee are silent fame,
Forgotten arts, and wisdom disappeared.

Thine for a space are they—
Yet shalt thou yield thy treasures up at last:
Thy gates shall yet give way,
Thy bolts shall fall, inexorable Past! 40

All that of good and fair
Has gone into thy womb from earliest time,
Shall then come forth to wear
The glory and the beauty of its prime.

They have not perished—no!
Kind words, remembered voices once so sweet,
Smiles, radiant long ago,
And features, the great soul's apparent seat.

All shall come back; each tie
Of pure affection shall be knit again;
Alone shall Evil die, 50
And Sorrow dwell a prisoner in thy reign.

And then shall I behold
Him, by whose kind paternal side I sprung,
And her, who, still and cold,
Fills the next grave—the beautiful and young.

1828   1828

THE EVENING WIND

Spirit that breathest through my lattice, thou
    That cool'st the twilight of the sultry day,
Gratefully flows thy freshness round my brow;
    Thou hast been out upon the deep at play,
Riding all day the wild blue waves till now,
    Roughening their crests, and scattering high their spray,
And swelling the white sail. I welcome thee
To the scorched land, thou wanderer of the sea!

Nor I alone; a thousand bosoms round
    Inhale thee in the fulness of delight;   10
And languid forms rise up, and pulses bound
    Livelier, at coming of the wind of night;
And, languishing to hear thy grateful sound,
    Lies the vast inland stretched beyond the sight.
Go forth into the gathering shade; go forth,
God's blessing breathed upon the fainting earth!

Go, rock the little wood-bird in his nest,
    Curl the still waters, bright with stars, and rouse
The wide old wood from his majestic rest,
    Summoning from the innumerable boughs   20
The strange, deep harmonies that haunt his breast:
    Pleasant shall be thy way where meekly bows
The shutting flower, and darkling waters pass,
And where the o'ershadowing branches sweep the grass.

The faint old man shall lean his silver head
    To feel thee; thou shalt kiss the child asleep,
And dry the moistened curls that overspread
    His temples, while his breathing grows more deep:
And they who stand about the sick man's bed,
    Shall joy to listen to thy distant sweep,   30
And softly part his curtains to allow
Thy visit, grateful to his burning brow.

Go—but the circle of eternal change,
    Which is the life of Nature, shall restore,
With sounds and scents from all thy mighty range,
    Thee to thy birthplace of the deep once more;
Sweet odors in the sea-air, sweet and strange,
    Shall tell the homesick mariner of the shore;
And, listening to thy murmur, he shall deem
He hears the rustling leaf and running stream.   40

1829   1829

THE SIESTA

FROM THE SPANISH

> Vientecico murmurador,
> Que lo gozas y andas todo, etc.

Airs, that wander and murmur round,
    Bearing delight where'er ye blow!
Make in the elms a lulling sound,
    While my lady sleeps in the shade below.

Lighten and lengthen her noonday rest,
    Till the heat of the noonday sun is o'er.
Sweet be her slumbers! though in my breast
    The pain she has waked may slumber no more.

Breathing soft from the blue profound,
    Bearing delight where'er ye blow,   10
Make in the elms a lulling sound,
    While my lady sleeps in the shade below.

Airs! that over the bending boughs,
    And under the shade of pendent leaves,
Murmur soft, like my timid vows
    Or the secret sighs my bosom heaves—

Gently sweeping the grassy ground,
    Bearing delight where'er ye blow,

Make in the elms a lulling sound,
While my lady sleeps in the shade below.   20

1829

TO COLE, THE PAINTER, DEPARTING FOR EUROPE

Thine eyes shall see the light of distant skies;
Yet, COLE! thy heart shall bear to Europe's strand
A living image of our own bright land,
Such as upon thy glorious canvas lies;
Lone lakes—savannas where the bison roves—
Rocks rich with summer garlands—solemn streams—
Skies, where the desert eagle wheels and screams—
Spring bloom and autumn blaze of boundless groves.
Fair scenes shall greet thee where thou goest—fair,
But different—everywhere the trace of men,   10
Paths, homes, graves, ruins, from the lowest glen
To where life shrinks from the fierce Alpine air—
Gaze on them, till the tears shall dim thy sight,
But keep that earlier, wilder image bright.

1829   1829

TO THE FRINGED GENTIAN

Thou blossom bright with autumn dew
And colored with the heaven's own blue,
That openest when the quiet light
Succeeds the keen and frosty night—

Thou comest not when violets lean
O'er wandering brooks and springs unseen,
Or columbines, in purple dressed,
Nod o'er the ground-bird's hidden nest.

Thou waitest late and com'st alone,
When woods are bare and birds are flown,   10
And frosts and shortening days portend
The aged year is near his end.

Then doth thy sweet and quiet eye
Look through its fringes to the sky,
Blue—blue—as if that sky let fall
A flower from its cerulean wall.

I would that thus, when I shall see
The hour of death draw near to me,
Hope, blossoming within my heart,
May look to heaven as I depart.   20

1829   1832

HYMN OF THE CITY

Not in the solitude
Alone may man commune with Heaven, or see,
        Only in savage wood
And sunny vale, the present Deity;
        Or only hear his voice
Where the winds whisper and the waves rejoice.

        Even here do I behold
Thy steps, Almighty!—here, amid the crowd
        Through the great city rolled,
With everlasting murmur deep and loud—   10
        Choking the ways that wind
'Mong the proud piles, the work of human kind.

        Thy golden sunshine comes
From the round heaven, and on their dwellings lies
        And lights their inner homes;
For them thou fill'st with air the unbounded skies,
        And givest them the stores
Of ocean, and the harvests of its shores.

        Thy Spirit is around,
Quickening the restless mass that sweeps along;   20
        And this eternal sound—
Voices and footfalls of the numberless throng—

Like the resounding sea,
Or like the rainy tempest, speaks of Thee.

And when the hour of rest
Comes, like a calm upon the mid-sea brine,
    Hushing its billowy breast—
The quiet of that moment too is thine;
    It breathes of Him who keeps
The vast and helpless city while it sleeps.   30

1830   1830

SONG OF MARION'S MEN

Our band is few but true and tried,
    Our leader frank and bold;
The British soldier trembles
    When Marion's name is told.
Our fortress is the good greenwood,
    Our tent the cypress-tree;
We know the forest round us,
    As seamen know the sea.
We know its walls of thorny vines,
    Its glades of reedy grass,   10
Its safe and silent islands
    Within the dark morass.

Woe to the English soldiery
    That little dread us near!
On them shall light at midnight
    A strange and sudden fear:
When, waking to their tents on fire,
    They grasp their arms in vain,
And they who stand to face us
    Are beat to earth again;   20
And they who fly in terror deem
    A mighty host behind,

And hear the tramp of thousands
   Upon the hollow wind.

Then sweet the hour that brings release
   From danger and from toil:
We talk the battle over,
   And share the battle's spoil.
The woodland rings with laugh and shout,
   As if a hunt were up,   30
And woodland flowers are gathered
   To crown the soldier's cup.
With merry songs we mock the wind
   That in the pine-top grieves,
And slumber long and sweetly
   On beds of oaken leaves.

Well knows the fair and friendly moon
   The band that Marion leads—
The glitter of their rifles,
   The scampering of their steeds.   40
'Tis life to guide the fiery barb
   Across the moonlit plain;
'Tis life to feel the night-wind
   That lifts his tossing mane.
A moment in the British camp—
   A moment—and away
Back to the pathless forest,
   Before the peep of day.

Grave men there are by broad Santee,
   Grave men with hoary hairs;   50
Their hearts are all with Marion,
   For Marion are their prayers.
And lovely ladies greet our band
   With kindliest welcoming,
With smiles like those of summer,
   And tears like those of spring.

For them we wear these trusty arms,
   And lay them down no more
Till we have driven the Briton,
   Forever, from our shore.   60

1831   1831

THE PRAIRIES

These are the gardens of the Desert, these
The unshorn fields, boundless and beautiful,
For which the speech of England has no name—
The Prairies. I behold them for the first,
And my heart swells, while the dilated sight
Takes in the encircling vastness. Lo! they stretch
In airy undulations, far away,
As if the Ocean, in his gentlest swell,
Stood still, with all his rounded billows fixed,
And motionless forever. Motionless?—   10
No—they are all unchained again. The clouds
Sweep over with their shadows, and, beneath,
The surface rolls and fluctuates to the eye;
Dark hollows seem to glide along and chase
The sunny ridges. Breezes of the South!
Who toss the golden and the flame-like flowers,
And pass the prairie-hawk that, poised on high,
Flaps his broad wings, yet moves not—ye have played
Among the palms of Mexico and vines
Of Texas, and have crisped the limpid brooks   20
That from the fountains of Sonora glide
Into the calm Pacific—have ye fanned
A nobler or a lovelier scene than this?
Man hath no part in all this glorious work:
The hand that built the firmament hath heaved
And smoothed these verdant swells, and sown their slopes
With herbage, planted them with island-groves,
And hedged them round with forests. Fitting floor
For this magnificent temple of the sky—
With flowers whose glory and whose multitude   30

Rival the constellations! The great heavens
Seem to stoop down upon the scene in love,—
A nearer vault, and of a tenderer blue,
Than that which bends above our Eastern hills.

    As o'er the verdant waste I guide my steed,
Among the high rank grass that sweeps his sides
The hollow beating of his footstep seems
A sacrilegious sound. I think of those
Upon whose rest he tramples. Are they here—
The dead of other days?—and did the dust   40
Of these fair solitudes once stir with life
And burn with passion? Let the mighty mounds
That overlook the rivers, or that rise
In the dim forest crowded with old oaks,
Answer. A race, that long has passed away,
Built them; a disciplined and populous race
Heaped, with long toil, the earth, while yet the Greek
Was hewing the Pentelicus to forms
Of symmetry, and rearing on its rock
The glittering Parthenon. These ample fields   50
Nourished their harvests, here their herds were fed,
When haply by their stalls the bison lowed,
And bowed his manèd shoulder to the yoke.
All day this desert murmured with their toils,
Till twilight blushed, and lovers walked, and wooed
In a forgotten language, and old tunes,
From instruments of unremembered form,
Gave the soft winds a voice. The red-man came—
The roaming hunter-tribes, warlike and fierce,
And the mound-builders vanished from the earth.   60
The solitude of centuries untold
Has settled where they dwelt. The prairie-wolf
Hunts in their meadows, and his fresh-dug den
Yawns by my path. The gopher mines the ground
Where stood their swarming cities. All is gone;
All—save the piles of earth that hold their bones,

The platforms where they worshipped unknown gods,
The barriers which they builded from the soil
To keep the foe at bay—till o'er the walls
The wild beleaguerers broke, and, one by one,   70
The strongholds of the plain were forced, and heaped
With corpses. The brown vultures of the wood
Flocked to those vast uncovered sepulchres,
And sat, unscared and silent, at their feast.
Haply some solitary fugitive,
Lurking in marsh and forest, till the sense
Of desolation and of fear became
Bitterer than death, yielded himself to die.
Man's better nature triumphed then. Kind words
Welcomed and soothed him; the rude conquerors   80
Seated the captive with their chiefs; he chose
A bride among their maidens, and at length
Seemed to forget—yet ne'er forgot—the wife
Of his first love, and her sweet little ones,
Butchered, amid their shrieks, with all his race.

    Thus change the forms of being. Thus arise
Races of living things, glorious in strength,
And perish, as the quickening breath of God
Fills them, or is withdrawn. The red-man, too,
Has left the blooming wilds he ranged so long,   90
And, nearer to the Rocky Mountains, sought
A wilder hunting-ground. The beaver builds
No longer by these streams, but far away,
On waters whose blue surface ne'er gave back
The white man's face—among Missouri's springs,
And pools whose issues swell the Oregon—
He rears his little Venice. In these plains
The bison feeds no more. Twice twenty leagues
Beyond remotest smoke of hunter's camp,
Roams the majestic brute, in herds that shake   100
The earth with thundering steps—yet here I meet
His ancient footprints stamped beside the pool.

Still this great solitude is quick with life.
Myriads of insects, gaudy as the flowers
They flutter over, gentle quadrupeds,
And birds, that scarce have learned the fear of man,
Are here, and sliding reptiles of the ground,
Startlingly beautiful. The graceful deer
Bounds to the wood at my approach. The bee,
A more adventurous colonist than man, 110
With whom he came across the eastern deep,
Fills the savannas with his murmurings,
And hides his sweets, as in the golden age,
Within the hollow oak. I listen long
To his domestic hum, and think I hear
The sound of that advancing multitude
Which soon shall fill these deserts. From the ground
Comes up the laugh of children, the soft voice
Of maidens, and the sweet and solemn hymn
Of Sabbath worshippers. The low of herds 120
Blends with the rustling of the heavy grain
Over the dark brown furrows. All at once
A fresher wind sweeps by, and breaks my dream,
And I am in the wilderness alone.

1832   1833

EARTH

A midnight black with clouds is in the sky;
I seem to feel, upon my limbs, the weight
Of its vast brooding shadow. All in vain
Turns the tired eye in search of form; no star
Pierces the pitchy veil; no ruddy blaze,
From dwellings lighted by the cheerful hearth,
Tinges the flowering summits of the grass.
No sound of life is heard, no village hum,
Nor measured tramp of footstep in the path,
Nor rush of wind, while, on the breast of Earth, 10
I lie and listen to her mighty voice:

A voice of many tones—sent up from streams
That wander through the gloom, from woods unseen
Swayed by the sweeping of the tides of air,
From rocky chasms where darkness dwells all day,
And hollows of the great invisible hills,
And sands that edge the ocean, stretching far
Into the night—a melancholy sound!

O Earth! dost thou too sorrow for the past
Like man thy offspring? Do I hear thee mourn   20
Thy childhood's unreturning hours, thy springs
Gone with their genial airs and melodies,
The gentle generations of thy flowers,
And thy majestic groves of olden time,
Perished with all their dwellers? Dost thou wail
For that fair age of which the poets tell,
Ere yet the winds grew keen with frost, or fire
Fell with the rains or spouted from the hills,
To blast thy greenness, while the virgin night
Was guiltless and salubrious as the day?   30
Or haply dost thou grieve for those that die—
For living things that trod thy paths awhile,
The love of thee and heaven—and now they sleep
Mixed with the shapeless dust on which thy herds
Trample and graze? I too must grieve with thee,
O'er loved ones lost. Their graves are far away
Upon thy mountains; yet, while I recline
Alone, in darkness, on thy naked soil,
The mighty nourisher and burial-place
Of man, I feel that I embrace their dust.   40

Ha! how the murmur deepens! I perceive
And tremble at its dreadful import. Earth
Uplifts a general cry for guilt and wrong,
And heaven is listening. The forgotten graves
Of the heart-broken utter forth their plaint.
The dust of her who loved and was betrayed,

And him who died neglected in his age;
The sepulchres of those who for mankind
Labored, and earned the recompense of scorn;
Ashes of martyrs for the truth, and bones   50
Of those who, in the strife for liberty,
Were beaten down, their corses given to dogs,
Their names to infamy, all find a voice.
The nook in which the captive, overtoiled,
Lay down to rest at last, and that which holds
Childhood's sweet blossoms, crushed by cruel hands,
Send up a plaintive sound. From battle-fields,
Where heroes madly drave and dashed their hosts
Against each other, rises up a noise,
As if the armèd multitudes of dead   60
Stirred in their heavy slumber. Mournful tones
Come from the green abysses of the sea—
A story of the crimes the guilty sought
To hide beneath its waves. The glens, the groves,
Paths in the thicket, pools of running brook,
And banks and depths of lake, and streets and lanes
Of cities, now that living sounds are hushed,
Murmur of guilty force and treachery.

Here, where I rest, the vales of Italy
Are round me, populous from early time,   70
And field of the tremendous warfare waged
'Twixt good and evil. Who, alas! shall dare
Interpret to man's ear the mingled voice
That comes from her old dungeons yawning now
To the black air, her amphitheatres,
Where the dew gathers on the mouldering stones,
And fanes of banished gods, and open tombs,
And roofless palaces, and streets and hearths
Of cities dug from their volcanic graves?
I hear a sound of many languages,   80
The utterance of nations now no more,
Driven out by mightier, as the days of heaven

Chase one another from the sky. The blood
Of freemen shed by freemen, till strange lords
Came in their hour of weakness, and made fast
The yoke that yet is worn, cries out to Heaven.

    What then shall cleanse thy bosom, gentle Earth,
From all its painful memories of guilt?
The whelming flood, or the renewing fire,
Or the slow change of time?—that so, at last,   90
The horrid tale of perjury and strife,
Murder and spoil, which men call history,
May seem a fable, like the inventions told
By poets of the gods of Greece. O thou,
Who sittest far beyond the Atlantic deep,
Among the sources of thy glorious streams,
My native Land of Groves! a newer page
In the great record of the world is thine;
Shall it be fairer? Fear, and friendly Hope,
And Envy, watch the issue, while the lines,   100
By which thou shalt be judged, are written down.

1834   1835

TO THE APENNINES

Your peaks are beautiful, ye Apennines!
    In the soft light of these serenest skies;
From the broad highland region, black with pines,
    Fair as the hills of Paradise they rise,
Bathed in the tint Peruvian slaves behold
In rosy flushes on the virgin gold.

There, rooted to the aërial shelves that wear
    The glory of a brighter world, might spring
Sweet flowers of heaven to scent the unbreathed air,
    And heaven's fleet messengers might rest the wing
To view the fair earth in its summer sleep,   11
Silent, and cradled by the glimmering deep.

Below you lie men's sepulchres, the old
    Etrurian tombs, the graves of yesterday;
The herd's white bones lie mixed with human mould,
    Yet up the radiant steeps that I survey
Death never climbed, nor life's soft breath, with pain,
Was yielded to the elements again.

Ages of war have filled these plains with fear;
    How oft the hind has started at the clash   20
Of spears, and yell of meeting armies here,
    Or seen the lightning of the battle flash
From clouds, that rising with the thunder's sound,
Hung like an earth-born tempest o'er the ground!

Ah me! what armèd nations—Asian horde,
    And Libyan host, the Scythian and the Gaul—
Have swept your base and through your passes poured,
    Like ocean-tides uprising at the call
Of tyrant winds—against your rocky side
The bloody billows dashed, and howled, and died!   30

How crashed the towers before beleaguering foes,
    Sacked cities smoked and realms were rent in twain;
And commonwealths against their rivals rose,
    Trode out their lives and earned the curse of Cain!
While, in the noiseless air and light that flowed
Round your fair brows, eternal Peace abode.

Here pealed the impious hymn, and altar-flames
    Rose to false gods, a dream-begotten throng,
Jove, Bacchus, Pan, and earlier, fouler names;
    While, as the unheeding ages passed along,   40
Ye, from your station in the middle skies,
Proclaimed the essential Goodness, strong and wise.

In you the heart that sighs for freedom seeks
    Her image; there the winds no barrier know,

Clouds come and rest and leave your fairy peaks;
　　While even the immaterial Mind, below,
And Thought, her wingèd offspring, chained by power,
　　Pine silently for the redeeming hour.

1835   1835

LIFE

O LIFE! I breathe thee in the breeze,
　　I feel thee bounding in my veins,
I see thee in the stretching trees,
　　These flowers, this still rock's mossy stains.

This stream of odors flowing by
　　From clover-field and clumps of pine,
This music, thrilling all the sky,
　　From all the morning birds, are thine.

Thou fill'st with joy this little one,
　　That leaps and shouts beside me here,   10
Where Isar's clay-white rivulets run
　　Through the dark woods like frighted deer.

Ah! must thy mighty breath, that wakes
　　Insect and bird, and flower and tree,
From the low-trodden dust, and makes
　　Their daily gladness, pass from me—

Pass, pulse by pulse, till o'er the ground
　　These limbs, now strong, shall creep with pain,
And this fair world of sight and sound
　　Seem fading into night again?   20

The things, O LIFE! thou quickenest, all
　　Strive upward toward the broad bright sky.
Upward and outward, and they fall
　　Back to earth's bosom when they die.

All that have borne the touch of death,
    All that shall live, lie mingled there,
Beneath that veil of bloom and breath,
    That living zone 'twixt earth and air.

There lies my chamber dark and still,
    The atoms trampled by my feet   30
There wait, to take the place I fill
    In the sweet air and sunshine sweet.

Well, I have had my turn, have been
    Raised from the darkness of the clod,
And for a glorious moment seen
    The brightness of the skirts of God;

And knew the light within my breast,
    Though wavering oftentimes and dim,
The power, the will, that never rest,
    And cannot die, were all from him.   40

Dear child! I know that thou wilt grieve
    To see me taken from thy love,
Wilt seek my grave at Sabbath eve
    And weep, and scatter flowers above.

Thy little heart will soon be healed,
    And being shall be bliss, till thou
To younger forms of life must yield
    The place thou fill'st with beauty now.

When we descend to dust again,
    Where will the final dwelling be   50
Of thought and all its memories then,
    My love for thee, and thine for me?

1835   1842

CATTERSKILL FALLS

Midst greens and shades the Catterskill leaps,
   From cliffs where the wood-flower clings;
All summer he moistens his verdant steeps
   With the sweet light spray of the mountain-springs,
And he shakes the woods on the mountain-side,
When they drip with the rains of autumn-tide.

But when, in the forest bare and old,
   The blast of December calls,
He builds, in the starlight clear and cold,
   A palace of ice where his torrent falls,   10
With turret, and arch, and fretwork fair,
And pillars blue as the summer air.

For whom are those glorious chambers wrought,
   In the cold and cloudless night?
Is there neither spirit nor motion of thought
   In forms so lovely, and hues so bright?
Hear what the gray-haired woodmen tell
Of this wild stream and its rocky dell:

'Twas hither a youth of dreamy mood,
   A hundred winters ago,   20
Had wandered over the mighty wood,
   When the panther's track was fresh on the snow,
And keen were the winds that came to stir
The long dark boughs of the hemlock-fir.

Too gentle of mien he seemed and fair,
   For a child of those rugged steeps;
His home lay low in the valley where
   The kingly Hudson rolls to the deeps:
But he wore the hunter's frock that day,
And a slender gun on his shoulder lay.   30

And here he paused, and against the trunk
   Of a tall gray linden leant,
When the broad clear orb of the sun had sunk,
   From his path in the frosty firmament,
And over the round dark edge of the hill
A cold green light was quivering still.

And the crescent moon, high over the green,
   From a sky of crimson shone,
On that icy palace, whose towers were seen
   To sparkle as if with stars of their own,   40
While the water fell with a hollow sound,
'Twixt the glistening pillars ranged around.

Is that a being of life, that moves
   Where the crystal battlements rise?
A maiden watching the moon she loves,
   At the twilight hour, with pensive eyes?
Was that a garment which seemed to gleam
Betwixt the eye and the falling stream?

'Tis only the torrent tumbling o'er,
   In the midst of those glassy walls,   50
Gushing, and plunging, and beating the floor
   Of the rocky basin in which it falls.
'Tis only the torrent—but why that start?
Why gazes the youth with a throbbing heart?

He thinks no more of his home afar,
   Where his sire and sister wait.
He heeds no longer how star after star
   Looks forth on the night as the hour grows late,
He heeds not the snow-wreaths, lifted and cast
From a thousand boughs, by the rising blast.   60

His thoughts are alone of those who dwell
   In the halls of frost and snow,

Who pass where the crystal domes upswell
    From the alabaster floors below,
Where the frost-trees shoot with leaf and spray,
And frost-gems scatter a silvery day.

"And oh that those glorious haunts were mine!"
    He speaks, and throughout the glen
Thin shadows swim in the faint moonshine,
    And take a ghastly likeness of men,   70
As if the slain by the wintry storms
Came forth to the air in their earthly forms.

There pass the chasers of seal and whale,
    With their weapons quaint and grim,
And bands of warriors in glittering mail,
    And herdsmen and hunters huge of limb,
There are naked arms, with bow and spear,
And furry gauntlets the carbine rear.

There are mothers—and oh, how sadly their eyes
    On their children's white brows rest!   80
There are youthful lovers—the maiden lies,
    In a seeming sleep, on the chosen breast;
There are fair wan women with moonstruck air,
The snow-stars flecking their long loose hair.

They eye him not as they pass along,
    But his hair stands up with dread,
When he feels that he moves with that phantom throng,
    Till those icy turrets are over his head,
And the torrent's roar as they enter seems
Like a drowsy murmur heard in dreams.   90

The glittering threshold is scarcely passed,
    When there gathers and wraps him round
A thick white twilight, sullen and vast,
    In which there is neither form nor sound;

The phantoms, the glory, vanish all,
With the dying voice of the waterfall.

Slow passes the darkness of that trance,
 And the youth now faintly sees
Huge shadows and gushes of light that dance
 On a rugged ceiling of unhewn trees, 100
And walls where the skins of beasts are hung,
And rifles glitter on antlers strung.

On a couch of shaggy skins he lies;
 As he strives to raise his head,
Hard-featured woodmen, with kindly eyes,
 Come round him and smooth his furry bed,
And bid him rest, for the evening star
Is scarcely set and the day is far.

They had found at eve the dreaming one
 By the base of that icy steep, 110
When over his stiffening limbs begun
 The deadly slumber of frost to creep,
And they cherished the pale and breathless form,
Till the stagnant blood ran free and warm.

1836   1836

THE BATTLE-FIELD

Once this soft turf, this rivulet's sands,
 Were trampled by a hurrying crowd,
And fiery hearts and armèd hands
 Encountered in the battle-cloud.

Ah! never shall the land forget
 How gushed the life-blood of her brave—
Gushed, warm with hope and courage yet,
 Upon the soil they fought to save.

Now all is calm, and fresh, and still;
    Alone the chirp of flitting bird,   10
And talk of children on the hill,
    And bell of wandering kine, are heard.

No solemn host goes trailing by
    The black-mouthed gun and staggering wain;
Men start not at the battle-cry,
    Oh, be it never heard again!

Soon rested those who fought; but thou
    Who minglest in the harder strife
For truths which men receive not now,
    Thy warfare only ends with life.   20

A friendless warfare! lingering long
    Through weary day and weary year;
A wild and many-weaponed throng
    Hang on thy front, and flank, and rear.

Yet nerve thy spirit to the proof,
    And blench not at thy chosen lot,
The timid good may stand aloof,
    The sage may frown—yet faint thou not.

Nor heed the shaft too surely cast,
    The foul and hissing bolt of scorn;   30
For with thy side shall dwell, at last,
    The victory of endurance born.

Truth, crushed to earth, shall rise again;
    Th' eternal years of God are hers;
But Error, wounded, writhes in pain,
    And dies among his worshippers.

Yea, though thou lie upon the dust,
    When they who helped thee flee in fear,

Die full of hope and manly trust,
    Like those who fell in battle here. 40

Another hand thy sword shall wield,
    Another hand the standard wave,
Till from the trumpet's mouth is pealed
    The blast of triumph o'er thy grave.

1837   1837

THE DEATH OF SCHILLER

'Tis said, when Schiller's death drew nigh,
    The wish possessed his mighty mind,
To wander forth wherever lie
    The homes and haunts of humankind.

Then strayed the poet, in his dreams,
    By Rome and Egypt's ancient graves;
Went up the New World's forest-streams,
    Stood in the Hindoo's temple-caves;

Walked with the Pawnee, fierce and stark,
    The sallow Tartar, midst his herds, 10
The peering Chinese, and the dark
    False Malay, uttering gentle words.

How could he rest? even then he trod
    The threshold of the world unknown;
Already, from the seat of God,
    A ray upon his garments shone;—

Shone and awoke the strong desire
    For love and knowledge reached not here,
Till, freed by death, his soul of fire
    Sprang to a fairer, ampler sphere. 20

1838   1838

THE FUTURE LIFE

How shall I know thee in the sphere which keeps
    The disembodied spirits of the dead,
When all of thee that time could wither sleeps
    And perishes among the dust we tread?

For I shall feel the sting of ceaseless pain
    If there I meet thy gentle presence not;
Nor hear the voice I love, nor read again
    In thy serenest eyes the tender thought.

Will not thy own meek heart demand me there?
    That heart whose fondest throbs to me were given— 10
My name on earth was ever in thy prayer,
    And wilt thou never utter it in heaven?

In meadows fanned by heaven's life-breathing wind,
    In the resplendence of that glorious sphere,
And larger movements of the unfettered mind,
    Wilt thou forget the love that joined us here?

The love that lived through all the stormy past,
    And meekly with my harsher nature bore,
And deeper grew, and tenderer to the last,
    Shall it expire with life, and be no more? 20

A happier lot than mine, and larger light,
    Await thee there, for thou hast bowed thy will
In cheerful homage to the rule of right,
    And lovest all, and renderest good for ill.

For me, the sordid cares in which I dwell
    Shrink and consume my heart, as heat the scroll;
And wrath has left its scar—that fire of hell
    Has left its frightful scar upon my soul.

Yet, though thou wear'st the glory of the sky,
    Wilt thou not keep the same belovèd name,   30
The same fair thoughtful brow, and gentle eye,
    Lovelier in heaven's sweet climate, yet the same?

Shalt thou not teach me, in that calmer home,
    The wisdom that I learned so ill in this—
The wisdom which is love—till I become
    Thy fit companion in that land of bliss?

1839   1839

THE FOUNTAIN

Fountain, that springest on this grassy slope,
Thy quick cool murmur mingles pleasantly,
With the cool sound of breezes in the beech,
Above me in the noontide. Thou dost wear
No stain of thy dark birthplace; gushing up
From the red mould and slimy roots of earth,
Thou flashest in the sun. The mountain-air,
In winter, is not clearer, nor the dew
That shines on mountain-blossom. Thus doth God
Bring, from the dark and foul, the pure and bright.   10

This tangled thicket on the bank above
Thy basin, how thy waters keep it green!
For thou dost feed the roots of the wild-vine
That trails all over it, and to the twigs
Ties fast her clusters. There the spice-bush lifts
Her leafy lances; the viburnum there,
Paler of foliage, to the sun holds up
Her circlet of green berries. In and out
The chipping-sparrow, in her coat of brown,
Steals silently lest I should mark her nest.   20

Not such thou wert of yore, ere yet the axe
Had smitten the old woods. Then hoary trunks

Of oak, and plane, and hickory, o'er thee held
A mighty canopy. When April winds
Grew soft, the maple burst into a flush
Of scarlet flowers. The tulip-tree, high up,
Opened, in airs of June, her multitude
Of golden chalices to humming-birds
And silken-wingèd insects of the sky.

Frail wood-plants clustered round thy edge in spring; 30
The liver-leaf put forth her sister blooms
Of faintest blue. Here the quick-footed wolf,
Passing to lap thy waters, crushed the flower
Of sanguinaria, from whose brittle stem
The red drops fell like blood. The deer, too, left
Her delicate footprint in the soft moist mould,
And on the fallen leaves. The slow-paced bear,
In such a sultry summer noon as this,
Stopped at thy stream, and drank, and leaped across.

But thou hast histories that stir the heart   40
With deeper feeling; while I look on thee
They rise before me. I behold the scene
Hoary again with forests; I behold
The Indian warrior, whom a hand unseen
Has smitten with his death-wound in the woods,
Creep slowly to thy well-known rivulet,
And slake his death-thirst. Hark, that quick fierce cry
That rends the utter silence! 'tis the whoop
Of battle, and a throng of savage men
With naked arms and faces stained like blood,   50
Fill the green wilderness; the long bare arms
Are heaved aloft, bows twang and arrows stream;
Each makes a tree his shield, and every tree
Sends forth its arrow. Fierce the fight and short,
As is the whirlwind. Soon the conquerors
And conquered vanish, and the dead remain
Mangled by tomahawks. The mighty woods

Are still again, the frighted bird comes back
And plumes her wings; but thy sweet waters run
Crimson with blood. Then, as the sun goes down,   60
Amid the deepening twilight I descry
Figures of men that crouch and creep unheard,
And bear away the dead. The next day's shower
Shall wash the tokens of the fight away.

I look again—a hunter's lodge is built,
With poles and boughs, beside thy crystal well,
While the meek autumn stains the woods with gold,
And sheds his golden sunshine. To the door
The red-man slowly drags the enormous bear
Slain in the chestnut-thicket, or flings down   70
The deer from his strong shoulders. Shaggy fells
Of wolf and cougar hang upon the walls,
And loud the black-eyed Indian maidens laugh,
That gather, from the rustling heaps of leaves,
The hickory's white nuts, and the dark fruit
That falls from the gray butternut's long boughs.

So centuries passed by, and still the woods
Blossomed in spring, and reddened when the year
Grew chill, and glistened in the frozen rains
Of winter, till the white man swung the axe   80
Beside thee—signal of a mighty change.
Then all around was heard the crash of trees,
Trembling awhile and rushing to the ground,
The low of ox, and shouts of men who fired
The brushwood, or who tore the earth with ploughs;
The grain sprang thick and tall, and hid in green
The blackened hill-side; ranks of spiky maize
Rose like a host embattled; the buckwheat
Whitened broad acres, sweetening with its flowers
The August wind. White cottages were seen   90
With rose-trees at the windows; barns from which
Came loud and shrill the crowing of the cock;

Pastures where rolled and neighed the lordly horse,
And white flocks browsed and bleated. A rich turf
Of grasses brought from far o'ercrept thy bank,
Spotted with the white clover. Blue-eyed girls
Brought pails, and dipped them in thy crystal pool;
And children, ruddy-cheeked and flaxen-haired,
Gathered the glistening cowslip from thy edge.

Since then, what steps have trod thy border! Here   100
On thy green bank, the woodman of the swamp
Has laid his axe, the reaper of the hill
His sickle, as they stooped to taste thy stream.
The sportsman, tired with wandering in the still
September noon, has bathed his heated brow
In thy cool current. Shouting boys, let loose
For a wild holiday, have quaintly shaped
Into a cup the folded linden-leaf,
And dipped thy sliding crystal. From the wars
Returning, the plumed soldier by thy side   110
Has sat, and mused how pleasant 'twere to dwell
In such a spot, and be as free as thou,
And move for no man's bidding more. At eve,
When thou wert crimson with the crimson sky,
Lovers have gazed upon thee, and have thought
Their mingled lives should flow as peacefully
And brightly as thy waters. Here the sage,
Gazing into thy self-replenished depth,
Has seen eternal order circumscribe
And bound the motions of eternal change,   120
And from the gushing of thy simple fount
Has reasoned to the mighty universe.

Is there no other change for thee, that lurks
Among the future ages? Will not man
Seek out strange arts to wither and deform
The pleasant landscape which thou makest green?
Or shall the veins that feed thy constant stream

Be choked in middle earth, and flow no more
For ever, that the water-plants along
Thy channel perish, and the bird in vain   130
Alight to drink? Haply shall these green hills
Sink, with the lapse of years, into the gulf
Of ocean waters, and thy source be lost
Amidst the bitter brine? Or shall they rise,
Upheaved in broken cliffs and airy peaks,
Haunts of the eagle and the snake, and thou
Gush midway from the bare and barren steep?

1839   1839

THE WINDS

I.

Ye winds, ye unseen currents of the air,
    Softly ye played a few brief hours ago;
Ye bore the murmuring bee; ye tossed the air
    O'er maiden cheeks, that took a fresher glow;
Ye rolled the round white cloud through depths of blue;
Ye shook from shaded flowers the lingering dew;
Before you the catalpa's blossoms flew,
    Light blossoms, dropping on the grass like snow.

II.

What change is this! Ye take the cataract's sound;
    Ye take the whirlpool's fury and its might;   10
The mountain shudders as ye sweep the ground;
    The valley woods lie prone beneath your flight.
The clouds before you shoot like eagles past:
The homes of men are rocking in your blast;
Ye lift the roofs like autumn leaves, and cast,
    Skyward, the whirling fragments out of sight.

III.

The weary fowls of heaven make wing in vain,
    To escape your wrath; ye seize and dash them dead;

Against the earth ye drive the roaring rain;
 The harvest-field becomes a river's bed;   20
And torrents tumble from the hills around,
Plains turn to lakes, and villages are drowned,
And wailing voices, midst the tempest's sound,
 Rise, as the rushing waters swell and spread.

IV.

Ye dart upon the deep, and straight is heard
 A wilder roar, and men grow pale, and pray;
Ye fling its floods around you, as a bird
 Flings o'er his shivering plumes the fountain's spray,
See! to the breaking mast the sailor clings;
Ye scoop the ocean to its briny springs,   30
And take the mountain-billow on your wings,
 And pile the wreck of navies round the bay.

V.

Why rage ye thus?—no strife for liberty
 Has made you mad; no tyrant, strong through fear,
Has chained your pinions till ye wrenched them free,
 And rushed into the unmeasured atmosphere;
For ye were born in freedom where ye blow;
Free o'er the mighty deep to come and go;
Earth's solemn woods were yours, her wastes of snow,
 Her isles where summer blossoms all the year. 40

VI.

O ye wild winds! a mightier power than yours
 In chains upon the shore of Europe lies;
The sceptred throng whose fetters he endures
 Watch his mute throes with terror in their eyes;
And armèd warriors all around him stand,
And, as he struggles, tighten every band,
And lift the heavy spear, with threatening hand,
 To pierce the victim, should he strive to rise.

VII.

Yet oh, when that wronged Spirit of our race
　Shall break, as soon he must, his long-worn chains,　50
And leap in freedom from his prison-place,
　Lord of his ancient hills and fruitful plains,
Let him not rise, like these mad winds of air,
To waste the loveliness that time could spare,
To fill the earth with woe, and blot her fair
　Unconscious breast with blood from human veins.

VIII.

But may he like the spring-time come abroad,
　Who crumbles winter's gyves with gentle might,
When in the genial breeze, the breath of God,
　The unsealed springs come spouting up to light;　60
Flowers start from their dark prisons at his feet,
The woods, long dumb, awake to hymnings sweet,
And morn and eve, whose glimmerings almost meet,
　Crowd back to narrow bounds the ancient night.

1839   1839

THE OLD MAN'S COUNSEL

　Among our hills and valleys, I have known
Wise and grave men, who, while their diligent hands
Tended or gathered in the fruits of earth,
Were reverent learners in the solemn school
Of Nature. Not in vain to them were sent
Seed-time and harvest, or the vernal shower
That darkened the brown tilth, or snow that beat
On the white winter hills. Each brought, in turn,
Some truth, some lesson on the life of man,
Or recognition of the Eternal mind　　　　　　10
Who veils his glory with the elements.

　One such I knew long since, a white-haired man,
Pithy of speech, and merry when he would;

A genial optimist, who daily drew
From what he saw his quaint moralities.
Kindly he held communion, though so old,
With me a dreaming boy, and taught me much
That books tell not, and I shall ne'er forget.

The sun of May was bright in middle heaven,
And steeped the sprouting forests, the green hills,   20
And emerald wheat-fields, in his yellow light.
Upon the apple-tree, where rosy buds
Stood clustered, ready to burst forth in bloom,
The robin warbled forth his full clear note
For hours, and wearied not. Within the woods,
Whose young and half-transparent leaves scarce cast
A shade, gay circles of anemones
Danced on their stalks; the shad-bush, white with flowers,
Brightened the glens; the new-leaved butternut
And quivering poplar to the roving breeze   30
Gave a balsamic fragrance. In the fields
I saw the pulses of the gentle wind
On the young grass. My heart was touched with joy
At so much beauty, flushing every hour
Into a fuller beauty; but my friend,
The thoughtful ancient, standing at my side,
Gazed on it mildly sad. I asked him why.

"Well mayst thou join in gladness," he replied,
"With the glad earth, her springing plants and flowers,
And this soft wind, the herald of the green   40
Luxuriant summer. Thou art young like them,
And well mayst thou rejoice. But while the flight
Of seasons fills and knits thy spreading frame,
It withers mine, and thins my hair, and dims
These eyes, whose fading light shall soon be quenched
In utter darkness. Hearest thou that bird?"

I listened, and from midst the depth of woods
Heard the love-signal of the grouse, that wears

A sable ruff around his mottled neck;
Partridge they call him by our northern streams,   50
And pheasant by the Delaware. He beat
His barred sides with his speckled wings, and made
A sound like distant thunder; slow the strokes
At first, then fast and faster, till at length
They passed into a murmur and were still.

  "There hast thou," said my friend, "a fitting type
Of human life. 'Tis an old truth, I know,
But images like these revive the power
Of long familiar truths. Slow pass our days
In childhood, and the hours of light are long   60
Betwixt the morn and eve; with swifter lapse
They glide in manhood, and in age they fly;
Till days and seasons flit before the mind
As flit the snow-flakes in a winter storm,
Seen rather than distinguished. Ah! I seem
As if I sat within a helpless bark,
By swiftly-running waters hurried on
To shoot some mighty cliff. Along the banks
Grove after grove, rock after frowning rock,
Bare sands and pleasant homes, and flowery nooks,   70
And isles and whirlpools in the stream, appear
Each after each, but the devoted skiff
Darts by so swiftly that their images
Dwell not upon the mind, or only dwell
In dim confusion; faster yet I sweep
By other banks, and the great gulf is near.

  "Wisely, my son, while yet thy days are long,
And this fair change of seasons passes slow,
Gather and treasure up the good they yield—
All that they teach of virtue, of pure thoughts   80
And kind affections, reverence for thy God
And for thy brethren; so when thou shalt come
Into these barren years, thou mayst not bring
A mind unfurnished and a withered heart."

Long since that white-haired ancient slept—but still,
When the red flower-buds crowd the orchard-bough,
And the ruffed grouse is drumming far within
The woods, his venerable form again
Is at my side, his voice is in my ear.

1840   1840

THE ANTIQUITY OF FREEDOM

Here are old trees, tall oaks, and gnarlèd pines,
That stream with gray-green mosses; here the ground
Was never trenched by spade, and flowers spring up
Unsown, and die ungathered. It is sweet
To linger here, among the flitting birds
And leaping squirrels, wandering brooks, and winds
That shake the leaves, and scatter, as they pass,
A fragrance from the cedars, thickly set
With pale-blue berries. In these peaceful shades—
Peaceful, unpruned, immeasurably old—   10
My thoughts go up the long dim path of years,
Back to the earliest days of liberty.

O FREEDOM! thou art not, as poets dream,
A fair young girl, with light and delicate limbs,
And wavy tresses gushing from the cap
With which the Roman master crowned his slave
When he took off the gyves. A bearded man,
Armed to the teeth, art thou; one mailèd hand
Grasps the broad shield, and one the sword; thy brow,
Glorious in beauty though it be, is scarred   20
With tokens of old wars; thy massive limbs
Are strong with struggling. Power at thee has launched
His bolts, and with his lightnings smitten thee;
They could not quench the life thou hast from heaven;
Merciless Power has dug thy dungeon deep,
And his swart armorers, by a thousand fires,
Have forged thy chain; yet, while he deems thee bound,

The links are shivered, and the prison-walls
Fall outward; terribly thou springest forth,
As springs the flame above a burning pile,
And shoutest to the nations, who return
Thy shoutings, while the pale oppressor flies.

Thy birthright was not given by human hands:
Thou wert twin-born with man. In pleasant fields,
While yet our race was few, thou sat'st with him,
To tend the quiet flock and watch the stars,
And teach the reed to utter simple airs.
Thou by his side, amid the tangled wood,
Didst war upon the panther and the wolf,
His only foes; and thou with him didst draw
The earliest furrow on the mountain-side,
Soft with the deluge. Tyranny himself,
Thy enemy, although of reverend look,
Hoary with many years, and far obeyed,
Is later born than thou; and as he meets
The grave defiance of thine elder eye,
The usurper trembles in his fastnesses.

Thou shalt wax stronger with the lapse of years,
But he shall fade into a feebler age—
Feebler, yet subtler. He shall weave his snares,
And spring them on thy careless steps, and clap
His withered hands, and from their ambush call
His hordes to fall upon thee. He shall send
Quaint maskers, wearing fair and gallant forms
To catch thy gaze, and uttering graceful words
To charm thy ear; while his sly imps, by stealth,
Twine round thee threads of steel, light thread on thread,
That grow to fetters; or bind down thy arms
With chains concealed in chaplets. Oh! not yet
Mayst thou unbrace thy corslet, nor lay by
Thy sword; nor yet, O Freedom! close thy lids,
In slumber; for thine enemy never sleeps,

30

40

50

60

And thou must watch and combat till the day
Of the new earth and heaven. But wouldst thou rest
Awhile from tumult and the frauds of men,
These old and friendly solitudes invite
Thy visit. They, while yet the forest-trees
Were young upon the unviolated earth,
And yet the moss-stains on the rock were new,
Beheld thy glorious childhood, and rejoiced.   70
1842   1842

A HYMN OF THE SEA

The sea is mighty, but a mightier sways
His restless billows. Thou, whose hands have scooped
His boundless gulfs and built his shore, thy breath,
That moved in the beginning o'er his face,
Moves o'er it evermore. The obedient waves
To its strong motion roll, and rise and fall.
Still from that realm of rain thy cloud goes up,
As at the first, to water the great earth,
And keep her valleys green. A hundred realms
Watch its broad shadow warping on the wind,   10
And in the dropping shower, with gladness hear
Thy promise of the harvest. I look forth
Over the boundless blue, where joyously
The bright crests of innumerable waves
Glance to the sun at once, as when the hands
Of a great multitude are upward flung
In acclamation. I behold the ships
Gliding from cape to cape, from isle to isle,
Or stemming toward far lands, or hastening home
From the Old World. It is thy friendly breeze   20
That bears them, with the riches of the land,
And treasure of dear lives, till, in the port,
The shouting seaman climbs and furls the sail.

But who shall bide thy tempest, who shall face
The blast that wakes the fury of the sea?

O God! thy justice makes the world turn pale,
When on the armèd fleet, that royally
Bears down the surges, carrying war, to smite
Some city, or invade some thoughtless realm,
Descends the fierce tornado. The vast hulks   30
Are whirled like chaff upon the waves; the sails
Fly, rent like webs of gossamer; the masts
Are snapped asunder; downward from the decks,
Downward are slung, into the fathomless gulf,
Their cruel engines; and their hosts, arrayed
In trappings of the battle-field, are whelmed
By whirlpools, or dashed dead upon the rocks.
Then stand the nations still with awe, and pause,
A moment, from the bloody work of war.

These restless surges eat away the shores   40
Of earth's old continents; the fertile plain
Welters in shallows, headlands crumble down,
And the tide drifts the sea-sand in the streets
Of the drowned city. Thou, meanwhile, afar
In the green chambers of the middle sea,
Where broadest spread the waters and the line
Sinks deepest, while no eye beholds thy work,
Creator! thou dost teach the coral-worm
To lay his mighty reefs. From age to age,
He builds beneath the waters, till, at last,   50
His bulwarks overtop the brine, and check
The long wave rolling from the southern pole
To break upon Japan. Thou bidd'st the fires,
That smoulder under ocean, heave on high
The new-made mountains, and uplift their peaks,
A place of refuge for the storm-driven bird.
The birds and wafting billows plant the rifts
With herb and tree; sweet fountains gush; sweet airs
Ripple the living lakes that, fringed with flowers,
Are gathered in the hollows. Thou dost look   60
On thy creation and pronounce it good.

Its valleys, glorious in their summer green,
Praise thee in silent beauty, and its woods,
Swept by the murmuring winds of ocean, join
The murmuring shores in a perpetual hymn.

1842   1842

THE STREAM OF LIFE

Oh silvery streamlet of the fields,
    That flowest full and free,
For thee the rains of spring return,
    The summer dews for thee;
And when thy latest blossoms die
    In autumn's chilly showers,
The winter fountains gush for thee,
    Till May brings back the flowers.

Oh Stream of Life! the violet springs
    But once beside thy bed;   10
But one brief summer, on thy path,
    The dews of heaven are shed.
Thy parent fountains shrink away,
    And close their crystal veins,
And where thy glittering current flowed
    The dust alone remains.

1845   1845

"OH MOTHER OF A MIGHTY RACE"

Oh mother of a mighty race,
Yet lovely in thy youthful grace!
The elder dames, thy haughty peers,
Admire and hate thy blooming years.
            With words of shame
And taunts of scorn they join thy name.

For on thy cheeks the glow is spread
That tints thy morning hills with red;
Thy step—the wild-deer's rustling feet

Within thy woods are not more fleet;
    Thy hopeful eye
Is bright as thine own sunny sky.

Ay, let them rail—those haughty ones,
While safe thou dwellest with thy sons.
They do not know how loved thou art,
How many a fond and fearless heart
    Would rise to throw
Its life between thee and the foe.

They know not, in their hate and pride,
What virtues with thy children bide;
How true, how good, thy graceful maids
Make bright, like flowers, the valley-shades;
    What generous men
Spring, like thine oaks, by hill and glen.

What cordial welcomes greet the guest
By thy lone rivers of the West;
How faith is kept, and truth revered,
And man is loved, and God is feared,
    In woodland homes,
And where the ocean-border foams.

There's freedom at thy gates and rest
For Earth's down-trodden and opprest,
A shelter for the hunted head,
For the starved laborer toil and bread.
    Power, at thy bounds,
Stops and calls back his baffled hounds.

Oh, fair young mother! on thy brow
Shall sit a nobler grace than now.
Deep in the brightness of thy skies
The thronging years in glory rise,
    And, as they fleet,
Drop strength and riches at thy feet.

Thine eye, with every coming hour,
Shall brighten, and thy form shall tower;
And when thy sisters, elder born,
Would brand thy name with words of scorn,
        Before thine eye,
Upon their lips the taunt shall die.

1846   1847

THE PLANTING OF THE APPLE-TREE

Come, let us plant the apple-tree.
Cleave the tough greensward with the spade;
Wide let its hollow bed be made;
There gently lay the roots, and there
Sift the dark mould with kindly care,
    And press it o'er them tenderly,
As, round the sleeping infant's feet,
We softly fold the cradle-sheet;
    So plant we the apple-tree.

What plant we in this apple-tree?   10
Buds, which the breath of summer days
Shall lengthen into leafy sprays;
Boughs where the thrush, with crimson breast,
Shall haunt and sing and hide her nest;
    We plant, upon the sunny lea,
A shadow for the noontide hour,
A shelter from the summer shower,
    When we plant the apple-tree.

What plant we in this apple-tree?
Sweets for a hundred flowery springs   20
To load the May-wind's restless wings,
When, from the orchard-row, he pours
Its fragrance through our open doors;
    A world of blossoms for the bee,

Flowers for the sick girl's silent room,
For the glad infant sprigs of bloom,
   We plant with the apple-tree.

What plant we in this apple-tree?
Fruits that shall swell in sunny June,
And redden in the August noon,   30
And drop, when gentle airs come by,
That fan the blue September sky,
   While children come, with cries of glee,
And seek them where the fragrant grass
Betrays their bed to those who pass,
   At the foot of the apple-tree.

And when, above this apple-tree,
The winter stars are quivering bright,
And winds go howling through the night,
Girls, whose young eyes o'erflow with mirth,   40
Shall peel its fruit by cottage-hearth,
   And guests in prouder homes shall see,
Heaped with the grape of Cintra's vine
And golden orange of the line,
   The fruit of the apple-tree.

The fruitage of this apple-tree
Winds and our flag of stripe and star
Shall bear to coasts that lie afar,
Where men shall wonder at the view,
And ask in what fair groves they grew;   50
   And sojourners beyond the sea
Shall think of childhood's careless day,
And long, long hours of summer play,
   In the shade of the apple-tree.

Each year shall give this apple-tree
A broader flush of roseate bloom,
A deeper maze of verdurous gloom,

And loosen, when the frost-clouds lower,
The crisp brown leaves in thicker shower.
 The years shall come and pass, but we 60
Shall hear no longer, where we lie,
The summer's songs, the autumn's sigh,
 In the boughs of the apple-tree.

 And time shall waste this apple-tree.
Oh, when its aged branches throw
Thin shadows on the ground below,
Shall fraud and force and iron will
Oppress the weak and helpless still?
 What shall the tasks of mercy be,
Amid the toils, the strifes, the tears 70
Of those who live when length of years
 Is wasting this little apple-tree?

 "Who planted this old apple-tree?"
The children of that distant day
Thus to some aged man shall say;
And, gazing on its mossy stem,
The gray-haired man shall answer them:
 "A poet of the land was he,
Born in the rude but good old times;
'Tis said he made some quaint old rhymes, 80
 On planting the apple-tree."

1849   1864

"THE MAY SUN SHEDS AN AMBER LIGHT"

The May sun sheds an amber light
 On new-leaved woods and lawns between;
But she who, with a smile more bright,
 Welcomed and watched the springing green,
  Is in her grave,
  Low in her grave.

The fair white blossoms of the wood
    In groups beside the pathway stand;
But one, the gentle and the good,
    Who cropped them with a fairer hand,   10
            Is in her grave,
            Low in her grave.

Upon the woodland's morning airs
    The small birds' mingled notes are flung;
But she, whose voice, more sweet than theirs,
    Once bade me listen while they sung,
            Is in her grave,
            Low in her grave.

That music of the early year
    Brings tears of anguish to my eyes;   20
My heart aches when the flowers appear;
    For then I think of her who lies
            Within her grave,
            Low in her grave.

1849   1852

ROBERT OF LINCOLN

Merrily swinging on brier and weed,
    Near to the nest of his little dame,
Over the mountain-side or mead,
    Robert of Lincoln is telling his name:
            Bob-o'-link, bob-o'-link,
            Spink, spank, spink;
Snug and safe is that nest of ours,
Hidden among the summer flowers.
            Chee, chee, chee.

Robert of Lincoln is gayly drest,   10
    Wearing a bright black wedding-coat;

White are his shoulders and white his crest.
　　Hear him call in his merry note:
　　　　Bob-o'-link, bob-o'-link,
　　　　Spink, spank, spink;
Look, what a nice new coat is mine,
Sure there was never a bird so fine.
　　　　　　Chee, chee, chee.

Robert of Lincoln's Quaker wife,
　　Pretty and quiet, with plain brown wings,　　20
Passing at home a patient life,
　　Broods in the grass while her husband sings:
　　　　Bob-o'-link, bob-o'-link,
　　　　Spink, spank, spink;
Brood, kind creature; you need not fear
Thieves and robbers while I am here.
　　　　　　Chee, chee, chee.

Modest and shy as a nun is she;
　　One weak chirp is her only note.
Braggart and prince of braggarts is he,　　30
　　Pouring boasts from his little throat:
　　　　Bob-o'-link, bob-o'-link,
　　　　Spink, spank, spink;
Never was I afraid of man;
Catch me, cowardly knaves, if you can!
　　　　　　Chee, chee, chee.

Six white eggs on a bed of hay,
　　Flecked with purple, a pretty sight!
There as the mother sits all day,
　　Robert is singing with all his might:　　40
　　　　Bob-o'-link, bob-o'-link,
　　　　Spink, spank, spink;
Nice good wife, that never goes out,
Keeping house while I frolic about.
　　　　　　Chee, chee, chee.

Soon as the little ones chip the shell,
    Six wide mouths are open for food;
Robert of Lincoln bestirs him well,
    Gathering seeds for the hungry brood.
        Bob-o'-link, bob-o'-link,   50
        Spink, spank, spink;
This new life is likely to be
Hard for a gay young fellow like me.
                Chee, chee, chee.

Robert of Lincoln at length is made
    Sober with work, and silent with care;
Off is his holiday garment laid,
    Half forgotten that merry air:
        Bob-o'-link, bob-o'-link,
        Spink, spank, spink;   60
Nobody knows but my mate and I
Where our nest and our nestlings lie.
                Chee, chee, chee.

Summer wanes; the children are grown;
    Fun and frolic no more he knows;
Robert of Lincoln's a humdrum crone;
    Off he flies, and we sing as he goes:
        Bob-o'-link, bob-o'-link,
        Spink, spank, spink;
When you can pipe that merry old strain,   70
Robert of Lincoln, come back again.
                Chee, chee, chee.

1855   1855

AN INVITATION TO THE COUNTRY

Already, close by our summer dwelling,
    The Easter sparrow repeats her song;
A merry warbler, she chides the blossoms—
    The idle blossoms that sleep so long.

The bluebird chants, from the elm's long branches,
   A hymn to welcome the budding year.
The south wind wanders from field to forest,
   And softly whispers, "The Spring is here."

Come, daughter mine, from the gloomy city,
   Before those lays from the elm have ceased;   10
The violet breathes, by our door, as sweetly
   As in the air of her native East.

Though many a flower in the wood is waking,
   The daffodil is our doorside queen;
She pushes upward the sward already,
   To spot with sunshine the early green.

No lays so joyous as these are warbled
   From wiry prison in maiden's bower;
No pampered bloom of the green-house chamber
   Has half the charm of the lawn's first flower.   20

Yet these sweet sounds of the early season,
   And these fair sights of its sunny days,
Are only sweet when we fondly listen,
   And only fair when we fondly gaze.

There is no glory in star or blossom
   Till looked upon by a loving eye;
There is no fragrance in April breezes
   Till breathed with joy as they wander by.

Come, Julia dear, for the sprouting willows,
   The opening flowers, and the gleaming brooks,   30
And hollows, green in the sun, are waiting
   Their dower of beauty from thy glad looks.

1857   1857

THE SONG OF THE SOWER

I.

The maples redden in the sun;
  In autumn gold the beeches stand;
Rest, faithful plough, thy work is done
  Upon the teeming land.
Bordered with trees whose gay leaves fly
On every breath that sweeps the sky,
The fresh dark acres furrowed lie,
  And ask the sower's hand.
Loose the tired steer and let him go
To pasture where the gentians blow,   10
And we, who till the grateful ground,
Fling we the golden shower around.

II.

Fling wide the generous grain; we fling
O'er the dark mould the green of spring.
For thick the emerald blades shall grow,
When first the March winds melt the snow,
And to the sleeping flowers, below,
    The early bluebirds sing.
Fling wide the grain; we give the fields
  The ears that nod in summer's gale,   20
The shining stems that summer gilds,
  The harvest that o'erflows the vale,
And swells, an amber sea, between
The full-leaved woods, its shores of green.
Hark! from the murmuring clods I hear
Glad voices of the coming year;
The song of him who binds the grain,
The shout of those that load the wain,
And from the distant grange there comes
  The clatter of the thresher's flail,   30
And steadily the millstone hums
  Down in the willowy vale.

III.

Fling wide the golden shower; we trust
The strength of armies to the dust.
This peaceful lea may haply yield
Its harvest for the tented field.
Ha! feel ye not your fingers thrill,
   As o'er them, in the yellow grains,
Glide the warm drops of blood that fill,
   For mortal strife, the warrior's veins;   40
Such as, on Solferino's day,
Slaked the brown sand and flowed away—
Flowed till the herds, on Mincio's brink,
Snuffed the red stream and feared to drink;—
Blood that in deeper pools shall lie,
   On the sad earth, as time grows gray,
When men by deadlier arts shall die,
And deeper darkness blot the sky
     Above the thundering fray;
And realms, that hear the battle-cry,   50
     Shall sicken with dismay;
And chieftains to the war shall lead
Whole nations, with the tempest's speed,
     To perish in a day;—
Till man, by love and mercy taught,
Shall rue the wreck his fury wrought,
     And lay the sword away!
Oh strew, with pausing, shuddering hand,
The seed upon the helpless land,
As if, at every step, ye cast   60
The pelting hail and riving blast.

IV.

Nay, strew, with free and joyous sweep,
   The seed upon the expecting soil;
For hence the plenteous year shall heap
   The garners of the men who toil.

Strew the bright seed for those who tear
The matted sward with spade and share,
And those whose sounding axes gleam
Beside the lonely forest-stream,
    Till its broad banks lie bare;   70
And him who breaks the quarry-ledge,
  With hammer-blows, plied quick and strong,
And him who, with the steady sledge,
  Smites the shrill anvil all day long.
Sprinkle the furrow's even trace
  For those whose toiling hands uprear
The roof-trees of our swarming race,
  By grove and plain, by stream and mere;
Who forth, from crowded city, lead
  The lengthening street, and overlay   80
Green orchard-plot and grassy mead
  With pavement of the murmuring way.
Cast, with full hands the harvest cast,
For the brave men that climb the mast,
When to the billow and the blast
  It swings and stoops, with fearful strain,
And bind the fluttering mainsail fast,
  Till the tossed bark shall sit, again,
  Safe as a sea-bird on the main.

v.

Fling wide the grain for those who throw   90
The clanking shuttle to and fro,
In the long row of humming rooms,
  And into ponderous masses wind
The web that, from a thousand looms,
  Comes forth to clothe mankind.
Strew, with free sweep, the grain for them,
  By whom the busy thread
Along the garment's even hem
  And winding seam is led;
A pallid sisterhood, that keep   100

The lonely lamp alight,
In strife with weariness and sleep,
    Beyond the middle night.
Large part be theirs in what the year
Shall ripen for the reaper here.

VI.

Still, strew, with joyous hand, the wheat
On the soft mould beneath our feet,
        For even now I seem
To hear a sound that lightly rings
From murmuring harp and viol's strings,   110
        As in a summer dream.
The welcome of the wedding-guest,
    The bridegroom's look of bashful pride,
    The faint smile of the pallid bride,
And bridemaid's blush at matron's jest,
And dance and song and generous dower
Are in the shining grains we shower.

VII.

Scatter the wheat for shipwrecked men,
Who, hunger-worn, rejoice again
    In the sweet safety of the shore,   120
And wanderers, lost in woodlands drear,
Whose pulses bound with joy to hear
    The herd's light bell once more.
    Freely the golden spray be shed
For him whose heart, when night comes down
On the close alleys of the town,
    Is faint for lack of bread.
In chill roof-chambers, bleak and bare,
Or the damp cellar's stifling air,
She who now sees, in mute despair,   130
        Her children pine for food,
Shall feel the dews of gladness start
To lids long tearless, and shall part

The sweet loaf with a grateful heart,
Among her thin pale brood.
Dear, kindly Earth, whose breast we till!
Oh, for thy famished children, fill,
Where'er the sower walks,
Fill the rich ears that shade the mould
With grain for grain, a hundredfold,   140
To bend the sturdy stalks.

VIII.

Strew silently the fruitful seed,
As softly o'er the tilth ye tread,
For hands that delicately knead
The consecrated bread—
The mystic loaf that crowns the board,
When, round the table of their Lord,
Within a thousand temples set,
In memory of the bitter death
Of Him who taught at Nazareth,   150
His followers are met,
And thoughtful eyes with tears are wet,
As of the Holy One they think,
The glory of whose rising yet
Makes bright the grave's mysterious brink.

IX.

Brethren, the sower's task is done.
The seed is in its winter bed.
Now let the dark-brown mould be spread,
To hide it from the sun,
And leave it to the kindly care   160
Of the still earth and brooding air,
As when the mother, from her breast,
Lays the hushed babe apart to rest,
And shades its eyes, and waits to see
How sweet its waking smile will be.
The tempest now may smite, the sleet

All night on the drowned furrow beat,
And winds that, from the cloudy hold,
Of winter breathe the bitter cold,
Stiffen to stone the mellow mould,   170
   Yet safe shall lie the wheat;
Till, out of heaven's unmeasured blue,
   Shall walk again the genial year,
To wake with warmth and nurse with dew
   The germs we lay to slumber here.

x.

Oh blessed harvest yet to be!
   Abide thou with the Love that keeps,
In its warm bosom, tenderly,
   The Life which wakes and that which sleeps.
The Love that leads the willing spheres   180
Along the unending track of years,
And watches o'er the sparrow's nest,
Shall brood above thy winter rest,
And raise thee from the dust, to hold
   Light whisperings with the winds of May,
And fill thy spikes with living gold,
   From summer's yellow ray;
Then, as thy garners give thee forth,
   On what glad errands shalt thou go,
Wherever, o'er the waiting earth,   190
   Roads wind and rivers flow!
The ancient East shall welcome thee
To mighty marts beyond the sea,
And they who dwell where palm-groves sound
To summer winds the whole year round,
Shall watch, in gladness, from the shore,
The sails that bring thy glistening store.

1859   1864

THE CLOUD ON THE WAY

See, before us, in our journey, broods a mist upon the ground;
Thither leads the path we walk in, blending with that gloomy
    bound.
Never eye hath pierced its shadows to the mystery they screen;
Those who once have passed within it never more on earth are
    seen.
Now it seems to stoop beside us, now at seeming distance
    lowers,
Leaving banks that tempt us onward bright with summer-green
    and flowers.
Yet it blots the way forever; there our journey ends at last;
Into that dark cloud we enter, and are gathered to the past.
Thou who, in this flinty pathway, leading through a stranger-
    land,   9
Passest down the rocky valley, walking with me hand in hand,
Which of us shall be the soonest folded to that dim Unknown?
Which shall leave the other walking in this flinty path alone?
Even now I see thee shudder, and thy cheek is white with fear,
And thou clingest to my side as comes that darkness sweeping
    near.
"Here," thou sayest, "the path is rugged, sown with thorns that
    wound the feet;
But the sheltered glens are lovely, and the rivulet's song is
    sweet;
Roses breathe from tangled thickets; lilies bend from ledges
    brown;
Pleasantly between the pelting showers the sunshine gushes
    down;
Dear are those who walk beside us, they whose looks and voices
    make
All this rugged region cheerful, till I love it for their sake.   20
Far be yet the hour that takes me where that chilly shadow lies,
From the things I know and love, and from the sight of loving
    eyes!"

So thou murmurest, fearful one; but see, we tread a rougher
way:

Fainter grow the gleams of sunshine that upon the dark rocks
play;

Rude winds strew the faded flowers upon the crags o'er which
we pass;

Banks of verdure, when we reach them, hiss with tufts of withered grass.

One by one we miss the voices which we loved so well to hear;

One by one the kindly faces in that shadow disappear.

Yet upon the mist before us fix thine eyes with closer view;

See, beneath its sullen skirts, the rosy morning glimmers
through.   30

One whose feet the thorns have wounded passed that barrier
and came back,

With a glory on His footsteps lighting yet the dreary track.

Boldly enter where He entered; all that seems but darkness here,

When thou once hast passed beyond it, haply shall be crystal-
clear.

Viewed from that serener realm, the walks of human life may lie,

Like the page of some familiar volume, open to thine eye;

Haply, from the o'erhanging shadow, thou mayst stretch an
unseen hand,

To support the wavering steps that print with blood the rugged
land.

Haply, leaning o'er the pilgrim, all unweeting thou art near,

Thou mayst whisper words of warning or of comfort in his ear,

Till, beyond the border where that brooding mystery bars the
sight,   41

Those whom thou hast fondly cherished stand with thee in
peace and light.

1860   1860

THE TIDES

The moon is at her full, and, riding high,
    Floods the calm fields with light;
The airs that hover in the summer sky
    Are all asleep to-night.

There comes no voice from the great woodlands round
    That murmured all the day;
Beneath the shadow of their boughs the ground
    Is not more still than they.

But ever heaves and moans the restless Deep;
    His rising tides I hear,   10
Afar I see the glimmering billows leap;
    I see them breaking near.

Each wave springs upward, climbing toward the fair
    Pure light that sits on high—
Springs eagerly, and faintly sinks, to where
    The mother-waters lie.

Upward again it swells; the moonbeams show
    Again its glimmering crest;
Again it feels the fatal weight below,
    And sinks, but not to rest.   20

Again and yet again; until the Deep
    Recalls his brood of waves;
And, with a sullen moan, abashed, they creep
    Back to his inner caves.

Brief respite! they shall rush from that recess
    With noise and tumult soon,
And fling themselves, with unavailing stress,
    Up toward the placid moon.

O restless Sea, that, in thy prison here,
    Dost struggle and complain;   30
Through the slow centuries yearning to be near
    To that fair orb in vain;

The glorious source of light and heat must warm
    Thy billows from on high,
And change them to the cloudy trains that form
    The curtains of the sky.

Then only may they leave the waste of brine
    In which they welter here,
And rise above the hills of earth, and shine
    In a serener sphere.   40

1860   1860

ITALY

Voices from the mountains speak,
    Apennines to Alps reply;
Vale to vale and peak to peak
    Toss an old-remembered cry:
        "Italy
        Shall be free!"
Such the mighty shout that fills
All the passes of her hills.

All the old Italian lakes
    Quiver at that quickening word;   10
Como with a thrill awakes;
    Garda to her depths is stirred;
        Mid the steeps
        Where he sleeps,
Dreaming of the elder years,
Startled Thrasymenus hears.

Sweeping Arno, swelling Po,
    Murmur freedom to their meads.
Tiber swift and Liris slow
    Send strange whispers from their reeds.   20
        "Italy
        Shall be free!"

Sing the glittering brooks that slide,
Toward the sea, from Etna's side.

Long ago was Gracchus slain;
　　Brutus perished long ago;
Yet the living roots remain
　　Whence the shoots of greatness grow,
　　　　　Yet again,
　　　　　Godlike men,　　　　　　30
Sprung from that heroic stem,
Call the land to rise with them.

They who haunt the swarming street,
　　They who chase the mountain-boar,
Or, where cliff and billow meet,
　　Prune the vine or pull the oar,
　　　　　With a stroke
　　　　　Break their yoke;
Slaves but yestereve were they—
Freemen with the dawning day.　　　　40

Looking in his children's eyes,
　　While his own with gladness flash,
"These," the Umbrian father cries,
　　"Ne'er shall crouch beneath the lash!
　　　　　These shall ne'er
　　　　　Brook to wear
Chains whose cruel links are twined
Round the crushed and withering mind."

Monarchs! ye whose armies stand
　　Harnessed for the battle-field!　　50
Pause, and from the lifted hand
　　Drop the bolts of war ye wield.
　　　　　Stand aloof
　　　　　While the proof
Of the people's might is given;
Leave their kings to them and Heaven!

Stand aloof, and see the oppressed
   Chase the oppressor, pale with fear,
As the fresh winds of the west
   Blow the misty valleys clear.   60
        Stand and see
        Italy
Cast the gyves she wears no more
To the gulfs that steep her shore.

1860   1860

OUR COUNTRY'S CALL

Lay down the axe; fling by the spade;
   Leave in its track the toiling plough;
The rifle and the bayonet-blade
   For arms like yours were fitter now;
And let the hands that ply the pen
   Quit the light task, and learn to wield
The horseman's crooked brand, and rein
   The charger on the battle-field.

Our country calls; away! away!
   To where the blood-stream blots the green.   10
Strike to defend the gentlest sway
   That Time in all his course has seen.
See, from a thousand coverts—see,
   Spring the armed foes that haunt her track;
They rush to smite her down, and we
   Must beat the banded traitors back.

Ho! sturdy as the oaks ye cleave,
   And moved as soon to fear and flight,
Men of the glade and forest! leave
   Your woodcraft for the field of fight.   20
The arms that wield the axe must pour
   An iron tempest on the foe;
His serried ranks shall reel before
   The arm that lays the panther low.

And ye, who breast the mountain-storm
   By grassy steep or highland lake,
Come, for the land ye love, to form
   A bulwark that no foe can break.
Stand, like your own gray cliffs that mock
   The whirlwind, stand in her defence;   30
The blast as soon shall move the rock
   As rushing squadrons bear ye thence.

And ye, whose homes are by her grand
   Swift rivers, rising far away,
Come from the depth of her green land,
   As mighty in your march as they;
As terrible as when the rains
   Have swelled them over bank and bourne,
With sudden floods to drown the plains
   And sweep along the woods uptorn.   40

And ye, who throng, beside the deep,
   Her ports and hamlets of the strand,
In number like the waves that leap
   On his long-murmuring marge of sand—
Come like that deep, when, o'er his brim,
   He rises, all his floods to pour,
And flings the proudest barks that swim,
   A helpless wreck, against his shore!

Few, few were they whose swords of old
   Won the fair land in which we dwell;   50
But we are many, we who hold
   The grim resolve to guard it well.
Strike, for that broad and goodly land,
   Blow after blow, till men shall see
That Might and Right move hand in hand,
   And glorious must their triumph be!

1861   1861

CASTLES IN THE AIR

"But there is yet a region of the clouds
Unseen from the low earth. Beyond the veil
Of these dark volumes rolling through the sky,
Its mountain summits glisten in the sun,—
The realm of Castles in the Air. The foot
Of man hath never trod those shining streets;
But there his spirit, leaving the dull load
Of bodily organs, wanders with delight,
And builds its structures of the impalpable mist,
Glorious beyond the dream of architect,   10
And populous with forms of nobler mould
Than ever walked the earth."

                    So said my guide,
And led me, wondering, to a headland height
That overlooked a fair broad vale shut in
By the great hills of Cloudland. "Now behold
The Castle-builders!" Then I looked; and, lo!
The vale was filled with shadowy forms, that bore
Each a white wand, with which they touched the banks
Of mist beside them, and at once arose,
Obedient to their wish, the walls and domes   20
Of stately palaces, Gothic or Greek,
Or such as in the land of Mohammed
Uplift the crescent, or, in forms more strange,
Border the ancient Indus, or behold
Their gilded friezes mirrored in the lakes
Of China—yet of ampler majesty,
And gorgeously adorned. Tall porticos
Sprang from the ground; the eye pursued afar
Their colonnades, that lessened to a point
In the faint distance. Portals that swung back   30
On musical hinges showed the eye within
Vast halls with golden floors, and bright alcoves,
And walls of pearl, and sapphire vault besprent

With silver stars. Within the spacious rooms
Were banquets spread; and menials, beautiful
As wood-nymphs or as stripling Mercuries,
Ran to and fro, and laid the chalices,
And brought the brimming wine-jars. Enters now
The happy architect, and wanders on
From room to room, and glories in his work.   40

  Not long his glorying: for a chill north wind
Breathes through the structure, and the massive walls
Are folded up; the proud domes roll away
In mist-wreaths; pinnacle and turret lean
Forward, like birds prepared for flight, and stream,
In trains of vapor, through the empty air.
Meantime the astonished builder, dispossessed,
Stands 'mid the drifting rack. A brief despair
Seizes him; but the wand is in his hand,
And soon he turns him to his task again.   50
"Behold," said the fair being at my side,
"How one has made himself a diadem
Out of the bright skirts of a cloud that lay
Steeped in the golden sunshine, and has bound
The bauble on his forehead! See, again,
How from these vapors he calls up a host
With arms and banners! A great multitude
Gather and bow before him with bare heads.
To the four winds his messengers go forth,
And bring him back earth's homage. From the ground   60
Another calls a wingèd image, such
As poets give to Fame, who, to her mouth
Putting a silver trumpet, blows abroad
A loud, harmonious summons to the world,
And all the listening nations shout his name.
Another yet, apart from all the rest,
Casting a fearful glance from side to side,
Touches the ground by stealth. Beneath his wand
A glittering pile grows up, ingots and bars

Of massive gold, and coins on which earth's kings   70
Have stamped their symbols." As these words were said,
The north wind blew again across the vale,
And, lo! the beamy crown flew off in mist;
The host of armèd men became a scud
Torn by the angry blast; the form of Fame
Tossed its long arms in air, and rode the wind,
A jagged cloud; the glittering pile of gold
Grew pale and flowed in a gray reek away.
Then there were sobs and tears from those whose work
The wind had scattered; some had flung themselves   80
Upon the ground in grief; and some stood fixed
In blank bewilderment; and some looked on
Unmoved, as at a pageant of the stage
Suddenly hidden by the curtain's fall.

"Take thou this wand," my bright companion said.
I took it from her hand, and with it touched
The knolls of snow-white mist, and they grew green
With soft, thick herbage. At another touch
A brook leaped forth, and dashed and sparkled by;
And shady walks through shrubberies cool and close   90
Wandered; and where, upon the open grounds,
The peaceful sunshine lay, a vineyard nursed
Its pouting clusters; and from boughs that drooped
Beneath their load an orchard shed its fruit;
And gardens, set with many a pleasant herb
And many a glorious flower, made sweet the air.
    I looked, and I exulted; yet I longed
For Nature's grander aspects, and I plied
The slender rod again; and then arose
Woods tall and wide, of odorous pine and fir,   100
And every noble tree that casts the leaf
In autumn. Paths that wound between their stems
Led through the solemn shade to twilight glens,
To thundering torrents and white waterfalls,
And edge of lonely lakes, and chasms between

The mountain-cliffs. Above the trees were seen
Gray pinnacles and walls of splintered rock.

But near the forest margin, in the vale,
Nestled a dwelling half embowered by trees,
Where, through the open window, shelves were seen   110
Filled with old volumes, and a glimpse was given
Of canvas, here and there along the walls,
On which the hands of mighty men of art
Had flung their fancies. On the portico
Old friends, with smiling faces and frank eyes,
Talked with each other: some had passed from life
Long since, yet dearly were remembered still.
My heart yearned toward them, and the quick, warm tears
Stood in my eyes. Forward I sprang to grasp
The hands that once so kindly met my own,—   120
I sprang, but met them not: the withering wind
Was there before me. Dwelling, field, and brook,
Dark wood, and flowery garden, and blue lake,
And beetling cliff, and noble human forms,
All, all had melted into that pale sea
Of billowy vapor rolling round my feet.
1862   1866

THE POET

Thou, who wouldst wear the name
    Of poet mid thy brethren of mankind,
And clothe in words of flame
    Thoughts that shall live within the general mind!
Deem not the framing of a deathless lay
The pastime of a drowsy summer day.

But gather all thy powers,
    And wreak them on the verse that thou dost weave,
And in thy lonely hours,
    At silent morning or at wakeful eve,   10

While the warm current tingles through thy veins,
Set forth the burning words in fluent strains.

No smooth array of phrase,
    Artfully sought and ordered though it be,
Which the cold rhymer lays
    Upon his page with languid industry,
Can wake the listless pulse to livelier speed,
Or fill with sudden tears the eyes that read.

The secret wouldst thou know
    To touch the heart or fire the blood at will?   20
Let thine own eyes o'erflow;
    Let thy lips quiver with the passionate thrill;
Seize the great thought, ere yet its power be past,
And bind, in words, the fleet emotion fast.

Then, should thy verse appear
    Halting and harsh, and all unaptly wrought,
Touch the crude line with fear,
    Save in the moment of impassioned thought;
Then summon back the original glow, and mend
The strain with rapture that with fire was penned.   30

Yet let no empty gust
    Of passion find an utterance in thy lay,
A blast that whirls the dust
    Along the howling street and dies away;
But feelings of calm power and mighty sweep,
Like currents journeying through the windless deep.

Seek'st thou, in living lays,
    To limn the beauty of the earth and sky?
Before thine inner gaze
    Let all that beauty in clear vision lie;   40
Look on it with exceeding love, and write
The words inspired by wonder and delight.

Of tempests wouldst thou sing,
   Or tell of battles—make thyself a part
Of the great tumult; cling
   To the tossed wreck with terror in thy heart;
Scale, with the assaulting host, the rampart's height,
And strike and struggle in the thickest fight.

So shalt thou frame a lay
   That haply may endure from age to age,   50
And they who read shall say:
   "What witchery hangs upon this poet's page!
What art is his the written spells to find
That sway from mood to mood the willing mind!"

1863   1864

From THE FIFTH BOOK OF HOMER'S ODYSSEY

    * * * The great Ulysses spread
His canvas joyfully, to catch the breeze,
And sat and guided with nice care the helm,
Gazing with fixed eye on the Pleiades,
Boötes setting late, and the Great Bear,
By others called the Wain, which, wheeling round,
Looks ever toward Orion, and alone
Dips not into the waters of the deep.
For so Calypso, glorious goddess, bade   330
That, on his ocean journey, he should keep
That constellation ever on his left.
Now seventeen days were in the voyage past,
And on the eighteenth shadowy heights appeared,
The nearest point of the Pheacian land,
Lying on the dark ocean like a shield.
   But mighty Neptune, coming from among
The Ethiopians, saw him. Far away
He saw, from mountain-heights of Solyma,
The voyager, and burned with fiercer wrath,   340
And shook his head, and said within himself:

"Strange! now I see the gods have new designs
For this Ulysses, formed while I was yet
In Ethiopia. He draws near the land
Of the Pheacians, where it is decreed
He shall o'erpass the boundary of his woes;
But first, I think, he will have much to bear."

He spoke, and round about him called the clouds
And roused the ocean, wielding in his hand
The trident, summoned all the hurricanes   350
Of all the winds, and covered earth and sky
At once with mists, while from above, the night
Fell suddenly. The east wind and the south
Rushed forth at once, with the strong-blowing west,
And the clear north rolled up his mighty waves.
Ulysses trembled in his knees and heart,
And thus to his great soul, lamenting, said:

"What will become of me? unhappy man!
I fear that all the goddess said was true,
Foretelling what disasters should o'ertake   360
My voyage, ere I reach my native land.
Now are her words fulfilled. How Jupiter
Wraps the great heaven in clouds and stirs the deep
To tumult! Wilder grow the hurricanes
Of all the winds, and now my fate is sure.
Thrice happy, four times happy they, who fell
On Troy's wide field, warring for Atreus' sons:
Oh, had I met my fate and perished there,
That very day on which the Trojan host,
Around the dead Achilles, hurled at me   370
Their brazen javelins! I had then received
Due burial and great glory with the Greeks;
Now must I die a miserable death."

As thus he spoke, upon him, from on high,
A huge and frightful billow broke; it whirled
The raft around, and far from it he fell.
His hands let go the rudder; a fierce rush
Of all the winds together snapped in twain

The mast; far off the yard and canvas flew
Into the deep; the billow held him long   380
Beneath the waters, and he strove in vain
Quickly to rise to air from that huge swell
Of ocean, for the garments weighed him down
Which fair Calypso gave him. But, at length,
Emerging, he rejected from his throat
The bitter brine that down his forehead streamed.
Even then, though hopeless with dismay, his thought
Was on the raft, and, struggling through the waves,
He seized it, sprang on board, and seated there
Escaped the threatened death. Still to and fro   390
The rolling billows drove it. As the wind
In autumn sweeps the thistles o'er the field,
Clinging together, so the blasts of heaven
Hither and thither drove it o'er the sea.
And now the south wind flung it to the north
To buffet; now the east wind to the west.

   Ino Leucothea saw him clinging there,
The delicate-footed child of Cadmus, once
A mortal, speaking with a mortal voice;
Though now within the ocean-gulfs, she shares   400
The honors of the gods. With pity she
Beheld Ulysses struggling thus distressed,
And, rising from the abyss below, in form
A cormorant, the sea-nymph took her perch
On the well-banded raft, and thus she said:

   "Ah, luckless man, how hast thou angered thus
Earth-shaking Neptune that he visits thee
With these disasters? Yet he cannot take,
Although he seek it earnestly, thy life.
Now do my bidding, for thou seemest wise.   410
Laying aside thy garments, let the raft
Drift with the winds, while thou, by strength of arm,
Makest thy way in swimming to the land
Of the Pheacians, where thy safety lies.
Receive this veil and bind its heavenly woof

Beneath thy breast, and have no further fear
Of hardship or of danger. But, as soon
As thou shalt touch the island, take it off,
And turn away thy face, and fling it far
From where thou standest, into the black deep."   420
The goddess gave the veil as thus she spoke,
And to the tossing deep went down, in form
A cormorant; the black wave covered her,
But still Ulysses, mighty sufferer,
Pondered, and thus to his great soul he said:

   "Ah me! perhaps some god is planning here
Some other fraud against me, bidding me
Forsake my raft. I will not yet obey,
For still far off I see the land in which
'Tis said my refuge lies. This will I do,   430
For this seems wisest. While the fastenings last
That hold these timbers, I will keep my place
And bide the tempest here. But when the waves
Shall dash my raft in pieces, I will swim,
For nothing better will remain to do."

   As he revolved this purpose in his mind,
Earth-shaking Neptune sent a mighty wave,
Horrid, and huge, and high, and where he sat
It smote him. As a violent wind uplifts
The dry chaff heaped upon a threshing-floor,   440
And sends it scattered through the air abroad,
So did that wave fling loose the ponderous beams.
To one of these, Ulysses, clinging fast,
Bestrode it, like a horseman on his steed;
And now he took the garments off, bestowed
By fair Calypso, binding round his breast
The veil, and forward plunged into the deep,
With palms outspread, prepared to swim. Meanwhile,
Neptune beheld him, Neptune, mighty king,
And shook his head, and said within himself: 450

   "Go thus, and, laden with mischances, roam
The waters, till thou come among the race

Cherished by Jupiter; but well I deem
Thou wilt not find thy share of suffering light."

Thus having spoke, he urged his coursers on,
With their fair-flowing manes, until he came
To Ægæ, where his glorious palace stands.

But Pallas, child of Jove, had other thoughts.
She stayed the course of every wind beside,
And bade them rest, and lulled them into sleep,   460
But summoned the swift north to break the waves,
That so Ulysses, the high-born, escaped
From death and from the fates, might be the guest
Of the Pheacians, men who love the sea.

Two days and nights, among the mighty waves
He floated, oft his heart foreboding death,
But when the bright-haired Eos had fulfilled
The third day's course, and all the winds were laid,
And calm was on the watery waste, he saw
That land was near, as, lifted on the crest   470
Of a huge swell, he looked with sharpened sight;
And as a father's life preserved makes glad
His children's hearts, when long time he has lain
Sick, wrung with pain, and wasting by the power
Of some malignant genius, till, at length,
The gracious gods bestow a welcome cure;
So welcome to Ulysses was the sight
Of woods and fields. By swimming on he thought
To climb and tread the shore, but when he drew
So near that one who shouted could be heard   480
From land, the sound of ocean on the rocks
Came to his ear, for there huge breakers roared
And spouted fearfully, and all around
Was covered with the sea-foam. Haven here
Was none for ships, nor sheltering creek, but shores
Beetling from high, and crags and walls of rock.
Ulysses trembled both in knees and heart,
And thus, to his great soul, lamenting, said:

"Now woe is me! as soon as Jove has shown

What I had little hoped to see, the land,   490
And I through all these waves have ploughed my way,
I find no issue from the hoary deep.
For sharp rocks border it, and all around
Roar the wild surges; slippery cliffs arise
Close to deep gulfs, and footing there is none,
Where I might plant my steps and thus escape.
All effort now were fruitless to resist
The mighty billow hurrying me away
To dash me on the pointed rocks. If yet
I strive, by swimming further, to descry   500
Some sloping shore or harbor of the isle,
I fear the tempest, lest it hurl me back,
Heavily groaning, to the fishy deep.
Or huge sea-monster, from the multitude
Which sovereign Amphitrite feeds, be sent
Against me by some god, for well I know
The power who shakes the shores is wroth with me."
     While he revolved these doubts within his mind,
A huge wave hurled him toward the rugged coast.
Then had his limbs been flayed, and all his bones   510
Broken at once, had not the blue-eyed maid,
Minerva, prompted him. Borne toward the rock,
He clutched it instantly, with both his hands,
And panting clung till that huge wave rolled by,
And so escaped its fury. Back it came,
And smote him once again, and flung him far
Seaward. As to the claws of polypus,
Plucked from its bed, the pebbles thickly cling,
So flakes of skin, from off his powerful hands,
Were left upon the rock. The mighty surge   520
O'erwhelmed him; he had perished ere his time,
Hapless Ulysses, but the blue-eyed maid,
Pallas, informed his mind with forecast. Straight
Emerging from the wave that shoreward rolled,
He swam along the coast and eyed it well,
In hope of sloping beach or sheltered creek.

But when, in swimming, he had reached the mouth
Of a soft-flowing river, here appeared
The spot he wished for, smooth, without a rock,
And here was shelter from the wind. He felt   530
The current's flow, and thus devoutly prayed:
   "Hear me, O sovereign power, whoe'er thou art!
To thee, the long-desired, I come. I seek
Escape from Neptune's threatenings on the sea.
The deathless gods respect the prayer of him
Who looks to them for help, a fugitive,
As I am now, when to thy stream I come,
And to thy knees, from many a hardship past,
O thou that here art ruler, I declare
Myself thy suppliant; be thou merciful."   540
   He spoke; the river stayed his current, checked
The billows, smoothed them to a calm, and gave
The swimmer a safe landing at his mouth.
Then dropped his knees and sinewy arms, at once
Unstrung, for faint with struggling was his heart.
His body was all swollen; the brine gushed forth
From mouth and nostrils; all unnerved he lay,
Breathless and speechless; utter weariness
O'ermastered him. But when he breathed again,
And his flown senses had returned, he loosed   550
The veil that Ino gave him from his breast,
And to the salt flood cast it. A great wave
Bore it far down the stream; the goddess there
In her own hands received it. He, meanwhile,
Withdrawing from the brink, lay down among
The reeds, and kissed the harvest-bearing earth,
And thus to his great soul, lamenting, said:
   "Ah me! what must I suffer more! what yet
Will happen to me? If, by the river's side,
I pass the unfriendly watches of the night,   560
The cruel cold and dews that steep the bank
May, in this weakness, end me utterly,
For chilly blows the river-air at dawn.

But should I climb this hill, to sleep within
The shadowy wood, among thick shrubs, if cold
And weariness allow me, then I fear,
That, while the pleasant slumbers o'er me steal,
I may become the prey of savage beasts."
    Yet, as he longer pondered, this seemed best.
He rose and sought the wood, and found it near   570
The water, on a height, o'erlooking far
The region round. Between two shrubs, that sprung
Both from one spot, he entered—olive-trees,
One wild, one fruitful. The damp-blowing wind
Ne'er pierced their covert; never blazing sun
Darted his beams within, nor pelting shower
Beat through, so closely intertwined they grew.
Here entering, Ulysses heaped a bed
Of leaves with his own hands; he made it broad
And high, for thick the leaves had fallen around.   580
Two men and three, in that abundant store,
Might bide the winter-storm, though keen the cold.
Ulysses, the great sufferer, on his couch
Looked and rejoiced, and placed himself within,
And heaped the leaves high o'er him and around.
As one who, dwelling in the distant fields,
Without a neighbor near him, hides a brand
In the dark ashes, keeping carefully
The seeds of fire alive, lest he, perforce,
To light his hearth must bring them from afar;   590
So did Ulysses, in that piles of leaves,
Bury himself, while Pallas o'er his eyes
Poured sleep and closed his lids, that he might take,
After his painful toils, the fitting rest.

1863   1865

THE DEATH OF LINCOLN

Oh, slow to smite and swift to spare,
    Gentle and merciful and just!
Who, in the fear of God, didst bear
    The sword of power, a nation's trust!

In sorrow by thy bier we stand,
    Amid the awe that hushes all,
And speak the anguish of a land
    That shook with horror at thy fall.

Thy task is done; the bond are free:
    We bear thee to an honored grave,   10
Whose proudest monument shall be
    The broken fetters of the slave.

Pure was thy life; its bloody close
    Hath placed thee with the sons of light,
Among the noble host of those
    Who perished in the cause of Right.

1865   1865

THE DEATH OF SLAVERY

O thou great Wrong, that, through the slow-paced years,
    Didst hold thy millions fettered, and didst wield
    The scourge that drove the laborer to the field,
And turn a stony gaze on human tears,
        Thy cruel reign is o'er;
        Thy bondmen crouch no more
In terror at the menace of thine eye;
    For He who marks the bounds of guilty power,
Long-suffering, hath heard the captive's cry,
    And touched his shackles at the appointed hour,   10
And lo! they fall, and he whose limbs they galled
Stands in his native manhood, disenthralled.

A shout of joy from the redeemed is sent;
    Ten thousand hamlets swell the hymn of thanks;
    Our rivers roll exulting, and their banks

Send up hosannas to the firmament!
              Fields where the bondman's toil
              No more shall trench the soil,
Seem now to bask in a serener day;
    The meadow-birds sing sweeter, and the airs   20
Of heaven with more caressing softness play,
    Welcoming man to liberty like theirs.
A glory clothes the land from sea to sea,
For the great land and all its coasts are free.

Within that land wert thou enthroned of late,
    And they by whom the nation's laws were made,
    And they who filled its judgment-seats obeyed
Thy mandate, rigid as the will of Fate.
              Fierce men at thy right hand,
              With gesture of command,   30
Gave forth the word that none might dare gainsay;
    And grave and reverend ones, who loved thee not,
Shrank from thy presence, and in blank dismay
    Choked down, unuttered, the rebellious thought;
While meaner cowards, mingling with thy train,
Proved, from the book of God, thy right to reign.

Great as thou wert, and feared from shore to shore,
    The wrath of Heaven o'ertook thee in thy pride;
    Thou sitt'st a ghastly shadow; by thy side
Thy once strong arms hang nerveless evermore.   40
              And they who quailed but now
              Before thy lowering brow,
Devote thy memory to scorn and shame,
    And scoff at the pale, powerless thing thou art.
And they who ruled in thine imperial name,
    Subdued, and standing sullenly apart,
Scowl at the hands that overthrew thy reign,
And shattered at a blow the prisoner's chain.

Well was thy doom deserved; thou didst not spare
    Life's tenderest ties, but cruelly didst part   50

Husband and wife, and from the mother's heart
Didst wrest her children, deaf to shriek and prayer;
       Thy inner lair became
       The haunt of guilty shame;
Thy lash dropped blood; the murderer, at thy side,
   Showed his red hands, nor feared the vengeance due.
Thou didst sow earth with crimes, and, far and wide,
   A harvest of uncounted miseries grew,
Until the measure of thy sins at last
Was full, and then the avenging bolt was cast!   60

Go now, accursed of God, and take thy place
   With hateful memories of the elder time,
   With many a wasting plague, and nameless crime,
And bloody war that thinned the human race;
       With the Black Death, whose way
       Through wailing cities lay,
Worship of Moloch, tyrannies that built
   The Pyramids, and cruel creeds that taught
To avenge a fancied guilt by deeper guilt—
   Death at the stake to those that held them not.   70
Lo! the foul phantoms, silent in the gloom
Of the flown ages, part to yield thee room.

I see the better years that hasten by
   Carry thee back into that shadowy past,
   Where, in the dusty spaces, void and vast,
The graves of those whom thou hast murdered lie.
       The slave-pen, through whose door
       Thy victims pass no more,
Is there, and there shall the grim block remain
   At which the slave was sold; while at thy feet   80
Scourges and engines of restraint and pain
   Moulder and rust by thine eternal seat.
There, mid the symbols that proclaim thy crimes,
Dwell thou, a warning to the coming times.

1866   1866

AMONG THE TREES

O ye who love to overhang the springs,
And stand by running waters, ye whose boughs
Make beautiful the rocks o'er which they play,
Who pile with foliage the great hills, and rear
A paradise upon the lonely plain,
Trees of the forest, and the open field!
Have ye no sense of being?   Does the air,
The pure air, which I breathe with gladness, pass
In gushes o'er your delicate lungs, your leaves,
All unenjoyed?   When on your winter's sleep   10
The sun shines warm, have ye no dreams of spring?
And when the glorious spring-time comes at last,
Have ye no joy of all your bursting buds,
And fragrant blooms, and melody of birds
To which your young leaves shiver?   Do ye strive
And wrestle with the wind, yet know it not?
Feel ye no glory in your strength when he,
The exhausted Blusterer, flies beyond the hills,
And leaves you stronger yet?   Or have ye not
A sense of loss when he has stripped your leaves,   20
Yet tender, and has splintered your fair boughs?
Does the loud bolt that smites you from the cloud
And rends you, fall unfelt?   Do there not run
Strange shudderings through your fibres when the axe
Is raised against you, and the shining blade
Deals blow on blow, until, with all their boughs,
Your summits waver and ye fall to earth?
Know ye no sadness when the hurricane
Has swept the wood and snapped its sturdy stems
Asunder, or has wrenched, from out the soil,   30
The mightiest with their circles of strong roots,
And piled the ruin all along his path?

    Nay, doubt we not that under the rough rind,
In the green veins of these fair growths of earth,

There dwells a nature that receives delight
From all the gentle processes of life,
And shrinks from loss of being. Dim and faint
May be the sense of pleasure and of pain,
As in our dreams; but, haply, real still.

Our sorrows touch you not. We watch beside   40
The beds of those who languish or who die,
And minister in sadness, while our hearts
Offer perpetual prayer for life and ease
And health to the belovèd sufferers.
But ye, while anxious fear and fainting hope
Are in our chambers, ye rejoice without.
The funeral goes forth; a silent train
Moves slowly from the desolate home; our hearts
Are breaking as we lay away the loved,
Whom we shall see no more, in their last rest,   50
Their little cells within the burial-place.
Ye have no part in this distress; for still
The February sunshine steeps your boughs
And tints the buds and swells the leaves within;
While the song-sparrow, warbling from her perch,
Tells you that spring is near. The wind of May
Is sweet with breath of orchards, in whose boughs
The bees and every insect of the air
Make a perpetual murmur of delight,
And by whose flowers the humming-bird hangs poised   60
In air, and draws their sweets and darts away.
The linden, in the fervors of July,
Hums with a louder concert. When the wind
Sweeps the broad forest in its summer prime,
As when some master-hand exulting sweeps
The keys of some great organ, ye give forth
The music of the woodland depths, a hymn
Of gladness and of thanks. The hermit-thrush
Pipes his sweet note to make your arches ring.
The faithful robin, from the wayside elm,   70

Carols all day to cheer his sitting mate,
And when the autumn comes, the kings of earth,
In all their majesty, are not arrayed
As ye are, clothing the broad mountain-side
And spotting the smooth vales with red and gold;
While, swaying to the sudden breeze, ye fling
Your nuts to earth, and the brisk squirrel comes
To gather them, and barks with childish glee,
And scampers with them to his hollow oak.

    Thus, as the seasons pass, ye keep alive   80
The cheerfulness of Nature, till in time
The constant misery which wrings the heart
Relents, and we rejoice with you again,
And glory in your beauty; till once more
We look with pleasure on your varnished leaves,
That gayly glance in sunshine, and can hear,
Delighted, the soft answer which your boughs
Utter in whispers to the babbling brook.

    Ye have no history.   I cannot know
Who, when the hill-side trees were hewn away,   90
Haply two centuries since, bade spare this oak,
Leaning to shade, with his irregular arms,
Low-bent and long, the fount that from his roots
Slips through a bed of cresses toward the bay.
I know not who, but thank him that he left
The tree to flourish where the acorn fell,
And join these later days to that far time
While yet the Indian hunter drew the bow
In the dim woods, and the white woodman first
Opened these fields to sunshine, turned the soil,   100
And strewed the wheat.   An unremembered Past
Broods, like a presence, 'mid the long gray boughs
Of this old tree, which has outlived so long
The flitting generations of mankind.

Ye have no history. I ask in vain
Who planted on the slope this lofty group
Of ancient pear-trees that with spring-time burst
Into such breadth of bloom. One bears a scar
Where the quick lightning scored its trunk, yet still
It feels the breath of Spring, and every May   110
Is white with blossoms. Who it was that laid
Their infant roots in earth, and tenderly
Cherished the delicate sprays, I ask in vain,
Yet bless the unknown hand to which I owe
This annual festival of bees, these songs
Of birds within their leafy screen, these shouts
Of joy from children gathering up the fruit
Shaken in August from the willing boughs.

Ye that my hands have planted, or have spared,
Beside the way, or in the orchard-ground,   120
Or in the open meadow, ye whose boughs
With every summer spread a wider shade,
Whose herd in coming years shall lie at rest
Beneath your noontide shelter? who shall pluck
Your ripened fruit? who grave, as was the wont
Of simple pastoral ages, on the rind
Of my smooth beeches some belovèd name?
Idly I ask; yet may the eyes that look
Upon you, in your later, nobler growth,
Look also on a nobler age than ours;   130
An age when, in the eternal strife between
Evil and Good, the Power of Good shall win
A grander mastery; when kings no more
Shall summon millions from the plough to learn
The trade of slaughter, and of populous realms
Make camps of war; when in our younger land
The hand of ruffian Violence, that now
Is insolently raised to smite, shall fall
Unnerved before the calm rebuke of Law,

And Fraud, his sly confederate, shrink, in shame,   140
Back to his covert, and forego his prey.

1868   1869

TREE–BURIAL

Near our southwestern border, when a child
Dies in the cabin of an Indian wife,
She makes its funeral-couch of delicate furs,
Blankets and bark, and binds it to the bough
Of some broad branching tree with leathern thongs
And sinews of the deer.   A mother once
Wrought at this tender task, and murmured thus:
    "Child of my love, I do not lay thee down
Among the chilly clods where never comes
The pleasant sunshine.   There the greedy wolf   10
Might break into thy grave and tear thee thence,
And I should sorrow all my life.   I make
Thy burial-place here, where the light of day
Shines round thee, and the airs that play among
The boughs shall rock thee.   Here the morning sun,
Which woke thee once from sleep to smile on me,
Shall beam upon thy bed and sweetly here
Shall lie the red light of the evening clouds
Which called thee once to slumber.   Here the stars
Shall look upon thee—the bright stars of heaven   20
Which thou didst wonder at.   Here too the birds,
Whose music thou didst love, shall sing to thee,
And near thee build their nests and rear their young
With none to scare them.   Here the woodland flowers
Whose opening in the spring-time thou didst greet
With shouts of joy, and which so well became
Thy pretty hands when thou didst gather them,
Shall spot the ground below thy little bed.
    "Yet haply thou hast fairer flowers than these,
Which, in the land of souls, thy spirit plucks   30
In fields that wither not, amid the throng

Of joyous children, like thyself, who went
Before thee to that brighter world and sport
Eternally beneath its cloudless skies.
Sport with them, dear, dear child, until I come
To dwell with thee, and thou, beholding me,
From far, shalt run and leap into my arms,
And I shall clasp thee as I clasped thee here
While living, oh most beautiful and sweet
Of children, now more passing beautiful,   40
If that can be, with eyes like summer stars—
A light that death can never quench again.
   "And now, oh wind, that here among the leaves
Dost softly rustle, breathe thou ever thus
Gently, and put not forth thy strength to tear
The branches and let fall their precious load,
A prey to foxes. Thou, too, ancient sun,
Beneath whose eye the seasons come and go,
And generations rise and pass away,
While thou dost never change—oh, call not up   50
With thy strong heats, the dark, grim thunder-cloud,
To smite this tree with bolts of fire, and rend
Its trunk and strew the earth with splintered boughs.
Ye rains, fall softly on the couch that holds
My darling. There the panther's spotted hide
Shall turn aside the shower; and be it long,
Long after thou and I have met again,
Ere summer wind or winter rain shall waste
This couch and all that now remains of thee,
To me thy mother. Meantime, while I live,   60
With each returning sunrise I shall seem
To see thy waking smile, and I shall weep;
And when the sun is setting I shall think
How, as I watched thee, o'er thy sleepy eyes
Drooped the smooth lids, and laid on the round cheek
Their lashes, and my tears will flow again;
And often, at those moments, I shall seem
To hear again the sweetly prattled name

Which thou didst call me by, and it will haunt
My home till I depart to be with thee."   70
1872   1872

A LIFETIME

I sit in the early twilight,
    And, through the gathering shade,
I look on the fields around me
    Where yet a child I played.

And I peer into the shadows,
    Till they seem to pass away,
And the fields and their tiny brooklet
    Lie clear in the light of day.

A delicate child and slender,
    With locks of light-brown hair,   10
From knoll to knoll is leaping
    In the breezy summer air.

He stoops to gather blossoms
    Where the running waters shine;
And I look on him with wonder,
    His eyes are so like mine.

I look till the fields and brooklet
    Swim like a vision by,
And a room in a lowly dwelling
    Lies clear before my eye.   20

There stand, in the clean-swept fireplace,
    Fresh boughs from the wood in bloom,
And the birch-tree's fragrant branches
    Perfume the humble room.

And there the child is standing
    By a stately lady's knee,

And reading of ancient peoples
   And realms beyond the sea.

Of the cruel King of Egypt
   Who made God's people slaves,   30
And perished, with all his army,
   Drowned in the Red Sea waves;

Of Deborah who mustered
   Her brethren long oppressed,
And routed the heathen army,
   And gave her people rest;

And the sadder, gentler story
   How Christ, the crucified,
With a prayer for those who slew him,
   Forgave them as he died.   40

I look again, and there rises
   A forest wide and wild,
And in it the boy is wandering,
   No longer a little child.

He murmurs his own rude verses
   As he roams the woods alone;
And again I gaze with wonder,
   His eyes are so like my own.

I see him next in his chamber,
   Where he sits him down to write   50
The rhymes he framed in his ramble,
   And he cons them with delight.

A kindly figure enters,
   A man of middle age,
And points to a line just written,
   And 'tis blotted from the page.

And next, in a hall of justice,
    Scarce grown to manly years,
Mid the hoary-headed wranglers
    The slender youth appears.   60

With a beating heart he rises,
    And with a burning cheek,
And the judges kindly listen
    To hear the young man speak.

Another change, and I see him
    Approach his dwelling-place
Where a fair-haired woman meets him,
    With a smile on her young face—

A smile that spreads a sunshine
    On lip and cheek and brow;   70
So sweet a smile there is not
    In all the wide earth now.

She leads by the hand their first-born,
    A fair-haired little one,
And their eyes as they meet him sparkle
    Like brooks in the morning sun.

Another change, and I see him
    Where the city's ceaseless coil
Sends up a mighty murmur
    From a thousand modes of toil.   80

And there, 'mid the clash of presses,
    He plies the rapid pen
In the battles of opinion,
    That divide the sons of men.

I look and the clashing presses
    And the town are seen no more,

But there is the poet wandering
  A strange and foreign shore.

He has crossed the mighty ocean
  To realms that lie afar,   90
In the region of ancient story,
  Beneath the morning star.

And now he stands in wonder
  On an icy Alpine height;
Now pitches his tent in the desert
  Where the jackal yells at night;

Now, far on the North Sea islands,
  Sees day on the midnight sky,
Now gathers the fair strange fruitage
  Where the isles of the Southland lie.   100

I see him again at his dwelling,
  Where, over the little lake,
The rose-trees droop in their beauty
  To meet the image they make.

Though years have whitened his temples,
  His eyes have the first look still,
Save a shade of settled sadness,
  A forecast of coming ill.

For in that pleasant dwelling,
  On the rack of ceaseless pain,   110
Lies she who smiled so sweetly,
  And prays for ease in vain.

And I know that his heart is breaking,
  When, over those dear eyes,
The darkness slowly gathers,
  And the loved and loving dies.

A grave is scooped on the hill-side
    Where often, at eve or morn,
He lays the blooms of the garden—
    He, and his youngest born.   12

And well I know that a brightness
    From his life has passed away,
And a smile from the green earth's beauty,
    And a glory from the day.

But I behold, above him,
    In the far blue deeps of air,
Dim battlements shining faintly,
    And a throng of faces there;

See over crystal barrier
    The airy figures bend,   13
Like those who are watching and waiting
    The coming of a friend.

And one there is among them,
    With a star upon her brow,
In her life a lovely woman,
    A sinless seraph now.

I know the sweet calm features;
    The peerless smile I know,
And I stretch my arms with transport
    From where I stand below.   14

And the quick tears drown my eyelids,
    But the airy figures fade,
And the shining battlements darken
    And blend with the evening shade.

I am gazing into the twilight
    Where the dim-seen meadows lie,

And the wind of night is swaying
The trees with a heavy sigh.

1876

THE FLOOD OF YEARS

A mighty Hand, from an exhaustless Urn,
Pours forth the never-ending Flood of Years,
Among the nations. How the rushing waves
Bear all before them! On their foremost edge,
And there alone, is Life. The Present there
Tosses and foams, and fills the air with roar
Of mingled noises. There are they who toil,
And they who strive, and they who feast, and they
Who hurry to and fro. The sturdy swain—
Woodman and delver with the spade—is there,   10
And busy artisan beside his bench,
And pallid student with his written roll.
A moment on the mounting billow seen,
The flood sweeps over them and they are gone.
There groups of revellers whose brows are twined
With roses, ride the topmost swell awhile,
And as they raise their flowing cups and touch
The clinking brim to brim, are whirled beneath
The waves and disappear. I hear the jar
Of beaten drums, and thunders that break forth   20
From cannon, where the advancing billow sends
Up to the sight long files of armèd men,
That hurry to the charge through flame and smoke.
The torrent bears them under, whelmed and hid
Slayer and slain, in heaps of bloody foam.
Down go the steed and rider, the plumed chief
Sinks with his followers; the head that wears
The imperial diadem goes down beside
The felon's with cropped ear and branded cheek.
A funeral-train—the torrent sweeps away   30
Bearers and bier and mourners. By the bed

Of one who dies men gather sorrowing,
And women weep aloud; the flood rolls on;
The wail is stifled and the sobbing group
Borne under. Hark to that shrill, sudden shout,
The cry of an applauding multitude,
Swayed by some loud-voiced orator who wields
The living mass as if he were its soul!
The waters choke the shout and all is still.
Lo! next a kneeling crowd, and one who spreads   40
The hands in prayer, the engulfing wave o'ertakes
And swallows them and him. A sculptor wields
The chisel, and the stricken marble grows
To beauty; at his easel, eager-eyed,
A painter stands, and sunshine at his touch
Gathers upon his canvas, and life glows;
A poet, as he paces to and fro,
Murmurs his sounding lines. Awhile they ride
The advancing billow, till its tossing crest
Strikes them and flings them under, while their tasks   50
Are yet unfinished. See a mother smile
On her young babe that smiles to her again;
The torrent wrests it from her arms; she shrieks
And weeps, and midst her tears is carried down.
A beam like that of moonlight turns the spray
To glistening pearls; two lovers, hand in hand,
Rise on the billowy swell and fondly look
Into each other's eyes. The rushing flood
Flings them apart: the youth goes down; the maid
With hands outstretched in vain, and streaming eyes,   60
Waits for the next high wave to follow him.
An aged man succeeds; his bending form
Sinks slowly. Mingling with the sullen stream
Gleam the white locks, and then are seen no more.
    Lo! wider grows the stream—a sea-like flood
Saps earth's walled cities; massive palaces
Crumble before it; fortresses and towers
Dissolve in the swift waters; populous realms

Swept by the torrent see their ancient tribes
Engulfed and lost; their very languages   70
Stifled, and never to be uttered more.
    I pause and turn my eyes, and looking back
Where that tumultuous flood has been, I see
The silent ocean of the Past, a waste
Of waters weltering over graves, its shores
Strewn with the wreck of fleets where mast and hull
Drop away piecemeal; battlemented walls
Frown idly, green with moss, and temples stand
Unroofed, forsaken by the worshipper.
There lie memorial stones, whence time has gnawed   80
The graven legends, thrones of kings o'erturned,
The broken altars of forgotten gods,
Foundations of old cities and long streets
Where never fall of human foot is heard,
On all the desolate pavement. I behold
Dim glimmerings of lost jewels, far within
The sleeping waters, diamond, sardonyx,
Ruby and topaz, pearl and chrysolite,
Once glittering at the banquet on fair brows
That long ago were dust, and all around   90
Strewn on the surface of that silent sea
Are withering bridal wreaths, and glossy locks
Shorn from dear brows, by loving hands, and scrolls
O'er written, haply with fond words of love
And vows of friendship, and fair pages flung
Fresh from the printer's engine. There they lie
A moment, and then sink away from sight.
    I look, and the quick tears are in my eyes,
For I behold in every one of these
A blighted hope, a separate history   100
Of human sorrows, telling of dear ties
Suddenly broken, dreams of happiness
Dissolved in air, and happy days too brief
That sorrowfully ended, and I think
How painfully must the poor heart have beat

In bosoms without number, as the blow
Was struck that slew their hope and broke their peace
   Sadly I turn and look before, where yet
The Flood must pass, and I behold a mist
Where swarm dissolving forms, the brood of Hope, 11
Divinely fair, that rest on banks of flowers,
Or wander among rainbows, fading soon
And reappearing, haply giving place
To forms of grisly aspect such as Fear
Shapes from the idle air—where serpents lift
The head to strike, and skeletons stretch forth
The bony arm in menace. Further on
A belt of darkness seems to bar the way
Long, low, and distant, where the Life to come
Touches the Life that is. The Flood of Years   12
Rolls toward it near and nearer. It must pass
That dismal barrier. What is there beyond?
Hear what the wise and good have said. Beyond
That belt of darkness, still the Years roll on
More gently, but with not less mighty sweep.
They gather up again and softly bear
All the sweet lives that late were overwhelmed
And lost to sight, all that in them was good,
Noble, and truly great, and worthy of love—
The lives of infants and ingenuous youths,   13
Sages and saintly women who have made
Their households happy; all are raised and borne
By that great current in its onward sweep,
Wandering and rippling with caressing waves
Around green islands fragrant with the breath
Of flowers that never wither. So they pass
From stage to stage along the shining course
Of that bright river, broadening like a sea.
As its smooth eddies curl along their way
They bring old friends together; hands are clasped 14
In joy unspeakable; the mother's arms
Again are folded round the child she loved

And lost. Old sorrows are forgotten now,
Or but remembered to make sweet the hour
That overpays them; wounded hearts that bled
Or broke are healed forever. In the room
Of this grief-shadowed present, there shall be
A Present in whose reign no grief shall gnaw
The heart, and never shall a tender tie
Be broken; in whose reign the eternal Change   150
That waits on growth and action shall proceed
With everlasting Concord hand in hand.

1876

PROSE SELECTIONS

ON THE USE OF TRISYLLABIC FEET
IN IAMBIC VERSE

The only feet of three syllables which can be employed in English Iambics, are either those which have the two first short, and the third long, or those which have all three short—the anapest, and the tribrachys. A certain use of these feet, in that kind of verse, has been allowed from the very beginnings of English poetry. This takes place either when the two first syllables in these feet are vowels or diphthongs, as in the following instance—

To scorn | delights | and live | labo- | *riŏŭs dāys.*

or when the letter *r*, only, is interposed between the vowels, as in the following—

And ev- | ery flower | that sad | embroid- | *erў wēar.*

or when the consonant *n* comes between the vowels, and the vowel preceding this letter is so obscurely or rapidly pronounced, as to leave it doubtful whether it may be considered as forming a distinct syllable, as in this instance.

Under | the op- | *ĕnĭng eўe-* | lids of | the morn.

Sometimes the letter *l*, in a like position, gives the poet a like liberty, as in the following example.

Wafted | the trav- | *ĕllĕr tō* | the beau- | teous west.

In all these cases, the three syllables were, until lately, written with a contraction which shortened them into two, and it came at length to be regarded as a rule, by most critics and authors, that no trisyllabic feet should be admitted in Iambic measure, where such a contraction was not allowed, or where the two first syllables might not, by some dexterity of pronunciation, be blended into one. This was, in effect, excluding all trisyllabic feet whatever; but they are now generally written without the contraction, and in reading poetry it is not, I believe, usually observed.

There is a freer use of trisyllabic feet in Iambic verse, of equal antiquity with the former, but which was afterwards proscribed as irregular and inharmonious, and particularly avoided by those who wrote in rhyme. I allude to all those cases where the two first syllables will not admit of a contraction, or which is nearly the same thing, refuse to coalesce in the pronunciation. These may be called pure trisyllabic feet, and the following is an example of this kind.

Impos- | tor, do | not charge | most in- | nŏcĕnt nāture.

In excluding liberties of this description, it is difficult to tell what has been gained, but it is easy to see what has been lost— the rule has been observed to the frequent sacrifice of beauty of expression, and variety and vivacity of numbers.

I think that I can show, by examples drawn from some of our best poets, that the admission of pure trisyllabic feet into Iambic verse is agreeable to the genius of that kind of measure, as well as to the habits of our language. I begin with those who have written in blank verse. The sweetest passages of Shakspeare— those which appear to have been struck out in the ecstasy of genius, and flow with that natural melody which is peculiar to him, are generally sprinkled with freedoms of this kind. Take the following specimen among a thousand others—part of the eloquent apostrophe of Timon to gold.

> Thou ever young, fresh, loved and *delicate wooer*
> Whose blush doth thaw the consecrated snow
> That lies in Dian's lap! thou *visible god*
> That solderest close impossibilities
> And mak'st them kiss!

Most of the older dramatists have done the same thing,— some more frequently than others,—but none appear to have avoided it with much care. I will next point to the most perfect master of poetic modulation perhaps in our language—a man to whom nature had given an exquisite ear, whose taste had been improved and exalted by a close study of the best models in the most harmonious tongues we know, and who emulated, in their own languages, the sweetness of the Latin and Italian poets. The heroic verse of Milton abounds with instances of pure trisyllabic feet. The following passage is certainly not deficient in harmony.

> And where the *river of bliss*, through midst of heaven,
> Rolls o'er Elysian flowers her amber stream,
> With these, that never fade, the *spirits elect*
> Bind their resplendent locks inwreathed with beams.

Dryden sometimes admits feet of this kind in his tragedies in blank verse, and many other dramatic poets, his contemporaries and successors, have taken the same liberty. In the celebrated work of Young, I find no instance of this sort, and it is not hard to tell the reason. Young was a profound and blind admirer of Pope, nor is it to be wondered at that he, who, at the recommendation of his friend, gave his days and nights to the study of Thomas Aquinas, as a system of divinity, should take that friend for a model in poetry. Young, in his Night Thoughts, endeavoured to do that for which, of all things, his genius least fitted him—to imitate the manner of Pope; and the consequence was that he injured the fine flow of his own imagination by violent attempts at point and an awkward sententiousness. It was like setting the Mississippi to spout little *jets d'eau* and turn children's water-wheels. He was probably afraid to use feet of three syllables, because he did not find them in the works of his master. About this time, and for some years afterwards, the exclusion of pure trisyllabic feet from blank verse seems to have been complete. I find no traces of them in Thomson and Dyer, nor in the heavy writings of Glover and Cumberland. Akenside's Pleasures of Imagination has been highly esteemed for the art with which the numbers are modulated, and the pauses adjusted. In this poem, as it was first written, I find no instances of the sort of which I am speaking—but when, in the maturity of his faculties, he revised, and partly wrote over the work, he seems to have been, in some measure, dissatisfied with that versification which the world had praised so much. In looking over this second draught of his work, I have noted the following deviations from his former practice.

> Furies which curse the earth, and make the blows,
> The heaviest blows, of nature's *innocent hand*
> Seem sport—
> I checked my prow and thence with eager steps,
> The *city of Minos* entered—
> But the chief
> Are poets, *eloquent men*, who dwell on earth.

Armstrong has given us some examples of a similar license in versification, Cowper's Task abounds with them, and they may be frequently found in the blank verse of some of our latest poets.

In accompanying me in the little retrospect which I have taken of the usage of our poets who have written in blank verse, I think the reader must be convinced, that there is something not incompatible with the principles of English versification, nor displeasing to an unperverted taste, in a practice, that in spite of rules and prejudices, is continually showing itself in the works of most of our sweetest and most valued poets, which prevailed in the best age of English poetry, and has now returned to us endeared by its associations with that venerable period. I will not here multiply examples to show how much it may sometimes improve the beauty of the numbers. I will only refer the reader to those already laid before him. I do not believe that he would be contented to exchange any of the words marked in the quotations which I have made, for tame Iambics, could it ever be done by the use of phrases equally proper and expressive. For my part, when I meet with such passages, amidst a dead waste of dissyllabic feet, their spirited irregularity refreshes and relieves me, like the sight of eminences and forests breaking the uniformity of a landscape.

If pure trisyllabic feet are allowed in blank verse, it would seem difficult to give any good reason why they should not be employed in rhyme. If they have any beauty in blank verse they cannot lose it merely because the ends of the lines happen to coincide in sound. The distinction between prose and verse is more strongly marked in rhymes than in blank verse, and the former therefore stands less in need than the latter, of extreme regularity of quantity, to make the distinction more obvious. Besides, the restraint which rhyme imposes on the diction is a good reason why it should be freed from any embarrassments which cannot contribute to its excellence. But whatever may be the reasons for admitting trisyllabic feet into Iambic rhyme, it is certain that most of our rhyming poets, from the time of Dryden, have carefully excluded them.

Spenser's verse is harmonious—but its harmony is of a peculiar kind. It is a long-drawn, diffuse, redundant volume of music, sometimes, indeed, sinking into languor, but generally filling the ear agreeably. His peculiar dialect has been called the Doric of the English language. I would rather call it the Ionic. It delights in adding vowels and resolving contractions, and instead of shortening two syllables into one, it often dilates one syllable into two. It is not in Spenser, therefore, that we are to look for frequent examples of pure trisyllabic feet in Iambic verse. They have an air of compression not well suited to the loose and liquid flow of his numbers. Yet he has occasionally admitted them, and without any apparent apprehension that he was sinning against propriety, for by a little variation of phrase he might have avoided them. In turning over his Fairy Queen, I meet, without any very laborious search, the following instances.

> Unweeting of the *perĭloŭs* wāndering ways.
> The sight whereof so *thoroŭghlў hĭm* dismayed.
> That still it breathed forth sweet *spirĭt ănd* whōlesome smell.
> When oblique Saturn sate *ĭn thĕ hoūse* of agonies.

That Milton did not think the use of these feet in rhyme, incompatible with correct versification, is evident from the following passages in his Lycidas—no unworthy or hasty effort of his genius.

> Fame is the spur that the clear *spir̆it dŏth raīse*.
> Oh, fountain *Ar̆eth̆use! ānd* thou, honoured flood,
> Smooth-sliding Mincius—
> To all that wander in that *p̆eril̆ous floōd*.

Cowley employed pure trisyllabic feet in Iambics without scruple. Waller and Denham sometimes admitted them, but Dryden and his successors rigidly excluded them; or when in too great haste to do this, disguised them by some barbarous and almost unpronounceable elision. Pope, in one of his earlier poems, has an instance of this sort.

> The courtier's learning, policy o' th' gown.

Who, at this day, would attempt to pronounce this line as it is written? I have observed some instances of pure trisyllabic feet in Garth's Dispensary; and a few even occur, at remote distances, to break the detestable monotony of Darwin's Iambics.

Some of our latest modern poets in rhyme have restored the old practice, and, as I think, with a good effect. Will the reader forgive me for setting before him an example of this kind, from one of those authors—an admirable specimen of representative versification?

> Alone Mokanna, midst the general flight,
> Stands, like the red moon in some stormy night,
> Among the *fugitive clouds* that hurrying by
> Leave only her unshaken in the sky.

Here the anapest in the third line quickens the numbers, and gives additional liveliness to the image which we receive of the rapid flight of the clouds over the face of heaven.

The liberty for which I have been contending, has often been censured and ridiculed. The utmost favour which it has, at any time, to my knowledge, received from the critics, is to have been silently allowed—no one has openly defended it. It has not been my aim to mark its limits or to look for its rules. I have only attempted to show that it is an ancient birthright of the poets, and ought not to be given up.

1811–19   1819

From REVIEW OF SOLYMAN BROWN, *AN ESSAY ON
AMERICAN POETRY*

[EARLY AMERICAN VERSE]

Of the poetry of the United States different opinions have
been entertained, and prejudice on the one side, and partiality
on the other, have equally prevented a just and rational estimate
of its merits. Abroad, our literature has fallen under unmerited
contumely, from those who were but slenderly acquainted
with the subject on which they professed to decide; and at
home, it must be confessed, that the swaggering and pompous
pretensions of many have done not a little to provoke and
excuse the ridicule of foreigners. Either of these extremes
exerts an injurious influence on the cause of letters in our
country. To encourage exertion and embolden merit to come
forward, it is necessary that they should be acknowledged and
rewarded—few will have the confidence to solicit what has
been withheld from claims as strong as theirs, or the courage to
tread a path which presents no prospect but the melancholy
wrecks of those who have gone before them. National gratitude—national pride—every high and generous feeling that
attaches us to the land of our birth, or that exalts our characters
as individuals, ask of us that we should foster the infant literature of our country, and that genius and industry, employing
their efforts to hasten its perfection, should receive, from our
hands, that celebrity which reflects as much honour on the
nation which confers it as on those to whom it is extended.
On the other hand, it is not necessary for these purposes—
it is even detrimental to bestow on mediocrity the praise due
to excellence, and still more so is the attempt to persuade ourselves and others into an admiration of the faults of favourite
writers. We make but a contemptible figure in the eyes of the
world, and set ourselves up as objects of pity to our posterity,
when we affect to rank the poets of our own country with

those mighty masters of song who have flourished in Greece, Italy and Britain. Such extravagant admiration may spring from a praise-worthy and patriotic motive, but it seems to us that it defeats its own object of encouraging our literature, by seducing those, who would aspire to the favour of the public, into an imitation of imperfect models, and leading them to rely too much on the partiality of their countrymen to overlook their deficiencies. Were our rewards to be bestowed only on what is intrinsically meritorious, merit alone would have any apology for appearing before the public. The poetical adventurer should be taught that it is only the production of genius, taste, and diligence that can find favour at the bar of criticism— that his writings are not to be applauded merely because they are written by an American, and are not decidedly bad; and that he must produce some more satisfactory evidence of his claim to celebrity than an extract from the parish register. To show him what we expect of him, it is as necessary to point out the faults of his predecessors, as to commend their excellences. He must be taught, as well what to avoid, as what to imitate. This is the only way of diffusing and preserving a pure taste, both among those who read and those who write, and, in our opinion, the only way of affording merit a proper and effectual encouragement.

It must, however, be allowed, that the poetry of the United States, though it has not reached that perfection to which some other countries have carried theirs, is yet even better than we could have been expected to produce, considering that our nation has scarcely seen two centuries since the first of its founders erected their cabins on its soil, that our literary institutions are yet in their infancy, and that our citizens are just beginning to find leisure to attend to intellectual refinements and indulge in intellectual luxury, and the means of rewarding intellectual excellence.

For the first century after the settlement of this country, the few quaint and unskilful specimens of poetry which yet remain to us, are looked upon merely as objects of curiosity, are preserved only in the cabinet of the antiquary, and give little pleasure, if read without reference to the age and people which produced them. A purer taste began after this period to prevail —the poems of the Rev. John Adams, written in the early part of the eighteenth century, which have been considered as no bad specimen of the poetry of his time, are tolerably free from the faults of the generation that preceded him, and show the dawnings of an ambition of correctness and elegance. The poetical writings of Joseph Green, Esq. who wrote about the middle of the same century, have been admired for their humour and the playful ease of their composition.

But, previous to the contest which terminated in the independence of the United States, we can hardly be said to have had any national poetry. Literary ambition was not then frequent amongst us—there was little motive for it, and few rewards. We were contented with considering ourselves as participating in the literary fame of that nation, of which we were a part, and of which many of us were natives, and aspired to no separate distinction. And indeed we might well lay an equal claim, with those who remained on the British soil, to whatever glory the genius and learning as well as the virtue and bravery of other times reflected on the British name. These were qualities which ennobled our common ancestors; and though their graves were not with us, and we were at a distance from the scenes and haunts which were hallowed by their deeds, their studies, and their contemplations, yet we brought with us, and preserved all the more valuable gifts which they left to their posterity and to mankind—their illumination—their piety —their spirit of liberty—reverence for their memory and example and all the proud tokens of a generous descent.

Yet here was no theatre for the display of literary talent— the worshippers of fame could find no altars erected to that divinity in America, and he who would live by his pen must seek patronage in the parent country. Some men of taste and learning amongst us, might occasionally amuse their leisure with poetical trifles, but a country struggling with the difficulties of colonization, and possessing no superfluous wealth, wanted any other class of men rather than poets. Accordingly we find the specimens of American poetry, before this period, mostly desultory and occasional—rare and delicate exotics, cultivated only by the curious.

On our becoming an independent empire, a different spirit began to manifest itself, and the general ambition to distinguish ourselves as a nation was not without its effect on our literature. It seems to us, that it is from this time only that we can be said to have poets of our own, and from this period it is that we must date the origin of American poetry. About this time, flourished Francis Hopkinson, whose humorous ballad, entitled The Battle of the Kegs, is in most of our memories, and some of whose attempts, though deficient in vigour, are not inelegant. The keen and forcible invectives of Dr. Church, which are still recollected by his contemporaries, received an additional edge and sharpness from the exasperated feelings of the times. A writer in verse of inferior note was Philip Freneau, whose pen seems to have been chiefly employed on political subjects, and whose occasional productions, distinguished by a coarse strength of sarcasm, and abounding with allusions to passing events, which is perhaps their greatest merit, attracted in their time considerable notice, and in the year 1786 were collected into a volume. But the influence of that principle which awoke and animated the exertions of all who participated in the political enthusiasm of that time, was still more strongly exemplified in the Connecticut poets—Trumbull, Dwight, Barlow, Humphreys, and Hopkins—who began to write about this period. In all the productions of these authors, there is a pervading spirit of *nationality* and patriotism—a desire to reflect credit on the country to which they belonged, which seems, as much as individual ambition, to have prompted their efforts, and which at times gives a certain glow and interest to their manner.

McFingal, the most popular of the writings of the former of these poets, first appeared in the year 1782. This pleasant satire on the adherents of Britain in those times, may be pronounced a tolerably successful imitation of the great work of Butler—though, like every other imitation of that author, it wants that varied and inexhaustible fertility of allusion, which made all subjects of thought—the lightest and most abstruse parts of learning—every thing in the physical and moral world —in art or nature, the playthings of his wit. The work of Trumbull cannot be much praised for the purity of its diction. Yet perhaps great scrupulousness in this particular was not consistent with the plan of the author, and, to give the scenes of his poem their full effect, it might have been thought necessary to adopt the familiar dialect of the country and the times. We think his Progress of Dulness a more pleasing poem, as more finished, and more perfect in its kind, and, though written in the same manner, more free from the constraint and servility of imitation. The graver poems of Trumbull contain some vigorous and animated declamation.

Of Dr. Dwight we would speak with all the respect due to talents, to learning, to piety, and a long life of virtuous usefulness—but we must be excused from feeling any high admiration of his poetry. It seems to us modelled upon a manner altogether too artificial and mechanical. There is something strained, violent, and out of nature, in all his attempts. His Conquest of Canaan will not secure immortality to its author. In this work the author has been considered by some as by no means happy in the choice of his fable—however this may be, he has certainly failed to avail himself of the advantages it offered him— his epic wants the creations and colourings of an inventive and poetical fancy—the charm, which, in the hands of genius, communicates an interest to the simplest incidents, and something of the illusion of reality to the most improbable fictions. The versification is remarkable for its unbroken monotony. Yet it contains splendid passages, which, separated from the body of the work, might be admired, but a few pages pall both on the ear and the imagination. It has been urged in its favor that the writer was young—the poetry of his maturer years does not however seem to possess greater beauties or fewer faults. The late Mr. Dennie at one time exerted his ingenuity to render this poem popular with his countrymen; in the year 1800 he published, in the Farmer's Museum, a paper printed at Walpole, of which he was the editor, a series of observations and criticisms on the Conquest of Canaan, after the manner of Addison in those numbers of the Spectator which made Milton a favourite with the English people. But this attempt did not meet with success—the work would not sell, and loads of copies yet cumber the shelves of our booksellers. In the other poems of Dr. Dwight, which are generally obnoxious [*sic*] to the same criticisms, he sometimes endeavours to descend to a more familiar style, and entertains his reader with laborious attempts at wit, and here he is still unsuccessful. Parts of his Greenfield Hill, and that most unfortunate of his productions, the Triumph of Infidelity, will confirm the truth of this remark.

Barlow, when he began to write, was a poet of no inconsiderable promise. His Hasty Pudding, one of his earliest productions, is a good specimen of mock-heroic poetry, and his Vision of Columbus, at the time of its first appearance, attracted much attention and was hailed as an earnest of better things. It is no small praise to say, that when appointed by the General Assembly of Churches in Connecticut to revise Watts' Version of the Psalms and to versify such as were omitted in that work, he performed the task in a manner which made a near approach to the simplicity and ease of that poet who according to Dr. Johnson, 'has done better than any body else what nobody has done well.' In his maturer years, Barlow became ambitious of distinguishing himself and doing honour to his country by some more splendid and important exertion of his talents, and, for this purpose, projected a national epic, in which was sung the Discovery of America, the successful struggle of the states in the defence of their liberties, and the exalted prospects which were opening before them. It is to be regretted that a design, so honourable and so generously conceived, should have failed. In 1807 appeared the Columbiad, which was his poem of the Vision of Columbus, much enlarged, and with such variations as the feelings and reflections of his riper age and judgment led him to make. The Columbiad is not, in our opinion, so pleasing a poem, in its present form as in that in which it was originally written. The plan of the work is utterly destitute of interest, and that, which was at first sufficiently wearisome, has become doubly so by being drawn out to its present length. Nor are the additions of much value, on account of the taste in which they are composed. Barlow, in his later poetry, attempted to invigorate his style, but instead of drawing strength and salubrity, from the pure wells of ancient English, he corrupted and debased it with foreign infusions. The imposing but unchaste glitter, which distinguished the manner of Darwin and his imitators, appears likewise to have taken strong hold on his fancy, and he has not scrupled to bestow on his poem much of this meretricious decoration. But notwithstanding the bad taste in which his principal work is composed—notwithstanding he cannot be said to write with much pathos, or many of the native felicities of fancy, there is yet enough, in the poetry of Mr. Barlow to prove that, had he fixed his eye on purer models, he might have excelled, not indeed in epic or narrative poetry nor in the delineation of passion and feeling, but in that calm, lofty, sustained style, which suits best with topics of morality and philosophy, and for which the vigour and spirit of his natural manner, whenever he permits it to appear, shew him to have been well qualified.

Humphreys was a poet of humbler pretensions. His writings, which were first collected in 1790, are composed in a better taste than those of the two last, and, if he has less genius, he has likewise fewer faults. Some of his lighter pieces are sufficiently pretty. He is most happy when he aims at nothing beyond an elegant mediocrity, and to do him justice this is generally the extent of his ambition. On the whole, he may be considered as sustaining a respectable rank among the poets of our country.

A writer of a different cast from those we have mentioned, and distinguished by a singular boldness of imagination, as well as great humour, was Dr. Lemuel Hopkins, who, in 1786, and the year following, in conjunction with Trumbull, Barlow, and Humphreys, and other wits of that time, wrote the Anarchiad, a satire, on a plan similar to that of the Rolliad, which appeared in the New Haven Gazette of those years, and of which the wildest parts are attributed to him. He was likewise author of the Speech of Hesper, and some smaller poems, which have been praised for their wit. There is a coarseness and want of polish in his style; and his imagination, daring and original, but unrestrained by a correct judgment, often wanders into absurdities and extravagances. Still, if he had all the madness, he must be allowed to have possessed some of the inspiration of poetry.

One material error of taste pervades the graver productions of these authors, into which it should seem they were led by copying certain of the poets of England, who flourished near the period in which they began to write. It was their highest ambition to attain a certain lofty, measured, declamatory manner—an artificial elevation of style, from which it is impossible to rise or descend without abruptness and violence, and which allows just as much play and freedom to the faculties of the writer as a pair of stilts allows the body. The imagination is confined to one trodden circle, doomed to the chains of a perpetual mannerism, and condemned to tinkle the same eternal tune with its fetters. Their versification, though not equally exceptionable in all, is formed upon the same stately model of balanced and wearisome regularity. Another fault, which arises naturally enough out of the peculiar style which we have imputed to these poets, is the want of pathos and feeling in their writings—the heart is rarely addressed, and never with much power or success. Amidst this coldness of manner, sameness of imagery and monotony of versification, the reader lays down his book, dazzled and fatigued.

In 1800 appeared the poems of William Cliffton, who fell, at the age of twenty seven, a victim to that scourge of our climate which ceases not to waste when other diseases are sated—the pulmonary consumption. There is none of our American poetry, on which we dwell with more pleasure, mingled indeed with regret at the untimely fate of the writer, than these charming remains. Amidst many of the immature effusions of his greener years, and unfinished productions which were never meant to meet the eye of the world, there are to be found specimens of poetry, not only more delicate, classical and polished, but more varied in imagery, and possessing more of that flexibility of style of the want of which in others we have complained, and more faithful to nature and the feelings, than it has often been our lot to meet with, in the works of our native poets. In his later and more finished productions, his diction is refined to an unusual degree of purity, and through this lucid medium the creations of his elegant fancy appear with nothing to obscure their loveliness.

Several respectable additions have been made to the mass of American poetry by Mr. Alsop. His monody on the death of Washington was admired at the time of its appearance. The public is likewise indebted to him for a version of the poem of Silius Italicus on the Punic war, and another of the Second Canto of Berni's Orlando Inamorato. Often elegant, but occasionally relapsing into feebleness and languor, his poetry is that of a man of correct and cultivated taste, but of no very fervid genius, nor bending the faculties of his mind with much intensity to the work in which he was engaged.

The posthumous works of St. John Honeywood, Esq. were published in the year 1801. These modest remains, the imperfect but vigorous productions of no common mind, have not been noticed as they deserved. They contain many polished and nervous lines.

We should not expect to be easily pardoned, were we to pass by the writings of a poet who enjoyed, during his life time, so extensive a popularity as the late Mr. [Robert Treat] Paine. The first glow of admiration, which the splendid errors of his manner excited in the public, is now over, and we can calmly estimate his merits and defects. He must be allowed to have possessed an active and fertile fancy. Even in the misty obscurity, which often shrouds his conceptions not only from the understanding of the reader, but, it should seem, from that of the writer himself, there sometimes break out glimpses of greatness and majesty. Yet with a force and exuberance of imagination which, if soberly directed, might have gained him the praise of magnificence, he is perpetually wandering in search of conceits and extravagances. He is ambitious of the epigrammatic style, and often bewilders himself with attempts to express pointedly what he does not conceive clearly. More instances of the false sublime might perhaps be selected from the writings of this poet, than from those of any other of equal talents, who lived in the same period. The brilliancy of Paine's poetry is like the brilliancy of frost-work—cold and fantastic. Who can point out the passage in his works, in which he speaks to the heart in its own language? He was a fine, but misguided genius.

With respect to the prevailing style of poetry, at the present day, in our country, we apprehend that it will be found, in too many instances, tinged with a sickly and affected imitation of the peculiar manner of some of the late popular poets of England. We speak not of a disposition to emulate whatever is beautiful and excellent in their writings—still less would we be understood as intending to censure that sort of imitation which, exploring all the treasures of English poetry, culls from all a diction, that shall form a natural and becoming dress for the conceptions of the writer,—this is a course of preparation which every one ought to go through before he appears before the public—but we desire to set a mark on that servile habit of copying, which adopts the vocabulary of some favourite author, and apes the fashion of his sentences, and cramps and forces the ideas into a shape, which they would not naturally have taken, and of which the only recommendation is, not that it is most elegant or most striking, but that it bears some resemblance to the manner of him who is proposed as a model. This way of writing has an air of poverty and meanness—it seems to indicate a paucity of reading as well as perversion of taste—it might almost lead us to suspect that the writer had but one or two examples of poetical composition in his hands, and was afraid of expressing himself, except according to some formula which they might contain—and it ever has been, and ever will be, the resort of those who are sensible that their works need some factitious recommendation to give them even a temporary popularity.

We have now given a brief summary of what we conceived to be the characteristic merits and defects of our most celebrated American poets. Some names, of which we are not at present aware, equally deserving of notice with those whom we have mentioned, may have been omitted—some we have passed over, because we were not willing to disturb their passage to that oblivion, towards which, to the honour of our country, they are hastening—and some elegant productions of later date we have not commented on, because we were unwilling to tire our readers with a discussion which they may think already exhausted.

On the whole there seems to be more good taste among those who read, than those who write poetry in our country. With respect to the poets whom we have enumerated, and whose merits we have discussed, we think the judgment pronounced on their works by the public will be found, generally speaking, just. They hold that station in our literature to which they are entitled, and could hardly be admired more than they are, without danger to the taste of the nation. We know of no instance in which great poetical merit has come forward, and finding its claims unallowed, been obliged to retire to the shade from which it emerged. Whenever splendid talents of this description shall appear, we believe that there will be found a disposition to encourage and reward them. The fondness for literature is fast increasing in our country—and if this were not the case, the patrons of literature have multiplied, of course, and will continue to multiply with the mere growth of our population. The popular English works of the day are reprinted in our country—they are dispersed all over the union—they are to be found in every body's hands—they are made the subject of every body's conversation. What should hinder our native works, if equal in merit, from meeting an equally favourable reception? * * *

1818   1818

From REVIEW OF CATHERINE M. SEDGWICK, *REDWOOD*

[ROMANCE]

* * * There is a strong love of romance inherent in the human mind. We all remember how our childhood was captivated with stories of sorcerers and giants. We do not, in our riper age, forget with what a fearful and thrilling interest we hung over tales of the interpositions of supernatural beings, of acts of desperate heroism, followed by incredible successes, of impossible dangers, and equally impossible deliverances. And when our maturer judgment has caused us to turn with disgust, from the relation of what is contrary to the known laws of nature, we transfer the same intense attention to narratives that keep within the bounds of possibility. We love to read of imminent perils, and hairbreadth escapes, of adventures in strange lands and among strange races of men, or in times of great public commotion or unusual public calamity. Something of this taste exists in every mind, though variously modified and diversified, and contented with a greater or less degree of verisimilitude, according as the imagination is more or less inflammable. Some preserve a fondness for fictions almost as wild as those, which amused their earlier years, while others can be pleased only with the recital of what is strictly probable. Some will listen with interest to stories of 'antres vast and deserts idle,' and the adventures of the intrepid voyager who traverses them, while others delight to have their blood curdle at being told of

> The Anthropophagi, and men whose heads
> Do grow beneath their shoulders.

In reading narratives of the romantic kind, our curiosity comes in aid of the author. We are eager to learn the issue of adventures so new to us. The imagination of the reader is also ready with its favorable offices. This faculty, always busiest when we are told of scenes and events out of the range of men's ordinary experience, expatiates at large upon the suggestions of the author, and, as we read, rapidly fills up the outline he gives with bright colors and deep shades of its own. From all these causes it may happen, that by the mere fortunate invention and happy arrangement of striking incidents, a work of fiction shall succeed in gaining the public favor, without any considerable proportion of the higher merits of that kind of writing, without any uncommon beauty of style, or any unusual degree either of pathos or humor, or splendor of imagination, or vivacity of description, or powerful delineation of character. * * *

[AMERICAN SOCIETY AS A FIELD FOR FICTION]

* * * On more than one occasion, we have already given somewhat at large our opinion of the fertility of our country, and its history, in the materials of romance. If our reasonings needed any support from successful examples of that kind of writing, as a single fact is worth a volume of ingenious theorising, we have had the triumph of seeing them confirmed beyond all controversy, by the works of a popular American author, who has shown the literary world into what beautiful creations those materials may be wrought. In like manner, we look upon the specimen before us as a conclusive argument, that the writers of works of fiction, of which the scene is laid in familiar and domestic life, have a rich and varied field before them in the United States. Indeed, the opinion on this subject, which, till lately, prevailed pretty extensively among us, that works of this kind, descriptive of the manners of our countrymen, could not succeed, never seemed to us to rest on a very solid foundation. It was rather a sweeping inference drawn from the fact, that no highly meritorious work of the kind had appeared, and the most satisfactory and comfortable way of accounting for this, was to assert, that no such could be written. But it is not always safe to predict what a writer of genius will make of a given subject. Twenty years ago, what possible conception could an English critic have had of the admirable productions of the author of

Waverley, and of the wonderful improvement his example has
effected in that kind of composition? Had the idea of one of
those captivating works, destined to take such strong hold on
all minds, been laid before him by the future author, he would
probably only have wondered at his vanity.

* * * It has been objected, that the habits of our countrymen
are too active and practical; that they are too universally and
continually engrossed by the cares and occupations of business
to have leisure for that intrigue, those plottings and counter
plottings, which are necessary to give a sufficient degree of action and eventfulness to the novel of real life. It is said that we
need for this purpose a class of men, whose condition in life
places them above the necessity of active exertion, and who are
driven to the practice of intrigue, because they have nothing else
to do. It remains, however, to be proved that any considerable
portion of this ingredient is necessary in the composition of a
successful novel. To require that it should be made up of nothing better than the manœuvres of those, whose only employment is to glitter at places of public resort, to follow a perpetual
round of amusements, and to form plans to outshine, thwart, and
vex each other, is confining the writer to a narrow and most barren circle. It is requiring an undue proportion of heartlessness,
selfishness, and vice in his pictures of society. It is compelling
him to go out of the wholesome atmosphere of those classes,
where the passions and affections have their most salutary and
natural play, and employ his observations on that where they
are most perverted, sophisticated, and corrupt.

But will it be seriously contended, that he can have no other
resource but the rivalries and machinations of the idle, the
frivolous, and the dissolute, to keep the reader from yawning
over his pictures? Will it be urged that no striking and interesting incidents can come to pass without their miserable aid? If
our country be not the country of intrigue, it is at least the
country of enterprise; and nowhere are the great objects that
worthily interest the passions, and call forth the exertions of men,
pursued with more devotion and perseverance. The agency of
chance too is not confined to the shores of Europe; our country-

men have not attained a sufficient degree of certainty in their calculations to exclude it from ours. It would really seem to us, that these two sources, along with that proportion of the blessed quality of intrigue, which even the least favorable view of our society will allow us, are abundantly fertile in interesting occurrences, for all the purposes of the novelist. Besides, it should be recollected, that it is not in any case the dull diary of ordinary occupations, or amusements, that forms the groundwork of his plot. On the contrary, it is some event, or at least a series of events, of unusual importance, standing out in strong relief from the rest of the biography of his principal characters, and to which the daily habits of their lives, whatever may be their rank or condition, are only a kind of accompaniment.

But the truth is, that the distinctions of rank, and the amusements of elegant idleness, are but the surface of society, and only so many splendid disguises put upon the reality of things. They are trappings which the writer of real genius, the anatomist of the human heart, strips away when he would exhibit his characters as they are, and engage our interest for them as beings of our own species. He reduces them to the same great level where distinctions of rank are nothing, and difference of character everything. It is here that James First and Charles Second and Louis Ninth and Rob Roy, and Jeanie Deans, and Meg Merrilies are, by the great author of the Waverley Novels, made to meet. The monarch must come down from the dim elevation of his throne, he must lay aside the assumed and conventional manners of his station, and unbend and unbosom himself with his confidants, before that illustrious master will condescend to describe him. In the artificial sphere in which the great move, they are only puppets and pageants, but here they are men. A narrative, the scene of which is laid at the magnificent levees of princes, in the drawing rooms of nobles, and the bright assemblies of fashion, may be a very pretty, showy sort of thing, and so may a story of the glittering dances and pranks of fairies. But we soon grow weary of all this, and ask for objects of sympathy and regard, for something the recollection of which shall dwell on the heart, and to which it will love to recur; for something, in short, which is natural, the uneffaced traits of strength and weakness, of the tender and the comic, all which the pride of rank either removes from observation or obliterates.

If these things have any value, we hesitate not to say, that they are to be found abundantly in the characters of our countrymen, formed as they are under the influence of our free institutions, and shooting into a large and vigorous, though sometimes irregular luxuriance. They exist most abundantly in our more ancient settlements, and amidst the more homogeneous races of our large populations, where the causes that produce them have operated longest and with most activity. It is there that the human mind has learned best to enjoy our fortunate and equal institutions, and to profit by them. In the countries of Europe the laws chain men down to the condition in which they were born. This observation, of course, is not equally true of all those countries, but when they are brought into comparison with ours, it is in some degree applicable to them all. Men spring up, and vegetate, and die without thinking of passing from the sphere in which they find themselves any more than the plants they cultivate think of removing from the places where they are rooted. It is the tendency of this rigid and melancholy destiny to contract and stint the intellectual faculties, to prevent the development of character, and to make the subjects of it timid, irresolute, and imbecile. With us, on the contrary, where the proudest honors in the state, and the highest deference in society, are set equally before all our citizens, a wholesome and quickening impulse is communicated to all parts of the social system. All are possessed with a spirit of ambition and a love of adventure, an intense competition calls forth and exalts the passions and faculties of men, their characters become strongly defined, their minds acquire a hardihood and activity which can be gained by no other discipline, and the community, throughout all its conditions, is full of bustle, and change, and action.

Whoever will take the pains to pursue this subject a little into its particulars, will be surprised at the infinite variety of forms of character, which spring up under the institutions of our country. Religion is admitted on all hands to be a mighty agent in moulding the human character; and accordingly, with the perfect allowance and toleration of all religions, we see among us their innumerable and diverse influences upon the manners and temper of our people. Whatever may be his religious opinions, no one is restrained by fear of consequences from avowing them, but is left to nurse his peculiarities of doctrine into what importance he pleases. The Quaker is absolved from submission to the laws in those particulars, which offend his conscience, the Moravian finds no barriers in the way of his work of proselytism and charity, the Roman Catholic is subjected to no penalty for pleasing himself with the magnificent ceremonial of his religion, and the Jew worships unmolested in his synagogue. In many parts of our country we see communities of that strange denomination, the Shakers, distinguished from their neighbors by a garb, a dialect, an architecture, a way of worship, of thinking, and of living, as different, as if they were in fact of a different origin, instead of being collected from the families around them. In other parts we see small neighborhoods of the Seventh Day Baptists, retaining the simplicity of manners and quaintness of language delivered down from their fathers. Here we find the austerities of puritanism preserved to this day, there the rights and doctrines of the Church of England are shown in their effect on the manners of the people, and yet in another part of the country springs up a new and numerous sect, who wash one another's feet, and profess to revive the primitive habits of the apostolic times.

It is in our country also, that these differences of character, which grow naturally out of geographical situation, are least tampered with and repressed by political regulations. The adventurous and roving natives of our seacoast and islands, are a different race of men from those who till the interior, and the hardy dwellers of our mountainous districts are not like the inhabitants of the rich plains, that skirt our mighty lakes and rivers. The manners of the northern states are said to be characterised by the keenness and importunity of their climate, and those of the southern to partake of the softness of theirs. In our cities you will see the polished manners of the European capitals, but pass into the more quiet and unvisited parts of the country, and you will find men, whom you might take for the first planters of our colonies. The descendants of the Hollanders have not forgotten the traditions of their fathers, and the legends of Germany are still recited, and the ballads of Scotland still sung, in settlements whose inhabitants derive their origin from those countries. It is hardly possible that the rapid and continual growth and improvement of our country, a circumstance wonderfully exciting to the imagination, and altogether unlike anything witnessed in other countries, should not have some influence in forming our national character. At all events, it is a most fertile source of incident. It does for us in a few short years, what, in Europe, is the work of centuries. The hardy and sagacious native of the eastern states, settles himself in the wilderness by the side of the emigrant from British Isles; the pestilence of the marshes is braved and overcome; the bear, and wolf and catamount are chased from their haunts; and then you see cornfields and roads and towns springing up as if by enchantment. In the mean time pleasant Indian villages, situated on the skirts of their hunting grounds, with their beautiful green plats for dances and martial exercises, are taken into the bosom of our extending population, while new states are settled and cities founded far beyond them. Thus a great deal of history is crowded into a brief space. Each little hamlet, in a few seasons has more events and changes to tell of, than a European village can furnish in a course of ages.

But, if the writer of fictitious history does not find all the variety he wishes in the various kinds of our population, descended, in different parts of our country, from ancestors of different nations, and yet preserving innumerable and indubitable tokens of their origin, if the freedom with which every man is suffered to take his own way, in all things not affecting the peace and good order of society, does not furnish him with a sufficient diversity of characters, employments, and modes of life, he has yet other resources. He may bring into his plots men, whose characters and manners were formed by the institutions and modes of society in the nations beyond the Atlantic, and he may describe them faithfully, as things which he has observed and studied. If he is not satisfied with indigenous virtue, he may take for the model of his characters men of whom the old world is not worthy, and whom it has cast out from its bosom. If domestic villany be not dark enough for his pictures, here are fugitives from the justice of Europe come to prowl in America. If the coxcombs of our own country are not sufficiently exquisite, affected, and absurd, here are plenty of silken fops from the capitals of foreign kingdoms. If he finds himself in need of a class of men more stupid and degraded than are to be found among the natives of the United States, here are crowds of the wretched peasantry of Great Britain and Germany, flying for refuge from intolerable suffering, in every vessel that comes to our shores. Hither also resort numbers of that order of men who, in foreign countries, are called the middling class, the most valuable part of the communities they leave, to enjoy a moderate affluence, where the abuses and exactions of a distempered system of government cannot reach them, to degrade them to the condition of the peasantry. Our country is the asylum of the persecuted preachers of new religions, and the teachers of political doctrines, which Europe will not endure; a sanctuary for dethroned princes, and the consorts of slain emperors. When we consider all these innumerable differences of character, native and foreign, this infinite variety of pursuits and objects, this endless diversity and change of fortunes, and behold them gathered and grouped into one vast assemblage in our own country, we shall feel little pride in the sagacity or the skill of that native author, who asks for a richer or a wider field of observation. * * *

1825   1825

LECTURES ON POETRY

LECTURE I. ON THE NATURE OF POETRY

In treating of the subject which has been assigned me, it is obvious that it will be impossible for me to compress into four lectures anything like a complete view of it. I am to speak of one of the most ancient of all arts, of the very earliest and most venerable branch of literature—one which even now exists in many countries that have no other; one, which although it has not in every period been cultivated with the same degree of success, has yet in no age of the world ceased to attract a large degree of the attention of mankind. Not only have the writers of poetry been exceedingly numerous—more so, perhaps, than those of any other class—but poetry has shot forth another branch of literature, her handmaid and satellite, and raised up a large body of authors, who speculate upon what the poets have written, who define the elements and investigate the principles of the art, and fix the degrees of estimation in which its several productions should be held. Not only has the poetry of one age been exceedingly different from that of another, but different styles of poetry have prevailed at the same time in different nations, different schools of poetry have arisen in the same nation, and different forms of poetical composition have been preferred by the several writers of the same school. So much poetry has been written, and that poetry has been the subject of so much criticism, so much matter for speculation has been collected, and so many reasonings and theories have been framed out of it, that the subject has grown to be one of the most comprehensive in the whole province of literature.

If I were to treat of either of its great subdivisions—if, for example, I were to attempt its history from its earliest origin, through its various stages, to the present time; if I were to analyze the several forms of poetical composition, or to point out the characteristics of the various kinds of poetry that have prevailed at different periods, or to compare the genius of the most illustrious poets—in either case, I could do little more than pass rapidly over the principal topics. The view would be so brief that it would seem like a dry table of the contents of a large work, and would become tedious from its very brevity. I shall, therefore, in the short course of lectures which I have undertaken, attempt no entire view of the subject assigned to me; but shall only endeavor to select a few of the topics which seem to me among the most interesting, and on which I may imagine that I shall weary you the least.

Of the nature of poetry different ideas have been entertained. The ancient critics seemed to suppose that they did something toward giving a tolerable notion of it by calling it a mimetic or imitative art, and classing it with sculpture and painting. Of its affinity with these arts there can be no doubt; but that affinity seems to me to consist almost wholly in the principles by which they all produce their effect, and not in the manner in which those principles are reduced to practice. There is no propriety in applying to poetry the term *imitative* in a literal and philosophical sense, as there is in applying it to painting and sculpture. The latter speak to the senses; poetry speaks directly to the mind. They reproduce sensible objects, and, by means of these, suggest the feeling or sentiment connected with them; poetry, by the symbols of words, suggests both the sensible object and the association. I should be glad to learn how a poem descriptive of a scene or an event is any more an imitation of that scene or that event than a prose description would be. A prose composition giving an account of the proportions and dimensions of a building, and the materials of which it is constructed, is certainly, so far as mere exactness is concerned, a better imitation of it than the finest poem that could be written about it. Yet who, after all, ever thought of giving such a composition the name of an imitation? The truth is, painting and sculpture are, literally, imitative arts, while poetry is only metaphorically so. The epithet as applied to poetry may be well enough, perhaps, as a figure of speech, but to make a metaphor the foundation of a philosophical classification is putting it to a service in which it is sure to confuse what it professes to make clear.

I would rather call poetry a suggestive art. Its power of affecting the mind by pure suggestion, and employing, instead of a visible or tangible imitation, arbitrary symbols, as unlike as possible to the things with which it deals, is what distinguishes this from its two sister arts. It is owing to its operation by means of suggestion that it affects different minds with such different degrees of force. In a picture or a statue the colors and forms employed by the artist impress the senses with the greatest distinctness. In painting, there is little—in sculpture, there is less—for the imagination to supply. It is true that different minds, according to their several degrees of cultivation, will receive different degrees of pleasure from the productions of these arts, and that the moral associations they suggest will be variously felt, and in some instances variously interpreted. Still, the impression made on the senses is in all cases the same; the same figures, the same lights and shades, are seen by all beholders alike. But the creations of Poetry have in themselves nothing of this precision and fixedness of form, and depend greatly for their vividness and clearness of impression upon the mind to which they are presented. Language, the great machine with which her miracles are wrought, is contrived to have an application to all possible things; and wonderful as this contrivance is, and numerous and varied as are its combinations, it is still limited and imperfect, and, in point of comprehensiveness, distinctness, and variety, falls infinitely short of the mighty and diversified world of matter and mind of which it professes to be the representative. It is, however, to the very limitation of this power of language, as it seems to me, that Poetry owes her magic. The most detailed of her descriptions, which, by the way, are not always the most striking, are composed of a few touches; they are glimpses of things thrown into the mind; here and there a trace of the outline; here a gleam of light, and there a dash of shade. But these very touches act like a spell upon the imagination and awaken it to greater activity, and fill it, perhaps, with greater delight than the best defined objects could do. The imagination is the most active and the least susceptible of fatigue of all the faculties of the human mind; its more intense exercise is tremendous, and sometimes unsettles the reason; its repose is only a gentle sort of activity; nor am I certain that it is ever quite unemployed, for even in our sleep it is still awake and busy, and amuses itself with fabricating our dreams. To this restless faculty—which is unsatisfied when the whole of its work is done to its hands, and which is ever wandering from the combination of ideas directly presented to it to other combinations of its own—it is the office of poetry to furnish the exercise in which it delights. Poetry is that art which selects and arranges the symbols of thought in such a manner as to excite it the most powerfully and delightfully. The imagination of the reader is guided, it is true, by the poet, and it is his business to guide it skilfully and agreeably; but the imagination in the mean time is by no means passive. It pursues the path which the poet only points out, and shapes its visions from the scenes and allusions which he gives. It fills up his sketches of beauty with what suits its own highest conceptions of the beautiful, and completes his outline of grandeur with the noblest images its own stores can furnish. It is obvious that the degree of perfection with which this is done must depend greatly upon the strength and cultivation of that faculty. For example, in the following passage, in which Milton describes the general mother passing to her daily task among the flowers:

> "With goddess-like demeanor forth she went
>   Not unattended, for on her as queen
>   A pomp of winning graces waited still."

The coldest imagination, on reading it, will figure to itself, in the person of Eve, the finest forms, attitudes, and movements of female loveliness and dignity, which, after all, are not described, but only hinted at by the poet. A warmer fancy, kindling at the delicate allusions in these lines, will not only bestow these attractions on the principal figure, but will fill the air around her with beauty, and people it with the airy forms of the graces; it will see the delicate proportions of their limbs, the lustre of their flowing hair, and the soft light of their eyes. Take, also, the following passage from the same poet, in which, speaking of Satan, he says:

> "His face
> Deep scars of thunder had entrenched, and care
> Sat on his faded cheek—but under brows
> Of dauntless courage and considerate pride
> Waiting revenge; cruel his eye but cast
> Signs of remorse and passion to behold
> The fellows of his crime, the followers rather,
> (Far other once beheld in bliss), condemned
> For evermore to have their lot in pain."

The imagination of the reader is stimulated by the hints in this powerful passage to form to itself an idea of the features in which reside this strong expression of malignity and dejection— the brow, the cheek, the eye of the fallen angel, bespeaking courage, pride, the settled purpose of revenge, anxiety, sorrow for the fate of his followers, and fearfully marked with the wrath of the Almighty. There can be no doubt that the picture which this passage calls up in the minds of different individuals will vary accordingly as the imagination is more or less vivid, or more or less excited in the perusal. It will vary, also, accordingly as the individual is more or less experienced in the visible expression of strong passion, and as he is in the habit of associating the idea of certain emotions with certain configurations of the countenance.

There is no question that one principal office of poetry is to excite the imagination, but this is not its sole, nor perhaps its chief, province; another of its ends is to touch the heart, and, as I expect to show in this lecture, it has something to do with the understanding. I know that some critics have made poetry to consist solely in the exercise of the imagination. They distinguish poetry from pathos. They talk of pure poetry, and by this phrase they mean passages of mere imagery, with the least possible infusion of human emotion. I do not know by what authority these gentlemen take the term poetry from the people, and thus limit its meaning.

In its ordinary acceptation, it has, in all ages and all countries, included something more. When we speak of a poem, we do not mean merely a tissue of striking images. The most beautiful poetry is that which takes the strongest hold of the feelings, and, if it is really the most beautiful, then it is poetry in the highest sense. Poetry is constantly resorting to the language of the passions to heighten the effect of her pictures; and, if this be not enough to entitle that language to the appellation of poetical, I am not aware of the meaning of the term. Is there no poetry in the wrath of Achilles? Is there no poetry in the passage where Lear, in the tent of Cordelia, just recovered from his frenzy, his senses yet infirm and unassured, addresses his daughter as she kneels to ask his blessing?

> "Pray do not mock me;
> I am a very foolish, fond old man,
> Fourscore and upward:
> Not an hour more or less, and to deal plainly
> I fear I am not in my perfect mind."

Is there no poetry in the remorse of Othello, in the terrible consciousness of guilt which haunts Macbeth, or the lamentations of Antony over the body of his friend, the devoted love of Juliet, and the self-sacrificing affection of Cleopatra? In the immortal work of Milton, is there no poetry in the penitence of Adam, or in the sorrows of Eve at being excluded from Paradise? The truth is, that poetry which does not find its way to the heart is scarcely deserving of the name; it may be brilliant and ingenious, but it soon wearies the attention. The feelings and the imagination, when skilfully touched, act reciprocally on each other. For example, when the poet introduces Ophelia, young, beautiful, and unfortunate, the wildness of frenzy in her eye, dressed with fantastic garlands of wild flowers, and singing snatches of old tunes, there is a picture for the imagination, but it is one which affects the heart. But when, in the midst of her incoherent talk, she utters some simple allusion to her own sorrows, as when she says,

> "We know what we are, but know not what we may be,"

this touching sentence, addressed merely to our sympathy,

strongly excites the imagination. It sets before us the days when she knew sorrow only by name, before her father was slain by the hand of her lover, and before her lover was estranged, and makes us feel the heaviness of that affliction which crushed a being so gentle and innocent and happy.

Those poems, however, as I have already hinted, which are apparently the most affluent of imagery, are not always those which most kindle the reader's imagination. It is because the ornaments with which they abound are not naturally suggested by the subject, not poured forth from a mind warmed and occupied by it; but a forced fruit of the fancy, produced by labor, without spontaneity or excitement.

The language of passion is naturally figurative, but its figures are only employed to heighten the intensity of the expression; they are never introduced for their own sake. Important, therefore, as may be the office of the imagination in poetry, the great spring of poetry is emotion. It is this power that holds the key of the storehouse where the mind has laid up its images, and that alone can open it without violence. All the forms of fancy stand ever in its sight, ready to execute its bidding. Indeed, I doubt not that most of the offences against good taste in this kind of composition are to be traced to the absence of emotion. A desire to treat agreeably or impressively a subject by which the writer is himself little moved, leads him into great mistakes about the means of effecting his purpose. This is the origin of cold conceits, of prosing reflections, of the minute painting of uninteresting circumstances, and of the opposite extremes of tameness and extravagance. On the other hand, strong feeling is always a sure guide. It rarely offends against good taste, because it instinctively chooses the most effectual means of communicating itself to others. It gives a variety to the composition it inspires, with which the severest taste is delighted. It may sometimes transgress arbitrary rules, or offend against local associations, but it speaks a language which reaches the heart in all countries and all times. Everywhere are the sentiments of fortitude and magnanimity uttered in strains that brace our own nerves, and the dead mourned in accents that draw our tears.

But poetry not only addresses the passions and the imagination; it appeals to the understanding also. So far as this position relates to the principles of taste which lie at the foundation of all poetry, and by which its merits are tried, I believe its truth will not be doubted. These principles have their origin in the reason of things, and are investigated and applied by the judgment. True it is that they may be observed by one who has never speculated about them, but it is no less true that their observance always gratifies the understanding with the fitness, the symmetry, and the congruity it produces. To write fine poetry requires intellectual faculties of the highest order, and among these, not the least important, is the faculty of reason. Poetry is the worst mask in the world behind which folly and stupidity could attempt to hide their features. Fitter, safer, and more congenial to them is the solemn discussion of unprofitable questions. Any obtuseness of apprehension or incapacity for drawing conclusions, which shows a deficiency or want of cultivation of the reasoning power, is sure to expose the unfortunate poet to contempt and ridicule.

But there is another point of view in which poetry may be said to address the understanding—I mean in the direct lessons of wisdom that it delivers. Remember that it does not concern itself with abstract reasonings, nor with any course of investigation that fatigues the mind. Nor is it merely didactic; but this does not prevent it from teaching truths which the mind instinctively acknowledges. The elements of moral truth are few and simple, but their combinations with human actions are as innumerable and diversified as the combinations of language. Thousands of inductions resulting from the application of great principles to human life and conduct lie, as it were, latent in our minds, which we have never drawn for ourselves, but which we admit the moment they are hinted at, and which, though not abstruse, are yet new. Nor are these of less value because they require no laborious research to discover them. The best riches of the earth are produced on its surface, and we need no reasoning to teach us the folly of a people who should leave its harvests ungathered to dig for its ores. The truths of which I have spoken, when possessing any peculiar force or beauty, are properly within the province of the art of which I am treating, and, when recommended by harmony of numbers, become poetry of the highest kind. Accordingly, they abound in the works of the most celebrated poets. When Shakespeare says of mercy,

> "it is twice blessed—
> It blesses him that gives and him that takes,"

does he not utter beautiful poetry as well as unquestionable truth? There are passages also in Milton of the same kind, which sink into the heart like the words of an oracle. For instance:

> "Evil into the mind of God or man
> May come and go so unapproved, and leave
> No spot or blame behind."

Take, also, the following example from Cowper, in which he bears witness against the guilt and folly of princes:

> "War is a game which, were their subjects wise,
> Kings should not play at. Nations would do well
> To extort their truncheons from the puny hands
> Of heroes whose infirm and baby minds
> Are gratified with mischief, and who spoil,
> Because men suffer it, their toy—the world."

I call these passages poetry, because the mind instantly acknowledges their truth and feels their force, and is moved and filled and elevated by them. Nor does poetry refuse to carry on a sort of process of reasoning by deducing one truth from another. Her demonstrations differ, however, from ordinary ones by requiring that each step should be in itself beautiful or striking, and that they all should carry the mind to the final conclusion without the consciousness of labor.

All the ways by which poetry affects the mind are open also to the prose-writer. All that kindles the imagination, all that excites emotion, all those moral truths that find an echo in our bosoms, are his property as well as that of the poet. It is true that in the ornaments of style the poet is allowed a greater license, but there are many excellent poems which are not distinguished by any liberal use of the figures of speech from prose writings composed with the same degree of excitement. What, then, is the ground of the distinction between prose and poetry? This is a question about which there has been much debate, but one which seems to me of easy solution to those who are not too ambitious of distinguishing themselves by profound researches into things already sufficiently clear. I suppose that poetry differs from prose, in the first place, by the employment of metrical harmony. It differs from it, in the next place, by excluding all that disgusts, all that tasks and fatigues the understanding, and all matters which are too trivial and common to excite any emotion whatever. Some of these, verse cannot raise into dignity; to others, verse is an encumbrance: they are, therefore, all unfit for poetry; put them into verse, and they are prose still.

A distinction has been attempted to be made between poetry and eloquence, and I acknowledge that there is one; but it seems to me that it consists solely in metrical arrangement. Eloquence is the poetry of prose; poetry is the eloquence of verse. The maxim that the poet is born and the orator made is a pretty antithesis, but a moment's reflection will convince us that one can become neither without natural gifts improved by cultivation. By eloquence I do not mean mere persuasiveness: there are many processes of argument that are not susceptible of eloquence, because they require close and painful attention. But by eloquence I understand those appeals to our moral perceptions that produce emotion as soon as they are uttered. It is in these that the orator is himself affected with the feelings he would communicate, that his eyes glisten, and his frame seems to dilate, and his voice acquires an unwonted melody, and his sentences arrange themselves into a sort of measure and harmony, and the listener is chained in involuntary and breathless attention. This is the very enthusiasm that is the parent of poetry. Let the same man go to his closet and clothe in numbers conceptions full of the same fire and spirit, and they will be poetry.

In conclusion, I will observe that the elements of poetry make a part of our natures, and that every individual is more or less a poet. In this "bank-note world," as it has been happily denominated, we sometimes meet with individuals who declare that they have no taste for poetry. But by their leave I will assert they are mistaken; they have it, although they may have never cultivated it. Is there any one among them who will confess himself insensible to the beauty of order or to the pleasure of variety—two principles, the happy mingling of which makes the perfection of poetic numbers? Is there any one whose eye is undelighted with beautiful forms and colors, whose ear is not charmed by sweet sounds, and who sees no loveliness in the returns of light and darkness, and the changes of the seasons? Is there any one for whom the works of Nature have no associations but such as relate to his animal wants? Is there any one to whom her great courses and operations show no majesty, to whom they impart no knowledge, and from whom they hide no secrets? Is there any one who is attached by no ties to his fellow-beings, who has no hopes for the future, and no memory of the past? Have they all forgotten the days and the friends of their childhood, and do they all shut their eyes to the advances of age? Have they nothing to desire and nothing to lament, and are their minds never darkened with the shadows of fear? Is it, in short, for these men that life has no pleasures and no pains, the grave no solemnity, and the world to come no mysteries? All these things are the sources of poetry, and they are not only part of ourselves, but of the universe, and will expire only with the last of the creatures of God.

LECTURE II. ON THE VALUE AND USES OF POETRY

In my last lecture I attempted to give some notion of the nature of poetry. In the present I intend to examine its value and uses, to inquire into its effects upon human welfare and happiness, and to consider some of the objections that have been urged against an indulgence in its delights. It is of no little consequence that we should satisfy ourselves of the tendency of a class of compositions which forms so large a part of the literature of all nations and times, so that, if it is found beneficial, we may estimate the degree in which it is worthy of encouragement; if pernicious, that we may bethink ourselves of a remedy. In what I have to say on this head I cannot by any means be certain that my partiality for the art will permit me to treat the subject with that coolness of judgment and freedom from prejudice which might be desirable. I only ask your frank assent to whatever may be true in the apology I shall make for it. It is not for my hands to hold the balance in which it is weighed.

I shall consider the influence of poetry on the welfare and happiness of our race in the three points of view in which I placed it in my last lecture—namely, as it addresses itself to the imagination, to the passions, and to the intelligence. As it respects the imagination, I believe the question may be soon and easily disposed of; for, so far as that faculty merely is excited by poetry without taking into account the effect produced on the passions, its activity is an amusement, an agreeable intellectual exercise—no more. A great deal of poetry, doubtless, has no higher object than this, and excites no stronger emotion than that complacency which proceeds from being agreeably employed. This is something in a world whose inhabitants are perpetually complaining of its labors, fatigues, and miseries. It has, however, a still higher value when regarded as in some sort the support of our innocence, for there is ever something pure and elevated in the creations of poetry. Its spirit is an aspiration after superhuman beauty and majesty, which, if it has no affinity with, has at least some likeness to, virtue. We cannot eradicate the imagination, but we may cultivate and regulate it; we cannot keep it from continual action, but we can give it a salutary direction. Certainly it is a noble occupation to shape the creations of the mind into perfect forms according to those laws which man learns from observing the works of his Maker.

There are exercises of the imagination, it must be confessed, of too gross and sordid a nature to be comprised within the confines of any divine art—revellings of the fancy amid the images of base appetites and petty and ridiculous passions. These are the hidden sins of the heart, that lurk in its darkest recesses, where shame and the opinion of men cannot come to drive them out, and which pollute and debase it the more because they work in secrecy and at leisure. Is it not well, therefore, to substitute something better in the place of these, or, at least, to preoccupy the mind with what may prevent their entrance, and to create imaginative habits that may lead us to regard them with contempt and disgust? Poetry is well fitted for this office. It has no community with degradation, nor with things that degrade. It utters nothing that cannot be spoken without shame. Into the window of his bosom who relishes its pleasures, all the world may freely look. The tastes from which it springs, the sentiments it awakens, the objects on which it dwells with fondness, and which it labors to communicate to mankind, are related to the best and most universal sympathies of our nature.

In speaking of the influences of poetry on the happiness of mankind as connected with its effects on the imagination, I have been obliged to anticipate a part of what I had to say in regard to its power over the passions. These two topics, indeed, are closely connected; they may be separated in classification, but it is difficult to speculate upon them separately; for, as I observed in my last lecture, the excitement of the imagination awakens the feelings, and the excitement of the feelings kindles the imagination. It is the dominion of poetry over the feelings and passions of men that gives it its most important bearing upon the virtue and the welfare of society. Everything that affects our sensibilities is a part of our moral education, and the habit of being rightly affected by all the circumstances by which we are surrounded is the perfection of the moral character. The purest of all religions agrees with the soundest philosophy in referring the practice of virtue to the affections. Every good action has its correspondent emotion of the heart given to impel us to our duty, and to reward us for doing it. Now, it is admitted that poetry moves these springs of moral conduct powerfully; but it has sometimes been disputed whether it moves them in a salutary way, or whether it perverts them to evil. This question may be settled by inquiring what kind of sentiments it ordinarily tends to encourage. Has it any direct connection with vice? for, if it has not, the emotions it inspires must be innocent, and innocent emotions are emphatically healthful. Is there any poetry in cruelty? are the vivid descriptions of human and animal suffering it sets before us such as make us to rejoice in that suffering, or even such as leave us unmoved? Is there any poetry in injustice? Is there any poetry in fraud and treachery? The stronger the colors in which the former is painted, the more thoroughly do we detest it; the more forcibly the latter is presented to our minds, the more cordially do we despise it. Has poetry any kindred with covetousness and selfishness? or, rather, are they not a blight, and death itself, to that enthusiasm to which poetry owes its birth? On the other hand, do we not know that poetry delights in inspiring compassion, the parent of all kind offices? Does it not glory in sentiments of fortitude and magnanimity, the fountain of disinterested sacrifices? It cherishes patriotism, the incitement to vigorous toils endured for the welfare of communities. It luxuriates among the natural affections, the springs of all the gentle charities of domestic life. It has so refined and transformed and hallowed the love of the sexes that piety itself has sometimes taken the language of that passion to clothe its most fervent aspirations. It delights to infold not only the whole human race, but all the creatures of God, in the wide circle of its sympathies. It loves to point man to the beginning and end of his days, and to the short and swift passage between; to linger about the cradle and about the grave, and to lift the veil of another life. All moral lessons which are uninteresting and unimpressive, and, therefore, worthless, it leaves to prose; but all those which touch the heart, and are, therefore, important and effectual, are its own. One passion, indeed, is excited by poetry, about the worth of which moralists differ—the love of glory. I cannot stay to inquire into the moral quality of this passion; but this I will say, that, if it be not a virtue, it is frequently an excellent substitute for one, and becomes the motive of great and generous actions. At all events, a regard for the good opinion of our fellow-creatures is so interwoven with our natures, is of so much value to the order and welfare of society, does so much good and prevents so much evil, that I cannot bring myself to think ill of anything that encourages and directs it. None the less, poetry teaches us, also, lessons of profoundest humility. Reverence for that boundless goodness and infinite power which pervade and uphold all things that exist is one of its elements, and is the source of some of its loftiest meditations and deepest emotions. Much as we all glory in the power that is our own, the mind delights quite as naturally to raise its view to power that is above it, and to lose itself in the contemplation of strength and wisdom without bound. The poet who wrote atheist after his name knew not of what manner of spirit he was. He, too, paid a willing and undissembled homage to the Divinity. He called it Nature, but it was the Great First Cause whom we all worship, whatever its essence, and whatever its name.

One of the great recommendations of poetry in that point of view in which I am now considering it is, that it withdraws us from the despotism of many of those circumstances which mislead the moral judgment. It is dangerous to be absorbed continuously in our own immediate concerns. Self-interest is the most ingenious and persuasive of all the agents that deceive our consciences, while by means of it our unhappy and stubborn prejudices operate in their greatest force. But poetry lifts us to a sphere where self-interest cannot exist, and where the prejudices that perplex our every-day life can hardly enter. It restores us to our unperverted feelings, and leaves us at liberty to compare the issues of life with our unsophisticated notions of good and evil. We are taught to look at them as they are in themselves, and not as they may affect our present convenience, and then we are sent back to the world with our moral perceptions cleared and invigorated.

Among the most remarkable of the influences of poetry is the exhibition of those analogies and correspondences which it beholds between the things of the moral and of the natural world. I refer to its adorning and illustrating each by the other—infusing a moral sentiment into natural objects, and bringing images of visible beauty and majesty to heighten the effect of moral sentiment. Thus it binds into one all the passages of human life and connects all the varieties of human feeling with the works of creation. Any one who will make the experiment for himself will see how exceedingly difficult it is to pervert this process into an excitement of the bad passions of the soul. There are a purity and innocence in the appearances of Nature that make them refuse to be allied to the suggestions of guilty emotion. We discern no sin in her grander operations and vicissitudes, and no lessons of immorality are to be learned from them, as there are from the examples of the world. They cannot be studied without inducing the love, if they fail of giving the habit, of virtue. In so far as poetry directly addresses the understanding, it would be preposterous to apprehend any injurious consequences from it, which in my last lecture I said was by means of those moral truths which the mind instinctively acknowledges, and of which it immediately feels the force. The simplicity and clearness of the truths with which it deals prevent any mistake in regard to their meanings or tendencies. They strike the mind by their own brightness, and win its assent by their manifest and beautiful agreement with the lessons of our own experience. It belongs to more subtle and abstruse speculations than any into which poetry can enter, to unsettle the notions of men respecting right and wrong. Ingenious casuistry and labored sophistry may confuse and puzzle the understanding, and lead it through their own darkness to false conclusions; but poetry abhors their assistance. It may be said, however, that the power which poetry exercises over the mind is liable to abuse. It is so, undoubtedly, like all power. Its influences may be, and unquestionably have been, perverted; but my aim has been to show that they are beneficial in their nature, intrinsically good, and, if so, not to be rejected because accidentally mischievous. To confound the abuses of a thing with the thing itself is to sophisticate. Why do not they who set up this objection to poetry talk in the same manner of the common and universal sources of human enjoyment? When you tell them of the element which diffuses comfort through our habitations, when the earth and the air are frozen, and enables us to support life through the inclemency of the season, do they deny its utility, or endeavor to convince you of your error, by pointing you to dwellings laid waste by conflagrations, or by telling you tales of martyrs roasted at the stake? When you speak of the beneficent influences of the sun, why do they not meet you with the scorched and barren deserts of Africa, with diseases born under his heat, the plague of Europe, and the yellow fever of America? When you are simple enough to rejoice in the kind provision of rains for the refreshment of the earth and the growth of its plants, why do they not silence you with stories of harvest and cattle and human beings swept away by inundations? Well, when we are persuaded to part with our hearth-fires, and to refuse the fruits which sunshine and showers have ripened for our sustenance, let us give up poetry. In the mean time, instead of putting it by with scorn, let us cherish it as we do the other gifts of Heaven.

In those works which have met with merited reprehension on account of their pernicious tendencies, it is not of the poetry that the friends of virtue have reason to complain; it is of the foul ingredients mingled with it; it is of the leaven of corruption interspersed with what is in itself pure and innocent. The elements of poetry are the beautiful and noble in the creation and in man's nature; and, so far as anything vicious is mingled with these, the compound is incongruous. Indeed, I am apt to think that those poems which are objectionable on account of their immoral character have won for their authors the reputation of greater powers than they really possessed. The passages of real beauty and excellence which they contain appear the more beautiful and excellent from the contrast they offer to the grossness by which they are surrounded. Those bursts of true feeling, those fine moral touches, those apprehensions of the glory and beauty of the universe, and the language it speaks to the heart of man, delight us there by a certain unexpectedness. Their innocence appears more spotless, their pathos more touching, because such qualities refresh the mind in the midst of its horror and disgust.

The heroic poems of the ancients are said to inspire a sanguinary spirit, the love of war, and an indifference to the miseries of which war is the cause; but I cannot believe that they produce this effect to the extent which many suppose, and, so far as they do produce it, it is from an imperfection in the poetry. Poetry that is unfeeling and indifferent to suffering is no poetry at all. It is but justice, however, to these writers to say that, if they do encourage a fondness for war, it is rather by what they leave undone than what they do. War, like all other situations of danger and of change, calls forth the exertion of admirable intellectual qualities and great virtues, and it is only by dwelling on these, and keeping out of sight the sufferings and sorrows, and all the crimes and evils that follow in its train, that it has its glory in the eyes of men. We do not admire the heroes of Homer because they shed blood and cut throats—any highwayman may do this—but we admire them for the greatness of mind they show in the dreadful scenes in which they are engaged. We reverence that hardy spirit that faces danger without shrinking, and voluntarily exposes the body to pain, for it is a modification of that noble principle which gives birth to all virtue and all greatness—the endurance of present toils and submission to present sacrifices, in order to insure great good for the future. We love, also, to contemplate strong and skilful action of the body, which in the personal combats he describes is prompted and ordered by strong action of the mind, by intense emotion, and clear sagacity. But the purer and gentler spirit of the Father of Verse and the humanizing influences of poetry show themselves strongly in his great works, and set him far in advance of the age in which he wrote. The poet often stops to lament those whom his favorite heroes slew without remorse—old men cut off in the honors of a blameless age, young men in the bloom of their years and the promise of their virtues—and to sympathize with the unavailing and unappeasable sorrow of those to whom they were dear. Nay, it would seem that his mind was ever haunted with a secret sentiment of the emptiness of the very glory he was celebrating, for not only the Odyssey, but the Iliad itself, is full of allusions to the final fate of those who earned renown at the siege of Troy, to their wanderings, their hardships, their domestic calamities, and their violent and unhonored deaths.

I shall close this lecture with an extract from an eloquent writer, who has replied to some other objections that have been raised against poetry in such a manner that I should not feel myself justified in using any other words than his own: "It is objected to poetry," he says, "that it gives wrong views and excites false expectations of life, peoples the mind with shadows and illusions, and builds up imaginations on ruins of wisdom. That there is a wisdom against which poetry wars— the wisdom of the senses, which makes physical comfort the chief good, and wealth the chief interest of life—is not denied; nor can it be denied, the least service which poetry renders to mankind, that it redeems them from the thraldom of this earth-born prudence. But, passing over this topic, it may be observed that the complaint against poetry as abounding in illusion and deception is in the main groundless. In many poems there is more of truth than in many histories and philo-sophic theories. The fictions of genius are often the vehicles of the sublimest verities, and its flashes often open new regions of thought, and throw new light on the mysteries of our being. In poetry the letter is falsehood, but the spirit is often the pro-foundest wisdom. And, if truth thus dwells in the boldest fictions of the poet, much more may it be expected in his delineations of life; for the present life, which is the first stage of the immortal mind, abounds in the materials of poetry, and it is the high office of the bard to detect this divine element among the grosser labors and pleasures of our earthly being. The present life is not wholly prosaic, precise, tame, and finite. To the gifted eye it abounds in the poetic. The affections, which spread beyond ourselves and stretch far into futurity; the workings of mighty passions, which seem to arm the soul with an almost superhuman energy; the innocent and irrepres-sible joy of infancy; the bloom and buoyancy and dazzling hopes of youth; the throbbings of the heart when it first wakes to love, and dreams of a happiness too vast for earth; woman, with her beauty and grace and gentleness and freshness of feeling and depth of affection, and her blushes of purity, and the tones and looks which only a mother's heart can inspire—these are all poetical. It is not true that the poet paints a life which does not exist. He only extracts and concentrates, as it were, life's ethereal essence, arrests and condenses its volatile fragrance, brings together its scattered beauties, and prolongs its more refined but evanescent joys; and in this he does well; for it is good to feel that life is not wholly usurped by cares for subsistence and physical gratification, but admits, in measures which may be indefinitely enlarged, sentiments and delights worthy of a higher being. This power of poetry to refine our views of life and happiness is more and more needed as society advances. It is needed to withstand the encroachments of heartless and artificial manners which make civilization so tame and uninteresting. It is needed to counteract the tendency of physical science, which—being now sought, not, as formerly, for intellectual gratification, but for multiplying bodily comforts—requires a new development of imagination, taste, and poetry to preserve men from sinking into an earthly, material, epicurean life."*

LECTURE III.   ON POETRY IN ITS RELATION TO OUR AGE AND COUNTRY

An opinion prevails, which neither wants the support of respectable names nor of plausible reasonings, that the art of poetry, in common with its sister arts, painting and sculpture, cannot in the present age be cultivated with the same degree of success as formerly. It has been supposed that the progress of reason, of science, and of the useful arts has a tendency to narrow the sphere of the imagination, and to repress the enthusiasm of the affections. Poetry, it is alleged, whose office it was to nurse the infancy of the human race, and to give it its first lessons of wisdom, having fulfilled the part to which she was appointed, now resigns her charge to severer instructors. Others, again, refining upon this idea, maintain that not only

*William Ellery Channing. [*Godwin's* note.]

the age in which we live must fail to produce anything to rival the productions of the ancient masters of song, but that our own country, of all parts of the globe, is likely to remain the most distant from such a distinction.

Our citizens are held to possess, in a remarkable degree, the heedful, calculating, prosaic spirit of the age, while our country is decried as peculiarly barren of the materials of poetry. The scenery of our land these reasoners admit to be beautiful, but they urge that it is the beauty of a face without expression; that it wants the associations of tradition which are the soul and interest of scenery; that it wants the national superstitions which linger yet in every district in Europe, and the legends of distant and dark ages and of wild and unsettled times of which the old world reminds you at every step. Nor can our country, they say, ever be more fruitful of these materials than at present. For this is not an age to give birth to new superstitions, but to explode and root out old, however harmless and agreeable they may be, while half the world is already wondering how little the other half will finally believe. Is it likely, then, that a multitude of interesting traditions will spring up in our land to ally themselves with every mountain, every hill, every forest, every river, and every tributary brook? There may be some passages of our early history which associate themselves with particular places, but the argument is that the number of these will never be greatly augmented. The genius of our nation is quiet and commercial. Our people are too much in love with peace and gain, the state of society is too settled, and the laws too well enforced and respected, to allow of wild and strange adventures. There is no romance either in our character, our history, or our condition of society; and, therefore, it is neither likely to encourage poetry, nor capable of supplying it with those materials—materials drawn from domestic traditions and manners—which render it popular.

If these views of the tendency of the present age, and the state of things in our own country, are to be received as true, it must be acknowledged that they are not only exceedingly discouraging to those who make national literature a matter of pride, but, what is worse, that they go far toward causing that very inferiority on which they so strongly insist. Not that there is any danger that the demand for contemporary poetry will entirely cease. Verses have always been, and always will be written, and will always find readers; but it is of some consequence that they should be good verses, that they should exert the healthful and beneficial influences which I consider as belonging to the highest productions of the art; not feebly and imperfectly, but fully and effectually.

If, however, excellence in any art is believed to be unattainable, it will never be attained. There is, indeed, no harm in representing it as it really is, in literature as in every other pursuit, as rare and difficult, for by this means they who aspire to it are incited to more vigorous exertions. The mind of man glories in nothing more than in struggling successfully with difficulty, and nothing more excites our interest and admiration than the view of this struggle and triumph. The distinction of having done what few are able to do is the more enviable from its unfrequency, and attracts a multitude of competitors who catch each other's ardor and imitate each other's diligence. But if you go a step farther, and persuade those who are actuated by a generous ambition that this difficulty amounts to an impossibility, you extinguish their zeal at once. You destroy hope, and with it strength; you drive from the attempt those who were most likely and most worthy to succeed, and you put in their place a crowd of inferior contestants, satisfied with a low measure of excellence, and incapable of apprehending anything higher. Should, then, the views of this subject of which I have spoken be untrue, we may occasion much mischief by embracing them; and it becomes us, before we adopt them, to give them an attentive examination, and to be perfectly satisfied of their soundness.

But, if it be a fact that poetry in the present age is unable to attain the same degree of excellence as formerly, it cannot certainly be ascribed to any change in the original and natural faculties and dispositions of mind by which it is produced and by which it is enjoyed. The theory that men have degenerated in their mental powers and moral temperament is even more absurd than the notion of a decline in their physical strength, and is too fanciful to be combated by grave reasoning. It would be difficult, I fancy, to persuade the easiest credulity that the imagination of man has become, with the lapse of ages, less active and less capable of shaping the materials at its command into pictures of majesty and beauty. Is anybody whimsical enough to suppose that the years that have passed since the days of Homer have made men's hearts cold and insensible, or deadened the delicacy of their moral perceptions, or rendered them less susceptible of cultivation? All the sources of poetry in the mind, and all the qualities to which it owes its power over the mind, are assuredly left us. Degeneracy, if it has taken place, must be owing to one of two things—either to the absence of those circumstances which, in former times, developed and cherished the poetical faculty to an extraordinary degree, or to the existence of other intellectual interests which, in the present age, tend to repress its natural exercise.

What, then, were the circumstances which fostered the art of poetry in ancient times? They have been defined to be the mystery impressed on all the operations of nature as yet not investigated and traced to their laws—the beautiful systems of ancient mythology, and, after their extinction, the superstitions that linger like ghosts in the twilight of a later age. Let us examine separately each of these alleged advantages. That there is something in whatever is unknown and inscrutable which strongly excites the imagination and awes the heart, particularly when connected with things of unusual vastness and grandeur, is not to be denied. But I deny that much of this mystery is apparent to an ignorant age, and I maintain that no small degree of inquiry and illumination is necessary to enable the mind to perceive it. He who takes all things to be as they appear, who supposes the earth to be a great plain, the sun a moving ball of fire, the heavens a vault of sapphire, and the stars a multitude of little flames lighted up in its arches—what does he think of mysteries, or care for them? But enlighten him a little further. Teach him that the earth is an immense sphere; that the wide land whose bounds he knows so imperfectly is an isle in the great oceans that flow all over it; talk to him of the boundlessness of the skies, and the army of worlds that move through them—and, by means of the knowledge that you communicate, you have opened to him a vast field of the unknown and the wonderful. Thus it ever was and ever will be with the human mind; everything which it knows introduces to its observation a greater multitude of things which it does not know; the clearing up of one mystery conducts it to another; all its discoveries are bounded by a circle of doubt and ignorance which is wide in proportion to the knowledge it enfolds. It is a pledge of the immortal destinies of the human intellect that it is forever drawn by a strong attraction to the darker edge of this circle, and forever attempting to penetrate the obscurities beyond. The old world, then, is welcome to its mysteries; we need not envy it on that account: for, in addition to our superior knowledge and as a consequence of it, we have even more of them than it, and they are loftier, deeper, and more spiritual.

But the mythologies of antiquity!—in particular, the beautiful mythologies of Greece and Rome, of which so much enters into the charming remains of ancient poetry! Beautiful those mythologies unquestionably were, and exceedingly varied and delightfully adapted to many of the purposes of poetry; yet it may be doubted whether, on the whole, the art gained more by them than it lost. For remark that, so far as mystery is a quality of poetry, it has been taken away almost entirely by the myth. The fault of the myth was that it accounted for everything. It had a god for every operation of nature—a Jupiter to distil the showers and roll the thunder, a Phœbus to guide the chariot of the sun, a divinity to breathe the winds, a divinity to pour out every fountain. It left nothing in obscurity; everything was seen. Its very beauty consisted in minute disclosures. Thus the imagination was delighted, but neither the imagination nor the feelings were stirred up from their utmost depths. That system gave us the story of a superior and celestial race of beings, to whom human passions were attributed, and who were, like ourselves, susceptible of suffering; but it elevated them so far above the creatures of earth in power, in knowledge, and in security from the calamities of our condition, that they could be the subjects of little sympathy. Therefore it is that the mythological poetry of the ancients is as cold as it is beautiful, as unaffecting as it is faultless. And the genius of this mythological poetry, carried into the literature of a later age, where it was cultivated with a less sincere and earnest spirit, has been the destruction of all nature and simplicity. Men forsook the sure guidance of their own feelings and impressions, and fell into gross offences against taste. They wished to describe the passion of love, and they talked of Venus and her boy Cupid and his bow; they would speak of the freshness and glory of morning, and they fell to prattling of Phœbus and his steeds. No wonder that poetry has been thought a trifling art when thus practiced. For my part I cannot but think that human beings, placed among the things of this earth, with their affections and sympathies, their joys and sorrow, and the accidents of fortune to which they are liable, are infinitely a better subject for poetry than any imaginary race of creatures whatever. Let the fountain tell me of the flocks that have drunk at it; of the village girl that has gathered spring flowers on its margin; the traveller that has slaked his thirst there in the hot noon, and blessed its waters; the schoolboy that has pulled the nuts from the hazels that hang over it as it leaps and sparkles in its cool basin; let it speak of youth and health and purity and gladness, and I care not for the naiad that pours it out. If it must have a religious association, let it murmur of the invisible goodness that fills and feeds its reservoirs in the darkness of the earth.* The admirers of poetry, then, may give up the ancient mythology without a sigh. Its departure has left us what is better than all it has taken away: it has left us men and women; it has left us the creatures and things of God's universe, to the simple charm of which the cold splendor of that system blinded men's eyes, and to the

*See Mr. Bryant's own poem of "The Fountain," written thirteen years later, for a beautiful illustration of his principles. [*Godwin's note.*]

magnificence of which the rapid progress of science is every day adding new wonders and glories. It has left us, also, a more sublime and affecting religion, whose truths are broader, higher, nobler than any outlook to which its random conjectures ever attained.

With respect to later superstitions, traces of which linger yet in many districts of the civilized world—such as the belief in witchcraft, astrology, the agency of foul spirits in the affairs of men, in ghosts, fairies, water-sprites, and goblins of the wood and the mine—I would observe that the ages which gave birth to this fantastic brood are not those which have produced the noblest specimens of poetry. Their rise supposes a state of society too rude for the successful cultivation of the art. Nor does it seem to me that the bigoted and implicit reception of them is at all favorable to the exercise of poetic talent. Poetry, it is true, sometimes produces a powerful effect by appealing to that innate love of the supernatural which lies at the bottom of every man's heart and mind, and which all are willing to indulge, some freely and some by stealth, but it does this for the most part by means of those superstitions which exist rather in tradition than in serious belief. It finds them more flexible and accommodating; it is able to mould them to its purposes, and at liberty to reject all that is offensive. Accordingly, we find that even the poets of superstitious ages have been fond of going back to the wonders and prodigies of elder days. Those who invented fictions for the age of chivalry, which one would be apt to think had marvels enough of its own, delighted to astonish their readers with tales of giants, dragons, hippogriffs, and enchanters, the home of which was laid in distant ages, or, at least, in remote countries. The best witch ballad, with the exception, perhaps, of "Tam o' Shanter," that I know of is Hogg's "Witch of Fife," yet both these were written long after the belief in witches had been laughed out of countenance.

It is especially the privilege of an age which has no engrossing superstitions of its own, to make use in its poetry of those of past ages; to levy contributions from the credulity of all time, and thus to diversify indefinitely the situations in which its human agents are placed. If these materials are managed with sufficient skill to win the temporary assent of the reader to the probability of the supernatural circumstances related, the purpose of the poet is answered. This is precisely the condition of the present age; it has the advantage over all ages that have preceded it in the abundance of those collected materials, and its poets have not been slow to avail themselves of their aid.

In regard to the circumstances which are thought in the present age to repress and limit the exercise of the poetical faculty, the principal if not the only one is supposed to be the prevalence of studies and pursuits unfavorable to the cultivation of the imagination and to enthusiasm of feeling. True it is that there are studies and pursuits which principally call into exercise other faculties of the mind, and that they are competitors with Poetry for the favor of the public. But it is not certain that the patronage bestowed on them would be extended to her, even if they should cease to exist. Nay, there is strong reason to suppose that they have done something to extend her influence, for they have certainly multiplied the number of readers, and everybody who reads at all sometimes reads poetry, and generally professes to admire what the best judges pronounce excellent, and, perhaps, in time come to enjoy it. Various inclinations continue, as heretofore, to impel one individual to one pursuit, and another to another—one to chemistry and another to poetry—yet I cannot see that their different labors interfere with each other, or that, because the chemist prosecutes his science successfully, therefore the poet should lose his inspiration. Take the example of Great Britain. In no country are the sciences studied with greater success, yet in no country is poetry pursued with more ardor. Spring and autumn reign hand in hand in her literature; it is loaded at once with blossoms and fruits. Does the poetry of that island of the present day—the poetry of Wordsworth, Scott, Coleridge, Byron, Southey, Shelley, and others—smack of the chilling tendencies of the physical sciences? Or, rather, is it not bold, varied, impassioned, irregular, and impatient of precise laws, beyond that of any former age? Indeed, has it not the freshness, the vigor, and perhaps also the disorder, of a new literature?

The amount of knowledge necessary to be possessed by all who would keep pace with the age, as much greater as it is than formerly, is not, I apprehend, in danger of oppressing and smothering poetical talent. Knowledge is the material with which Genius builds her fabrics. The greater its abundance, the more power is required to dispose it into order and beauty, but the more vast and magnificent will be the structure. All great poets have been men of great knowledge. Some have gathered it from books, as Spenser and Milton; others from keen observation of men and things, as Homer and Shakespeare. On the other hand, the poetry of Ossian, whether genuine or not, is an instance of no inconsiderable poetical talent struggling with the disadvantages of a want of knowledge. It is this want which renders it so singularly monotonous. The poverty of the poet's ideas confined his mind to a narrow circle, and his poems are a series of changes rung upon a few thoughts and a few images. Single passages are beautiful and affecting, but each poem, as a whole, is tiresome and uninteresting.

I come, in the last place, to consider the question of our own expectations in literature, and the probability of our producing in the new world anything to rival the immortal poems of the old. Many of the remarks already made on the literary spirit of the present age will apply also to this part of the subject. Indeed, in this point of view, we should do ill to despair of our country, at least until the lapse of many years shall seem to have settled the question against us. Where the fountains of knowledge are by the roadside, and where the volumes from which poetic enthusiasms are caught and fed are in everybody's hands, it would be singularly strange if, amid the multitude of pursuits which occupy our citizens, nobody should think of taking verse as a path to fame. Yet, if it shall be chosen and pursued with the characteristic ardor of our countrymen, what can prevent its being brought to the same degree of perfection here as in other countries? Not the want of encouragement surely, for the literary man needs but little to stimulate his exertions, and with that little his exertions are undoubtedly greater. Who would think of fattening a race-horse? Complaints of the poverty of poets are as old as their art, but I never heard that they wrote the worse verses for it. It is enough, probably, to call forth their most vigorous efforts, that poetry is admired and honored by their countrymen. With respect to the paucity of national traditions, it will be time to complain of it when all those of which we are possessed are exhausted. Besides, as I have already shown, it is the privilege of poets, when they suppose themselves in need of materials, to seek them in other countries. The best English poets have done this. The events of Spenser's celebrated poem take place within the shadowy limits of fairy-land. Shakespeare has laid the scene of many of his finest tragedies in foreign countries. Milton went out of the world for the subject of his two epics. Byron has taken the incidents of all his poems from outside of England. Southey's best work is a poem of Spain— of chivalry, and of the Roman Church. For the story of one of his narrative poems, Moore went to Persia; for that of another, to the antediluvian world. Wordsworth and Crabbe, each in a different way, and each with great power, abjuring all heroic traditions and recollections, and all aid from the supernatural and the marvellous, have drawn their subjects from modern manners and the simple occurrences of common life. Are they read, for that reason, with any the less avidity by the multitudes who resort to their pages for pastime, for edification, for solace, for noble joy, and for the ecstasies of pure delight?

It has been urged by some, as an obstacle to the growth of elegant literature among us, that our language is a transplanted one, framed for a country and for institutions different from ours, and, therefore, not likely to be wielded by us with such force, effect, and grace, as it would have been if it had grown up with our nation, and received its forms and its accessions from the exigences of our experience. It seems to me that this is one of the most unsubstantial of all the brood of phantoms which have been conjured up to alarm us. Let those who press this opinion descend to particulars. Let them point out the peculiar defects of our language in its application to our natural and political situation. Let them show in what respects it refuses to accommodate itself easily and gracefully to all the wants of expression that are felt among us. Till they do this, let us be satisfied that the copious and flexible dialect we speak is as equally proper to be used at the equator as at the poles, and at any intermediate latitude; and alike in monarchies or republics. It has grown up, as every forcible and beautiful language has done, among a simple and unlettered people; it has accommodated itself, in the first place, to the things of nature, and, as civilization advanced, to the things of art; and thus it has become a language full of picturesque forms of expression, yet fitted for the purposes of science. If a new language were to arise among us in our present condition of society, I fear that it would derive too many of its words from the roots used to signify canals, railroads, and steam-boats— things which, however well thought of at present, may perhaps a century hence be superseded by still more ingenious inventions. To try this notion about a transplanted dialect, imagine one of the great living poets of England emigrated to this country. Can anybody be simple enough to suppose that his poetry would be the worse for it?

I infer, then, that all the materials of poetry exist in our own country, with all the ordinary encouragements and opportunities for making a successful use of them. The elements of beauty and grandeur, intellectual greatness and moral truth, the stormy and the gentle passions, the casualties and the changes of life, and the light shed upon man's nature by the story of past times and the knowledge of foreign manners, have not made their sole abode in the old world beyond the waters. If under these circumstances our poetry should finally fail of rivalling that of Europe, it will be because Genius sits idle in the midst of its treasures.

LECTURE IV.   ON ORIGINALITY AND IMITATION

I propose in this lecture to say a few words on the true
use and value of imitation in poetry. I mean not what is tech-
nically called the imitation of nature, but the studying and
copying of models of poetic composition. There is hardly any
praise of which writers in the present age, particularly writers
in verse, are more ambitious than that of originality. This
ambition is a laudable one, for a captivating originality is
everything in the art. Whether it consists in presenting familiar
things in a new and striking yet natural light, or in revealing
secrets of emotion and thought which have lain undetected
from the birth of literature, it is one of the most abundant and
sure sources of poetic delight. It strikes us with the same sort
of feeling as the finding of some beautiful spot in our familiar
walks which we had never observed before, or the exhibition
of some virtue in the character of a friend which we were
ignorant that he possessed. It is of itself a material addition to
the literary riches of the country in which it is produced; and
it impresses something of its character upon that literature,
which lasts as long as the productions in which it is contained
are read and remembered.

Nor does it lose its peculiar charm with the lapse of time,
for there is an enduring freshness and vividness in its pictures
of nature, of action and emotion, that fade not with years.
The poetry of Shakespeare, for instance, maintains its original
power over the mind, and no more loses its living beauty by
the lapse of ages than the universe grows dim and deformed
in the sight of men.

It is not at all strange that a quality of so much importance
to the poet should be sought after with great ardor, and that,
in the zeal of pursuit, mistakes should sometimes be made as
to that characteristic of it which alone is really valuable. Poets
have often been willing to purchase the praise of it at the sacrifice of what is better. They have been led, by their overeager-
ness to attain it, into puerile conceits, into extravagant vagaries
of imagination, into overstrained exaggerations of passion, into

mawkish and childish simplicity. It has given birth to outrages upon moral principle, upon decency, upon common sense; it has produced, in short, irregularities and affectations of every kind. The grandiloquous nonsense of euphuism, which threatened to overlay and smother English literature in its very cradle, the laborious wit of the metaphysical poets who were contemporaries of Milton, the puling effeminacy of the cockney school, which has found no small favor at the present day—are all children of this fruitful parent.

It seems to me that all these errors arise from not paying sufficient attention to the consideration that poetry is an art; that, like all other arts, it is founded upon a series of experiments—experiments, in this instance, made upon the imagination and the feelings of mankind; that a great deal of its effect depends upon the degree of success with which a sagacious and strong mind seizes and applies the skill of others, and that to slight the experiences of our predecessors on this subject is a pretty certain way to go wrong. For, if we consider the matter a little more narrowly, we shall find that the most original of poets is not without very great obligations to his predecessors and his contemporaries. The art of poetry is not perfected in a day. It is brought to excellence, by slow degrees, from the first rude and imperfect attempts at versification to the finished productions of its greatest masters. The gorgeousness of poetic imagery, the curious felicities of poetic language, the music of poetic numbers, the spells of words that act like magic on the heart, are not created by one poet in any language, in any country. An innumerable multitude of sentiments, of illustrations, of impassioned forms of expression, of harmonious combinations of words, both fixed in books and floating in conversation, must previously exist either in the vernacular language of the poet or in some other which he has studied, and whose beauties and riches he seeks to transplant into his own, before he can produce any work which is destined to live.

Genius, therefore, with all its pride in its own strength, is but a dependent quality, and cannot put forth its whole powers nor claim all its honors without an amount of aid from the talents and labors of others which it is difficult to calculate. In those fortunate circumstances which permit its most perfect exercise, it takes, it is true, a pre-eminent station; but, after all, it is elevated upon the shoulders of its fellows. It may create something in literature, but it does not create all, great as its merit may be. What it does is infinitely less than what is done for it; the new treasures it finds are far less in value than the old of which it makes use. There is no warrant for the notion maintained by some, that the first poets in any language were great poets, or that, whatever their rank, they did not learn their art from the great poets in other languages. It might as well be expected that a self-taught architect would arise in a country whose inhabitants live in caves, and, without models or instruction, raise the majestic Parthenon and pile up St. Peter's into the clouds.

That there were poets in the English language before Chaucer, some of whom were not unworthy to be his predecessors, is attested by extant monuments of their verse; and, if there had not been, he might have learned his art from the polished poets of Italy, whom he studied and loved. Italy had versifiers before Dante, and, if they were not his masters, he at least found masters in the harmonious poets of a kindred dialect, the Provençal. In the Provençal language, the earliest of the cultivated tongues of modern Europe, there arose no great poet. The reason was that their literature had scarcely been brought to that degree of perfection which produces the finest specimens of poetry when the hour of its decline had come. It possessed, it is true, authors innumerable, revivers of the same art, enrichers of the same idiom, and polishers of the same system of versification, yet they never looked for models out of their own literature; they did not study the remains of ancient poetry to avail themselves of its riches; they confined themselves to such improvements and enlargements of the art as were made among themselves; and therefore their progress, though wonderful for the circumstances in which they were placed, was yet limited in comparison with that of those nations who have had access to the treasures they neglected.

In Roman literature there were poets before Lucretius, who is thought to have carried the poetry of the Latins to its highest measure of perfection; before even Ennius, who boasted of having introduced the melody of the hexameter into Latin verse. But Ennius and Lucretius and Horace and Virgil, and all the Roman poets, were, moreover, disciples of the Greeks, and sought to transfuse the spirit of the Grecian literature into their domestic tongue. Of the Greeks we discover no instructors. The oldest of their poems which we possess, the writings of Homer, are also among the most perfect. Yet we should forget all reverence for probability were we to suppose that the art of poetry was born with him. The inferior and more mechanical parts of it must have been the fruit of long and zealous cultivation; centuries must have elapsed, and thousands of trials must have been made, before the musical and various hexameter could have been brought to the perfection in which we find it in his works. His poems themselves are full of allusions to a long antiquity of poetry. All the early traditions of Greece are sprinkled with the names of its minstrels, and the heroic fables of that country are probably, in a great measure, the work of these primitive bards. Orpheus, whose verse recalled the dead, Sinus and Musæus, whom Virgil, the disciple of Homer, seats in that elysium where he forgets to place his master, are examples of a sort of immortality conferred on mere names in literature, the dim but venerable shadows of the fathers of poetry, whose works have been lost for thousands of years. These were undoubtedly the ancient bards from whose compositions Homer kindled his imagination, and, catching a double portion of their spirit, emulated and surpassed them.

At the present day, however, a writer of poems writes in a language which preceding poets have polished, refined, and filled with forcible, graceful, and musical expressions. He is not only taught by them to overcome the difficulties of rhythmical construction, but he is shown, as it were, the secrets of the mechanism by which he moves the mind of his reader; he is shown ways of kindling the imagination and of interesting the passions which his own sagacity might never have discovered; his mind is filled with the beauty of their sentiments, and their enthusiasm is breathed into his soul. He owes much, also, to his contemporaries as well as to those who have gone before him. He reads their works, and whatever excellence he beholds in them, inspires him with a strong desire to rival it—stronger, perhaps, than that excited by the writings of his predecessors; for such is our reverence for the dead that we are willing to concede to them that superiority which we are anxious to snatch from the living. Even if he should refuse to read the writings of his brethren, he cannot escape the action of their minds on his own. He necessarily comes to partake somewhat of the character of their genius, which is impressed not only on all contemporary literature, but even on the daily thoughts of those with whom he associates. In short, his mind is in a great degree formed by the labors of others; he walks in a path which they have made smooth and plain, and is supported by their strength. Whoever would entirely disclaim imitation, and aspire to the praises of complete originality, should be altogether ignorant of any poetry written by others, and of all those aids which the cultivation of poetry has lent to prose. Deprive an author of these advantages, and what sort of poetry does any one imagine that he would produce? I dare say it would be sufficiently original, but who will affirm that it could be read?

The poet must do precisely what is done by the mathematician, who takes up his science where his predecessors have left it, and pushes its limits as much farther, and makes as many new applications of its principles, as he can. He must found himself on the excellence already attained in his art, and if, in addition to this, he delights us with new modes of sublimity, of beauty, and of human emotion, he deserves the praise of originality and of genius. If he has nothing of all this, he is entitled to no other honor than belongs to him who keeps alive the practice of a delightful and beautiful art.

This very necessity, however, of a certain degree of dependence upon models in poetry has at some periods led into an opposite fault to the inordinate desire of originality. The student, instead of copying nature with the aid of knowledge derived from these models, has been induced to make them the original, from which the copy was to be drawn. He has been led to take an imperfect work—and all human works are imperfect—as the standard of perfection, and to dwell upon it with such reverence that he comes to see beauties where no beauties are, and excellence in place of positive defects. Thus the study of poetry, which should encourage the free and unlimited aspirations of the mind after all that is noble and beautiful, has been perverted into a contrivance to chill and repress them. It has seduced its admirers from an admiration of the works of God to an idolatry for the works of men; it has carried them from living and inexhaustible sources of poetic inspiration to drink at comparatively scanty and impure channels; it has made them to linger by the side of these instead of using them as guides to ascend to their original fountain.

It is of high importance, then, to inquire what are the proper limits of poetic imitation, or, in other words, by what means the examples and labors of others may be made use of in strengthening, and prevented from enfeebling, the native vigor of genius. No better rule has been given for this purpose than to take no particular poem nor poet, nor class of poets, as the pattern of poetic composition, but to study the beauties of all. All good poems have their peculiar merits and faults, all great poets their points of strength and weakness, all schools of poetry their agreements with good taste and their offences against it. To confine the attention and limit the admiration to one particular sort of excellence, not only tends to narrow the range of the intellectual powers, but most surely brings along with it the peculiar defects to which that sort of excellence is allied, and into which it is most apt to deviate. Thus, a poet of the Lake school, by endeavoring too earnestly after simplicity, may run into childishness; a follower of Byron, in his pursuit of energy of thought, and the intense expression of passion, may degenerate into abruptness, extravagance, or obscurity; a disciple of Scott, in his zeal for easy writing, may find himself inditing something little better than doggerel, or, at least, very dull and feeble verse; an imitator of Leigh Hunt, too intent on keeping up the vivacity and joyousness of the poetic temperament, may forget his common sense; and a poet of the school of Pope may write very polished, well-balanced verses with a great deal of antithesis and very little true feeling.

Still, these several schools have all their excellences; they have all some qualities to be admired and loved and dwelt upon. Let the student of poetry dwell upon them as long as he pleases, let him study them until they are incorporated into his mind, but let him give his admiration to no one of them exclusively. It is remarkable to what a degree the great founders of the several styles of English poetry, even of the least lofty, varied, and original, have pursued this universal search after excellence. When Pope—brilliant, witty, harmonious, and, within a certain compass, a great master of language—had fixed the poetical taste of his age, we all know what a crowd of imitators arose in his train, and how rapidly poetry declined. But the imitators of Pope failed to do what Pope did. Great as was his partiality for the French school, and closely as he had formed himself on the model of Boileau, he yet disdained not to learn much from other instructors. He went back for gems of thought and graces of style to the earlier writers of English verse—to the poets of the Elizabethan age, and, farther still, to the venerable Chaucer. He was a passionate admirer and a restorer of Shakespeare, and, by recommending him to the English people, prepared the way for the downfall of his own school, but not, I hope, for the oblivion of his own writings.

This relish of poetic excellence in all its forms, and in whatever school or style of poetry it is found, does not, I apprehend, lead to a less lively apprehension of the several merits of these styles, while at the same time it opens the eyes of the student to their several defects and errors. In this way the mind forms to itself a higher standard of excellence than exists in any of them—a standard compounded of the characteristic merits of all, and free from any of their imperfections. To this standard it will refer all their compositions; to this it will naturally aspire; and, by the contemplation of this, it will divest itself of that blind and idolatrous reverence for certain models of composition and certain dogmas of ancient criticism which are the death of the hopes and inspirations of the poet.

It is long since the authority of great names was disregarded in matters of science. Ages ago the schools shook themselves loose from the fetters of Aristotle. He no more now delivers the oracles of philosophy than the priests of Apollo deliver the oracles of religion. Why should the chains of authority be worn any longer by the heart and the imagination than by the reason? This is a question which the age has already answered. The genius of modern times has gone out in every direction in search of originality. Its ardor has not always been compensated by the discovery of its object, but under its auspices a fresh, vigorous, and highly original poetry has grown up. The fertile soil of modern literature has thrown up, it is true, weeds among the flowers, but the flowers are of immortal bloom and fragrance, and the weeds are soon outworn. It is no longer necessary that a narrative poem should be written on the model of the ancient epic; a lyric composition is not relished the more, perhaps not so much, for being Pindaric or Horatian; and it is not required that a satire should remind the reader of Juvenal. It is enough for the age if beautiful diction, glowing imagery, strong emotion, and fine thought are so combined as to give them their fullest effect upon the mind. The end of poetry is then attained, no matter by what system of rules.

If it were to be asked which is the more likely to produce specimens of poetry worthy of going down to posterity, which is the more favorable to the enlargement of the human mind and the vigorous action of all its faculties on the variety of objects and their relations by which it is surrounded—an age distinguished for too great carefulness of imitation, or an age remarkable for an excessive ambition of originality—I think that a wise decision must be in favor of the latter. Whatever errors in taste may spring from the zeal for new developments of genius and the disdain of imitation, their influence is of short duration. The fantastic brood of extravagances and absurdities to which they give birth soon die and are forgotten, for nothing is immortal in literature but what is truly excellent. On the other hand, such an age may and does produce poems worthy to live. The works of the early Italian poets were composed in such an age; the proudest monuments of English verse are the growth of such a spirit; the old poetry of Spain, the modern poetry of Germany, grew into beauty and strength under such auspices. Men walked, as they should ever do, with a confident step by the side of these ancient masters, of whom they learned this art; they studied their works, not that they might resemble, but that they might surpass them.

But one of the best fruits of such an age is the remarkable activity into which it calls the human intellect. Those things which are ours rather by memory than by the natural growth of the mind lie on its surface, already wrought into distinct shape, and are brought into use with little effort. But for the native conceptions of the mind, the offspring of strong mental excitement, it is necessary to go deeper and to toil more intensely. It is not without a vigorous exercise that the intellect searches for these among its stores, extricates them from the obscurity in which they are first beheld, ascertains their parts and detains them until they are moulded into distinctness and symmetry, and embodied in language.

But when once a tame and frigid taste has possessed the tribe of poets, when all their powers are employed in servilely copying the works of their predecessors, it is not only impossible that any great work should be produced among them, but the period of a literary reformation, of the awakening of genius, is postponed to a distant futurity. It is the quality of such a state of literature, by the imposing precision of its rules and the ridicule it throws on everything out of its own beaten track, to perpetuate itself indefinitely. The happy appearance of some extraordinary genius, educated under different influences than those operating on the age, and compelling admiration by the force of his talents; or, perhaps, some great moral or political revolution, by unsettling old opinions and familiarizing men to daring speculations—can alone have any effect to remove it. The mind grows indolent, or, at least, enfeebled, by the want of those higher exercises to which it was destined. At the same time, the spirit of poetry, as seen in its power of elevating the mind, of humanizing the affections, and expelling sordid appetites, is no longer felt, or only felt by a few, who conceal in their own bosoms the secret of its power over them.

1825–6   1884

A BORDER TRADITION

In travelling through the western part of New England, not long since, I stopped for a few days at one of the beautiful villages of that region. It was situated on the edge of some fine rich meadows, lying about one of the prettiest little rivers in the world. While there, I went one morning to the top of a little round hill, which commanded a view of the surrounding country. I saw the white houses under the shade of the old elms, the neat painted fences before them, and the border of bright green turf on either side of the road, which the inhabitants kept as clean as the grass plots of their gardens. I saw the river winding away to the south, between leaning trees, and thick shrubs and vines, the hills, rising gently to the west of the village, covered with orchards and woods and openings of pasture ground, the rich level meadows to the east, and beyond them, at no great distance, the craggy mountains rising almost perpendicularly, as if placed there to heighten, by their rugged aspect, the soft beauty of the scene below them. If the view was striking in itself, it was rendered still more so by circumstances of life and splendor belonging to the weather, the hour, and the season. The wide circle of verdure, in the midst of which I stood, was loaded and almost crushed by one of those profuse dews, which fall in our climate of a clear summer night, and glittered under a bright sun and a sky of transparent blue. The trees about me were noisy with birds, the bob-o' lincoln rose singing from the grass to sink in the grass again when his strain was ended, and the cat-bird squalled in the thicket, in spite of the boy who was trying to stone it out. Then there was the whistle of the quail, the resounding voice of the hang-bird, the mysterious note of the post-driver, and the chatter of swallows darting to and fro. As a sort of accompaniment to this natural music, there was heard at times the deep and tremulous sound of the river breaking over a mill-dam at some distance.

There is an end of gazing at the finest sights, and of listening to the most agreeable sounds. I had turned to go down the hill, when I observed a respectable looking old man sitting near me, on the edge of a rock that projected a little way out of the ground. At the very first glance I set him down for one of the ancient yeomanry of our country; for his sturdy frame and large limbs had evidently been rendered sturdier and larger by labor and hardship, and old age had only taken away the appearance of agility without impairing his natural air of strength. I am accustomed to look with a feeling of gratitude, as well as respect, on these remnants of a hardy and useful generation. I see in them the men, who have hewed down the forests and tamed the soil of the fair country we inhabit; who built the roads we travel, over mountains and across morasses, and who planted the hill sides with orchards, of which we idly gather the fruit. From the attention with which the old man was looking at the surrounding prospect, I judged that he was come to the hill on the same errand with myself, and, on entering into conversation with him, I found that I was not mistaken. He had lived in the village when a boy; he had been absent from it nearly sixty years, and now, having occasion to pass through it on a journey from a distant part of the country, he was trying to recollect its features from the little eminence by which it was overlooked. "I can hardly," said he, "satisfy myself that this is the place in which I passed my boyish days. It is true, that the river is still yonder, and this is the hill where I played when a child, and those mountains, with their rocks and woods, look to me as they did then. That small peak lies still in the lap of the larger and loftier ridge that stretches like a semicircle around it. There are the same smooth meadows to the east, and the same fine ascent to the west of the village. But the old dwellings have been pulled down, and new ones built in their stead, the trees under which I sat in my childhood have decayed or been cut down, and others have been planted; the very roads have changed their places, and the rivulets, that turned my little machinery, are dried up. Do you see," said he, pointing with his staff, "that part of the meadow that runs up like a little creek or bay between the spurs of the upland, and comes close to the highway? A brook formerly came down to that spot, and lost itself in the marshy soil, but its bed, as you see, is now dry, and only serves as a channel to carry off the superabundance of the rains. That part of the meadow is now covered with thick and tall grass, but I well remember when it was overgrown with bushes and water-flags, among which many old decaying trunks of trees served as a kind of causeys over a quagmire, that otherwise would have been impassable. It was a spot of evil report in the village, for it was said that lights had been seen at night moving among the thickets, and strange noises had been heard from the ground,— gurgling and half-smothered sounds, as of a living creature strangled in the midst of sods and water. It was said, also, that glimpses of something white had been seen gliding among the bushes, and that often the rank vegetation had been observed to be fearfully agitated, as if the earth shuddered at the spot where innocent blood had been shed. Some fearful deed, it was said, had doubtless been done there. It was thought by some, that a child had been strangled and thrown into the quagmire by its unnatural mother; and by others, that a traveller had been murdered there, for the sake of his money. Nobody cared, after dark, to travel the road, which formerly wound about the base of this hill, and thus kept longer beside the edge of the fen than it does now. I remember being drawn once or twice by curiosity to visit the place, in company with another lad of my age. We stole in silence along the old logs, speaking to each other in whispers, and our hair stood on end at the sight of the white bones lying about. They were the bones of cattle, who had sunk into the mire, and could not be dragged out, or had perished before they were found. There is a story about that spot," continued the old man, "which it may be worth your while to hear, and if you will please to be seated on this rock, I will tell it."

There was something in the old man's conversation which denoted a degree of intelligence and education superior to what I expected from his appearance. I was curious to know what sort of story would follow such an introduction; I sat down, therefore, by his side, on the edge of the rock, and he went on as follows.

It is a story that I heard from my grandmother, a good old Dutch lady, belonging to a family of the first settlers of the place. The Dutch from the North River, and the Yankees from the Connecticut, came into the valley about the same time, and settled upon these rich meadows. Which were the first comers, I am unable to tell; I have heard different accounts of the matter, but the traditions of the Dutch families give the priority to their own ancestors, and I am inclined to think them in the right; for, although it was not uncommon, in those days, for the restless Yankee to settle in a neighbourhood of Dutchmen, yet it was a rare thing for the quiet Hollander voluntarily to plant himself in the midst of a bustling Yankee settlement. However this may be, it is certain, that, about ninety years ago, a little neighbourhood had been formed of the descendants of both the emigrants from Holland and those from England. At first, the different races looked sourly upon each other, but the daily sight of each other's faces, and the need of each other's kindness and assistance soon brought them to live upon friendly terms. The Dutchman learned to salute his neighbour in bad English, and the Yankee began to make advances towards driving a bargain, in worse Dutch.

Jacob, or, as he was commonly called, Yok Suydam, was one of these early Dutch planters, and Jedidiah Williams, his neighbour, one of the first Yankees who sat down on the banks of this river. Williams was a man of a hard countenance and severe manners, who had been a deacon of the church in the parish he had left, and who did not, as I have known some people do, forget his religion when it ceased to be of any service to him in his worldly concerns. He was as grave in his demeanour, as guarded in his speech, and as constant in his devotions, as ever, notwithstanding that these qualities in his character were less prized in his new situation than they had been in Connecticut. The place had as yet no minister; but

Williams contrived to collect every Sunday a few of the neigh-
bours at his house to perform the weekly worship. On a still
summer morning you might hear him doling out a portion of
the Scriptures, or reading a sermon of some godly divine of
the day, in a sort of nasal recitation, which could be distinguished, swelling over the noises of his pigs and poultry, at
the distance of a quarter of a mile from his dwelling. Honest
Yok read his Bible too, but he read it in Dutch, and excused
himself from attending the meetings at Williams's house, on
account of his ignorance of the language in which the exercises
were held. Instead, however, of confining himself to the house
during the whole Sunday like Williams, he would sometimes
stray out into his fields, to look at his cattle and his crops, and
was known once or twice to lie down on the grass under a tree,
in the corner of one of his inclosures, where the rustling of his
Indian corn, and the hum of the bees among the pumpkin
blossoms, would put him to sleep. The rest of the day, when
the weather was fine, he passed in smoking his pipe under a
rude kind of piazza in front of his house, looking out over the
rich meadows which he had lately cleared of their wood, or
listening to a chapter of the New Testament, read to him by one
of his daughters. He was also less guarded in his language
than suited the precise notions of Williams; the words "duyvel"
or "donner," or some such unnecessary exclamation, would
often slip out of his mouth in the haste of conversation. But
there was another practice of Yok's, which was still less to the
taste of his neighbour. As was the case with most of the Dutch
planters at that time, his house swarmed with negro domestics,
and among the merry, sleek-faced blacks, that jabbered Dutch
and ate sour crout in his kitchen, there was one who could
play tolerably on the fiddle. Yok did not suffer this talent to
lie useless. On every New Year's eve, and not on that alone,
but on many a long and bright winter evening that followed
it, when the snow looked whiter than ever in the moonlight, and
you could see the little wedges of frost floating and glistening
in the air, the immense fireplace in the long kitchen was piled
with dry hickory, the negro Orpheus was mounted on a high

bench, and the brawny youths and ruddy girls of the place danced to the music till the cocks crew. Yok's own daughters, the prettiest maidens that ever ran in the woods of a new settlement, were allowed to acquit themselves exceedingly well on these occasions; but the performances of Yok himself extorted universal admiration. Old as he was, and he did not lack many winters of sixty, whenever he came on the floor, which was generally just before the breaking up of the revel, the youngest and most active of his guests acknowledged themselves outdone. He executed the double shuffle with incredible dexterity, drummed with his heels on the floor till you would have thought the drumming an accompaniment to the fiddle, and threw the joints of his limbs into the most gracefully acute angles that can be imagined.

Jedidiah, of course, did not suffer these irregularities of his neighbour to pass unrebuked, and Yok always took his admonitions kindly enough, although without much disposition to profit by them. He invariably apologized by saying that he was a Dutchman, that he followed the customs of his countrymen, and the practices of his fathers before him; and that it did not become the like of him to presume to be wiser or better than his ancestors, who were honest men, and who, he believed, had gone to heaven. The appearance of respect, however, with which he received these reproofs, went far to reconcile Jedidiah to his practical neglect of them, and a kind of friendship at length grew up between the two settlers and their families. Yok's pretty daughters came constantly to attend Williams's meetings, and Williams's son was a frequent and welcome visiter at the house of the hearty and hospitable Dutchman.

Yok's family, with the exception of the negro domestics I have mentioned, consisted only of himself and his two daughters. Mary, the elder, was somewhat tall, with a delicate shape, and a peaceful, innocent look. The climate, and three generations of American descent, had completely done away in her personal appearance all traces of her Dutch extraction, except the fair hair and the light blue eye. She was a sincere, single-hearted creature, whom the experience of eighteen years had not taught that there was such a thing as treachery in the world. It was no difficult matter to move her either to smiles or to tears, and had she lived in this novel-reading age, she would have been inevitably spoiled. As it was, the poor girl had no book but the Bible, of which there were in Yok's family several copies in the old Dutch letter, and she was forced to content herself with weeping over the fortunes of Ruth and the resurrection of Lazarus.   Geshie, her sister, little more than a year younger, had an appearance of firmer and more sanguine health than Mary, and all that excess of animal spirits and love of mirth, with which youth and high health are generally accompanied. She was ruddier, shorter in stature, and fuller in her proportions than the elder sister, and under the shade of her thick brown hair, her bright eye shone out with a look so arch and full of mischief, that, like the sun in June, it was not a thing to look long upon. The two sisters, though so little alike, were both as kind and good as the day is long, and were acknowledged to be the handsomest girls in the settlement. People, however, were divided in opinion as to which was the handsomer and more agreeable of the two. The greater number gave the preference to the blooming and sprightly Geshie, but James Williams, the son of Jedidiah, thought differently.

Young Williams, who had come with his father to the new settlement, was a frank, high-spirited, giddy young fellow. He had given some proofs of forwardness in early youth, and his father had set his heart upon seeing him one of the burning and shining lights of the church, emulating in the pulpit the eloquence of Solomon Stoddard, and the sound doctrine of Jonathan Edwards. He had sent him to Yale College to furnish his mind with the necessary worldly learning, trusting to his own prayers and to Providence for the piety that was to fit him for the work of the ministry. But his expectations were wretchedly disappointed, for the young man proved refractory under the discipline of a college, and made so good a use of his opportunities of rebellion, that in less than a year he was expelled. He came home to read Horace and shoot squirrels, and bear a part in the psalms sung at the meetings for religious worship held at his father's. He could not make up his mind to go back to the labors of husbandry, and yet was uncertain to what other course of life to betake himself.

Young men, who have nothing else to do, are apt to amuse themselves with making love. Time hung heavy on the hands of James Williams in the new and thinly inhabited settlement. He wandered the old woods, that stretched away on all sides, till he was weary; he found them altogether too gloomy and too silent for his taste, and when their echoes were awakened by the report of his own fowling-piece, by the cawing of the crow, or the shriek of the hawk, he could not help thinking that these sounds would interest him more, if they conveyed a human meaning. He grew tired of reading Horace in a place where nobody cared for his Latin. At length he would shut his book, and lay his gun on the two wooden hooks in his father's kitchen, and walk down to the house of honest Yok Suydam, where the good Dutchman greeted him with a cordial grasp of the hand, and his daughters with smiles. James was soon master of Dutch enough to tell the story of his college pranks, which usually called a hearty laugh from the old gentleman, a sentence or two of kind expostulation from the elder daughter, and a torrent of good humored raillery from the younger. In return for the proficiency which the society of the family enabled him to make in their language, James offered to teach the young ladies English, and the elder readily undertook to be his pupil. As for Geshie, she had no ambition that way; it was, she said, a silken, glozing tongue,—the tongue of pedlars and sharpers, fit only for those who wished to defraud and deceive; she was contented, for her part, with the plain household speech in which she had been brought up, the language of honesty and sincerity. James began to read the New Testament along with Mary, it being the only book with which she was familiar. After getting through with a few chapters, it was exchanged for a volume of Richardson's "Pamela," which had then just made its appearance. James had contrived to possess himself of a copy of this work while at New Haven, and concealed it as carefully from the eyes of his father as the quail hides her nest from the schoolboy. He knew, that if it should be discovered, the consequences could be no less than the great wrath of his father towards so graceless a son, and that the offending book would be burnt with fire.

Geshie soon had occasion to pay her sister a multitude of sly compliments on her proficiency in English. She had never known, she said, a tutor so assiduous, nor a pupil so teachable. It was not, indeed, extraordinary that James should fancy himself in love with the prettiest girl in the settlement, nor was it more so that she should be seriously in love with him. The young couple soon understood each other, and Geshie also, although not the confidant of her sister, understood enough of the matter to anticipate a merry wedding, and gay wedding-dresses. The language of Holland has been called barbarous and harsh; in the mouth of Mary, James thought it infinitely more musical than the Latin, and the whispers of affection in her imperfect English, seemed to give new graces to his native tongue. Their studies, however, were often interrupted by the frolics of Geshie. Sometimes the volume of "Pamela" was missing for several days, and James was obliged to defer his lessons till it could be found; sometimes the master and scholar, on attempting to rise, found themselves fastened to their chairs, and their chairs fastened together. James was somewhat of a superstitious turn; he had read Mather's "Magnalia," a copy of which by some accident belonged to his father, and had imbibed a deep respect for spirits and goblins. Geshie was not slow in discovering this weakness in his character, nor in making it contribute to her amusement. She had an abundance of stories of supernatural terrors, and always took care to relate them to James in the evening. On a moonlight night she would tell him of an apparition seen by moonlight, and on a cloudy evening, of a ghost that walked when you could not see your hand. She would then enjoy his evident alarm, as it grew late, and as he looked alternately at his hat and the window. In the mean time, Geshie, notwithstanding her pretended contempt for the English tongue, was making a progress in learning it equal at least to that of her sister. In truth, she was sufficiently indifferent as long as Mary was occupied with the English Testament; but when the first volume of "Pamela" was brought to the house, her curiosity to know its contents prevailed over every other consideration. After that she lost nothing of the lessons James gave her sister; she treasured up in her memory every English phrase she heard uttered; she read "Pamela" by stealth; and her talent for mimicry soon gave her a tolerable command of the English accent.

A year had now passed since James and Mary had become acquainted with each other. The settlement was growing every day more populous, and James had no difficulty of finding companions to cheat him of the tedious hours. There were also among the daughters of the new comers some who might be thought nearly as handsome and agreeable as Mary herself. His affection for her, by a perversity not uncommon in young men who are loved better than they deserve, began gradually to cool; his visits to her father's house became less and less frequent; the poor girl's English studies were wofully neglected, and finally discontinued altogether. Once she ventured to speak to him of his altered behaviour; but he gave her an indirect and trifling answer, and, after that, she spoke of it no more. But she felt it not the less deeply; her heart bled in silence and in secret; she became melancholy, was often found weeping by herself, and seemed going into a deep decline. The good old Suydam, who suspected nothing of the true cause of his daughter's malady, after prescribing all the household remedies he could think of, called in the doctor, notwithstanding she protested vehemently against it. The doctor came with his saddlebags on his arm,—a smock-faced young man just settled in the place, who thought himself happy if his prescriptions did not aggravate the disorder. He examined the patient, seemed to hesitate about her complaint, but, as he was called, he knew his duty too well not to prescribe; he therefore ordered her a little valerian, and took his leave. Geshie, who understood her sister's disorder better than the physician, and knew that it was not to be healed by medicine, threw the drug out of the window as soon as he was gone, and saved her the disgust of swallowing it.

This kind-hearted girl now undertook herself to be her sister's physician. She sung to her all the old songs she remembered, both sad and merry, composed by the mellifluous poets of Holland long ago, and handed down in the American settlements from mother to daughter, for a hundred years at least. She drew her forth to ramble in the meadows, and to pierce the great forest around them in various directions along dark and cool paths, leading to the sunny, cultivated openings lately made in its bosom. She collected for her entertainment all the gossip of her neighbourhood, mimicked the accent of the Yankees, danced, capered, and played a thousand monkey tricks to divert her. All her efforts were ineffectual to restore health and spirits to her sister, and she saw, with a sorrow almost increased to despair, that this was only to be hoped for from the return of her lover's affections.

It was now October. The forests around this valley, where there was then little else but forest, had put on their colors of yellow, orange, and crimson; and looked yet brighter in the golden sunshine of the season that lay upon them. The ripe apples were dropping from the young apple-trees by the cottages of the settlers; the chestnut, the oak, and the butternut were beginning to cast their fruit; squirrels were chirping and barking on the branches of the walnut; rabbits were scudding over the bright leaves that lay scattered below; and the heavy whirr of the partridge, as he rose from the gound, told how well he had been pampered by the abundance of the season. James Williams could not resist the temptation of such fine weather, and so much game. He was absent whole days in the depths of the woods; in the morning you might hear the report of his fowling-piece in the edge of the forest, in the neighbourhood of his father's; at noon its echoes would be sent faintly from the cliffs of that long rocky ridge which bounds the valley to the east.

One morning James passed by the house of Mary's father with his fowling-piece. He did not dare to raise his head as he went, nor to cast a look at the windows of the house, lest he should see the face of her with whose affections he had so unfeelingly trifled. He pretended to be very busy about the lock of his gun, until he had fairly passed the dwelling, when he quickened his pace, and was soon out of sight. Geshie observed him as he went, and determined to watch his return.

He did not return until after sunset. It was a clear night, except some scattered banks of mist from the river; the moon was shining brightly, and Geshie discerned at some distance the well known gait of James, and the glitter of his fowling-piece. She saw that this was the moment for the execution of a plan, which she had formed in the hope that it might be of some advantage to her sister, but which she had communicated to no one. A few minutes afterwards a figure in white was seen stealing down from the house between some high banks so as not to be observed by James, towards the swamp of which I have already spoken, and which is now changed into that beautiful meadow.

It was necessary for James, after passing Suydam's house, to follow the road for some distance along the edge of that swamp. The spot had already begun to have a bad name; the body of an Indian infant had been found in some bushes by the edge, and a drunken German carpenter, who had straggled into the settlement, had lost the road, and perished there in a flood, which covered the meadows, the swamp, and the road itself, with the waters of the river. Among the tales of ghosts and hobgoblins, with which Geshie had formerly entertained James, were one or two stories of strange sights seen about this swamp, to which, I suspect, she maliciously added some embellishments of her own.

James's heart did not beat with its usual calmness as he approached the swamp. But his timidity rose to fear, and his fear to agony, and his whole frame shook, and a cold sweat broke out at every pore, as he saw a figure in white come out from the bushes, and move slowly towards him. He stood rooted to the ground without the power to fly, but his hands instinctively fumbled with his fowling-piece, as though he would have used it against the object of his fears. The spectre raised its arm with a menacing gesture, and the piece fell from his hands to the ground. As the apparition drew nigh, he could perceive that it was wrapped in a linen sheet, and the white feet that showed themselves under the lower edge, left him no doubt that it was the tenant of a coffin who stood before him. He essayed to speak, but his throat seemed filled with ashes; nor was it necessary, for the arm of the spectre was again raised; he saw its eye glistening under the folds of the shroud; he saw its lips move; the words came forth in clear and solemn accents; he swooned, and fell to the ground.

The same evening, as Yok was quietly smoking his pipe by the fireside, and watching the changes in the embers, Geshie entered the room, quite out of breath, with an expression of unusual agitation and anxiety on her countenance. She seated herself, and after a moment's silence, 'I have been thinking,' said she, 'that you are not a very good neighbour to Williams.'

'Why so, my daughter?'

'It is so long since you have been to see him. I hope he has taken no offence at it; but, you know, he has not called at our house lately, and James, whom you used to be so fond of, and who diverted us so much, has not darkened our doors for many a long day.'

'That is true, girl; I will see Williams to-morrow evening.'

'Why not to-night; it is a beautiful night; the sky is so clear, and the moon so bright; it may be bad weather to-morrow, you know; besides, if Williams has really taken offence at your neglect of him, the sooner it is made up between you the better.'

'Why that is true, again; and I will even go to-night;'—and Geshie, with a pleasure she could hardly conceal, reached him his hat, and heard him walk away in the direction of Williams's house with a pace quickened by the dampness of the evening air. On the way, Yok found James lying in the road apparently lifeless, and a man who was passing about the same time, assisted in bearing him to his father's house, where, by proper applications, he was soon brought to himself. On his return, Yok related these circumstances to Geshie, who appeared as much surprised and interested, as if she had known nothing of the matter.

To the numerous questions put to him respecting the condition in which he was found, James returned no direct answer, but desired to be left to repose. Sleep did not visit his eyes that night; the event of the evening, which he had remembered but faintly on first coming out of the swoon, returned to him in all its circumstances, with an impression that grew stronger every moment. Again they seemed present to him; the haunted spot, the spectre, the shroud, the white feet and hand, the gleam of its eye, the perceptible motion of its lips, and the piercing and solemn tones of its voice. Then, also, the fearful words it uttered, returned, one by one, to his recollection, and, as they returned, engraved themselves there, as the diamond ploughs its characters on the rock; again he heard himself denounced as treacherous, faithless, and cruel, and warned to escape an untimely end by a speedy repentance. The morning found him haggard and exhausted, in a state of melancholy bordering on despair.

It happened at this time, that the minister of the parish in which Williams had formerly lived, was on a visit to his old neighbour. Williams, who had been one of the pillars of his church, had implored him so pathetically to come and dispense the word for a season in that destitute place, that he could not find it in his heart to deny him. He was one of that race of excellent old clergymen, of which some specimens yet remain, I am told, in New England, renowned equally for good sermons in the pulpit, and good stories out of it. His round and somewhat florid face was set off by a short fox-colored wig, and the severity of his brow tempered by the jollity of his cheeks and chin. The clergy, you know, were in those times the nobility of the country; their opinions were oracles, and their advice law. Those were good days, when the farmer sent the best of every thing he had to the minister; when every hat was doffed as he passed, and when, in every house he entered, the great easy-chair was instantly wheeled for him to the front of the fireplace, the housewife ran to comb her children, and the husband to broach the best barrel of cider in his cellar. Williams's minister was not a man to abuse the reverence in which he was held; the penitent are always ready to apply to a clergyman, but this good man was also the friend of the unfortunate and unhappy.

In the morning, as soon as the clergyman was up, James sent for him, and communicated to him the adventure of the night. A long conversation ensued. The clergyman examined James with great minuteness concerning all the circumstances, and satisfied himself of the truth of his story. He then inquired of him if there were any particulars of his late way of life, which might have given occasion to so remarkable a visitation. James hesitated for a while, and at last confessed that he had loved Mary; that he believed he had won her affections; that they had talked of marriage; that he had discontinued his visits; and that he had been told she was unhappy. Another series of questions ensued, and at the end of the conference it was settled, that James should immediately perform his engagement to Mary, and that the incident of the ghost should, in the mean time, be kept secret between him and the minister.

Mary did not know to what event she owed the return of her lover, for her sister had told nobody of the part she took in the affair. She received him without a word of reproach, but with a countenance in which tears and smiles contended for the mastery. She spoke with sorrow and concern of his altered and haggard appearance, and James wondered how he could ever have ceased to love her. The parents were consulted concerning the match. Yok was pleased, because he had always liked James; and Williams, because Yok was the owner of broad woodlands and goodly meadows. An early day was fixed for the marriage. The good parson came all the way from Connecticut to assist at the nuptials, and the doctor, to whose sagacious prescription Yok attributed the rapid amendment that was taking place in his daughter's health, was also of the party. After the ceremony was over, and the minister had retired, the company adjourned to the long kitchen. A great hickory fire was blazing in the chimney, and the negro fiddler who had been provided for the occasion, with an associate, was mounted on his bench with the instrument of music at his shoulder. The couples were soon arranged; the bride and bridegroom, in the gayest attire of the day, were at the head; and old Yok himself was on the floor. A November wind was howling in the woods, the old trees creaked and groaned, and showers of the red leaves were driven against the windows; but the bluster without was unheard amidst the merriment within. The black fiddlers threw themselves into the most violent contortions, and drew their bows from the head to the heel at every note. The sound of the instruments, the clatter of feet, the shouts of laughter, the jests that flew rapidly about, taken up by the shrill voices of the maidens, and echoed from the sonorous lungs of the rustic beaux, made the passer by to stop in amazement. But the guests remembered that it was only a wedding, and at midnight the house was as still and dark as ever.

James did not like the neighbourhood of the place where he had seen the spectre; and soon after his marriage, he went to settle in one of the villages on the banks of the Hudson, where he long lived quietly and respectably, and where his descendants reside to this day. Geshie was my grandmother by the mother's side, and from her lips I had the tale I have related. It is not known to many, for she never told it until she had arrived at extreme old age, when there were few in these parts who remembered either James Williams or her sister. As for the doctor who had prescribed for Mary, he rose almost immediately into great reputation and extensive practice, from being supposed to have cured a patient in the last stage of a consumption.

1826

RECOLLECTIONS OF THE SOUTH OF SPAIN

The National Ballads of Spain, entitled Romances, are perhaps the most interesting part of its literature, and not the least curious among them are those which pass under the name of *Romances Moriscos*, or Moriscan Romances. They are very ancient, having been mostly composed in the fourteenth century, but they bear no date or name of their authors. They relate the loves and chivalric deeds of the knights of Granada, and were probably many of them written by the Moors themselves, who at that period lived intermingled with Christians in the villages which had submitted to the Castilian dominions. However this may be, it is certain that the ancient songs in which Moslem heroism and Moslem beauty are celebrated, form an important part of the national literature of the most intolerant of all Christian countries. These poems are simple, spirited, and tender, and full of a sweet, natural melody. But to enjoy them as you ought, you should hear them sung by a Spanish maiden under a Spanish sky. You should hear them, as I have done—though rarely I confess, for the people of Spain have almost forgotten them in their late revolution— you should hear them from the small windows of one of those *casas morunas*, as they are called, those solid dwellings built centuries ago by Moorish architects, the floors of which, having settled below the level of the surrounding earth, give proof of their antiquity. You should hear them from the lips of one of the girls of Andalusia, whose cheeks seem to glow with the warmth of even a hotter sky than that of Spain, whose delicate hands and prettily turned ankles might serve for those of Mahometan Houries, who speak their language with a sort of oriental accent, and whose full black eyes seem to shoot forth revelations of the depth and mystery of eastern feeling. It is among the footsteps of Arabian beauty that you should listen to the last echoes of Arabian minstrelsy on the shores of western Europe.

I remember that one afternoon I was returning from a solitary excursion along the skirts of the Sierra Morena. I had arrived nearly at the foot of the mountain, following a stream which found its way among rocks of the most capricious forms, leaping over their bases in a series of cascades, and wetting the lower branches of the thorn-trees and wild olives that stooped over it. Finally it issued forth into the open meadows between two obelisks of rocks, forming a kind of fantastic gateway that straitened the current and added to its swiftness. I had scarcely ceased to hear the dash of the water as I proceeded, when a clear rich voice, singing what I could distinguish to be one of the ancient songs of the country, fell upon my ear. The sound proceeded from a dwelling at no great distance, built of dark coloured stone, united by that cement for which the Moors were so famous, and which has all the hardness and durability of the living rock. It was a high building, with small doors and narrow windows, whose depth showed the extraordinary thickness of the wall. At one of these jealous looking openings I could discern two youthful female faces, one of which I judged must belong to the singer. I stopped involuntarily, listening to the music, and struck with the beauty of the scene before me, for passing beautiful it was, in the rich reflection of the sun from the western heavens. The glow of the sky itself was scarcely less gorgeous than the aspect of the flowery ground and glittering stream beneath it. It was one of those charming spots you so often come upon in the province of Andalusia—natural gardens, uncultivated, but overspread with a spontaneous luxuriance and beauty of vegetation, and teeming with plenty which in other soils and climates require the tendance of man. The air was fragrant with a thousand trodden aromatic herbs, with fields of lavender, and with the brightest roses blushing in tufts all over the meadows, or breathing forth their sweetness from the secrecy of myrtle thickets and clumps of the fig tree and pomegranate. The sounds I had heard seemed worthy to mingle with this bright and perfumed atmosphere, and to thrill the beautiful scenery around me.

I was yet listening, when the strain suddenly ceased, and a good-looking Spaniard, with an olive complexion, clad in one of the short jackets of the country, came out to me and hospitably invited me to enter. I did so, and he presented me to his daughters, two pretty black-eyed Andalusian damsels, who placed before me the wines and fruits of the country. I took occasion to thank the young ladies for the pleasure they had afforded me without intending it, and ventured to request a repetition of the air that had pleased me so much. The young daughter Conchita, for so her father called her, a prettier and fonder name than her baptismal appellation, Conception, complied without any other apology or sign of reluctance than the slight blush that ran at first over her cheeks and forehead, and gave me, in her best manner, the romance beginning with

> "Diamante falso y fingido,
> Engastado en pedernal." &c.

The plaintive effect of the three first stanzas was skilfully contrasted by the singer with the sprightliness of the close, in which Raduan replies to the complaints of Fatima.

> "Cesad, hermosas estrellas!
> Que es bien que no lloreis mas;
> Que si a mi me llameis piedra,
> En piedras haceis senal." &c.

I am not a novelist, and cannot give my readers, from memory word for word, a song of several dozen lines, which I have heard but once. I desired, however, a copy of the words of the ballad, and Francisca the elder dictated them to me while I wrote them down with a pocket pencil upon the back of a letter from my old friend Mr. Adam Adrian Viellecour. When I had done I read them over, and the young ladies smiled at the bad Castilian which had naturally enough found its way into the lines of the ballad, and good-naturedly corrected it. I then took leave of my hospitable entertainer and his daughters, and was dismissed with abundance of Spanish courtesy. As it was late, they sent a servant to guide me to my lodgings,

which were distant about three miles, and which at that time
of night, and in a country without roads, I should not have
been able to find without such assistance. I have never since
that time seen either Conchita or Francisca, but I have often
met them in my dreams, and heard over again the plaintive
strain of "Diamante falso" with a distinctness that has sometimes awakened me from sleep. In the following lines I have
attempted to transfuse somewhat of its spirit into English
verse.

A MORISCAN ROMANCE

Diamante falso y fingido,
Engastado en pedernal, &c.

False diamond set in flint! proud heart with haughty brow!
The wild beasts of the wilderness have softer hearts than thou:
Thou art fickle as the sea, thou art wandering as the wind,
And the restless ever mounting flame is not more hard to bind.
If the tears I shed were tongues, yet all too few would be,
To tell of all the treachery that thou hast shown to me.
Oh! I could chide thee sharply,—but every maiden knows,
That she who chides her lover, forgives him ere he goes.

Thou hast called me oft the flower of all Granada's maids,
Thou hast said that by the side of me, the first and fairest fades;
And they thought thy heart was mine, and it seemed to every
    one
That what thou didst to win my love, from love of me was done.
Alas! if they but knew thee, as mine it is to know,
They well might see another mark to which thine arrows go;
But thou giv'st me little heed,—for I speak to one who knows
That she who chides her lover, forgives him ere he goes.

It wearies me, mine enemy, that I must weep and bear,
What fills thy heart with triumph, and fills my own with care.
Thou art leagued with those who hate me, and ah! thou know'st
    I feel,
That cruel words as surely kill as sharpest blades of steel.
'Twas the doubt that thou wert false, that wrung my heart with
    pain;

But, now I know thy perfidy, I shall be well again:
I would proclaim thee as thou art,—but every maiden knows
That she who chides her lover, forgives him ere he goes.

Thus Fatima complained to the valiant Raduan,
Where underneath the myrtles Alhambra's fountains ran:
The Moor was inly moved, and blameless as he was,
He took her white hand in his own, and pleaded thus his cause:
Oh, lady, dry those star-like eyes—their dimness does me
          wrong;
If my heart be made of flint, at least, 'twill keep thy image long:
Thou hast uttered cruel words—but I grieve the less for those,
Since she who chides her lover, forgives him ere he goes.
1828   1828

THE INDIAN SPRING

One of the adventures of my life upon which I have since oftenest reflected, and concerning which my imagination is most inclined to dispute the dictates of my reason, happened many years ago, when, quite a young man, I made an excursion into the interior of the state of New-York, and passed a few days in the region whose waters flow into the east branch of the Susquehannah. My readers will easily judge for themselves whether what I am going to relate can be accounted for from natural causes. For my own part, however, so vivid is the impression it has left upon my mind, and so difficult is it with me to distinguish my recollections of it from that of the absolute realities of my life, that I find it the easier belief to ascribe it to a cause above nature.

I think I have elsewhere intimated that I have great sympathy with believers in the supernatural. Theoretically, I am as much a philosopher, and have as little of what is commonly called superstition about me, as most persons of my acquaintance; but the luxury of a little superstition in practice, the strong and active play into which it calls the imagination, the fine thrill it sends through the veins, the alternate gushes of fear and courage that come over us when under its influence, are too agreeable a relief from the dull realities of the material world to be readily given up. My own individual experience also makes me indulgent to those whose credulity in these matters exceeds my own. Is it to be wondered at that the dogmas of philosophy should not gain credit when they have the testimony of our own senses against them? You say that this evidence is often counterfeited by the tricks of fancy, the hallucinations of the nerves, and by our very dreams. You are right—but who shall in all cases distinguish the false experience from the true?

The part of the country of which I am speaking had just been invaded by the footsteps of cultivation. Openings had been made here and there in the great natural forest, log houses had been built, the farmers were gathering in their first crops of tall grass, and the still taller harvests of wheat and rye stood up by the side of the woods in the clearings. It was then the month of June, and I sallied forth from my lodgings at a paltry log tavern to ramble in the woods with a friend of mine who had come with me from New-York. We set out amid the warblings of the birds, scarce waiting for the dew to be dried up from the herbage. I carried a fowling-piece on my shoulder; not that I meant to be the death of any living creature that fine morning, when everything seemed so happy, but because such a visible pretext for a stroll in the woods and fields satisfies at once the curiosity of those whom you meet, and saves you often a world of staring, and sometimes not a few impertinent questions. I hold it right and fair to kill game late in the autumn, when the animal has had his feast of fruits and nuts, and is left with a prospect of a long, hard, uncomfortable winter before him, and the dangers of being starved to death. But to take his life in the spring, or the beginning of summer, when he has so many fine sunny months of frolic and plenty before him—it is gratuitous cruelty, and I have ever religiously abstained from it.

My companion was much more corpulent than I, and as slow a walker as I was a fast one. However, he good-naturedly exerted himself to keep up with me, and I made more than one attempt to moderate my usual speed for his accommodation. The effort worried us both. At length he fairly gave out, and, bringing the butt of his fowling-piece smartly to the ground, stood still, with both hands grasping the muzzle.

"I beg," said he, "that you will go on at your own pace. I promise faithfully not to stir from the spot till you are fairly out of sight."

"But I am very willing to walk slower."

"No," rejoined my friend, "we did not set out together for the purpose of making each other uncomfortable, nor will we, if I can help it. Here we have been fretting and chafing each other for half an hour. Why, it is like yoking an ox with a race-horse. Go on, I beseech you, while I stop to recover my wind. I wish you a pleasant walk of it. I shall expect to see you back at our landlord's at one o'clock."

I took him at his word, and proceeded. I rambled through tall old groves clear of underwood, beside rivulets broken into little pools and cascades by rocks and fallen timber, along the edges of dark, shrubby swamps, and across sunny clearings, until I was tired. At length I came to a pleasant natural glade on the slope of a hill, and sat down under the shade of a tree to rest myself. It was a narrow opening in the woods, extending for some distance up the hill, and terminating in that quarter at the base of a ridge of rocks, above which rose the forest. At the lower end, near which I was, a spring rose up in a little hollow and formed a streamlet, which ran off under the trees. A most still, quiet nook it was, sheltered from all winds; the leaves were not waved, nor the grass bent by a breath of air, and the sun came down between the enclosing trees with so strong a heat that, except in the shade, I felt the warmth of the ground through the soles of my shoes.

As I lay with my head propped on my hand, and my elbow buried in a mass of herbage, my thoughts turned involuntarily upon the ancient inhabitants of these woods. Here, said I to myself, in this very spot, some Indian doubtless fixed his cabin; or haply some little neighborhood, the branch of a larger tribe, nestled in this sylvan enclosure. That circle of moldering timber is probably the remains of the wigwam of the last inhabitant, and that great vine which sprawls over it was probably once supported by its walls and, when they were abandoned and decaying, dragged them to the ground, as many a parasite has done by his credulous benefactor. Here the Indian woman planted her squashes and tended her maize; here the Indian father brought forth his boys to try their bows, and aim their little tomahawks at the trees, teaching—for even in the solemnity of my feelings I could not forbear the pun—teaching

> "The young idea how to shoot."

That spring, which gushes up so brightly and abundantly from the ground, yielding them, when their exercise was over, a beverage never mingled with the liquid poisons of the civilized world, and gave its cresses to season the simple repast. Gradually my imagination became both awed and kindled by these reflections. I felt rebuked by the wild genius of a place familiar for centuries only with the race of red men and hunters, and I almost expected to see some Indian, with his tomahawk and bow, walk up to me and ask me what I did there.

My thoughts were diverted from this subject by my eyes falling upon an earth-newt, as red as fire, crawling lazily and with an almost imperceptible motion over the grass. I yawned by a sort of sympathy with the sluggish creature, and, oppressed with fatigue and heat, for the sun was getting high, loosened my cravat and stretched out my legs to an easier position. All at once I found myself growing drowsy, my eyelids dropping involuntarily, my eyes rolling in their sockets with a laborious attempt to keep themselves open, and the landscape swimming and whirling before me, as if I saw it in a mirror suspended by a loose string and waving in the wind. Once or twice the scene was entirely lost for a moment to my vision, and I perceived that I had actually been asleep. It struck me that I might be better employed than in taking a nap at that time of day, and, accordingly, I rose and walked across the glade until I came to the foot of the rocks at the upper end of it, when I turned to take another look at the pleasant and quiet spot. Judge of my astonishment when I actually beheld, standing by the very circle of rubbish near which I had been reposing, and which I had taken for the remains of a wigwam, an Indian, a real Indian, the very incarnation of the images that had been floating in my fancy. I will not say that I did not spring from the ground when the figure met my eye—so sudden and startling was the shock it gave me. He was not one of that degenerate kind which I had seen in various parts of the country wearing hats, frock-coats, pantaloons, and Dutch blankets, but was dressed in the original garb of his nation. A covering of skin was wrapped about his loins, a mantle of the same was flung loosely over his shoulders, and his legs were bare from the middle of the thigh down to his ornamented moccasins [*sic*]. A single tuft of stiff, black hair on the top of his head, from which the rest was carefully plucked, was mingled with the gaudy plumage of different birds; a bow and a bundle of arrows peeped over his shoulder; a necklace of bears' claws hung down upon his breast; his right hand carried a tomahawk, and the fingers of his left were firmly closed, like those of one whose physical vigor and resoluteness of purpose suffered not the least muscle of his frame to relax for a moment. Notwithstanding the distance at which he stood, and which might be a hundred paces at least, I saw his whole figure, even to the minutest article of dress, with what seemed to me an unnatural distinctness. His countenance had that expression which has been so often remarked upon as peculiar to the aborigines of our country— a settled look of sullenness, sadness, and suspicion, as if when moulded by nature it had been visibly stamped with the presentiment of the decline and disappearance of their race. The features were strongly marked, hard, and stern; high cheek-bones, a broad forehead, an aquiline nose, garnished with an oblong piece of burnished copper; a mouth, somewhat wide, between a parenthesis of furrows, and a bony and fleshless chin. But then his eyes—such eyes I have never seen—distant as they were from me, they seemed close to my own, and to ray out an unpleasant brightness from their depths, like twin stars of evil omen. Their influence unstrung all my sinews, and a gush of sudden and almost suffocating heat came over my whole frame. I averted my look instantly and fixed it upon the feet of the savage, shod with their long moccasons, and standing motionless among the thick weeds; but I could not keep it there. Again my eyes returned upward; again they encountered his, glittering in the midst of that calm, sullen face, and again that oppressive, stifling sensation came over me. It was natural that I should feel an impulse to remove from so unpleasant a neighborhood; I therefore shouldered my fowling-piece, climbed the rock before me, and penetrated into the woods. As I proceeded, the idea took possession of me that I was followed by the Indian, and I walked pretty fast in order to shake it off; but I found this impossible. I had got into a state of fidgety, nervous excitement, and it seemed to me that I felt the rays of those bright, unnatural eyes on my shoulders, my back, my arms, and even my hands, as I flung them back in walking. At length I looked back, and, notwithstanding I half expected to see him, I was scarcely less surprised than at first, when I beheld the same figure, just at the same distance, standing motionless as then, his bright eyes gleaming upon me between the trunks of the trees. A third time I felt that flush of dissolving heat, and a violent sweat broke out all over me. I have heard of the cold, clammy sweat of fear; mine was not of that temperature; it was as the warmest summer rain, warm and free and profuse as the current of brooks in the hottest and moistest season of dog days. I walked on, keeping my sight fixed on the strange apparition. It did not seem to move, and, as I proceeded, gradually diminished by the natural effect of distance until I could scarcely distinguish it among the thick trunks and boughs of the forest. Happening to avert my eyes for a moment, I saw, as I turned again to the spot, that the figure had swiftly and silently gained upon me, and was now at the same distance as when I first beheld it. A clearing lay before me. I saw the sunshine and the grass between the trunks of the trees, and, rushing forward, found myself under the open sky, and felt relieved by a freer air. I looked back, and nothing was to be seen of my pursuer. A small log-house stood in the open space, with a well beside it, and a tall, rude machine of the kind they call a well-sweep leaning over it, loaded with a bucket at one end and a heavy stone at the other. A boy of about twelve years of age was drawing water. The sight of a human habitation, and a habitation of white men, was a welcome one to me; and, tormented as I was with heat and thirst, I rejoiced at the prospect of refreshing myself with a draught of the cool, pure element. Accordingly, I made for the well, and arrived at it just as the boy was pouring the contents of the bucket into a large stone pitcher. "You will give me a taste of the water?" said I to him.

"And welcome," replied the boy, "if you'll drink out of the pitcher, for the mug is broke, and we haven't got any glasses."

I stooped, and, raising the heavy vessel to my lips, took a

copious draught from the brim, where the cold water was yet sparkling with the bubbles raised by pouring it from the bucket. "Your water is very fine," said I, when I had recovered my breath.

"Yes, but not so fine as you'll get at the Indian spring," rejoined he. "That's the best water in all the country—the clearest, the coldest, and the sweetest. Father always sends me to the Indian spring when he wants the best water, when uncle comes up from York, or the minister makes us a visit."

"What is it that you call the Indian spring?" I inquired.

"Oh, I guess you must have passed it, by the way you came. Didn't you see a spring of water, east of a ledge of rocks, in a pretty spot of ground where there were no trees?"

"I believe I saw something of the kind," said I, recollecting the glade in which I had thrown myself to rest shortly before, and its fountain.

"That was the Indian spring; and, if you took notice, you must have seen some old logs and sticks lying in a heap, and a few stones that look as if there had been fire on them. It was thought that an Indian family lived there before the country was settled by our people."

"Are there any Indians in this neighborhood at present?" I inquired, with some eagerness.

"Oh, no, indeed; they are gone to the west'ard, so they say, though I am not big enough to know anything about it. It was before father came into the country—long before. The only Indian I ever saw was Jemmy Sunkum, who came about last summer, selling brooms and begging cider."

"A tall, spare, strong-looking man, was he?" asked I, "dressed in skins, and carrying a bow?" my thoughts naturally recurring to the figure I had just seen.

The boy grinned. "Not much taller than I am, and as fat as a woodchuck; and as for the skins he wore, I never see any but his own through the holes of his trousers, unless it be a squirrel-skin that he carried his tobacco and loose change in. He wore an old hat with the crown torn out, and had lost one of his eyes—they say it was by drinking so much cider. Father swapped an old pair of pantaloons with him for a broom. But I must take this pitcher to father, who is at work in the corn-field yonder; so good-morning to you, sir."

The lad tripped away, whistling, and I sat down on one of the broad, flat stones by the well-side, under the shade of a young tree of the kind commonly called yellow willow, which in a year or two shoots up from a slip of the size of a man's finger into a fine, shapely, overshadowing tree. I laid my hat and gun by my side and wiped my hot and sweaty forehead, upon which the wind, that swayed to and fro the long, flexible, depending branches, breathed with a luxurious coolness.

The Indian I have seen cannot be the one that the boy means, said I to myself, nor probably any other of which the inhabitants know anything. That fine, majestic savage is a very different being from the fat, one-eyed vagabond in the ragged trousers that the lad speaks of. It is probably some ancient inhabitant of the place, returned from the forest of the distant West to visit the scenes of his childhood. But what could he mean by following me in this manner, and why should he keep his eye fixed on me so strangely? As I said this, I looked along the forest I had just quitted, examining it carefully and with an eye sharpened by the excited state of my imagination, to see if I could discover anything of my late pursuer. All was quiet and motionless. I heard the bee as he flew by heavily from the cucumber-flowers in the garden near me, and the hum of the busy wheel from the open windows of the cottage; but face or form of human being I saw not. I replaced my hat on my head and my gun on my shoulder, crossed the clearing, and entered the opposite wood, intending to return home by a kind of circuit, for I did not care again to encounter the savage, whose demeanor was so mysterious.

I had proceeded but a few rods, when, a mingled sensation of uneasiness and curiosity inducing me to look over my shoulder, I started to behold the very figure, whose sight I was endeavoring to avoid, just entering the forest—the same brawny shoulders clad with skins, the same sad, stern, suspicious countenance, the same bright eyes thrilling and scorching me with their light. Again I felt that indescribable sensation of discomfort and heat, and the perspiration, which had ceased to flow while I sat by the well, again gushed forth from every pore. Involuntarily I stopped short. What was this being, and why should he dog my steps in this strange manner? What were his designs, pacific or hostile? and what method should I take to rid myself of his pursuit? I had tried walking away from him without effect; should I now adopt the expedient of walking up to him and asking his business? The thought struck me that, if his designs were malevolent, this step might bring me into danger— he was well armed with a tomahawk and arrows, and who could tell the force and certainty of his aim? This fear, on reflection, I rejected as groundless and unmanly; for what cause had he to seek my life? It was but prudent, however, to prepare myself for the worst that could happen. I therefore examined my priming, and, as I had nothing but small bird-shot with me, I kicked up the dry leaves from the earth under my feet, and, selecting a handful of the smallest, smoothest, and roundest pebbles from among the gravel, put two or three of them into the muzzle, and lodged the rest in my pocket. As I turned, there was that face still, at the very edge of the forest, glaring steadily upon me, and watching my operations with the unchanging, stony, stoical expression of the Indian race. I replaced the piece on my shoulder, and advanced toward it. Scarcely had I gone three paces when it suddenly disappeared behind the huge old trunk of an old buttonwood- or plane-tree, that stood just in the edge of the clearing. I approached the tree; there was no living thing behind it or near it. I looked out into the clearing, and scanned its whole extent for the object of my search, but in vain. There was the cottage, in which the wheel was still humming, and the well with its young willow waving restlessly over it. The clearing was long and narrow, and widened away toward the south, where was a field of Indian corn, in which I could distinguish my friend, the lad who had given me the water, in company with a man who, I suppose, was his father, diligently engaged in hoeing the corn; and at intervals I could hear the click of their hoes against the stones. Nothing else was to be seen, nothing else to be heard. I turned and searched the bushes about me; nothing was there. I looked up into the old plane-tree above my head; the clean and handsomely divided branches, speckled with white, guided my eye far into the very last of their verdurous recesses, but no creature, not even a bird, was to be seen there. Strange as it may seem, I found myself refreshed and cooled by this search, and relieved from the burning and suffocating heat that I felt while the eye of the savage rested upon me. My perplexity was, however, anything but lessened; and I resolved to pursue my way home with as little delay as possible, and spell out, if I could, the mystery at my leisure. Accordingly, I plunged again into the woods, and, after proceeding a little way, began to change my course, in a direction which I judged must bring me to the spot where I had rested in the Indian glade near the spring, from which I doubted not I could find my way home without difficulty. As I proceeded, the heat of the day seemed to grow more and more oppressive. There was shade about me and over my head—thick shade of oak, maple, and walnut—but it seemed to me as if beams of the hottest midsummer sun were beating upon my back and scorching the skin of my neck. I turned my head, and there again stood the Indian, with that eternal, intolerable glare of the eyes. I stopped not, but went on with a quicker pace. My face was flushed, my brow throbbed audibly, my head ached, the veins in my hands were swollen till they looked like ropes, and the sweat dropped from my hair like rain. A fine brook crossed my way, clear as diamond, full to the very brim, and sending up a cool vapor from its surface that promised for the grateful temperature of its waters. I longed to strip off my clothes, and lay myself down in its bed at full length, and steep my burning limbs in its current. Just then I remembered the story of Tam o' Shanter pursued by witches, and saved by crossing a running stream. If there be any witchcraft in this thing, said I to myself, it will not follow me beyond this brook. I was ashamed of the thought as it crossed my mind, but I leaped the brook notwithstanding, and hurried on. Turning afterward to observe the effect of my precaution, I saw the savage standing in the midst of the very current, the bright water flowing round his copper-colored ankles. The sight was as vexatious as it was singular, and did not by any means diminish my haste. A little opening, where the trees had been cut down and the ground sown with European grasses, came in my way, and I entered it. In this spot the red and white clover grew rankly, and blossomed side by side with columbine and cranesbill, the natives of the soil—flowers and verdure the more striking in their beauty for the unsightly and blackened stumps of trees standing thick among them—a sweet, still nook, a perpetual concert of humming-birds and bees, and a thousand beautiful winged insects, for which our common speech has no name, and exhaling from the herbage an almost overpowering stream of fragrance. I no longer saw my pursuer. What could this mean? Was this figure some restless shadow, that could haunt only its ancient wilderness, and was excluded from every spot reclaimed and cultivated by the white man? I took advantage of this respite to wipe my face and forehead; I unbuttoned my waistcoat, took off my cravat and put it in my pocket, threw back the collar of my coat from my shoulders, fanned myself awhile with my hat, and then went on. Soon after I again entered the wood, I perceived with surprise that my tormentor had gained upon me. He was twice as near to me as when I first saw him, and the strange light that seemed to shoot from his eyes was more intense and insufferable than ever. I was in a part of the forest which was thickly strewn with the fallen trunks of trees, wrenched up, as it seemed to me, long ago by some mighty wind. I hastened on, leaping from one to another, occasionally looking back at my pursuer. The air in my face, as I flew forward, seemed as if issuing from the mouth of a furnace. In leaping upon a spot where the earth was moist and soft, one of my shoes remained embedded fast in the soil. It is an old one, said I to myself; I shall be lighter and cooler without it. Immediately the low branch of a tree struck my hat from my head as I rushed onward. No matter, thought I—I will send a boy to look for it in the morning.

As I sprang from a rock my other shoe flew off, and dropped on the ground before me; I caught it up without stopping, and jerked it over my head with all my strength at the savage behind me. When I next looked back, I saw that he had decked himself with my spoils. He had strung both my shoes to his necklace of bears' claws, and had crowded down my hat upon his head over that tuft of long black hair mingled with feathers, the ends of which stood out under the brim in front, forming a wild, grotesque shade to those strangely bright eyes. Still I went on, and, in springing upon a log covered with green moss, and moist and slimy with decay, my foot slipped, and I could only keep from falling by dropping the fowling-piece I carried. I did not stop to pick it up, and the next instant it was upon the shoulder of the Indian, or demon, that chased me. I darted forward, panting, glowing, perspiring, ready to sink to the earth with heat and fatigue, until suddenly I found myself on the edge of that ridge of rocks which rose above the Indian glade, where I had thrown myself to rest under a tree in the morning, before my steps had been dogged by the savage. The whole scene lay beneath my feet, the spring, the ruins of the wigwam, the tree under which I reclined. A single desperate leap took me far down into the glade below me, and a few rapid strides brought me to the very spot where I had been reposing, and where the pressure of my form still remained on the grass. A shrill, wild shout, with which the woods rang in sharp echoes, rose upon the air, and instantly I perceived that my pursuer had leaped also, and was at my side, and had seized me with a strong and sudden grip that shook every fibre of my frame. A strange darkness came over all visible objects, and I sank to the ground.

An interval of insensibility followed, the duration of which I have no means of computing, and from which I was at last aroused by noises near me, and by motions of my body produced by some impulse from without. I opened my eyes on the very spot where I remembered to have reclined in the morning. My hat was off, my hair and clothes were steeped in sweat, my fowling-piece and shoes lay within a few feet of me, but scattered in different directions. My friend, who had accompanied me at the outset of my ramble, was shaking me by the shoulder, bawling my name in my ear, and asking me if I meant to lie there all day. I sat up, and found that the shade of the tree under which I was had shifted many feet from its original place, and that I was lying exposed to the burning beams of the sun. My old acquaintance, the red earth-newt, had made great progress in the grass, having advanced at least a yard from the place where I remembered to have seen him when I was beginning to grow drowsy, before my adventure with the savage. My friend complained that he had been looking for me for more than an hour, and hallooing himself hoarse without effect, and that he was sure we should be late for dinner.

I said nothing to my companion about what had happened until the next day, when I ventured to relate a part of the strange series of real or imaginary circumstances connected with my ramble. He laughed at the earnestness of my manner, and very promptly and flippantly said it was nothing but a dream. My readers may possibly be of the same opinion; and I myself, when in a philosophical mood, incline to this way of accounting for the matter. At other times, however, when I recall to mind the various images and feelings of that time, deeply and distinctly engraved on my memory, I find nothing in them which should lead me to class them with the illusions of sleep, and nothing to distinguish them from the waking experience of my life.

1829   1829

[A LETTER FROM ILLINOIS]

JACKSONVILLE, JUNE 19th, [1832]: I set out, as I wrote you I should do, from this place on Wednesday, the 13th of this month, on a little excursion toward the north. John accompanied me. The first day brought us to Springfield, the capital of Sangamon County, where the land office for this district is kept, and where I was desirous of making some inquiries as to the land in market. Springfield is thirty-five miles east of Jacksonville, situated just on the edge of a large prairie, on ground somewhat more uneven than Jacksonville, but the houses are not so good, a considerable proportion of them being log-cabins, and the whole town having an appearance of dirt and discomfort. The night we spent at a filthy tavern, and the next morning resumed our journey, turning toward the north. The general aspect of Sangamon County is like that of Morgan, except that the prairies are more extensive and more level. We passed over large tracts covered with hazel bushes, among which grew the red lily and the painted cup, a large scarlet flower. We then crossed a region thickly scattered with large trees, principally of black or white oak, at the extremity of which we descended to the bottom-lands of the Sangamon, covered with tall, coarse grass. About seven miles north of Springfield we forded the Sangamon, which rolls its transparent waters through a colonnade of huge button-wood trees and black maples, a variety of the sugar-maple. The immediate edge of the river was muddy, but the bottom was of solid rock, and the water was up to our saddle-skirts. We then mounted to the upland by a ravine, and, proceeding through another tract of scattered oaks, came out again on the open prairie. Having crossed a prairie of seven or eight miles in width, we came to a little patch of strawberries in the grass a little way from the edge of the woodland, where we alighted to gather them. My horse, in attempting to graze, twitched the bridle out of my hand, and, accidentally setting his foot on the rein, became very much frightened. I endeavored to catch him, but could not. He reared and plunged, shook off the saddle-bags which contained my clothing and some other articles, kicked the bags to pieces, and, getting into the wood by which we came, galloped furiously out of sight toward Springfield. I now thought my expedition at an end, and had the comfortable prospect of returning on foot or of adopting the method called "to ride and tie." I picked up the saddle-bags and their contents, and, giving them to John, I took charge of the umbrellas, which had also fallen off, and walked back for two miles under a hot sun, when I was met by a man riding a horse, which I was very glad to discover was the one that had escaped. A foot-passenger, who was coming on from Springfield, had stopped him after he had galloped about four miles, and had taken advantage of the circumstance to treat himself to a ride. I then went back to the strawberries and finished them.

As it was now three o'clock, we went to a neighboring house to get something to eat for ourselves and our horses. An old scarlet-faced Virginian gave our horses some corn, and his tall, prim-looking wife set a table for us with a rasher of bacon, a radish, bread and milk in pewter tumblers. They were Methodists, and appeared to live in a comfortable way, there being two rooms in their house, and in one of them only one bed. A little farther on we forded Salt Creek, a beautiful stream, perfectly clear, and flowing over pebbles and gravel—a rare sight in this country. A small prairie intervenes between this and Sugar Creek, which we also forded, but with better success than two travellers who came after us, who, attempting to cross it in another place, were obliged to swim their horses, and one of them was thrown into the water. At evening we stopped at a log-cabin on the edge of a prairie, the width of which we were told was fifteen miles, and on which there was not a house. The man had nothing for our horses but "a smart chance of pasture," as he called it, in a little spot of ground enclosed from the prairie, and which appeared, when we saw it the next morning, to be closely grazed to the very roots of the herbage. The dwelling was of the most wretched description. It consisted of but one room, about half of which was taken up with beds and cribs, on one of which lay a man sick with a fever, and on another sprawled two or three children, besides several who were asleep on the floor, and all of whom were brown with dirt. In a cavernous fireplace blazed a huge fire, built against an enormous back-log reduced to a glowing coal, and before it the hostess and her daughter were busy cooking a supper for several travellers, who were sitting under a kind of piazza or standing about in the yard. As it was a great deal too hot in the house, and a little too cool and damp in the night air, we endeavored to make the balance even by warming ourselves in the house and cooling ourselves out of doors alternately. About ten o'clock the sweaty hostess gave us our supper, consisting of warm cakes, bacon, coffee, and lettuce, with bacon-grease poured over it. About eleven, preparations were made for repose; the dirty children were picked up from the floor, and a feather bed was pulled out of a corner and spread before the great fire for John and myself, but on our intimating that we did not sleep on feathers, we had a place assigned to us near the door, where we stretched ourselves on our saddle-blankets for the night. The rest of the floor was taken up by the other travellers, with the exception of a small passage left for the sick man to get to the door. The floor of the piazza was also occupied with men wrapped in their blankets. The heat of the fire, the stifling atmosphere, the groans and tossings of the sick man, who got up once in fifteen minutes to take medicine or go to the door, the whimperings of the children, and the offensive odors of the place, prevented us from sleeping, and by four o'clock the next morning we had caught and saddled our horses and were on our journey.

We crossed the fifteen-mile prairie, and nearly three miles beyond came to the Mackinaw, a fine, clear stream (watering Tazewell County), which we forded, and about half a mile beyond came to a house where live a Quaker family of the name of Wilson. Here we got a nice breakfast, which we enjoyed with great relish, and some corn for our horses.

Seven or eight miles farther brought us to Pleasant Grove, a fine tract of country, and ten miles from Wilson's we came to a Mr. Shurtliff's, where we had been advised to stop for the purpose of making some inquiries about the country. Shurtliff lives near the north end of Pleasant Grove, and within four miles of the northern limit of the lands in market. The soil is fertile and well watered, the streams being rather more rapid than in Jacksonville, and the region more than usually healthy. It is within eight miles of Pekin, on the Illinois River, so that it is within convenient distance of a market; there is plenty of stone within a few miles, and saw-mills have been erected on some of the streams. I am strongly inclined to purchase a quarter-section in this place. We were now within two days' ride of Dixon's, where the American army is to be stationed; but, being already much fatigued with our journey, the weather being hot, and our horses, though young and strong, so very lazy and obstinate as to give us constant employment in whipping them to keep them on a gentle trot on the smoothest road, we concluded to proceed no farther. The next morning, therefore, we set out on our return. I should have mentioned that every few miles on our way we fell in with bodies of Illinois militia proceeding to the American camp, or saw where they had encamped for the night. They generally stationed themselves near a stream or a spring on the edge of a wood, and turned their horses to graze on the prairie. Their way was marked by trees barked or girdled, and the road through the uninhabited country was as much beaten and as dusty as the highways on New York Island. Some of the settlers complained that they made war upon the pigs and chickens. They were a hard-looking set of men, unkempt and unshaved, wearing shirts of dark calico, and sometimes calico capotes.*

In returning, we crossed the large prairie, already mentioned, by a newer way and more direct road to Jacksonville. In this direction the prairie was at least twenty-five miles across. In all

---

*One of these militia companies had for its captain a raw youth, in whose quaint and pleasant talk Mr. Bryant was much interested. He learned some years afterward that the name of the youth was Abraham Lincoln. [*Godwin's note.*]

this distance we found but one inhabited house, and one place, about a quarter of a mile from it, at which to water our horses. This house was stationed on the edge of a small wood on an eminence in the midst of the prairie. An old woman was spinning at the door, and a young woman and boy had just left, with some fire, to do the family washing at the watering-place I have just mentioned. Two or three miles farther on we came to another house on the edge of another grove, which appeared to have been built about two years, and which, with the surrounding enclosures, had been abandoned, as I afterward learned, on account of sickness and the want of water. We frequently passed the holes of the prairie-wolf, but saw none of the animals. The green-headed prairie-fly came around our horses whenever we passed a marshy spot of ground, and fastened upon them with the greediness of wolves, almost maddening them. A little before sunset we came to a wood of thinly scattered oaks, which marks the approach to a river in this country, and, descending a steep bluff, came to the moist and rich bottom-lands of the Sangamon. Next we passed through a thick wood of gigantic old elms, sycamores, mulberries, etc., and crossed the Sangamon in a ferry-boat. We had our horses refreshed at the ferry-house, and, proceeding three miles farther, roused up a Kentuckian of the name of Armstrong, who we understood had some corn. The man and his wife made no scruple in getting up to accommodate us. Every house on a great road in this country is a public house, and nobody hesitates to entertain the traveller or accept his money. The woman, who said she was Dutch (High Dutch, probably), bestirred herself to get our supper. We told her we wanted nothing but bread and milk, on which she lamented that she had neither buttermilk nor sour milk; but was answered that we were Yankees, and liked sweet milk best. She baked some cakes of corn-bread and set them before us, with a pitcher of milk and two tumblers. In answer to John, who said something of the custom of the Yankees to eat the bread cut into the milk, she said that she could give us spoons if we were in *yearnest*; but we answered they were quite unnecessary. On my saying that I had lived among the Dutch in New York and elsewhere, she remarked that she reckoned that was the reason why I did not talk like a Yankee. I replied that no doubt living among the Dutch had improved my English. We were early on the way next morning, and about ten o'clock came to Cox's Grove, a place about twenty-five miles from Jacksonville. In looking for a place to feed our horses, I asked for corn at the cabin of an old settler named Wilson, when I saw a fat, dusky-looking woman, barefoot, with six children as dirty as pigs and s[illegible] as bears. She was cleansing one of them and cracking [illegible]n unfortunate insects between her thumb-nails. I was very [illegible]when she told me she had no corn nor oats. At the next [illegible] we found corn, and, seeing a little boy of two years old [illegible]ng about with a clean face, I told John that we should get a [illegible] breakfast. I was right. The young man, whose name was [illegible]t, had a tall young wife in a clean cotton gown, and shoes [illegible] stockings. She baked us some cakes, fried some bacon, and [illegible]le a cup of coffee, which, being put on a clean table-cloth, [illegible] recommended by a good appetite, was swallowed with some [illegible]erness. Yet the poor woman had no teaspoons in the house, [illegible]d but one spoon for every purpose, and this was pewter and had but half the handle. With this implement she dipped up the brown sugar and stirred it in our cups before handing them to us. Short was also from Kentucky, or Kaintucky, as they call it, as indeed was every man whom I saw on my journey, except the Virginian, the Quaker family, who were from Pennsylvania, and Shurtliff, who is from Massachusetts, but who has a Kentucky wife. I forgot to tell you that at Armstrong's we were accommodated for the night after the Kentucky fashion—with a sheet under our persons and a blanket of cotton and wool over them. About nine in the evening we reached Wiswall's, very glad to repose from a journey which had been performed in exceedingly hot weather, on horses which required constant flogging to keep them awake, and during which we had not slept at the rate of more than three hours a night. What I have thought and felt amid these boundless wastes and awful solitudes I shall reserve for the only form of expression in which it can be properly uttered.

1832 1884

LETTERS OF A TRAVELLER

LETTER I. FIRST IMPRESSIONS OF AN AMERICAN IN FRANCE

Paris, *August* 9, 1834.

Since we first landed in France, every step of our jour as
reminded us that we were in an old country. Every th
saw spoke of the past, of an antiquity without limit; every
our eyes rested on the handiwork of those who had been
for ages, and we were in the midst of customs which the
bequeathed to their descendants. The churches were so va
solid, so venerable, and time-eaten; the dwellings so gray, a
such antique architecture, and in the large towns, like Ro
rose so high, and overhung with such quaint projections the
row and cavernous streets; the thatched cots were so mossy
so green with grass! The very hills about them looked scarc
as old, for there was youth in their vegetation—their shrubs a
flowers. The country-women wore such high caps, such long
waists, and such short petticoats!—the fashion of bonnets is an
innovation of yesterday, which they regard with scorn. We
passed females riding on donkeys, the Old Testament beast of
burden, with panniers on each side, as was the custom hundreds
of years since. We saw ancient dames sitting at their doors
with distaffs, twisting the thread by twirling the spindle between
the thumb and finger, as they did in the days of Homer. A
flock of sheep was grazing on the side of a hill; they were
attended by a shepherd, and a brace of prick-eared dogs,
which kept them from straying, as was done thousands of
years ago. Speckled birds were hopping by the sides of the
road; it was the magpie, the bird of ancient fable. Flocks of
what I at first took for the crow of our country were stalking
in the fields, or sailing in the air over the old elms; it was the
rook, the bird made as classical by Addison as his cousin the
raven by the Latin poets.

Then there were the old chateaus on the hills, built with an appearance of military strength, their towers and battlements telling of feudal times. The groves by which they were surrounded were for the most part clipped into regular walls, and pierced with regularly arched passages, leading in various directions, and the trees compelled by the shears to take the shape of obelisks and pyramids, or other fantastic figures, according to the taste of the middle ages. As we drew nearer to Paris, we saw the plant which Noah first committed to the earth after the deluge—you know what that was, I hope—trained on low stakes, and growing thickly and luxuriantly on the slopes by the side of the highway. Here, too, was the tree which was the subject of the first Christian miracle, the fig, its branches heavy with the bursting fruit just beginning to ripen for the market.

But when we entered Paris, and passed the Barrière d'Étoile, with its lofty triumphal arch; when we swept through the arch of Neuilly, and came in front of the Hotel des Invalides, where the aged or maimed soldiers, the living monuments of so many battles, were walking or sitting under the elms of its broad esplanade; when we saw the colossal statues of statesmen and warriors frowning from their pedestals on the bridges which bestride the muddy and narrow channel of the Seine; when we came in sight of the gray pinnacles of the Tuilleries, and the Gothic towers of Notre-Dame, and the Roman ones of St. Sulpice, and the dome of the Pantheon, under which lie the remains of so many of the great men of France, and the dark column of Place Vendôme, wrought with figures in relief, and the obelisk brought from Egypt to ornament the Place Louis Quatorze, the associations with antiquity which the country presents, from being general, became particular and historical. They were recollections of power, and magnificence, and extended empire; of valor and skill in war which had held the world in fear; of dynasties that had risen and passed away; of battles and victories which had left no other fruits than their monuments.

The solemnity of these recollections does not seem to press

with much weight upon the minds of the people. It has been said that the French have become a graver nation than formerly; if so, what must have been their gayety a hundred years ago? To me they seem as light-hearted and as easily amused as if they had done nothing but make love and quiz their priests since the days of Louis XIV—as if their streets had never flowed with the blood of Frenchmen shed by their brethren— as if they had never won and lost a mighty empire. I can not imagine the present generation to be less gay than that which listened to the comedies of Molière at their first representation; particularly when I perceive that even Molière's pieces are too much burdened with thought for a Frenchman of the present day, and that he prefers the lighter and more frivolous vaude-ville. The Parisian has his amusements as regularly as his meals, the theatre, music, the dance, a walk in the Tuilleries, a refection in the café, to which ladies resort as commonly as the other sex. Perpetual business, perpetual labor, is a thing of which he seems to have no idea. I wake in the middle of the night, and I hear the fiddle going, and the sound of feet keeping time, in some of the dependencies of the large building near the Tuilleries, in which I have my lodgings.

When a generation of Frenchmen

"Have played, and laughed, and danced, and drank their
     fill"—

when they have seen their allotted number of vaudevilles and swallowed their destined allowance of weak wine and bottled small-beer, they are swept off to the cemetery of Montmartre, or of Père la Chaise, or some other of the great burial-places which lie just without the city. I went to visit the latter of these the other day. You are reminded of your approach to it by the rows of stone-cutters' shops on each side of the street, with a glittering display of polished marble monuments. The place of the dead is almost a gayer-looking spot than the ordinary haunts of Parisian life. It is traversed with shady walks of elms and limes, and its inmates lie amidst thickets of ornamental shrubs and plantations of the most gaudy flowers. Their monuments are hung with wreaths of artificial flowers, or of those natural ones which do not lose their color and shape in drying, like the amaranth and the everlasting. Parts of the cemetery seem like a city in miniature; the sepulchral chapels, through the windows of which you see crucifixes and tapers, stand close to each other beside the path, intermingled with statues and busts.

There is one part of this repository of the dead which is little visited, that in which the poor are buried, where those who have dwelt apart from their more fortunate fellow-creatures in life lie apart in death. Here are no walks, no shade of trees, no planted shrubbery, but ridges of raw earth, and tufts of coarse herbage show where the bodies are thrown together under a thin

over the spot, but was repelled by the sickening exhalations that rose from it. * * *

1834   1850

From LETTER VII.   AN EXCURSION TO ROCK RIVER

Princeton, Illinois, *June* 21, 1841.

I have just returned from an excursion to Rock River, one of the most beautiful of our western streams.

We left Princeton on the 17th of the month, and after passing a belt of forest which conceals one of the branches of the Bureau River, found ourselves upon the wide, unfenced prairie, spreading away on every side until it met the horizon. Flocks of turtle-doves rose from our path scared at our approach; quails and rabbits were seen running before us; the prairie-squirrel, a little striped animal of the marmot kind, crossed the road; we started plovers by the dozen, and now and then a prairie-hen, which flew off heavily into the grassy wilderness. With these animals the open country is populous, but they have their pursuers and destroyers; not the settlers of the region, for they do not shoot often except at a deer or a wild turkey, or a noxious animal; but the prairie-hawk, the bald-eagle, the mink, and the prairie-wolf, which make merciless havoc among them and their brood.

About fifteen miles we came to Dad Joe's Grove, in the shadow of which, thirteen years ago, a settler named Joe Smith, who had fought in the battle of the Thames, one of the first white inhabitants of this region, seated himself, and planted his corn, and gathered his crops quietly, through the whole Indian war, without being molested by the savages, though he was careful to lead his wife and family to a place of security. As Smith was a settler of such long standing, he was looked to as a kind of patriarch in the county, and to distinguish him from other Joe Smiths, he received the venerable appellation of Dad. He has since removed to another part of the state, but his well-known, hospitable cabin, inhabited by another inmate, is still there, and his grove of tall trees, standing on a ridge amidst the immense savannahs, yet retains his name. As we descended into the prairie we were struck with the novelty and beauty of the prospect which lay before us. The ground sank gradually and gently into a low but immense basin, in the midst of which lies the marshy tract called the Winnebago Swamp. To the northeast the sight was intercepted by a forest in the midst of the basin, but to the northwest the prairies were seen swelling up again in the smoothest slopes to their usual height, and stretching away to a distance so vast that it seemed boldness in the eye to follow them.

The Winnebagoes and other Indian tribes which formerly possessed this country have left few memorials of their existence, except the names of places. Now and then, as at Indian-town, near Princeton, you are shown the holes in the ground where they stored their maize, and sometimes on the borders of the rivers you see the trunks of trees which they felled, evidently hacked by their tomahawks, but perhaps the most remarkable of their remains are the paths across the prairies or beside the large streams, called Indian trails—narrow and well-beaten ways, sometimes a foot in depth, and many of them doubtless trodden for hundreds of years.

As we went down the ridge upon which stands Dad Joe's

Grove, we saw many boulders of rock lying on the surface of the soil of the prairies. The western people, naturally puzzled to tell how they came there, give them the expressive name of "lost rocks." We entered a forest of scattered oaks, and after travelling for half an hour reached the Winnebago Swamp, a tract covered with tall and luxuriant water-grass, which we crossed on a causey built by a settler who keeps a toll-gate, and at the end of the causey we forded a small stream called Winnebago Inlet. Crossing another vast prairie we reached the neighborhood of Dixon, the approach to which was denoted by groves, farm-houses, herds of cattle, and inclosed corn fields, checkering the broad green prairie.

Dixon, named after an ancient settler of the place still living, is a country town situated on a high bank of Rock River. Five years ago two log-cabins only stood on the solitary shore, and now it is a considerable village, with many neat dwellings, a commodious court-house, several places of worship for the good people, and a jail for the rogues, built with a triple wall of massive logs, but I was glad to see that it had no inmate.

Rock River flows through high prairies, and not, like most streams of the West, through an alluvial country. The current is rapid, and the pellucid waters glide over a bottom of sand and pebbles. Its admirers declare that its shores unite the beauties of the Hudson and of the Connecticut. The banks on either side are high and bold; sometimes they are perpendicular precipices, the base of which stands in the running water; sometimes they are steep grassy or rocky bluffs, with a space of dry alluvial land between them and the stream; sometimes they rise by a gradual and easy ascent to the general level of the region, and sometimes this ascent is interrupted by a broad natural terrace. Majestic trees grow solitary or in clumps on the grassy acclivities, or scattered in natural parks along the lower lands upon the river, or in thick groves along the edge of the high country. Back of the bluffs, extends a fine agricultural region, rich prairies with an undulating surface, interspersed with groves. At the foot of the bluffs break forth copious springs of clear water, which hasten in little brooks to the river. In a drive which I took up the left bank of the river, I saw three of these in the space of as many miles. One of these is the spring which supplies the town of Dixon with water; the next is a beautiful fountain rushing out from the rocks in the midst of a clump of trees, as merrily and in as great a hurry as a boy let out of school; the third is so remarkable as to have received a name. It is a little rivulet issuing from a cavern six or seven feet high, and about twenty from the entrance to the further end, at the foot of a perpendicular precipice covered with forest-trees and fringed with bushes.

In the neighborhood of Dixon, a class of emigrants have established themselves, more opulent and more luxurious in their tastes than most of the settlers of the western country. Some of these have built elegant mansions on the left bank of the river, amidst the noble trees which seem to have grown up for that very purpose. Indeed, when I looked at them, I could hardly persuade myself that they had not been planted to overshadow older habitations. From the door of one of these dwellings I surveyed a prospect of exceeding beauty. The windings of the river allowed us a sight of its waters and its beautifully diversified banks to a great distance each way, and in one direction a high prairie region was seen above the woods that fringed the course of this river, of a lighter green than they, and touched with the golden light of the setting sun.

I am told that the character of Rock River is, throughout its course, much as I have described it in the neighborhood of Dixon, that its banks are high and free from marshes, and its waters rapid and clear, from its source in Wisconsin to where it enters the Mississippi amidst rocky islands. What should make its shores unhealthy I can not see, yet they who inhabit them are much subject to intermittent fevers. They tell you very quietly that every body who comes to live there must take a seasoning. I suppose that when this country becomes settled this will no longer be the case. Rock River is not much subject to inundations, nor do its waters become very low in summer. A project is on foot, I am told, to navigate it with steam-vessels of a light draught.

When I arrived at Dixon I was told that the day before a man named Bridge, living at Washington Grove, in Ogle county, came into town and complained that he had received notice from a certain association that he must leave the county before the seventeenth of the month, or that he would be looked upon as a proper subject for Lynch law. He asked for assistance to defend his person and dwelling against the lawless violence of these men. The people of Dixon county came together and passed a resolution to the effect, that they approved fully of what the inhabitants of Ogle county had done, and that they allowed Mr. Bridge the term of four hours to depart from the town of Dixon. He went away immediately, and in great trepidation. This Bridge is a notorious confederate and harborer of horse-thieves and counterfeiters. The thinly-settled portions of Illinois are much exposed to the depredations of horse-thieves, who have a kind of centre of operations in Ogle county, where it is said that they have a justice of the peace and a constable among their own associates, and where they contrive to secure a friend on the jury whenever any one of their number is tried. Trial after trial has taken place, and it has been found impossible to obtain a conviction on the clearest evidence, until last April, when two horse-thieves being on trial, eleven of the jury threatened the twelfth with a taste of the cowskin unless he would bring in a verdict of guilty. He did so, and the men were condemned. Before they were removed to the state-prison, the court-house was burnt down and the jail was in flames, but luckily they were extinguished without the liberation of the prisoners. Such at length became the general feeling of insecurity, that three hundred citizens of Ogle county, as I understand, have formed themselves into a company of volunteers for the purpose of clearing the county of these men. Two horse-thieves have been seized and flogged, and Bridge, their patron, has been ordered to remove or abide the consequences.

As we were returning from Dixon on the morning of the 19th, we heard a kind of humming noise in the grass, which one of the company said proceeded from a rattlesnake. We dismounted and found in fact it was made by a prairie-rattle-snake, which lay coiled around a tuft of herbage, and which we soon dispatched. The Indians call this small variety of the rattlesnake, the Massasauger. Horses are frequently bitten by it and come to the doors of their owners with their heads horribly swelled but they are recovered by the application of hartshorn. A little further on, one of the party raised the cry of wolf, and looking we saw a prairie-wolf in the path before us, a prick-eared animal of a reddish-gray color, standing and gazing at us with great composure. As we approached, he trotted off into the grass, with his nose near the ground, not deigning to hasten his pace for shouts, and shortly afterward we saw two others running in a different direction.

The prairie-wolf is not so formidable an animal as the name of wolf would seem to denote; he is quite as great a coward as robber, but he is exceeding mischievous. He never takes full-grown sheep unless he goes with a strong troop of his friends, but seizes young lambs, carries off sucking-pigs, robs the hen-roost, devours sweet corn in the gardens, and plunders the water-melon patch. A herd of prairie-wolves will enter a field of melons and quarrel about the division of the spoils as fiercely and noisily as so many politicians. It is their way to gnaw a hole immediately into the first melon they lay hold of. If it happens to be ripe, the inside is devoured at once, if not, it is dropped and another is sought out, and a quarrel is picked with the discoverer of a ripe one, and loud and shrill is the barking, and fierce the growling and snapping which is heard on these occasions. It is surprising, I am told, with what dexterity a wolf will make the most of a melon, absorbing every remnant of the pulp, and hollowing it out as clean as it could be scraped by a spoon. This is when the allowance of melons is scarce, but when they are abundant he is as careless and wasteful as a government agent. * * *

1841   1850

From DISCOURSE ON THE LIFE AND GENIUS OF
COOPER

[COOPER AS SOCIAL CRITIC]

✴ ✴ ✴ It happened to Cooper while he was abroad, as it not unfrequently happens to our countrymen, to hear the United States disadvantageously compared with Europe. He had himself been a close observer of things both here and in the old world, and was conscious of being able to refute the detractors of his country in regard to many points. He published in 1828, after he had been two years in Europe, a series of letters, entitled *Notions of the Americans, by a Travelling Bachelor*, in which he gave a favourable account of the working of our institutions, and vindicated his country from various flippant and ill-natured misrepresentations of foreigners. It is rather too measured in style, but is written from a mind full of the subject, and from a memory wonderfully stored with particulars. Although twenty-four years have elapsed since its publication, but little of the vindication has become obsolete.

Cooper loved his country and was proud of her history and her institutions, but it puzzles many that he should have appeared, at different times, as her eulogist and her censor. My friends, she is worthy both of praise and of blame, and Cooper was not the man to shrink from bestowing either, at what seemed to him the proper time. He defended her from detractors abroad; he sought to save her from flatterers at home. I will not say that he was in as good humour with his country when he wrote *Home as Found* as when he wrote his *Notions of the Americans*, but this I will say, that, whether he commended or censured, he did it in the sincerity of his heart, as a true American, and in the belief that it would do good. His *Notions of the Americans* were more likely to lessen than to increase his popularity in Europe, inasmuch as they were put forth without the slightest regard to European prejudices.

273

In 1829 he brought out the novel entitled the *Wept of Wish-ton-Wish*, one of the few of his works which we now rarely hear mentioned. He was engaged in the composition of a third nautical tale, which he afterward published under the name of *The Water-Witch*, when the memorable revolution of the Three Days of July broke out. He saw a government, ruling by fear and in defiance of public opinion, overthrown in a few hours, with little bloodshed; he saw the French nation, far from being intoxicated with their new liberty, peacefully addressing themselves to the discussion of the institutions under which they were to live. A work which Cooper afterward published, his *Residence in Europe*, gives the outline of a plan of government for France, furnished by him at that time to La Fayette, with whom he was then on habits of close and daily intimacy. It was his idea to give permanence to the new order of things by associating two strong parties in its support, the friends of legitimacy and the republicans. He suggested that Henry V. should be called to the hereditary throne of France, a youth yet to be educated as the head of a free people, that the peerage should be abolished, and a legislature of two chambers established, with a constituency of at least a million and a half of electors; the senate to be chosen by the general vote, as the representatives of the entire nation, and the members of the other house to be chosen by districts, as the representatives of the local interests. To the middle ground of politics so ostentatiously occupied by Louis Philippe at the beginning of his reign, he predicted a brief duration, believing that it would speedily be merged in despotism, or supplanted by the popular rule. His prophecy has been fulfilled more amply than he could have imagined—fulfilled in both its alternatives.

In one of the controversies of that time, Cooper bore a distinguished part. The *Révue Britannique*, a periodical published in Paris, boldly affirmed the government of the United States to be one of the most expensive in the world, and its people among the most heavily taxed of mankind. This assertion was supported with a certain show of proof, and the writer affected to have established the conclusion that a republic must necessarily be more expensive than a monarchy. The partisans of the court were delighted with the reasoning of the article, and claimed a triumph over our ancient friend La Fayette, who, during forty years, had not ceased to hold up the government of the United States as the cheapest in the world. At the suggestion of La Fayette, Cooper replied to this attack upon his country, in a letter which was translated into French, and together with another from General Bertrand, for many years a resident in America, was laid before the people of France.

These two letters provoked a shower of rejoinders, in which, according to Cooper, misstatements were mingled with scurrility. He commenced a series of letters on the question in dispute, which were published in the *National*, a daily sheet, and gave the first evidence of that extraordinary acuteness in controversy, which was no less characteristic of his mind than the vigour of his imagination. The enemies of La Fayette pressed into service Mr. Leavitt Harris, of New Jersey, afterward our *chargé d'affaires* at the court of France, but Cooper replied to Mr. Harris, in the *National* of May 2d, 1832, closing a discussion in which he had effectually silenced those who objected to our institutions on the score of economy. Of these letters, which would form an important chapter in political science, no entire copy, I have been told, is to be found in this country.

One of the consequences of earnest controversy is almost invariably personal ill-will. Cooper was told by one who held an official station under the French government, that the part he had taken in this dispute concerning taxation, would neither be forgotten nor forgiven. The dislike he had incurred in that quarter was strengthened by his novel of the *Bravo*, published in the year 1831, while he was in the midst of his quarrel with the aristocratic party. In that work, of which he has himself justly said, that it was thoroughly American, in all that belonged to it, his object was to show how institutions, professedly created to prevent violence and wrong, become, when perverted from their natural destination, the instruments of injustice, and how, in every system which makes power the exclusive property of the strong, the weak are sure to be oppressed. The work is written with all the vigour and spirit of his best novels; the magnificent city of Venice, in which the scene of the story is laid, stands continually before the imagination; and from time to time the gorgeous ceremonies of the Venetian republic pass under our eyes, such as the marriage of the Doge with the Adriatic, and the contest of the gondolas for the prize of speed. The Bravo himself and several of the other characters are strongly conceived and distinguished, but the most remarkable of them all is the spirited and generous-hearted daughter of the jailer.

It has been said by some critics, who judge of Cooper by his failures, that he had no skill in drawing female characters. By the same process it might, I suppose, be shown that Raphael was but an ordinary painter. It must be admitted that when Cooper drew a lady of high breeding, he was apt to pay too much attention to the formal part of her character, and to make her a mere bundle of cold proprieties. But when he places his heroines in some situation in life which leaves him nothing to do but to make them natural and true, I know of nothing finer, nothing more attractive or more individual than the portraitures he has given us.

Figaro, the wittiest of the French periodicals, and at that time on the liberal side, commended the *Bravo*; the journals on the side of the government censured it. *Figaro* afterward passed into the hands of the aristocratic party, and Cooper became the object of its attacks. He was not, however, a man to be driven from any purpose which he had formed, either by flattery or abuse, and both were tried with equal ill success. In 1832 he published his *Heidenmauer*, and in 1833 his *Headsman of Berne*, both with a political design similar to that of the *Bravo*, though neither of them takes the same high rank among his works.

In 1833, after a residence of seven years in different parts of Europe, but mostly in France, Cooper returned to his native country. The welcome which met him here was somewhat chilled by the effect of the attacks made upon him in France; and remembering with what zeal, and at what sacrifice of the universal acceptance which his works would otherwise have met, he had maintained the cause of his country against the wits and orators of the court party in France, we cannot wonder that he should have felt this coldness as undeserved. He published, shortly after his arrival in this country, *A Letter to his Countrymen*, in which he complained of the censures cast upon him in the American newspapers, gave a history of the part he had taken in exposing the misstatements of the *Révue Britannique*, and warned his countrymen against the too common error of resorting, with a blind deference, to foreign authorities, often swayed by national or political prejudices, for our opinions of American authors. Going beyond this topic, he examined and reprehended the habit of applying to the interpretation of our own constitution maxims derived from the practice of other governments, particularly that of Great Britain. The importance of construing that instrument by its own principles, he illustrated by considering several points in dispute between the parties of the day, on which he gave very decided opinions.

The principal effect of this pamphlet, as it seemed to me, was to awaken in certain quarters a kind of resentment that a successful writer of fiction should presume to give lessons in politics. I meddle not here with the conclusions to which he arrived, though I must be allowed to say that they were stated and argued with great ability. In 1835 Cooper published *The Monikins*, a satirical work, partly with a political aim; and in the same year appeared his *American Democrat*, a view of the civil and social relations of the United States, discussing more gravely various topics touched upon in the former work, and pointing out in what respects he deemed the American people in their practice to have fallen short of the excellence of their institutions.

He found time, however, for a more genial task, that of giving to the world his observations on foreign countries. In 1836 appeared his *Sketches of Switzerland*, a series of letters in four volumes, the second part published about two months after the first, a delightful work, written in a more fluent and flexible style than his *Notions of the Americans*. The first part of *Gleanings in Europe*, giving an account of his residence in France, followed in the same year, and the second part of the same work, containing his observations on England, was published in April, 1837. In these works, forming a series of eight volumes, he relates and describes with much of the same distinctness as in his novels; and his remarks on the manners and institutions of the different countries, often sagacious, and always peculiarly his own, derive, from their frequent reference to contemporary events, an historical interest.

In 1838 appeared *Homeward Bound* and *Home as Found*, two satirical novels, in which Cooper held up to ridicule a certain class of conductors of the newspaper press in America. These works had not the good fortune to become popular. Cooper did not, and, because he was too deeply in earnest, perhaps would not, infuse into his satirical works that gayety without which satire becomes wearisome. I believe, however, that if they had been written by any body else, they would have met with more favour; but the world knew that Cooper was able to give them something better, and would not be satisfied with any thing short of his best. Some childishly imagined that because, in the two works I have just mentioned, a newspaper editor is introduced, in whose character almost every possible vice of his profession is made to find a place, Cooper intended an indiscriminate attack upon the whole body of writers for the newspaper press, forgetting that such a portraiture was a satire only on those to whom it bore a likeness. We have become less sensitive and more reasonable of late, and the monthly periodicals make sport for their readers of the follies and ignorance of the newspaper editors, without awakening the slightest resentment; but Cooper led the way in this sort of discipline, and I remember some instances of towering indignation at his audacity expressed in the journals of that time. * * *

Scarce any thing in Cooper's life was so remarkable, or so strikingly illustrated his character, as his contest with the newspaper press. He engaged in it after provocations, many and long endured, and prosecuted it through years with great energy, perseverance, and practical dexterity, till he was left master of the field. In what I am about to say of it, I hope I shall not give offence to any one, as I shall speak without the slightest malevolence towards those with whom he waged this controversy. Over some of them, as over their renowned adversary, the grave has now closed. Yet where shall the truth be spoken, if not beside the grave?

I have already alluded to the principal causes which provoked the newspaper attacks upon Cooper. If he had never meddled with questions of government on either side of the Atlantic, and never satirized the newspaper press, I have little doubt that he would have been spared these attacks. I cannot, however, ascribe them all, or even the greater part of them, to personal malignity. One journal followed the example of another, with little reflection, I think, in most cases, till it became a sort of fashion, not merely to decry his works, but to arraign his motives.

It is related that, in 1832, while he was at Paris, an article was shown him in an American newspaper, purporting to be a criticism on one of his works, but reflecting with much asperity on his personal character. "I care nothing," he is reported to have said, "for the criticism, but I am not indifferent to the slander. If these attacks on my character should be kept up five years after my return to America, I shall resort to the New York courts for protection." He gave the newspaper press of this state the full period of forbearance on which he had fixed, but, finding that forbearance seemed to encourage assault, he sought redress in the courts of law.

When these litigations were first begun, I recollect it seemed to me that Cooper had taken a step which would give him a great deal of trouble, and effect but little good. I said to myself—

"Alas! Leviathan is not so tamed!"

As he proceeded, however, I saw that he had understood the matter better than I. He put a hook into the nose of this huge monster, wallowing in his inky pool and bespattering the passers-by; he dragged him to the land and made him tractable. One suit followed another; one editor was sued, I think, half-a-dozen times; some of them found themselves under a second indictment before the first was tried. In vindicating himself to his readers, against the charge of publishing one libel, the angry journalist often floundered into another. The occasions of these prosecutions seem to have been always carefully considered, for Cooper was almost uniformly successful in obtaining verdicts. In a letter of his, written in February, 1843, about five years, I think, from the commencement of the first prosecutions, he says: "I have beaten every man I have sued, who has not retracted his libels."

In one of these suits, commenced against the late William L. Stone, of the *Commercial Advertiser*, and referred to the arbitration of three distinguished lawyers, he argued, himself, the question of the authenticity of his account of the battle of Lake Erie, which was the matter in dispute. I listened to his opening; it was clear, skilful, and persuasive, but his closing argument was said to be splendidly eloquent. "I have heard nothing like it," said a barrister to me, "since the days of Emmet."

Cooper behaved liberally towards his antagonists, so far as pecuniary damages were concerned, though some of them wholly escaped their payment by bankruptcy. After, I believe, about six years of litigation, the newspaper press gradually subsided into a pacific disposition towards its adversary, and the contest closed with the account of pecuniary profit and loss, so far as he was concerned, nearly balanced. The occasion of these suits was far from honourable to those who provoked them, but the result was, I had almost said, creditable to all parties; to him, as the courageous prosecutor, to the administration of justice in this country, and to the docility of the newspaper press, which he had disciplined into good manners.

* * *

Before the appearance of his *Jack Tier*, Cooper published, in 1845 and the following year, a series of novels relating to the Anti-rent question, in which he took great interest. He thought that the disposition, manifested in certain quarters, to make concessions to what he deemed a denial of the rights of property, was a first step in a most dangerous path. To discourage this disposition, he wrote *Satanstoe, The Chainbearer*, and *The Redskins*. They are didactic in their design, and want the freedom of invention which belongs to Cooper's best novels; but if they had been written by any body but Cooper—by a member of Congress, for example, or an eminent politician of any class,—they would have made his reputation. It was said, I am told, by a distinguished jurist of our state, that they entitled the author to as high a place in law as his other works had won for him in literature. * * *

[THE MAN AND THE AUTHOR]

Of his failings I have said little; such as he had were obvious to all the world; they lay on the surface of his character; those who knew him least made the most account of them. With a character so made up of positive qualities—a character so independent and uncompromising, and with a sensitiveness far more acute than he was willing to acknowledge, it is not surprising that occasions frequently arose to bring him, sometimes into friendly collision, and sometimes into graver disagreements and misunderstandings with his fellow-men. For his infirmities, his friends found an ample counterpoise in the generous sincerity of his nature. He never thought of disguising his opinions, and he abhorred all disguise in others; he did not even deign to use that show of regard towards those of whom he did not think well, which the world tolerates, and almost demands. A manly expression of opinion, however different from his own, commanded his respect. Of his own works, he spoke with the same freedom as of the works of others; and never hesitated to express his judgment of a book for the reason that it was written by himself; yet he could bear with gentleness any dissent from the estimate he placed on his own writings. His character was like the bark of the cinnamon, a rough and astringent rind without, and an intense sweetness within. Those who penetrated below the surface found a genial temper, warm affections, and a heart with ample place for his friends, their pursuits, their good name, their welfare. They found him a philanthropist, though not precisely after the fashion of the day; a religious man, most devout where devotion is most apt to be a feeling rather than a custom, in the household circle; hospitable, and to the extent of his means, liberal-handed in acts of charity. They found, also, that though in general he would as soon have thought of giving up an old friend as of giving up an opinion, he was not proof against testimony, and could part with a mistaken opinion as one parts with an old friend who has been proved faithless and unworthy. In short, Cooper was one of those who, to be loved, must be intimately known.

Of his literary character I have spoken largely in the narrative of his life, but there are yet one or two remarks which must be made to do it justice. In that way of writing in which he excelled, it seems to me that he united, in a pre-eminent degree, those qualities which enabled him to interest the largest number of readers. He wrote not for the fastidious, the over-refined, the morbidly delicate; for these find in his genius something too robust for their liking—something by which their sensibilities are too rudely shaken; but he wrote for mankind at large—for men and women in the ordinary healthful state of feeling—and in their admiration he found his reward. It is for this class that public libraries are obliged to provide themselves with an extraordinary number of copies of his works: the number in the Mercantile Library, in this city, I am told, is forty. Hence it is, that he has earned a fame wider, I think, than any author of modern times—wider, certainly, than any author, of any age, ever enjoyed in his lifetime. All his excellences are translatable—they pass readily into languages the least allied in their genius to that in which he wrote, and in them he touches the heart and kindles the imagination with the same power as in the original English.

Cooper was not wholly without humour; it is sometimes

found lurking in the dialogue of Harvey Birch, and of Leather-stocking; but it forms no considerable element in his works; and, if it did, it would have stood in the way of his universal popularity, since, of all qualities, it is the most difficult to trans-fuse into a foreign language. Nor did the effect he produced upon the reader depend on any grace of style which would escape a translator of ordinary skill. With his style, it is true, he took great pains, and in his earlier works, I am told, some-times altered the proofs sent from the printer so largely that they might be said to be written over. Yet he attained no special felicity, variety, or compass of expression. His style, however, answered his purpose; it has defects, but it is manly and clear, and stamps on the mind of the reader the impression he desired to convey. I am not sure that some of the very defects of Cooper's novels do not add, by a certain force of contrast, to their power over the mind. He is long in getting at the interest of his narrative. The progress of the plot, at first, is like that of one of his own vessels of war, slowly, heavily, and even awkwardly working out of a harbour. We are impatient and weary, but when the vessel is once in the open sea, and feels the free breath of heaven in her full sheets, our delight and admiration are all the greater at the grace, the majesty and power with which she divides and bears down the waves, and pursues her course, at will, over the great waste of waters. * * *

1852   1852

From LETTER X.   BURGOS—THE CARTUJA—A BULL
FIGHT

MADRID, *November 1st,* 1857

In our way to the *Cartuja* we soon turned aside into a road
still more wretchedly uneven than the one which had led us to
Las Huelgas. After half an hour of severe jolting it took us
through a massive gateway, by which the possessions of the
convent were once entered; but the rest of the enclosure has
entirely disappeared. Half a mile from this, we stopped at an
imposing Gothic edifice on a hill. This was the convent, and
we turned to look at the extensive view it commanded—the
view of a broad, smooth vale, stretching league beyond league
—of the brown color of the soil, without trees and without
houses, except a village to the right, and the city of Burgos to
the left. "You should see it in early summer," said Don Pedro,
"when it is luxuriant with vegetation." A ragged fellow conducted us into the building, where we passed through long,
beautiful, silent cloisters, from the roof of which, in places,
the fresco flowers and stars were falling in small flakes, till we
reached the chapel, and here a priest, who was already occupied
with a French artist and his lady, took charge of us. From the
chapel and the other rooms, all the fine pictures have been
carried away, and we were shown in their stead what were not
worth looking at—some wretched things by a monastic
brother. But what most attract and repay the attention of the
visitor, are the monuments of the father and mother of Isabella
the Catholic, and of her youthful brother, quaintly and delicately carved in alabaster, with a singular combination of grace
and grotesqueness—the grace always predominating—in
which twining stems, foliage and flowers, figures of quadrupeds
and birds, of men and women, and, among these, warriors,
patriarchs and evangelists, all exquisitely and airily wrought,

are clustered together in marvellous and endless complication.

One of the cells of the Carthusian monks was shown us—a little chamber, with a plank bed on which he slept, covered only with his brown cloak. Opening from it was the little garden, with its separate wall, which he tilled alone; and on another side, the little oratory, where he knelt and prayed. "Here," said Don Pedro, pointing to a little opening from the cell to the cloister, "is the window through which the friar received his meals, to be eaten in solitude." As we were about to go out, I said to Don Pedro, "Is it the custom to give a fee here?" "No;" he replied, with some quickness, "not by any means." I could not help suspecting, however, that there was something in the rules of Spanish politeness which dictated this answer, for at that moment we passed into the *Campo Santo*, or burial-ground of the convent—a spacious area enclosed by the building, spotted with little hillocks, where the monks in utter silence dug their own graves, and Don Pedro said, "You see that part of the ground has been dug up and sown with grain. The ecclesiastics who take care of the building do this to piece out a scanty livelihood, for the government only allows them a *peseta*, the fifth part of a dollar, a day." The graves had no monuments, but close to the newest of them, where the earth had still a broken appearance, stood an iron cross, with the lower end driven into the ground. As we stepped from the burial-ground into the cloisters, and the priest locked the door after us, I put a trifle into his hand, which he received with an air that showed he expected it.

That afternoon, at the special urgency of Don Pedro—for I wished to postpone the spectacle till I should arrive at Madrid —I went with one of our party to a bull fight. "This is the last day," said our Spanish friend; "to-morrow the amphitheatre will be removed, every plank of it, and we shall have no more combats for a year." We found the place, which they told us was capable of containing six thousand persons, already full of people impatiently drumming with their feet, to hint that it was high time for the sport to begin. Nine-tenths or more of them were of the laboring class, and their bright-colored costumes, particularly those of the women, gave the crowd a gay appearance. Many children of various ages were among them, and some of these, showily dressed and attended by nurses, were evidently of opulent families. We took our places in the uppermost circle, under a narrow sort of roof which sheltered us from the sun; below us was range after range of seats open to the sky, descending to the central circle, the arena, in which the combats were to take place.

An alguazil, in black, first rode round the arena, proclaiming the regulations of the day. He was followed by a procession of the performers, in their gay dresses; the *picadores*, glittering with gold and silver lace, on horseback, with their broad-brimmed hats and long lances; the *chulos* on foot, with their red cloaks; the *banderilleros*, with their barbed shafts, wrapped in strips of white paper; the *matadores*, with their swords; and lastly, three mules, gayly caparisoned, with strings of little bells on their necks, who were to drag out the slain bulls. Loud shouts rose from the crowd, and then a door was opened, and an enormous bull, jet black, with massive chest and glaring eyes, bounded into the arena. He ran first at the *chulos*, who shook their cloaks at him, but his rage appeared soon to sub-side. A *picador* put his lance against the animal's forehead, but he shook it off and turned away. The *chulos* again came capering about him and trying to provoke him, but he pursued them only a few steps. Then rose the cry of, *Ah, que es manso! que es manso! cobarde! cobarde!** Finally, the people began to call for the dogs. *Los perros! los perros!* rose from a thousand throats. Three large dogs were brought, which, barking loudly, flew at the bull with great fury. He took them one after another on his horns, and threw them up in the air; one of them he caught in his fall, and tossed him again. The dogs tore his ears into strings, but they were soon either disabled or cowed, and only attacked him warily, while he kept them off by pre-senting to them first one horn and then the other. Then the

* "Ah, how tame he is! how tame he is! a coward! a coward!" [*Bryant's note.*]

dogs were withdrawn and the *chulos* tried him again, but he would not chase them far; the *picadores* poked at him with their lances, but he declined to gore their horses. The crowd shouted vigorously, "Away with him! away with him!" and at length the door by which the bull had entered was set wide open, that he might make his retreat. But the bull would not go; he was not minded either to fight or quit the field. "Kill him! kill him!" exclaimed a thousand throats—and the signal was given, in obedience to which one of the *matadores*—the *primera espada*, as the Spaniards call him, just as the Italians say *prima donna*—made his appearance with a red cloak on his arm, and a long, glittering, straight sword in his right hand. He shook the cloak at the bull, who made a rush at it, while the *matador* at the same moment attempted to pierce the animal to the heart through the chine. Three times he sought to make the fatal pass; at the third he was successful, burying the blade up to the hilt. A torrent of blood flowed from the creature's mouth, he staggered and fell; a sound of little bells was heard; the three mules, harnessed abreast, came in, and dragged out the lifeless carcase.

Another bull, of smaller size, but of more savage temper, was then let into the arena. He ran fiercely at the *chulos*, chasing them into the places of shelter built for them beside the barrier, and the crowd shouted, "*Es muy bravo, ese! muy bravo!*"* A *picador* touched with his lance the forehead of the animal, who instantly rushed towards him, raised with his horns the horse he rode, and laid him on the ground, ripping open his bowels. I then perceived, with a sort of horror, that the horse had been blindfolded, in order that he might not get out of the way of the bull. The *chulos* came up with their red cloaks, and diverted the attention of the bull from his victim, while the *picador*, who had fallen under his horse, was assisted to rise. Four other horses were brought forth blindfolded in this manner, and their lives put between the *picador* and the fury of the bull, and each was killed in its turn, amidst the shouts and applauses of the crowd.

* "He is very fierce, that fellow, very fierce!" [*Bryant's note.*]

One of the *banderilleros* now came forward, provoked the bull to rush at him, by shaking his cloak before his eyes, and leaping aside, planted one of his barbed shafts with its paper streamers, in each of the animal's shoulders. Others followed his example, till the bleeding shoulders of the bull were garnished with five or six *banderillas* on each side. The creature, however, was evidently becoming tired, and signal was given to finish him; a *matador* came forward and planted a sword in his heart, but he made a violent effort to keep his legs, and even while falling, seemed disposed to rush at the *chulos*.

I had now seen enough, and left the place amidst the thunders of applause which the creature's fall drew from the crowd. I heard that afterwards three more bulls and six horses were killed, and that an addition had been made to the usual entertainments of the *plaza*, with which the people were not well pleased. A class of combatants appeared, called *pegadores*, who literally took the bull by the horns, allowing him to toss them in the air, and one of them was much hurt by his fall. "It is a Portuguese innovation," said my friend Don Pedro, rather innocently, as it seemed to me, "and it is a horrible sight for us Spaniards. We do not like to see a man tossed like a dog."

* * *

1857   1859

From *A DISCOURSE ON THE LIFE, CHARACTER AND GENIUS OF WASHINGTON IRVING*

[*SALMAGUNDI* TO *THE SKETCH BOOK*]

When "Salmagundi" appeared, the quaint old Dutch town in which Irving was born had become transformed to a comparatively gay metropolis. Its population of twenty thousand souls had enlarged to more than eighty thousand, although its aristocratic class had yet their residences in what seems now to us the narrow space between the Battery and Wall street. The modes and fashions of Europe were imported fresh and fresh. "Salmagundi" speaks of leather breeches as all the rage for a morning dress, and flesh-colored smalls for an evening party. Gay equipages dashed through the streets. A new theatre had risen in Park Row, on the boards of which Cooper, one of the finest of declaimers, was performing to crowded houses. The churches had multiplied faster than the places of amusement; other public buildings of a magnificence hitherto unknown, including our present City Hall, had been erected; Tammany Hall, fresh from the hands of the builder, overlooked the Park. We began to affect a taste for pictures, and the rooms of Michael Paff, the famous German picture dealer in Broadway, were a favorite lounge for such connoisseurs as we then had, who amused themselves with making him talk of Michael Angelo. Ballston Springs were the great fashionable watering-place of the country, to which resorted the planters of the South with splendid equipages and troops of shining blacks in livery.

"Salmagundi" satirized the follies and ridiculed the humors of the time with great prodigality of wit and no less exuberance of good nature. In form it resembles the "Tatler," and that numerous brood of periodical papers to which the success of the "Tatler" and "Spectator" gave birth; but it is in no sense an imitation. Its gayety is its own; its style of humor is not that of Addison nor Goldsmith, though it has all the genial spirit of theirs; nor is it borrowed from any other writer. It is far more frolicsome and joyous, yet tempered by a native gracefulness. "Salmagundi" was manifestly written without the fear of criticism before the eyes of the authors, and to this sense of perfect freedom in the exercise of their genius the charm is probably owing which makes us still read it with so much delight. Irving never seemed to place much value on the part he contributed to this work, yet I doubt whether he ever excelled some of those papers in "Salmagundi" which bear the most evident marks of his style, and Paulding, though he has since acquired a reputation by his other writings, can hardly be said to have written anything better than the best of those which are ascribed to his pen.

Just before "Salmagundi" appeared, several of the authors who gave the literature of England its present character had begun to write. For five years the quarterly issues of the "Edinburgh Review," then in the most brilliant period of its existence, had been before the public. Hazlitt had taken his place among the authors, and John Foster had published his essays. Of the poets, Rogers, Campbell and Moore were beginning to be popular; Wordsworth had published his "Lyrical Ballads," Scott, his "Lay of the Last Minstrel," Southey, his "Madoc," and Joanna Baillie, two volumes of her plays. In this revival of the creative power in literature it is pleasant to see that our own country took part, contributing a work of a character as fresh and original as any they produced on the other side of the Atlantic.

Nearly two years afterward, in the autumn of 1809, appeared in the "Evening Post," addressed to the humane, an advertisement requesting information concerning a small elderly gentleman named Knickerbocker, dressed in a black coat and cocked hat, who had suddenly left his lodgings at the Columbian Hotel in Mulberry street, and had not been heard of afterward. In the beginning of November, a "Traveller" communicated to the same journal the information that he had seen a person answering to this description, apparently fatigued with his journey, resting by the road-side a little north of Kingsbridge.

Ten days later Seth Handaside, the landlord of the Columbian Hotel, gave notice, through the same journal, that he had found in the missing gentleman's chamber "a curious kind of written book," which he should print by way of reimbursing himself for what his lodger owed him. In December following, Inskeep and Bradford, booksellers, published "Diedrich Knickerbocker's History of New York."

"Salmagundi" had prepared the public to receive this work with favor, and Seth Handaside had no reason to regret having undertaken its publication. I recollect well its early and immediate popularity. I was then a youth in college, and having committed to memory a portion of it to repeat as a declamation before my class, I was so overcome with laughter, when I appeared on the floor, that I was unable to proceed, and drew upon myself the rebuke of the tutor.

I have just read this "History of New York" over again, and I found myself no less delighted than when I first turned its pages in my early youth. When I compare it with other works of wit and humor of a similar length, I find that, unlike most of them, it carries forward the reader to the conclusion without weariness or satiety, so unsought, spontaneous, self-suggested are the wit and the humor. The author makes us laugh, because he can no more help it than we can help laughing. Scott, in one of his letters, compared the humor of this work to that of Swift. The rich vein of Irving's mirth is of a quality quite distinct from the dry drollery of Swift, but they have this in common, that they charm by the utter absence of effort, and this was probably the ground of Scott's remark. A critic in the "London Quarterly," some years after its appearance, spoke of it as a "tantalizing book," on account of his inability to understand what he called "the point of many of the allusions in this political satire." I fear he must have been one of those respectable persons who find it difficult to understand a joke unless it be accompanied with a commentary opening and explaining it to the humblest capacity. Scott found no such difficulty. "Our sides," he says, in a letter to Mr. Brevoort, a friend of Irving, written just after he had read the book, "are absolutely sore with laughing." The mirth of the "History of New York" is of the most transparent sort, and the author, even in the later editions, judiciously abstained from any attempt to make it more intelligible by notes.

I find in this work more manifest traces than in his other writings of what Irving owed to the earlier authors in our language. The quaint poetic coloring and often the phraseology, betray the disciple of Chaucer and Spenser. We are conscious of a flavor of the olden time, as of a racy wine of some rich vintage—

"Cooled a long age in the deep-delvèd earth."

I will not say that there are no passages in this work which are not worthy of their context; that we do not sometimes meet with phraseology which we could wish changed; that the wit does not sometimes run wild and drop here and there a jest which we could willingly spare. We forgive, we overlook, we forget all this as we read, in consideration of the entertainment we have enjoyed, and of that which beckons us onward in the next page. Of all mock-heroic works, "Knickerbocker's History of New York" is the gayest, the airiest, and the least tiresome.

In 1848 Mr. Irving issued an edition of this work, to which he prefixed what he called an "Apology," intended in part as an answer to those who thought he had made too free with the names of our old Dutch families. To speak frankly, I do not much wonder that the descendants of the original founders of New Amsterdam should have hardly known whether to laugh or look grave on finding the names of their ancestors, of whom they never thought but with respect, now connected with ludicrous associations, by a wit of another race. In one of his excellent historical discourses Mr. Verplanck had gently complained of this freedom, expressing himself, as he said, more in sorrow than in anger. Even the sorrow, I believe, must have long since wholly passed away, when it is seen how little Irving's pleasantries have detracted from the honor paid to the early history of our city—at all events, I do not see how it could survive Irving's good-humored and graceful "Apology."

It was not long after the publication of the "History of New York" that Irving abandoned the profession of law, for which he had so decided a distaste as never to have fully tried his capacity for pursuing it. Two of his brothers were engaged in commerce, and they received him as a silent partner. He did not, however, renounce his literary occupations. He wrote, in 1810, a memoir of Campbell, the poet, prefaced to an edition of the writings of that author, which appeared in Philadelphia; and in 1813 and the following year, employed himself as editor of the "Analectic Magazine," published in the same city, making the experiment of his talent for a vocation to which men of decided literary tastes in this country are strongly inclined to betake themselves. Those who remember this magazine cannot have forgotten that it was a most entertaining miscellany, partly compiled from English publications, mostly periodicals, and partly made up of contributions of some of our own best writers. Paulding wrote for it a series of biographical accounts of the naval commanders of the United States, which added greatly to its popularity; and Verplanck contributed memoirs of Commodore Stewart and General Scott, Barlow, the poet, and other distinguished Americans, which were received with favor. "The Life of Campbell," with the exception, perhaps, of some less important contributions to the magazine, is the only published work of Irving between the appearance of the "History of New York," in 1809, and that of the "Sketch Book," in 1819.

It was during this interval that an event took place which had a marked influence on Irving's future life, affected the character of his writings, and, now that the death of both parties allows it to be spoken of without reserve, gives a peculiar interest to his personal history. He became attached to a young lady whom he was to have married. She died unwedded, in the flower of her age; there was a sorrowful leave-taking between her and her lover as the grave was about to separate them on the eve of what should have been her bridal; and Irving, ever after, to the close of his life, tenderly and faithfully cherished her memory. In one of the biographical notices published immediately after Irving's death, an old, well-worn copy of the Bible is spoken of, which was kept lying on the table in his chamber, within reach of his bedside, bearing her name on the title-page in a delicate female hand—a relic which we may presume to have been his constant companion. Those who are fond of searching, in the biographies of eminent men, for the circumstances which determined the bent of their genius, find in this sad event, and the cloud it threw over the hopeful and cheerful period of early manhood, an explanation of the transition from the unbounded playfulness of the "History of New York" to the serious, tender and meditative vein of the "Sketch Book."

In 1815, soon after our second peace with Great Britain, Irving sailed again for Europe, and fixed himself at Liverpool, where a branch of the large commercial house to which he belonged was established. His old love of rambling returned upon him; he wandered first into Wales, and over some of the finest counties of England, and then northward to the sterner region of the Scottish Highlands. His memoir of Campbell had procured him the acquaintance and friendship of that poet. Campbell gave him, more than a year after his arrival in England, a letter of introduction to Scott, who, already acquainted with him by his writings, welcomed him warmly to Abbotsford, and made him his friend for life. Scott sent a special message to Campbell, thanking him for having made him known to Irving. "He is one of the best and pleasantest acquaintances," said Scott, "that I have made this many a day."

In the same year that he visited Abbotsford his brothers failed. The changes which followed the peace of 1815, swept away their fortunes and his together, and he was now to begin the world anew.

In 1819, he began to publish the "Sketch Book." It was written in England and sent over to New York, where it was issued by Van Winkle in octavo numbers, containing from seventy to a hundred pages. In the preface he remarked that he was "unsettled in his abode," that he had "his cares and vicissitudes," and could not, therefore, give these papers the "tranquil attention necessary to finished composition." Several of them were copied with praise in the London "Literary Gazette," and an intimation was conveyed to the author, that some person in London was about to publish them entire. He preferred to do this himself, and accordingly offered the work to the famous bookseller, Murray. Murray was slow in giving the matter his attention, and Irving, after a reasonable delay, wrote to ask that the copy which he had left with him might be returned. It was sent back with a note, pleading excess of occupation, the great cross of all eminent booksellers, and alleging the "want of scope in the nature of the work," as a reason for declining it. This was discouraging, but Irving had the enterprise to print the first volume in London, at his own risk. It was issued by John Miller, and was well received, but in a month afterward the publisher failed. Immediately Sir Walter Scott came to London and saw Murray, who allowed himself to be persuaded, the more easily, doubtless, on account of the partial success of the first volume, that the work had more "scope" than he supposed, and purchased the copyright of both volumes for two hundred pounds, which he afterward liberally raised to four hundred.

Whoever compares the "Sketch Book" with the "History of New York" might at first, perhaps, fail to recognize it as the work of the same hand, so much graver and more thoughtful is the strain in which it is written. A more attentive examination, however, shows that the humor in the lighter parts is of the same peculiar and original cast, wholly unlike that of any author who ever wrote, a humor which Mr. Dana happily characterized as "a fanciful playing with common things, and here and there beautiful touches, till the ludicrous becomes half picturesque." Yet one cannot help perceiving that the author's spirit had been sobered since he last appeared before the public, as if the shadow of a great sorrow had fallen upon it. The greater number of the papers are addressed to our deeper sympathies, and some of them, as, for example, the Broken Heart, The Widow and Her Son, and Rural Funerals, dwell upon the saddest themes. Only in two of them—Rip Van Winkle and the Legend of Sleepy Hollow—does he lay the reins loose on the neck of his frolicsome fancy and allow it to dash forward without restraint; and these rank among the most delightful and popular tales ever written. In our country they have been read, I believe, by nearly everybody who can read at all.

The "Sketch Book," and the two succeeding works of Irving, "Bracebridge Hall" and the "Tales of a Traveller," abound with agreeable pictures of English life, seen under favorable lights and sketched with a friendly pencil. Let me say here, that it was not to pay court to the English that he thus described them and their country; it was because he could not describe them otherwise. It was the instinct of his mind to attach itself to the contemplation of the good and the beautiful, wherever he found them, and to turn away from the sight of what was evil, misshapen, and hateful. His was not a nature to pry for faults, or disabuse the world of good-natured mistakes; he looked for virtue, love and truth among men, and thanked God that he found them in such large measure. If there are touches of satire in his writings, he is the best-natured and most amiable of satirists, amiable beyond Horace; and in his irony—for there is a vein of playful irony running through many of his works—there is no tinge of bitterness.

I rejoice, for my part, that we have had such a writer as Irving to bridge over the chasm between the two great nations—that an illustrious American lived so long in England, and was so much beloved there, and sought so earnestly to bring the people of the two countries to a better understanding with each other, and to wean them from the animosities of narrow minds. I am sure that there is not a large-minded and large-hearted man in all our country who can read over the "Sketch Book" and the other writings of Irving, and disown one of the magnanimous sentiments they express with regard to England, or desire to abate the glow of one of his warm and cheerful pictures of English life. Occasions will arise, no doubt, for saying some things in a less accommodating spirit, and there are men enough on both sides of the Atlantic who can say them; but Irving was not sent into the world on that errand. A different work was assigned him in the very structure of his mind and the endowments of his heart—a work of peace and brotherhood, and I will say for him that he nobly performed it.

Let me pause here to speak of what I believe to have been the influence of the "Sketch Book" upon American literature. At the time it appeared the periodical lists of new American publications were extremely meagre, and consisted, to a great extent, of occasional pamphlets and dissertations on the questions of the day. The works of greater pretension were, for the most part, crudely and languidly made up, and destined to be little read. A work like the "Sketch Book," welcomed on both sides of the Atlantic, showed the possibility of an American author acquiring a fame bounded only by the limits of his own language, and gave an example of the qualities by which it might be won. Within two years afterward we had Cooper's "Spy" and Dana's "Idle Man;" the press of our country began, by degrees, to teem with works composed with a literary skill and a spirited activity of intellect until then little known among us. Every year the assertion that we had no literature of our own became less and less true: and now, when we look over a list of new works by native authors, we find, with an astonishment amounting almost to alarm, that the most voracious devourer of books must despair of being able to read half those which make a fair claim upon his attention. It was since 1819 that the great historians of our country, whose praise is in the mouths of all the nations, began to write. One of them built up the fabric of his fame long after Irving appeared as an author, and slept with Herodotus two years before Irving's death; another of the band lives yet to be the ornament of the association before which I am called to speak, and is framing the annals of his country into a work for future ages. Within that period has arisen among us the class who hold vast multitudes spell-bound in motionless attention by public discourses, the most perfect of their kind, such as make the fame of Everett. Within that period our theologians have learned to write with the elegance and vivacity of

the essayists. We had but one novelist before the era of the
"Sketch Book;" their number is now beyond enumeration by
any but a professed catalogue-maker, and many of them are
read in every cultivated form of human speech. Those whom
we acknowledge as our poets—one of whom is the special
favorite of our brothers in language who dwell beyond sea—
appeared in the world of letters and won its attention after Irving had become famous. We have wits, and humorists, and amus-
ing essayists, authors of some of the airiest and most graceful
compositions of the present century, and we owe them to the
new impulse given to our literature in 1819. I look abroad on
these stars of our literary firmament—some crowded together
with their minute points of light in a galaxy—some standing
apart in glorious constellations; I recognize Arcturus and Orion
and Perseus, and the glittering jewels of the Southern Cross,
and the Pleiades shedding sweet influences; but the Evening
Star, the soft and serene light that glowed in their van, the precursor of them all, has sunk below the horizon. The spheres,
meantime, perform their appointed courses; the same motion
which lifted them up to the mid-sky bears them onward to their
setting; and they, too, like their bright leader, must soon be
carried by it below the earth. * * *

[FINAL COMMENTS ON IRVING]

That amiable character which makes itself so manifest in the
writings of Irving was seen in all his daily actions. He was ever
ready to do kind offices, tender of the feelings of others, carefully just, but ever leaning to the merciful side of justice, averse
to strife, and so modest that the world never ceased to wonder
how it should have happened that one so much praised should
have gained so little assurance. He envied no man's success, he
sought to detract from no man's merits, but he was acutely sensitive both to praise and to blame—sensitive to such a degree that
an unfavorable criticism of any of his works would almost persuade him that they were as worthless as the critic represented
them. He thought so little of himself that he could never com-

prehend why it was that he should be the object of curiosity or reverence.

From the time that he began the composition of his "Sketch Book," his whole life was the life of an author. His habits of composition were, however, by no means regular. When he was in the vein, the periods would literally stream from his pen; at other times he would scarcely write anything. For two years after the failure of his brothers at Liverpool, he found it almost impossible to write a line. He was throughout life an early riser, and when in the mood, would write all the morning and till late in the day, wholly engrossed with his subject. In the evening he was ready for any cheerful pastime, in which he took part with an animation almost amounting to high spirits. These intervals of excitement and intense labor, sometimes lasting for weeks, were succeeded by languor, and at times by depression of spirits, and for months the pen would lie untouched; even to answer a letter at these times was an irksome task.

In the evening he wrote but very rarely, knowing—so, at least, I infer—that no habit makes severer demands upon the nervous system than this. It was owing, I doubt not, to this prudent husbanding of his powers, along with his somewhat abstinent habits and the exercise which he took every day, that he was able to preserve unimpaired to so late a period the faculties employed in original composition. He had been a vigorous walker and a fearless rider, and in his declining years he drove out daily, not only for the sake of the open air and motion, but to refresh his mind with the aspect of nature. One of his favorite recreations was listening to music, of which he was an indulgent critic, and he contrived to be pleased and soothed by strains less artfully modulated than fastidious ears are apt to require.

His facility in writing and the charm of his style were owing to very early practice, the reading of good authors and the native elegance of his mind, and not, in my opinion, to any special study of the graces of manner or any anxious care in the use of terms and phrases. Words and combinations of words are sometimes found in his writings to which a fastidious taste might object; but these do not prevent his style from being one

of the most agreeable in the whole range of our literature. It is transparent as the light, sweetly modulated, unaffected, the native expression of a fertile fancy, a benignant temper, and a mind which, delighting in the noble and the beautiful, turned involuntarily away from their opposites. His peculiar humor was, in a great measure, the offspring of this constitution of his mind. This "fanciful playing with common things," as Mr. Dana calls it, is never coarse, never tainted with grossness, and always in harmony with our better sympathies. It not only tinged his writings, but overflowed in his delightful conversation. * * *
1860   1860

[THE LUMINOUS STYLE]

There are two tendencies by which the seekers after poetic fame in our day are apt to be misled, through both the example of others and the applause of critics. One of these is the desire to extort admiration by striking novelties of expression; and the other, the ambition to distinguish themselves by subtilties of thought, remote from the common apprehension.

With regard to the first of these I have only to say what has been often said before, that, however favorable may be the idea which this luxuriance of poetic imagery and of epithet at first gives us of the author's talent, our admiration soon exhausts itself. We feel that the thought moves heavily under its load of garments, some of which perhaps strike us as tawdry and others as ill-fitting, and we lay down the book to take it up no more.

The other mistake, if I may so call it, deserves more attention, since we find able critics speaking with high praise of passages in the poetry of the day to which the general reader is puzzled to attach a meaning. This is often the case when the words themselves seem simple enough, and keep within the range of the Saxon or household element of our language. The obscurity lies sometimes in the phrase itself, and sometimes in the recondite or remote allusion. I will not say that certain minds are not affected by this, as others are by verses in plainer English. To the few it may be genuine poetry, although it may be a riddle to the mass of readers. I remember reading somewhere of a mathematician who was affected with a sense of sublimity by the happy solution of an algebraical or geometrical problem, and I have been assured by one who devoted himself to the science of mathematics that the phenomenon is no uncommon one. Let us beware, therefore, of assigning too narrow limits to the causes which produce the poetic exaltation of mind. The genius of those who write in this manner may be freely acknowledged, but they do not write for mankind at large.

To me it seems that one of the most important requisites for a great poet is a luminous style. The elements of poetry lie in natural òbjects, in the vicissitudes of human life, in the emotions of the human heart, and the relations of man to man. He who can present them in combinations and lights which at once affect the mind with a deep sense of their truth and beauty is the poet for his own age and the ages that succeed it. It is no disparagement either to his skill or his power that he finds them near at hand; the nearer they lie to the common track of the human intelligence, the more certain is he of the sympathy of his own generation, and of those which shall come after him. The metaphysician, the subtile thinker, the dealer in abstruse speculations, whatever his skill in versification, misapplies it when he abandons the more convenient form of prose and perplexes himself with the attempt to express his ideas in poetic numbers.

Let me say for the poets of the present day, that in one important respect they have profited by the example of their immediate predecessors; they have learned to go directly to nature for their imagery, instead of taking it from what had once been regarded as the common stock of the guild of poets. I have often had occasion to verify this remark with no less delight than surprise on meeting in recent verse new images in their untarnished lustre, like coins fresh from the mint, unworn and unsoiled by passing from pocket to pocket. It is curious, also, to observe how a certain set of hackneyed phrases, which Leigh Hunt, I believe, was the first to ridicule, and which were once used for the convenience of rounding out a line or supplying a rhyme, have disappeared from our poetry, and how our blank verse in the hands of the most popular writers has dropped its stiff Latinisms and all the awkward distortions resorted to by those who thought that by putting a sentence out of its proper shape they were writing like Milton. * * *

1870   1871

EDITORIALS IN THE *NEW YORK EVENING POST*

[THE REMOVAL OF THE DEPOSITS]

Hung be the heavens with black! Yield day to night!
Comets, importing change of time and states,
Brandish your crystal tresses in the sky,
And with them scourge the bad revolting stars,
That let the public money be removed
From Biddle's bank—too famous to live long!

Of this tenor are the Jeremiads of the Bank journals. It is heart-rending to hear their doleful lamentations on the occasion of the removal of the deposits. They lift up their voices and weep aloud. From the depth of their affliction come sounds of sublime denunciation. They grieve with an exceeding great grief over the fallen glory of their temple, and refuse to be comforted. The tears which stream from their eyes seem to have cleared their mental vision, and they see future events, as through a glass darkling. "A field of the dead rushes red on their sight." They foretell the ruin of their country, for "the Cabinet improper have triumphed!" and woe! woe! woe! is now the burden of their prediction. "The die is cast!" exclaims the National Intelligencer— "the evil counsellors by whom the President is surrounded have prevailed!" "The star of Olivier le Daim is in the ascendant!" "The evil consequences which we predicted *must* result from it to all the interests, public and private, of the country!" "If this be not tyranny—if this be not usurpation, what under heaven can constitute tyranny and usurpation?" "The law openly trampled on!" "its pernicious effects!"—"bankruptcy and ruin must result from it!" "Will the People stand by, and calmly see their authority thus spurned?—we asked if the People will quietly witness the restraints of the law broken down, and trodden under foot by their own servants? Will the Secretary of the Treasury suffer the sanctity of the law to be violated in his person?"

The National Gazette is not less sublimely dolorous, nor less fearfully prophetic. But however great its patriotic grief for the evil that has befallen its country, the event does not excite its surprise. "It was to be expected," says that pure and single-minded journal, "that the scheme of profligate and rancourous hostility against the Bank would be implacably pursued;" and it adds that "the case is fitted to awaken lively alarm and the gravest reflection." "To what does this lead?"—"to the result that the President of the United States will have usurped the command of the whole twenty-five millions of revenue!"—and "the power of distributing that revenue to whomsoever he pleases, whether to Banks, *or to individuals at Washington, or elsewhere, as managers of a political game!*" "This affair is equal in importance of fearful import [*sic*] to any thing that has occurred in our country;" it "outrages law!" and is a "scheme of usurpation!"

The rest of the purchased presses of the Bank are not less lachrymose and lugubrious, and all of them partake of a similar spirit of prescience. They all exclaim, almost in the words of Lord Byron,

> "The day of our destiny's over,
> The star of our fate has declined!"

"The times are out of joint!" they say—a disaster has befallen the country from which it can never recover—we are ruined, lost, utterly undone!—and like the misshapen dwarf in the Lay of the Last Minstrel, they wave their lean arms on high, and run to and fro, crying "lost! lost! lost!" Who can doubt the sincerity of their lamentations at the death-blow which has been given to the United States Bank, when it is remembered how munificent a patron that institution has been to them? Who can wonder that they appear at the head of the funeral train as chief mourners, and raise so loud their solemn wul-wullas, when he reflects how well their grief is paid for? No hired mourner at an English funeral ever earned his wages by so energetic a wail, or so lachrymose an aspect. They seem as wo-begone as pilgrims from the Cave of Trophonius, when

"—the sad sage, returning, smiled no more."

But their wailing is vain—"vainly they heap the ashes on their heads"—the fate of the Bank is sealed; and we, who are not paid to wet our cheeks with artificial tears, who have no cause to be a mourner, must be permitted to congratulate the country that a Monopoly, which, in the corrupt exercise of its dangerous power, threatened to sap the foundation of American independence, has, by this firm and timely act of the General Government, been reduced to a state of feebleness, which, we trust, is only the precursor of its final dissolution.

1833   1833

[*From* THE RIGHT OF WORKMEN TO STRIKE]

Sentence was passed on Saturday on the twenty "men who had determined not to work." The punishment selected, on due consideration, by the judge, was that officers appointed for the purpose should immediately demand from each of the delinquents a sum of money which was named in the sentence of the court. The amount demanded would not have fallen short of the savings of many years. Either the offenders had not parted with these savings, or their brother workmen raised the ransom money for them on the spot. The fine was paid over as required. All is now well; justice has been satisfied. But if the expenses of their families had anticipated the law, and left nothing in their hands, or if friends had not been ready to buy the freedom of their comrades, they would have been sent to prison, and there they would have staid, until their wives and children, besides earning their own bread, had saved enough to redeem the captives from their cells. Such has been their punishment. What was their offence? They had committed the crime of unanimously declining to go to work at the wages offered to them by their masters. They had said to one another, "Let us come out from the meanness and misery of our caste. Let us begin to do what every order more privileged and more honoured is doing everyday. By the means which we believe to be the best let us raise ourselves and our families above the humbleness of our condition. We may be wrong, but we cannot help believing that we might do much if we were true brothers to each other, and would resolve not to sell the only thing which is our own, the cunning of our hands, for less than it is worth." What other things they may have done is nothing to the purpose: it was for this they were condemned; it is for this they are to endure the penalty of the law.

We call upon a candid and generous community to mark that the punishment inflicted upon these twenty "men who had determined not to work" is not directed against the offence of conspiring to prevent others by force from working at low wages, but expressly against the offence of settling by pre-concert the compensation which they thought they were entitled to obtain. It is certainly superfluous to repeat, that this journal would be the very last to oppose a law levelled at any attempt to molest the labourer who chooses to work for less than the prices settled by the union. We have said, and to cut off cavil, we say it now again, that a conspiracy to deter, by threats of violence, a fellow workman from arranging his own terms with his employers, is a conspiracy to commit a felony—a conspiracy which, being a crime against liberty, we should be the first to condemn—a conspiracy which no strike should, for its own sake, countenance for a moment—a conspiracy already punishable by the statute, and far easier to reach than the one of which "the twenty" stood accused; but a conspiracy, we must add, that has not a single feature in common with the base and barbarous prohibition under which the offenders were indicted and condemned.

They were condemned because they had determined not to work for the wages that were offered them! Can any thing be imagined more abhorrent to every sentiment of generosity or justice, than the law which arms the rich with the legal right to fix, by assize, the wages of the poor? If this is not SLAVERY, we have forgotten its definition. Strike the right of associating for the sale of labour from the privileges of a freeman, and you may as well at once bind him to a master, or ascribe him to the soil. If it be not in the colour of his skin, and in the poor franchise of naming his own terms in a contract for his work, what advantage has the labourer of the north over the bondman of the south? Punish by human laws a "determination not to work," make it penal by any other penalty than idleness inflicts, and it matters little whether the task-masters be one or many, an individual or an order, the hateful scheme of slavery will have gained a foothold in the land. And then the meanness of this law, which visits with its malice those who cling to it for protection, and shelters with all its fences those who are raised above its threats. A late solicitation for its aid against employers, is treated with derision and contempt, but the moment the "masters" invoked its intervention, it came down from its high place with most indecent haste, and has now discharged its fury upon the naked heads of wretches so forlorn, that their worst faults multiply their titles to a liberty which they must learn to win from livelier sensibilities than the barren benevolence of Wealth, or the tardy magnanimity of Power. * * *

"Self-created societies," says Judge Edwards, "are unknown to the constitution and laws, and will not be permitted to rear their crest and extend their baneful influence over any portion of the community." If there is any sense in this passage it means that self-created societies are unlawful, and must be put down by the courts. Down then with every literary, every religious, and every charitable association not incorporated! What nonsense is this! Self-created societies *are* known to the constitution and laws, for they are not prohibited, and the laws which allow them will, if justly administered, protect them. But suppose in charity that the reporter has put this absurdity into the mouth of Judge Edwards, and that he meant only those self-created societies which have an effect upon trade and commerce. Gather up then and sweep to the penitentiary all those who are confederated to carry on any business or trade in concert, by fixed rules, and see how many men you would leave at large in this city. The members of every partnership in the place will come under the penalties of the law, and not only these, but every person pursuing any occupation whatever, who governs

himself by a mutual understanding with others that follow the
same occupation. * * *

1836   1836

[FREEDOM OF SPEECH]

A meeting of the people of Cincinnati have proclaimed the
right of silencing the expression of unpopular opinions by violence. We refer our readers to the proceedings of an anti-
abolition meeting lately held in that city. They will be found in
another part of this paper.

If the meeting had contented itself with declaring its disap-
probation of the tenets of the abolitionists, we should have had
nothing to say. They might have exhausted the resources of
rhetorick and of language—they might have indulged in the
very extravagance and wantonness of vehement condemnation,
for aught we cared; they would still have been in the exercise of
a right which the constitution and the laws secure to them. But
when they go further, and declare that they have not only a right
to condemn certain opinions in others, but the right to coerce
those who hold them to silence, it is time to make an immediate
and decided stand, and to meet the threat of coercion with defiance.

The Cincinnati meeting, in the concluding resolution offered
by Wilson N. Brown, and adopted with the rest, declare in so
many words that if they cannot put down the abolitionist press
by fair means they will do it by foul; if they cannot silence it by
remonstrance, they will silence it by violence; if they cannot persuade it to desist, they will stir up mobs against it, inflame them
to madness, and turn their brutal rage against the dwellings, the
property, the persons, the lives of the wretched abolitionists and
their families. In announcing that they will put them down by
force all this is included. Fire, robbery, bloodshed, are the common excesses of an enraged mob. There is no extreme of cruelty
and destruction to which in the drunkenness and delirium of its
fury it may not proceed. The commotions of the elements can
as easily be appeased by appeals to the quality of mercy as these
commotions of the human mind; the whirlwind and the light-

ning might as well be expected to pause and turn aside to spare the helpless and innocent, as an infuriated multitude.

If the abolitionists *must* be put down, and if the community are of that opinion, there is no necessity of violence to effect the object. The community have the power in their own hands; the majority may make a law declaring the discussion of slavery in a certain manner to be a crime, and imposing penalties. The law may then be put in force against the offenders, and their mouths may be gagged in due form, and with all the solemnities of justice.

What is the reason this is not done? The answer is ready. The community are for leaving the liberty of the press untrammelled—there is not a committee that can be raised in any of the State legislatures north of the Potomac who will report in favor of imposing penalties on those who declaim against slavery— there is not a legislature who would sanction such a report—and there is not a single free state the people of which would sustain a legislature in so doing. These are facts, and the advocates of mob law know them to be so.

Who then are the men that issue this invitation to silence the press by violence? Who but an insolent brawling minority, a few noisy fanatics who claim that their own opinions shall be the measure of freedom for the rest of the community, and who undertake to overawe a vast pacific majority by threats of wanton outrage and plunder? These men are for erecting an oligarchy of their own and riding rough shod over the people and the people's rights. They claim a right to repeal the laws established by the majority in favor of the freedom of the press. They make new laws of their own to which they require that the rest of the community shall submit, and in case of a refusal, they threaten to execute them by the ministry of a mob. There is no tyranny or oppression exercised in any part of the world more absolute or more frightful than that which they would establish.

So far as we are concerned we are determined that this despotism shall neither be submitted to nor encouraged. In whatever form it makes its appearance we shall raise our voice against it. We are resolved that the subject of slavery shall be as it ever

has been, as free a subject of discussion and argument and declamation, as the difference between whiggism and democracy,
or as the difference between the Arminians and the Calvinists.
If the press chooses to be silent on the subject it shall be the
silence of perfect free will, and not the silence of fear. We hold
that this combination of the few to govern the many by the
terror of illegal violence, is as wicked and indefensible as a conspiracy to rob on the highway. We hold it to be the duty of
good citizens to protest against it whenever and wherever it
shows itself, and to resist it if necessary to the death.

One piece of justice must be done to the South. Thousands
there are of persons in that quarter of the country who disap-
prove, as heartily as any citizen of the North can do, the employment of violence against the presses or the preachers of the anti-
slavery party. There are great numbers also, as we are well informed, who think that only harm could result from directing
the penalties of the law against those who discuss the question of
slavery. They are for leaving the mode of discussing this question solely to the calm and considerate good sense of the North,
satisfied that the least show of a determination to abridge the
liberty of speech in this matter is but throwing oil on the flames.

1836   1836

[THE DEATH OF LOVEJOY]

We have received by this morning's mail a slip from the
Missouri Argus, printed at St. Louis, containing intelligence
which has filled us with surprise and horror. A mob, in making
an attack upon an abolition press established at Alton, in
Illinois, murdered two persons, wounded several others, and
triumphing over the objects of their fury by this atrocious
violence, destroyed the press which these men had defended at
the cost of their blood and their lives.

We give the slip from the Missouri Argus as we received it,
but we cannot forbear expressing in the strongest language our
condemnation of the manner in which it speaks of this bloody
event. The right to discuss freely and openly, by speech, by
the pen, by the press, all political questions, and to examine and

animadvert upon all political institutions, is a right so clear and certain, so interwoven with our other liberties, so necessary, in fact, to their existence, that without it we must fall at once into despotism or anarchy. To say that he who holds unpopular opinions must hold them at the peril of his life, and that, if he expresses them in public, he has only himself to blame if they who disagree with him should rise and put him to death, is to strike at all rights, all liberties, all protection of law, and to justify or extenuate all crimes.

We regard not this as a question connected with the abolition of slavery in the South, but as a question vital to the liberties of the entire Union. We may have different opinions concerning the propriety of the measures which the abolitionists desire to recommend, but we marvel and we deplore that any difference can exist as to the freedom of discussion. We are astonished that even a single journal can be found, so forgetful of its own rights, to say nothing of its duties to the community, as to countenance, even indirectly, the idea of muzzling the press by the fear of violence.

For our own part we approve, we applaud, we would consecrate, if we could, to universal honor, the conduct of those who bled in this gallant defence of the freedom of the press. Whether they erred or not in their opinions, they did not err in the conviction of their right as citizens of a democratic government, to express them, nor did they err in defending this right with an obstinacy which yielded only to death and the uttermost violence. With these remarks we lay before our readers the brief narrative with which we are furnished of this bloody outrage.

Office of the Missouri Argus,⎫
St. Louis, Nov. 9, 1837.⎭

Mob at Alton, Illinois—The Rev. E. P. Lovejoy killed, and his Abolition press destroyed!!

The infatuated editor of the Alton Observer has at length fallen a victim to his obstinacy in the cause of the Abolitionists. Disregarding the known and expressed sentiments of a large portion of the citizens of Alton, in relation to his incendiary publications, and, as it would seem, bent upon his own destruction, he formed the determination to establish another press for the propagation of the odious and disorganizing principles of Tappan and his eastern confederates. But his temerity has received an awful retribution from the hands of an infuriated and lawless mob.—The following particulars of the tragical outrage is [*sic*] contained in a postscript to the Alton Telegraph of the 8th inst.:

LAMENTABLE OCCURRENCE.—It is with the deepest regret that we stop the press in order to state that, at a late hour last night, an attack was made by a large number of persons on the warehouse of Messrs. Godfrey, Gilman & Co., for the purpose of destroying a press intended for the revival of the Alton Observer, which, shocking to relate, resulted in the death of two individuals—the Rev. E. P. LOVEJOY, late editor of the Observer, and a man named —— BISHOP. Seven others were wounded, two severely, and the others slightly. We can add no more at this time, than that the assailants succeeded in effecting their object.

1837   1837

[MR. WEBSTER'S WIT]

That men of some wit and humor have lived before the present age is not, we believe, contested. Not to speak of the Greeks and Romans, there is wit in Boccaccio, and wit in Ariosto, and wit in Casti. Witty was Rabelais, and witty was Scarron, and witty, in another way, was Paul Courier. There are things in Cervantes which will make the reader laugh in spite of himself; Molière has been known to coax a grin from the most splenetic, and some passages in Shakspeare no man can read or hear without acknowledging that they are quite droll.

These authors were very well in their time, and some of their works are passable even now. We must not speak disparagingly of what made our fathers and mothers laugh. It would be irreverent.

But the age for wit is decidedly the present age, and the wittiest man of the time, beyond all question is Mr. Webster, the gentleman spoken of last summer as the whig candidate for the Presidency. Wit has hitherto been only in the bud,—Mr. Webster is the full blown flower; wit has till now remained in the clumsy chrysalis state,—Mr. Webster is the broad-winged butterfly. We have had indeed the promise of wit, but Mr. Webster is its fulfilment and perfection.

On Tuesday evening last a brilliant festival was given at East Boston, by John W. Fenno, Esquire, in honor of the recent glorious whig victories in New-York. It was held in Maverick House, the largest hotel in the city, gorgeously illuminated for the occasion. The festivity is duly chronicled in the columns of the Boston Centinel. Elbridge G. Austin presided at the dinner, and at his right was placed the witty Mr. Webster. Mr. Austin gave a toast in compliment to Mr. Webster, and Mr. Webster responded. We give his speech in the words of the Boston Centinel, cautioning our readers to look well to their diaphragms, and to hold their sides with both hands, for the drollery of this Mr. Webster is irresistible.

"Mr. Webster rose and pronounced a most eloquent and agreeable speech, which occupied the profound attention of his audience for three quarters of an hour. He touched happily on the great questions before the nation, and enlarged on the glorious results of the present and past week, and although now and then he spoke in the most serious and impressive tones, yet at other times he was sportive and humorous to admiration, and [kept] the company in roars of laughter. He remarked pleasantly that at the approaching session, when he should go to Washington, and call on the President, he should probably have occasion to say— 'How do you do, Mr. Van Buren? How go the times? What news from New York?'

"The effect of this frank colloquy was irresistible; the room was convulsed with laughter. It was all uttered with so much pleasantry and respect, and with such perfect good humor and *naiveté* of manner, that had Mr. Van Buren himself been present, he would have forgotten his own reverses, and joined heartily in the laughing all round the board. Mr. W. then added, that when he should see the Secretary of the Treasury, he might have occasion to say— 'How is Mr. Woodbury? What are the exact financial statements and plans that you propose to report for our consideration? What do the people say of your *sub-Treasury system?*' These words were accompanied by appropriate action, and the effect was such as may be imagined, but cannot be described."

Ah the wag! We are tempted to say to Mr. Webster as the negro boy said to Garrick when the great actor had stolen into the back yard and was personating the cock-turkey for his entertainment: "Massa Webster, you make-a me die wid laffin."

"How do you do, Mr. Van Buren? What news from New York?" "How is Mr. Woodbury? What do the people say of your sub-Treasury system?" Is there any mortal whose gravity is stern enough to stand any thing so superlatively comic as this? Why, it would have drawn a horse laugh from the lungs of the weeping philosopher.

We take it upon us to say that there is not so irresistible a jest in the works of all the wits who ever wrote, from Lucian down to the last number of the Pickwick papers by Boz.

In his True History of New York, Diedrich Knickerbocker relates the fate of a fat little Schepen who died of a Burgomaster's joke. If a mere Burgomaster's joke, a hundred and fifty years since, when wit was in its infancy, could do such execution, what must be the effect of the joke of so accomplished a wag as Mr. Webster? We have, however, looked carefully over the account given by the Boston Centinel, and we find no return of the killed. How is this? Is there no concealment of the consequences of Mr. Webster's waggery?

1837   1837

THE CORN LAW CONTROVERSY

A friend has placed in our hands numbers of the tracts which the corn law reformers of England circulate among the people. They are about the size and length of the religious tracts of this country, and are put up in an envelope, which is stamped with neat and appropriate devices. These little publications comprise essays on all the topics involved in the corn law controversy, sometimes in the form of dialogues, sometimes of tales, and sometimes of extracts from famous books and speeches. The arguments are arranged so as to be easily comprehended by the meanest capacities.

The friend to whom we are indebted for these, is well informed on the subject, and says that a more advanced state of opinion prevails among the people of England, in relation to the operation of tariffs, than in this nation generally so much more enlightened. It is a singular spectacle which is thus presented to the eyes of the civilized world. While the tendency of opinion, under an aristocratic monarchy, is towards the loosening of the restraints under which the labor of the people has long suffered, a large and powerful party in a nation, whose theory of government is nearly a century in advance of the world, is clamoring for their continuance and confirmation. Monarchical England is struggling to break the chains that an unwise legislation has forged for the limbs of its trade; but democratic America is urged to put on the fetters which older but less liberal nations are throwing off. The nations of Europe are seeking to extend their commercial relations, to expand the sphere of their mutual intercourse, to rivet the market for the products of their soil and skill, while the 'model-republic' of the new world is urged to stick to the silly and odious policy of a semi-barbarous age.

We look upon the attempt which is making in Great Britain, to procure a revision of the tariff laws, as one of the most important political movements of the age. It is a reform that contemplates benefits, whose effects would not be confined to any single nation, or any period of time. Should it be successful, it would be the beginning of a grand and universal scheme of commercial emancipation. Let England—that nation so extensive in her relations, and so powerful in her influences—let England adopt a more liberal policy, and it would remove the only obstacles now in the way of a complete freedom of industry throughout the globe. It is the apparent unwillingness of nations to reciprocate the advantages of mutual trade, that has kept back this desirable reform so long. The standing argument of the friends of exclusiveness—their defence under all assaults, their shelter in every emergency— has been that one nation cannot pursue a free system until all others do, or, in other words, that restriction is to be met by restriction. It is a flimsy pretence, but such as it is, has answered the purposes of those who have used it, for many centuries.

The practice of confining trade by the invisible, but potent chains of law, has been a curse wherever it has prevailed. In England, more dependent than other nations on the extent of its commercial intercourse, it may be said to have operated as a scourge. The most terrible inflictions of natural evil, storms, famine, and pestilence, have not produced an equal amount of suffering. Indeed, it has combined the characteristics of the worst of those evils. It has devastated, like the storm, the busy hives of industry; it has exhausted, like famine, the life and vital principle of trade; and, like the pestilence, it has "walked in the darkness and wasted at noon-day." When we read of thousands of miserable wretches, in all the cities and towns of a great nation, huddled together like so many swine in a pen; in rags, squalor, and want; without work, bread, or hope; dragging out from day to day, by begging, or the petty artifices of theft, an existence which is worthless and a burden; and when, at the same time, we see a system of laws, that has carefully drawn a band of iron around every mode of human exertion, which with lynx-eyed and omniscient vigilance, has dragged every product of industry from its retreat, to become the subject of a tax, can we fail in ascribing the effect to its cause, or suppress the utterance of our indignation at a policy so heartless and destructive?

Yet, this is the very policy that a certain class of politicians in this country would have us imitate. Misled by the selfish and paltry arguments of British statesmen, but unawed by the terrible experience of the British people, they would fasten upon us a system whose only recommendation, in its best form, is that it enriches a few, at the cost of the lives and happiness of many. They would assist a constrictor in wrapping his folds around us, until our industry shall be completely crushed.

1843   1843

FRIAR TUCK LEGISLATION

A famous thief was Robin Hood;
But Scotland had a thief as good,
It was—it was the great Rob Roy.
                                        Old Ballad.

A speaker, Mr. Thomas Gisborne, at one of the recent meetings of the Anti-Corn Law League, made a happy allusion to what he called Friar Tuck legislation. He had in his mind the story which is told in some of the old chronicles of Robin Hood and his merry foresters, when they were once assembled in Congress to deliberate upon the proper distribution of a pretty large amount of spoils. These legislators, persuaded by the soft and honied words of Friar Tuck, left it to him to frame a law for the proper adjustment of their claims. When the law was reported, by the able committee which had it in charge, it became instantly evident that Friar Tuck himself would get much the largest share. Public opinion, continues the history, thereupon went against the holy man, and a league was formed to resist the iniquity of his decision.

Now, what did the good Friar in the emergency? Why, he met the people boldly and openly, and said, "For whose benefit are laws made, I should like to know?" And then immediately answering his own question, lest some silly objector might give it another turn, he went on, "First, for the benefit of those who make them, and afterward as it may happen." Nor did the disinterested judge stop there, but he proceeded, "Am I not the lawmaker, and shall I not profit by my own law?" The story runs, we believe, that the good man next quietly pocketed his share of the booty, and left his unreasonable companions to make the best of what remained.

Friar Tuck represents a class; he is a type and pattern of a large circle of imitators; his peculiar method of legislation is not obsolete. There are many persons at this day whose morality seems to be framed according to the same standard. Members of the United States Congress, for instance, who pass tariff laws to put money into their own pockets, are the legitimate descendants of Friar Tuck.

It is quite remarkable how many are the points of resemblance between this legislation of Sherwood Forest and that of the manufacturers at Washington. In the first place, the plunder to be distributed is raised from the people, in either case, without their being formally consulted; in the one by high duties, and in the other by the strong arm. Then the persons who take upon themselves to decide how this plunder is to be divided, like Friar Tuck, have a deep interest in the result, and generally manage to appropriate to themselves the largest share. They are the owners of manufacturing capital, and they contrive to make this capital return an enormous interest. "For whose benefit," they gravely ask, "are laws made?" and then answer, "First for the benefit of those who make them, and afterward as it may happen." Let us impose high duties; let us fill our pockets; let us who make the laws take all that we can get— and as to the people, the mass of laborers and consumers, why that's as it may happen! This is virtually the reasoning of one sort of our just and disinterested legislators.

But there is one point in which the resemblance does not hold. Friar Tuck was a bold, straight-forward, open-mouthed statesman, willing to proclaim his principles and justify the consequences to which they led. His followers in Congress act upon precisely the same principles, but assign another reason. He avowed that he wished to cram his pocket; they hold up some mock pretense of public good. "Shall I not benefit by my own law?" he said, and gathered up his gains; but they gather the gain and leave the reason unsaid, or rather hypocritically resort to some more palatable reason. The advantage of consistency is on the side of Robin Hood's priest. There is a frankness in his philosophy which throws the sneaking duplicity of the legislators of the cotton mills quite into the shade.

A NEW PUBLIC PARK

The heats of summer are upon us, and while some are leaving the town for shady retreats in the country, others refresh themselves with short excursions to Hoboken or New Brighton, or other places among the beautiful environs of our city. If the public authorities, who expend so much of our money in laying out the city, would do what is in their power, they might give our vast population an extensive pleasure ground for shade and recreation in these sultry afternoons, which we might reach without going out of town.

On the road to Harlem, between Sixty-eighth street on the south and Seventy-seventh on the north, and extending from the Third Avenue to the East River, is a tract of beautiful woodland, comprising sixty or seventy acres, thickly covered with old trees, intermingled with a variety of shrubs. The surface is varied in a very striking and picturesque manner, with craggy eminences, and hollows, and a little stream runs through the midst. The swift tides of the East River sweep its rocky shores, and the fresh breeze of the bay comes in, on every warm summer afternoon, over the restless waters. The trees are of almost every species that grows in our woods:—the different varieties of oak, the birch, the beech, the linden, the mulberry, the tulip tree, and others; the azalea, the kalmia, and other flowering shrubs are in bloom here at their season, and the ground in spring is gay with flowers. There never was a finer situation for the public garden of a great city. Nothing is wanted but to cut winding paths through it, leaving the woods as they now are, and introducing here and there a jet from the Croton aqueduct, the streams from which would make their own water-falls over the rocks, and keep the brook running through the place always fresh and full. * * *

As we are now going on, we are making a belt of muddy docks all round the island. We should be glad to see one small part of the shore without them, one place at least where the tides may be allowed to flow pure, and the ancient brim of rocks which borders the waters left in its original picturesqueness and beauty. Commerce is devouring inch by inch the coast of the island, and if we would rescue any part of it for health and recreation it must be done now.

All large cities have their extensive public grounds and gardens, Madrid and Mexico City their Alamedas, London its Regent's Park, Paris its Champs Élysées, and Vienna its Prater. There are none of them, we believe, which have the same natural advantages of the picturesque and beautiful which belong to this spot. It would be of easy access to the citizens, and the public carriages which now rattle in almost every street in this city, would take them to its gates. The only objection which we can see to the plan would be the difficulty of persuading the owners of the soil to part with it.

If any of our brethren of the public press should see fit to support this project, we are ready to resign in their favor any claim to the credit of originally suggesting it.

1844   1844

A SHORT METHOD WITH DISUNIONISTS

The Richmond *Enquirer* calls the attention of its readers to an article in the Greenville *Patriot*, a South Carolina journal, the views of which, it observes, it "seconds most heartily," beginning thus:

"NORTHERN DISUNION.—We call the attention of southern disunionists to the article from the New Haven *Register*, headed 'The Disunionists Backing Out.' That the state of Massachusetts will back out from her abolition nullification whenever the issue comes, we have no doubt. But we do not wish these northern nullifiers and disunionists to back out. We wish to have the gratification of seeing them whipped out. The general government must give some signal instance of its ability to maintain itself. Old Massachusetts, 'the cradle of liberty,' is as fit place for this bloody contest as any other, and there is no blood more worthy of being shed to moisten the tree of liberty than that of abolitionists."

This is the language they use at the South when disunion shows its northern face; they defy it to do its worst, and give themselves no further trouble about it. The defiance is well enough, though the style of the Greenville print, we must acknowledge, is a little ruffianly. When any party or any state talks of disunion, the true method of dealing with them is not to yield to their complaints or their threats anything which is not called for by a simple regard to justice; but, on the contrary, to keep on in a firm and even course till the unreasonable clamorers become weary. A good nurse understands this in the treatment of children; when they cry for what they ought not to have, and refuse to be pacified without it, she lets them cry themselves to sleep. If they are permitted to learn that their most unreasonable desires will be gratified if they only cry loudly and perseveringly, they will keep the nursery in a perpetual uproar. The way to keep the place quiet, she knows well, is to let them see they can gain nothing by making a noise.

In our dealings with the South, we have for the most part taken a different method. The child has been allowed to have whatever it took a fancy to cry for. Missouri was received into our confederacy as a slave state under the threat of disunion. The compromise acts of 1850 were passed under the same threat. The Nebraska act was got through Congress, partly by bribery, it is true, but partly, also, by bluster. Now we are told that if Stringfellow and his associates succeed in their plan of getting up the show of an application to Congress from Kansas for admission into our confederacy, with a constitution drawn up to their own liking, and Congress reject it, the Union will be broken into fragments. The trick of threatening a dissolution of the Union has been so successful that it is tried on every occasion.

We have had one memorable example of refusing the demands of the South, which ought to have convinced us of the benefit of a firm policy towards that quarter of the Union— a policy looking only to the right, leaving the event to Providence. Andrew Jackson was not the man to be moved by any threat of the dissolution of the Union, coming from any quarter. When the politicians of South Carolina sought to engage the other southern states in a conspiracy to withdraw from the confederacy, Andrew Jackson held South Carolina in its place with a firm hand, and disconcerted the whole plot, by the mere exhibition of a calm determination to keep the states together.

All that we of the North have to do when the questions raised by the late events in Kansas come before Congress for its decision, when the dispute respecting the authority of the legislature imposed upon Kansas by Atchison and Stringfellow shall be brought into the House of Representatives, is to imitate the coolness and unconcern for the event shown by General Jackson in dealing with nullification in South Carolina, and we shall come out of the controversy with the same success.

1855   1855

THE NEW FEDERAL CONSTITUTION

Some of the journalists who support the cause of the administration are pleasing themselves with the fancy that the decision of the Supreme bench of the United States in the Dred Scott case will put an end to the agitation of the slavery question. They will soon find their mistake. The feeling in favor of liberty is not so easily smothered; discussion is not so readily silenced. One specific after another has been tried, with the same view and with the same success. The Fugitive Slave law, we are told, was to quiet all agitation, but it did not; the Nebraska bill was to stop all controversy on the slavery question, but it proved to be oil poured on the flames. The usurpation of the government of Kansas by the inroad from Missouri, was thought for a time to be a blow to the friends of liberty which they could not survive, but it only roused them to greater activity. The election of Mr. Buchanan as President in November was to put an end to the dispute, but since November the dispute has waxed warmer and warmer. It will never end till the cause of liberty has finally triumphed. Heap statute upon statute, follow up one act of Executive interference with another, add usurpation to usurpation, and judicial decision to judicial decision, the spirit against which they are levelled is indestructible. As long as the press and speech are free, the warfare will be continued, and every attempt to suppress it, by directing against it any part of the machinery of the government will only cause it to rage the more fiercely.

This has been the case hitherto. The more our Presidents have meddled with the matter—the more the majority in Congress have sought to stifle the discussion—the more force has been employed on the side of slavery, whether under the pretext of legal authority, as when Mr. Pierce called out the United States troops to enforce the pretended laws of Kansas, or, without that pretext, as when armed men crossed the border of that territory to make laws for the inhabitants, the more determined is the zeal by which the rights of freemen are asserted and upheld against the oligarchy. It will not cool the fiery temper of this zeal to know that slavery has enlisted the bench on its side; it will rather blow it into a stronger and more formidable flame.

Here are five slaveholding judges on the bench, disciples of this neologism of slavery—men who have espoused the doctrines lately invented by the southern politicians, and who seek to engraft them upon our code of constitutional law—men who alter our constitution for us, who find in it what no man of common sense, reading it for himself, could ever find, what its framers never thought of putting into it, what no man discerned in it till a very few years since it was seen, with the aid of optics sharpened by the eager desire to preserve the political ascendency of the slave states. We feel, in reading the opinions of these men, that local political prejudices have gained the mastery of that bench and tainted beyond recovery the minds of the majority of the judges. The constitution which they now profess to administer, is not the constitution under which this country has lived for seventy years; it is not the constitution which Washington, Franklin and Jefferson, and the able jurists who filled the seat of justice in the calmer days of our republic, recognized; this is not the constitution to which we have so long looked up with reverence and admiration; it is a new constitution, of which we never heard till it was invented by Mr.

Calhoun, and which we cannot see adopted by the judges of our federal courts without shame and indignation.

Hereafter, if this decision shall stand for law, slavery, instead of being what the people of the slave states have hitherto called it, their peculiar institution, is a federal institution, the common patrimony and shame of all the states, those which flaunt the title of free, as well as those which accept the stigma of being the Land of Bondage; hereafter, wherever our jurisdiction extends, it carries with it the chain and the scourge—wherever our flag floats, it is the flag of slavery. If so, that flag should have the light of the stars and the streaks of running red erased from it; it should be dyed black and its device should be the whip and the fetter.

Are we to accept, without question, these new readings of the constitution—to sit down contentedly under this disgrace —to admit that the constitution was never before rightly understood, even by those who framed it—to consent that hereafter it shall be the slaveholders' instead of the freemen's constitution? Never! Never! We hold that the provisions of the constitution, so far as they regard slavery, are now just what they were when it was framed, and that no trick of interpretation can change them. The people of the free states will insist on the old impartial construction of the constitution, adopted in calmer times—the construction given it by Washington and his contemporaries, instead of that invented by modern politicians in Congress and adopted by modern politicians on the bench.

What results will grow out of this decision—to what conflicts of legislation between the states and the federal government it may lead—with what difficulty these clashing views may be composed, or how this last attempt to sustain the cause of slavery, to spread it as widely and keep it in being as long as possible, may be overruled and rendered futile by causes now in operation, we do not undertake to conjecture.

1857   1857

[THE ELECTION OF LINCOLN]

What the more sagacious calculators of chances in the different political parties were prepared for has now become a fact; the Republican party has triumphed, and Abraham Lincoln, if he lives to the Fourth of March next, will be President of the United States. An immense majority in the free states are now rejoicing in the result; a large minority of the citizens of southern states, hitherto trampled under the iron heel of an oligarchy which has shown itself as impatient of the freedom of thought as any of the despotisms of the Old World, are rejoicing with still more intense delight. Even in the slave states the elections have taken a turn which shows how strongly a large proportion of their people sympathize with their brethren of the North. Virginia, the most powerful of them all, has emphatically rebuked the disunionists and their treasonable schemes by giving her voice for Bell and Everett. In Kentucky, one of the most flourishing of the offshoots from Virginia, the disunionists are beaten by a large majority; Breckinridge, one of her sons, who should have had her vote, if he had not held opinions and cherished views offensive to her people, is set aside, and electors who are to vote for Bell are chosen by a large majority. In Maryland the struggle between Bell and Breckinridge is close, but the state would have gone for Bell by a considerable majority had not the friends of Lincoln nominated and supported a ticket of their own. Wilmington, one of the most busy, enterprising and prosperous towns in any slave state, gives a majority of two hundred for the Lincoln ticket. Missouri turns her back on Breckinridge, and gives her vote to Douglas. It is impossible to regard these results of the election in that great belt of slave states which immediately adjoin the free, otherwise than as the strongest expression they could give of their inflexible determination to abide by our federal Union.

There are various causes of congratulation in this survey of our successes. It is most gratifying to see what we believe to be a righteous cause—the cause of justice and humanity—after a long and weary struggle, closed by a decisive triumph. It is consoling to those who cherish high hopes of the destinies of our race, to see a great people, after a long discussion, in which the subtlest skill has been employed to varnish over wrong and give it a semblance of fairness, and, after allowing itself for a time to be misled by these sophistries, at length breaking through them all, and deciding boldly and firmly for the right.

We congratulate the country, moreover, on having escaped the confusion, the agitations and the corruption which must almost necessarily attend the choice of a President by the House of Representatives. These dangers have of late been so strongly pressed upon the public attention that we need not dwell upon them here. This consideration had no doubt its effect in enabling us to foil the scheme of those who hoped, by a combination of all the factions opposed to the Republican party in the free states, to carry the choice of a President into Congress, and to convulse the Union with another series of manœuvres and intrigues, such as were put in motion last winter to prevent the election of a Republican Speaker.

We congratulate the country also in the termination of the almost frantic struggle of the slaveholders for the introduction of their baleful institution into the territories. How violent that struggle has been; how reckless those who were engaged in it have been of the plainest rules of justice, and how indifferent to the peace of the country, we need not stop to describe. The contest is now necessarily at an end; it can go no further. The controversy is closed. There can be no hope of influencing the Executive to favor their designs; the expectation of re-opening the slave trade to people these territories with African bondmen is at an end, never, probably, to be revived.

We might enlarge this list of reasons for congratulation to an indefinite extent; but we rather pass on to remark that our rejoicing at the success we have obtained should be sobered by the reflection that we have taken upon ourselves immense responsibilities which we must consider how we shall faithfully discharge. For two years to come we must expect to find a majority in both Houses of Congress influenced by a spirit of distrust, if not of hostility, to the Republican administration.

We must have patience to wait till, by a wise and impartial course of conduct, by a strict regard to the rights of the states, by a careful abstinence from every doubtful exercise of authority, by a frugal administration of the finances, and by the selection of wise, able and upright men as the agents of the government in every post, distrust shall be changed to confidence, and hostility disarmed of its weapons. We have pronounced in favor of a most conscientious as well as most able man to fill the Executive chair. The administration of the federal government must be conformed in all respects to the character of our Chief Magistrate, or the hold which we have obtained on the people is lost. Our success in the election, by deciding one question, the extension of slavery to the territories, has deprived our party of one important bond of union, one of the most powerful causes which have attracted to it the interest and favor of the people. Its place can only be supplied by an earnest endeavor to distinguish the Republican administration by an enlightened zeal for the public welfare.

In closing our remarks we take this occasion to congratulate the old friends of the EVENING POST, who have read it for the last score of years or thereabouts, on this new triumph of the principles which it maintains. The Wilmot Proviso is now consecrated as a part of the national public policy by this election; but earlier than the Wilmot Proviso was the opposition of our journal to the enlargement of slavery. It began with the first whisper of the scheme to annex Texas to the American Union, and it has been steadily maintained from that moment till now, when the right and justice of our cause is proclaimed, in a general election, by the mighty voice of a large majority of thirty millions of people.

1860   1860

From PEACEABLE SECESSION AN ABSURDITY

In behalf of the treachery and imbecility of the Administration at Washington the new doctrine is invoked that each state has a right peacefully to secede—that nullification of any particular law of Congress is to be resisted and punished by the government, but that secession, *i. e.*, the absolute nullification and defiance of all such laws, and of the Constitution and of the Union, is perfectly right and within the power, at all times, of each and every state. The faithless members of the cabinet seek thus to shelter themselves and their partisans in disunion from resistance by the general government, while the imbeciles aim in the same way to find an excuse from shrinking from their duty of affirmative and energetic action for which they lack courage if not principle.

A more monstrous and absurd doctrine than that of the right of any state at its pleasure to secede from the Union has never been put forth. The government in such case would indeed be a mere rope of sand. According to this dogma, Cuba, after we shall have paid $200,000,000 for her purchase, as a state may at once secede, and leave the United States Treasury to place that small item to the account of "profit and loss." Texas, when she came into the Union after we had paid many millions to discharge her debts, and other millions to go into her coffers, was and is entirely at liberty to secede with the booty. Each and all the states carved out of the Louisiana purchase, for which we also paid such an immense sum, may do the like.

So, too, states in which the largest amounts of the public property may be situated may at any time secede with that property. When the Pacific Railroad shall be constructed, at an expense of countless millions, paid from the common treasure, the two or three states through which it will run may decamp with the plunder and plant a custom-house on the site of our storehouses. Vermont, New Hampshire, Indiana, Illinois, Ohio, Kentucky, Tennessee, and the other inland states, which will have contributed to these great disbursements, and in which states hardly a dollar of the public treasure is even expended, are to look quietly and approvingly on the exodus of those which have been thus purchased and enriched at their expense, and to recognise the right of each of them to secede and take the property with them.

Again, if this right exists it exists at all times, until no two states remain united. What, then, would become of the national debt and the national credit? To whom would the creditors of the government look for payment? Should the government be, as it may at any time be, indebted on its stocks hundreds of millions of dollars, its creditors could look, in case of secession, only to the states which should remain united. Those which should have seceded and established independent governments could not be reached. The creditor could claim of them no percentage of liability. They would plead that they had never contracted, and that they had been only stockholders in a corporation in which there was no individual liability.

Nor could the continuing government of the United States compel the payment by the seceding state of a portion of the public debt. There would be no data from which a definite percentage could be assigned to it, nor would it have the ability to pay. If South Carolina finds it necessary to repudiate at the outset by suspending specie payments, and (as already foreshadowed) by annulling even private debts due by its citizens to those of other states, it is plain that both ability and principle will be lacking for payment of her share (if it could be allotted) of the public debt. There is no court by which any fixed amount could be established as due from her on account of that debt, or which could issue execution for its payment. It results therefore that the seceding state could only be compelled to pay any share of the national debt (contracted on her account, as well as that of the other states) by war and reprisals by the general government. This puts an end to the idea of peaceable secession and the right of secession.

But can any of the democratic book-keepers tell us how (if payment could be compelled) they could make out the account current between the seceding state and the government, so as to strike a balance between the debit and the credit sides? Large amounts have been expended by the government on her account and within her borders. Forts for her harbors, light-houses, court-houses, coast-surveys, custom-houses, nonpaying postoffices and post routes, and salaries of the swarms of officers and leeches attendant upon all these, in addition to her undefinable share of the public debt, have all been paid. But then she has a credit side of the account also, which it will be impossible to adjust. How are we to ascertain the values and the proportions thereof to which she is entitled of the public arms and ammunitions of war, arsenals, ceded places, public edifices, ships of war, and of the public lands? Is there any court, or is there any form of action by which partition can be made of the territories? This last item is a very material one, for the only point of principle on which the secessionists take issue with the Republicans as to the platform of the latter (adopted at Chicago) is that of carrying slavery into the territories. What foothold or property in the territories will the seceders retain on leaving the Union? They will be foreign states, and we believe it has not yet been claimed, even by Judge Taney, that the laws of foreign states extend *proprio vigore* over the territories.

Another difficulty in making up the account with *South Carolina* would result from her claiming an almost incalculable credit for the disproportion of the public burdens which she fancies she has borne in the confederacy, by reason of what she considered the unequal operation of the various revenue laws.

Now, this right of secession, if it exist at all, is an absolute one, and a state has as much right to exercise it at one time as at another. If she may secede at will, she may do so in anticipation of war, or in time of war. If she can secede when she chooses, she owes no allegiance to the government an hour after she decides to secede, but will then be just as independent of the government as she is of any other nation. In the midst of war, then, it will be the right of any state not only to desert our own government, but at the same time to ally herself to the enemy. The *Hartford Convention* complained that New England was heavily taxed, but not defended by the general government, and merely proposed to ask the consent of the government to expend in the defence of New England the taxes raised in New England. This was not claimed as a right, but the consent of the government was to be sought. This was hardly an approach to secession, but the democracy of that day did not tolerate even the proposition, and the Hartford Convention was execrated.

But the absurdity of this new doctrine of the right of secession is too palpable for serious argument. The government under such a principle could not have twenty-four hours of assured existence. Neither other nations, nor its own citizens, could have confidence in its permanence. It would lack the vital principle of existence, because it would wholly lack credit. Nobody would lend it a dollar, for nobody could be sure that it would hold together long enough to pay a six months' loan, to say nothing of loans for long terms of years. The *public faith*, on which alone all who deal with governments can repose, would be utterly lacking. Business could have no security or stability, for men would not embark either their industry or their capital, unless under the shelter of laws and institutions not liable to change.

No—if a state secedes it is revolution, and the seceders are traitors. Those who are charged with the executive branch of the government are recreant to their oaths if they fail to use all lawful means to put down such rebellion. The people of no party base any confidence either in the fidelity or nerve of the Administration at Washington, but fear they will prove; some of them from inclination and others from timidity, practical allies of the revolutionists. They and their partisans have done all in their power to inflame and mislead the South, by charging upon the northern states the design of interfering with the rights of the people of the South, and the mercenaries here have co-operated in this false clamor and deception. The Administration, in relinquishing the government will endeavor to leave all possible embarrassments in the way of its successors, but we much mistake if those of its partisans here who have been foremost in the false work, will not be the first with whom the consequent mischief will come home to roost. * * *

1860   1860

From WHAT THE "CONSERVATIVES" WANT

There have been several attempts of late, in New York, Washington and elsewhere, to raise up what is facetiously called a "conservative" party, and it is perhaps worth while to examine a little into the meaning of these hitherto abortive efforts. What do these self-styled "conservative" gentlemen want, that they endeavor to raise up a party in the nation in opposition to the government, and to the men who have gone forth to fight the battles of the Union? They *say* they want the war carried on. Well, the war is going on; and the general they laud to the skies as the greatest commander in the world, whom they have forced upon the Administration and the country, is now doing his best to get out of the difficulties in which he perversely or blunderingly placed the largest and finest army we have. They *say* they want the Union and the constitution preserved. Well, the President has, in the opinion of all loyal men shown himself scrupulously faithful to his oath, and means, with all his might and the nation's, to preserve both Union and constitution. They *say* they want an honest and economical administration of the government—but such of these "conservative" leaders as have the luck to be in Congress, have, with a few exceptions, steadfastly voted for every "job" which has been brought before that body. They *say* they want freedom of speech. Good—so do we. But we remember when these self-elected "conservative" leaders, who are now so loud-mouthed about free speech, did their best to put down this right in this city, in Philadelphia, Cincinnati and elsewhere at the North. We congratulate them on their conversion; we can only hope it will be as lasting as it is recent.

What these "conservative" gentlemen really want is the offices. When these languishing patriots whine about "the Union as it was," they mean the Union as it was under Buchanan, with honest John B. Floyd as Secretary of War, to arrange Fort Snelling jobs, Willett's Point purchases, and Utah expeditions, for the double purpose of enriching his friends and disarming the nation; with honest Jacob Thompson as Secretary of the Interior, to wink at the abstraction of millions of Indian Trust bonds; with honest James Buchanan himself, the elect of these "conservatives," in the Presidential chair, to dispense federal patronage to his friends to that extent that his administration was the most extravagant and the most corrupt the country has ever known—though he, too, came into office on the plea of economy, which his followers now echo.

The platform of these self-styled "conservatives" contains exactly seven political principles: five loaves and two fishes; and they are faithful to these, under all circumstances. They might indeed exclaim, with the pious editor in the Biglow Papers:

> "I *don't* believe in princerple,
> But, O, I *du* in interest."

The Union as it was under Pierce and Buchanan was what is called "rather a good thing" for our "conservative" friends. They had free access to the public treasury, and they emptied it. Buchanan abused poor Fillmore for spending forty millions a year; but in the first year of his own term he spent eighty millions, and left the treasury empty and bankrupt when he retired in disgrace from the high place in which he had foully betrayed a great nation. No wonder the conservative mouth waters for the flesh pots of Egypt. No wonder they cry out, like the Israelites of old, "We remember the fish which we did eat in Egypt freely; the cucumbers and the melons, and the leeks and the onions, and the garlic. But now our soul is dried away; there is nothing at all, besides this manna, before our eyes." No wonder they are tender towards their rebellious masters, who, if they used them, aforetimes, at least fed them—at the people's expense. * * *

1862   1862

From A CERTAIN AND AN UNCERTAIN POLICY

The political jumping-jacks who have constituted themselves leaders of the opposition are an unhappy set of people. They would like to go dead against the war; for that which is nearest their hearts is to make a new political alliance with the rebellious planters, to reinstate these aristocrats in their former supremacy over the southern people, and with their help once more to establish themselves in office, and prostitute the government to the uses of the planters. But, unhappy wretches, they feel that to declare for peace at any price, to favor the abasement of the nation at the feet of the rebels, squarely and openly, would be to court political ruin; therefore they straddle painfully a political fence, and endeavor to talk war and peace in the same breath * * *

The next four years will be, probably, the most important in our history. We have been sick and we are getting well; the treatment of the national physician has been cautious; he has avoided heroic methods; he has been, perhaps, slow—but he has been very careful, conscientious, watchful, and he has carried us thus far through a terrible disease in safety. He has gained experience in these three and a half years, and is a wiser and more capable physician at this moment than ever. We are getting well; but on the upward road we shall need the most skilful treatment, the most careful watching. At this moment up come Vallandigham, Wood, Cox, Voorhees, Long, Harris —a lot of fellows who have been flinging mud at the poor patient all the time he was ill, and have been constantly fore-telling his speedy decease—and these impudent fellows cry out: "Don't keep on that hum-drum old doctor; bundle him out neck and heels; allow us to recommend to you a gentleman who has invented a patent pill expressly to make you well. He will set you on your legs in a few days. He has not had much medical experience, to be sure; he never cured anybody; but just try his patent pill. *We* will guarantee its efficacy."

But the patient, who is *not* delirious or a natural fool, replies: Who are you, that recommend a quack to me? Are you not the same who so bitterly cursed me all these years, who flung mud at me, who prophesied my certain death? And do you now ask me to take a physician of your recommendation?

"Only try his patent pill," they reiterate. "We can't tell

you exactly how it will work; we can't explain to you of what drugs it is compounded; you must not ask any troublesome questions; shut your eyes and bolt it, and you will see, fast enough, what will come of it."

The policy of Mr. Lincoln is declared and known. He has now guided the ship of state for more than three years; in that time of tremendous difficulty he has perhaps made mistakes, but he has acted throughout conscientiously, honorably, and with an honest and patriotic desire to do right. He has gained wisdom by experience. Every year has seen our cause more successful; every year has seen abler generals, more skilful leaders, called to the head; every year has seen fewer errors, greater ability, greater energy, in the administration of public affairs. The timid McClellan has been superseded by Grant, the do-nothing Buell by Sherman; wherever a man has shown conspicuous merit he has been called forward; political and military rivalries have been as far as possible banished from the field and from the national councils; all have been forced either to work honestly for the good of the country, or else to give place to more patriotic men. The result is a success which has grown year after year, which has falsified every prophecy of our enemies abroad, and filled them with astonishment at the immense military power which could be developed under the faithful and admirable organization of a Stanton, and the command of such great and unselfish leaders as Grant, Sherman, Thomas, Rosecrans, Farragut, and a host of others. There is every reason to believe that, while Mr. Lincoln continues in power, this healthy and beneficial state of things will continue. The best men will be retained in command; the most effectual measures will be used against the public enemy; the most kindly and fraternal spirit will be displayed towards the unfortunate people who have been the unwilling tools of the rebellious planters. Under his guidance we have the assurance that the war will be conducted vigorously while an enemy remains on our territory and insults our flag; and when peace comes by that enemy's submission, we have an equal assurance that he will require no conditions which freemen may not grant; he will demand for the nation only, to use his own words, "Everything for security, but nothing for revenge."

And what are we asked to substitute for this well-defined and honorable and satisfactory policy? Nobody knows. The opposition have not yet agreed upon it. They attempted to tell the nation through their resolutions at Chicago; but they are already ashamed of those. They may presently get ashamed of their candidate's letter. Just now they are quarreling amongst themselves about its meaning. Some declare it means submission to Jeff. Davis; some that it means war, without the help of negro troops, and without conscription: war, that is to say, which shall begin by weakening the armies, and of course end in defeat. But whatever it may be found to mean, it includes subversion of all the most important measures of the present administration; it means disorganization of the war power; it means the substitution, for Grant and Sherman, of generals long since shelved as incapable, men who have had small experience to teach them, and who are to be resurrected only as political favorites. It includes, by the open assertion of opposition speakers, the return to slavery of more than a hundred thousand Union soldiers who now guard our detached posts and fight the enemy. It means weakening the army, and thus necessarily prolonging the war and ensuring a disgraceful peace.

1864   1864

MAZZINI

History, my friends, has recorded the deeds of Giuseppe Mazzini on a tablet which will endure while the annals of Italy are read. Art has been called to do her part in perpetuating his memory, and to-day a bust is unveiled which will make millions familiar with the divine image stamped on the countenance of one of the greatest men of our times.

The idea of Italian unity and liberty was the passion of Mazzini's life; it took possession of him in youth, it grew stronger as the years went on, and lost none of its power over him in his age. Nor is it at all surprising that it should have taken a strong hold on his youthful imagination. I recollect very well that when, forty-four years ago, I first entered Italy, then held down under the weight of a score of despotisms, the same idea forcibly suggested itself to my mind as I looked southward from the slopes of the mountain country. There lay a great sisterhood of provinces requiring only a confederate republican government to raise them to the rank of a great power, presenting to the world a single majestic front, and parcelling out the powers of local legislation and government among the different neighborhoods in such a manner as to educate the whole population in a knowledge of the duties and rights of freemen. There were the industrious Piedmontese, the enterprising Genoese, among whom Mazzini was born—a countryman of Columbus; there were the ambitious Venetians and the Lombards, rejoicing in their fertile plains; and there, as the imagination followed the ridge of the Apennines toward the Strait of Messina, were the Tuscans, famed in letters; the Umbrians, wearing in their aspect the tokens of Latin descent; the Romans in their centre of arts; the gay Neapolitans; and farther south the versatile Sicilians, over whose valleys rolls the smoke of the most famous volcano in the world. As we traverse these regions in thought we recognize them all as parts of one Italy, yet each inhabited by Italians of a different character from the rest, all speaking Italian, but with a difference in each province; each region cherishing its peculiar traditions, which reach back to the beginning of civilization, and its peculiar usages observed for ages.

Well might the great man whose bust we disclose at this time to the public gaze be deeply moved by this spectacle of his countrymen and kindred bound in the shackles of a brood of local tyrannies which kept them apart that they might with more ease be oppressed. When he further considered the many great men who had risen from time to time in Italy as examples of the intellectual endowments of her people—statesmen, legislators, men of letters, men eminent in philosophy, in arms, and in arts—I say that he might well claim for the birthplace of such men the unity of its provinces to make it great, and the liberty of its people to raise them up to the standard of their mental endowments. Who shall blame him—who in this land of freedom—for demanding in behalf of such a country a political constitution framed on the most liberal pattern which the world has seen?

For such a constitution he planned; for that he labored; that object he never suffered to be out of his sight. No proclaimer of a new religion was ever more faithful to his mission. Here, where we have lately closed a sanguinary but successful war in defence of the unity of the States which form our Republic; here, where we have just broken the chains of three millions of bondmen—is, above all others, the place where a memorial of the great champion of Italian unity and liberty should be set up amid a storm of acclamation from a multitude of freemen.

Yet, earnestly as he desired these ends and struggled to attain them, the struggle was a noble and manly one; he disdained to compass these ends by base or ferocious means; he abhorred bloodshed; he detested vengeance; he spoke little of rights, but much of duties, resolving the cares of an enlightened statesmanship into matters of duty. The only warfare which he would allow, and that as a sorrowful necessity, was an open warfare waged against that brute force that violates human duty and human right. In that warfare his courage rose always equal to the occasion—a courage worthy of the generous political philosophy which he professed. For there was no trial he would not endure, no sacrifice, no labor he would not undertake, no danger he would not encounter for the sake of that dream of his youth and pursuit of his manhood, the unity and liberty of Italy.

That country is now united under one political head—save a portion arbitrarily and unjustly added to France—and to the public opinion formed in Italy by the teachings of Mazzini the union is in large measure due. Italy has now a constitutional government, the best feature of which it owes to the principles of republicanism in which Mazzini trained a whole generation of the young men of Italy, however short the present government of the country may fall of the ideal standard at which he aimed.

One great result for which he labored was the perfect freedom of religious worship. Well has he deserved the honors of posterity who, holding enforced worship to be an abomination in the sight of God, took his life in his hand and went boldly forward until the yoke of the great tyranny exercised over the religious conscience in his native country was broken. Such a hero deserves a monument in a land where the Government knows no distinction between religious denominations and leaves their worship to their consciences.

I will not say that he whose image is to-day unveiled was prudent in all his proceedings; nobody is; timidity itself is not always prudence. But, wherever he went and whatever he did, he was a power on earth. He wielded an immense influence over men's minds; he controlled a vast agency; he made himself the centre of a wide diffusion of opinions; his footsteps are seen in the track of history by those who do not always reflect by whose feet they are impressed. Such was the celerity of his movements and so sure the attachment of his followers that he was the terror of the crowned heads of Europe. Kings trembled when they heard that he had suddenly disappeared from London, and breathed more freely when they learned that he was in his grave. In proportion as he was dreaded he was maligned.

Image of the illustrious champion of civil and religious liberty, cast in enduring bronze to typify the imperishable renown of thy original, remain for ages yet to come where we place thee, in this resort of millions; remain till the day shall dawn—far distant though it may be—when the rights and duties of human brotherhood shall be acknowledged by all the races of mankind!

1878   1878

THE EMBARGO,

OR SKETCHES OF THE TIMES; A SATIRE

"When private faith and public trust are sold,
  And traitors barter liberty for gold,
  When fell corruption, dark, and deep, like fate,
  Saps the foundations of a sinking state;
  Then warmer numbers glow through Satire's page,
  And all her smiles are darken'd into rage;
  Then keener indignation fires her eye,
  Then flash her lightnings and her thunders fly."
                          ESSAY ON SATIRE

Look where we will, and in whatever land,
Europe's rich soil, or Afric's burning sand;
Where the wild savage hunts his wilder prey,
Or art and science pour their brightest day;
The monster vice appears before our eyes,
In naked impudence or gay disguise.

But quit the lesser game, indignant Muse,
And to thy country turn thy nobler views.
Ill-fated clime! condemn'd to feel th' extremes
Of a weak ruler's philosophic dreams;   10
Driv'n headlong on to ruin's fateful brink
When will thy Country feel, when will she think!

Wake Muse of Satire, in the cause of trade,
Thou scourge of miscreants who the laws evade!
Dart thy keen glances, knit thy threat'ning brows,
And hurl thine arrows at fair Commerce's foes!

Much injur'd Commerce! 'tis thy falling cause,
Which, from obscurity, a stripling draws;

And were his powers but equal to his zeal,
Thy dastard foes his keen reproach should feel.   20
Curse of our Nation, source of countless woes,
From whose dark womb unreckon'd misery flows;
Th' embargo rages like a sweeping wind,
Fear low'rs before, and famine stalks behind.
What words, oh, Muse! can paint the mournful scene,
The saddening street, the desolated green;
How hungry labourers leave their toil and sigh,
And sorrow droops in each desponding eye!

See the bold sailor from the ocean torn,
His element, sink friendless and forlorn!   30
His suffering spouse the tear of anguish shed,
His starving children cry in vain for bread!

The farmer, since supporting trade is fled,
Leaves the rude yoke, and cheerless hangs his head;
Misfortunes fall, an unremitting shower,
Debts follow debts, on taxes, taxes pour.
See in his stores his hoarded produce rot,
Or sheriff sales his profits bring to naught;
Disheartening cares in thronging myriads flow,
Till down he sinks to poverty and woe!   40

Oh, ye bright pair, the blessing of mankind!
Whom time has sanction'd, and whom fate has join'd,
COMMERCE, that bears the trident of the main,
And AGRICULTURE, empress of the plain;
Who, hand in hand, and heav'n-directed, go
Diffusing gladness through the world below;
Whoe'er the wretch, would hurl the flaming brand,
Of dire disunion, palsied be his hand!
Like 'Cromwell damn'd to everlasting fame,'
Let unborn ages execrate his name!   50
Dark is the scene, yet darker prospects threat,
And ills may follow unexperienc'd yet!

Oh Heaven! defend, as future seasons roll,
This western world from Buonaparte's control,
Preserve our *Freedom*, and our rights secure,
While truth subsists, and virtue shall endure!

Lo, Austria crouches to the tyrant's stroke,
And Rome's proud states receive his galling yoke;
Kings fall before him, for his sway extends
Where'er his all-subduing course he bends.   60
See Lusitania's fate, and shall we, say,
Turn not our feet, that tread the self-same way?

Must we with Belgia, and Helvetia mourn,
In vile subjection, abject, and forlorn?
Our laws laid prostrate, and our freedom fled,
Our independence, boasted valour dead?

We, who seven years erst brav'd Britannia's power,
By Heaven supported in the gloomiest hour;
For whom our Sages plann'd, our Heroes bled,
Whom WASHINGTON, our pride and glory led;   70
Till Heaven, propitious did our efforts crown,
With freedom, commerce, plenty, and renown!

When shall this land, some courteous angel say,
Throw off a weak, and erring ruler's sway?
Rise, injur'd people, vindicate your cause!
And prove your love of Liberty and laws;
Oh wrest, sole refuge of a sinking land,
The sceptre from the slave's imbecile hand!
Oh ne'er consent, obsequious, to advance
The *willing vassal* of imperious France!   80
Correct that suffrage you misus'd before,
And lift your voice above a Congress' roar!
And thou, the scorn of every patriot name,
Thy country's ruin, and her council's shame!
Poor servile thing! derision of the brave!

Who erst from Tarleton fled to Carter's cave;
Thou, who, when menac'd by perfidious Gaul,
Didst prostrate to her whisker'd minion fall;
And when our cash her empty bags supplied,
Didst meanly strive the foul disgrace to hide;   90
Go, wretch, resign the presidential chair,
Disclose thy secret features foul or fair,
Go, search, with curious eyes, for horned frogs,
'Mongst the wild wastes of Louisianian bogs;
Or where Ohio rolls his turbid stream,
Digs for huge bones, thy glory and thy theme;
Go scan, Philosophist; thy ****** charms,
And sink supinely in her sable arms;
But quit to abler hands, the helm of state,
Nor image ruin on thy country's fate!   100

But vain are reason, eloquence and art,
And vain the warm effusions of the heart.
Ev'n while I sing, see, *faction* urge her claim,
Mislead with falsehood, and with zeal inflame,
Lift her broad banner, spread her empire wide,
And stalk triumphant, with a fury's stride.
She blows her brazen trump, and at the sound,
A motley throng obedient flock around;
A mist of changing hue o'er all she flings,
And darkness perches on her dragon wings!   110

As Johnson deep, as Addison refin'd,
And skill'd to pour conviction o'er the mind,
Oh might some Patriot rise! the gloom dispel,
Chase error's mist, and break her magic spell!

But vain the wish, for hark! the murmuring meed
Of hoarse applause, from yonder shed proceed;
Enter, and view the thronging concourse there,
Intent, with gaping mouth, and stupid stare,
While in the midst their supple leader stands,

Harangues aloud, and flourishes his hands; 120
To adulation tunes his servile throat,
And sues, successful, for each blockhead's vote.

"Oh, were I made a ruler in the land!
Your rights, no man can better understand;
For the dear people, how my bowels yearn!
That *such* may govern, be your chief concern:
Then federal tyranny shall flee away,
And *mild democracy* confirm her sway."
The powerful influence of the knave's address,
In capers droll, the foolish dupes confess, 130
With *horrid* shouts the affrighted sky is rent,
And high in air their tatter'd hats are sent.

But should truth shine, distinguishingly bright,
And lay his falsehoods naked to the sight;
He tries new arts to blind their willing eyes,
Feeds with new flatteries, hammers out new lies;
Exerts his influence, urges all his weight,
To blast the laurels of the good and great;
Till reconfirm'd the fools uphold him still,
Their creed, his *dictum*, and their laws, his will. 140

Now morning rises, borne on golden wings,
And fresh to toil the waking postboy springs;
Lo, trudging on his rawbon'd steed, he hies,
Dispersing Suns, and Chronicles, and Spys;
Men uninform'd, in rage for something new,
Howe'er unprincipled, howe'er untrue,
Suck in with greedy throat, the gilded pill,
Whose fatal sweetness pleases but to kill.
Wide, and more wide, the dire contagion flies,
Till half the town is overwhelm'd with lies. 150
Hence that delusion, hence that furious zeal,
Which wrong heads cherish, and which hot heads feel.

In vain *Italia* boasts her genial clime,
Her Rome's proud tow'rs, and palaces sublime;
In vain the hardy Swiss, inur'd to toil,
Draw scant subsistence from a stubborn soil;
Both doom'd alike, to feel, in evil hour,
The giant grasp of huge despotick power!
Touch not their shores, fair freedom is not there,
But far remote, she breathes Columbian air;   160
Yet here her temple totters to its fall,
Our rulers bowing to audacious Gaul!

Oh, let not prating *History* proclaim
The foul disgrace, the scandal to our name!
Write not the deed, my hand! Oh may it lie,
Plung'd deep, and mantled in obscurity!
Forbid it Heaven! that while true honor reigns,
And ancient valour glows within our veins;
(Our standard justice, and our shield our God,)
We e'er should tremble at a despot's nod!   170

Oh, may the laurels of unrivall'd fame,
For ever flourish round your honour'd name!
Ye, who unthrall'd by prejudice or power,
Determin'd stood in that eventful hour;
Tore the dire secret from the womb of night,
And bar'd your country's infamy to light!
Go boldly on, the deep laid plot unfold,
Though much is known, yet much remains untold.
But chief to thee our gratitude belongs,
Oh Pickering! who hast scann'd thy country's wrongs,   180
Whose ardent mind, and keen discerning eye,
Pierc'd the peep veil of Gallic policy;
And in whose well-tim'd labours we admire,
The sage's wisdom and the patriot's fire!

Rise then, Columbians! heed not France's wiles;
Her bullying mandates, her seductive smiles;

Send home Napoleon's slave, and bid him say,
No arts can lure us, and no threats dismay;
Determin'd yet to war with whom we will,
Choose our own allies or be neutral still.   190

Ye merchants, arm! the pirate Gaul repel,
Your prowess shall the naval triumph swell;
Send the marauders shatter'd, whence they came,
And Gallia's cheek suffuse with crimson shame.
But first select, our councils to direct,
One whose true worth entitles to respect;
In whom concentrates all that men admire,
The sage's prudence, and the soldier's fire;
Who scorns ambition, and the venal tribe,
And neither offers, nor receives a bribe;   200
Who firmly guards his country's every right,
And shines alike in council or in fight.

Then on safe seas the merchant's barque shall fly,
Our waving flag shall kiss the polar sky;
On canvas wings our thunders shall be borne,
Far to the west, or tow'rd the rising morn;
Then may we dare a haughty tyrant's rage,
And gain the blessings of an unborn age.

'Tis done, behold the cheerful prospects rise!
And splendid scenes the startled eye surprise;   210
Lo! busy commerce courts the prosperous main;
And peace and plenty glad our shores again!
Th' industrious swain sees nature smile around
His fields with fruit, with flocks, his pastures crown'd.

Thus in a fallen tree, from sprouting roots,
With sudden growth, a tender sapling shoots,
Improves from day to day, delights the eyes
With strength and beauty, stateliness and size,
Puts forth robuster arms, and broader leaves,
And high in air, its branching head upheaves.   220

Turn now our views to Europe's ravag'd plains,
Where murd'rous war, with grim oppression reigns;
There long and loud the storm of battle roars,
With direful portent to our distant shores;
The regal robber rages uncontrol'd,
No law restrains him, and no faith can hold;
Before his steps, lo! cow'ring terror flies,
And pil'd behind him heaps of carnage rise!
With fraud or force, he spreads his iron sway,
And blood and rapine mark his frightful way!　　　　230

Thus some huge rock of ice, on Greenland's shore,
When bound in frost, the surges cease to roar,
Breaks loosen'd from its base, with mighty sweep,
And thunders horrid o'er the frozen deep!

While thus, all Europe rings with his alarms,
Say, shall we rush, unthinking, to his arms?
No: let us dauntless all his fury brave,
Our fluttering flag, in freedom's gale shall wave,
Our guardian Sachem's errless shafts shall fly,
And terrors lighten from our eagle's eye!　　　　240

Here then I cease, rewarded, if my song
Shall prompt one honest mind though guided wrong,
To pause from party, view his country's state,
And lend his aid to stem approaching fate!
1808　　　　　　　　　　　　　　　　　　　　　　　1808

TO A FRIEND ON HIS MARRIAGE

While now the tepid skies and gentle rains
Of April bid the gushing brooks o'erflow;
While scarce their earliest verdure tints the plains
And cold in hollows lurks the lingering snow;—
Love, sauntering in the sunny glade to know
If yet upon the moss banks of the Grove

That little flower of golden vesture blow
Which first the spring receives of Flora's love;
I hum this careless strain as deviously I rove.

Yet not unlovely, nor with song uncheer'd   10
Is this pale month, and still I love to greet,
At misty dawn, the bluebird's carol heard,
And red breast, from the orchard warbling sweet;
The fogs, that, as the sun rises, meet
In snowy folds along the channell'd flood;
The squirrel issuing from his warm retreat,
The purple glow that tints the budding wood,
The sound of bursting streams by gathered mounds withstood.

And now the heaving breast, and glances meek,
The unbidden warmth in beauty's veins declare;   20
The gale that lifts the tresses from her cheek,
Can witness to the fires that kindle there;
Now is the time to woo the yielding fair;—
But thou, my friend, may'st woo the fair no more;
Thine are connubial joys and wedded care,
And scarce the hymenean moon is o'er,
Since first, in bridal hour, thy name Eliza bore.

And if thy poet's prayer be not denied,
The hymenean moon shall ever last;
The golden chain, indissolubly tied,   30
Shall heighten as the winged hours glide past;
And wheresoe'er in life thy lot be cast,
For life at best is bitterness and guile—
Still may thy own Eliza cheer the waste,
Soften its weary ruggedness the while,
And gild thy dreams of peace, and make thy sorrows smile.

Such be thy days.—O'er Coke's black letter page,
Trimming the lamp at eve, 't is mine to pore;
Well pleased to see the venerable sage
Unlock his treasur'd wealth of legal lore;   40

And I, that lov'd to trace the woods before,
And climb the hill a play mate of the breeze,
Have vow'd to tune the rural lay no more,
Have bid my useless classics sleep at ease,
And left the race of bards to scribble, starve and freeze.

Farewell.—When mildly through the naked wood,
The clear warm sun effus'd a mellow ray;
And livelier health propell'd the vital flood,
Loitering at large, I poured the incondite lay,
Forgot the cares and business of the day,   50
Forgot the quirks of Littleton and Coke,
Forgot the publick storms, and party fray;
And, as the inspiring flame across me broke,
To thee the lowly harp, neglected long, I woke.

1813   1813

"NOT THAT FROM LIFE, AND ALL ITS WOES"

Not that from life, and all its woes
    The hand of death shall set me free;
Not that this head, shall then repose
    In the low vale most peacefully.

Ah, when I touch time's farthest brink,
    A kinder solace must attend;
It chills my very soul, to think
    On that dread hour when life must end.

In vain the flatt'ring verse may breathe,
    Of ease from pain, and rest from strife,   10
There is a sacred dread of death
    Inwoven with the strings of life.

This bitter cup at first was given
    When angry *justice* frown'd severe,
And 'tis th' eternal doom of heaven
    That man must view the grave with fear.

Ca. 1814   1817

A CHORUS OF GHOSTS

Come to thy couch of iron rest,
  Come share our dreamless bed;
There's room, within the grave-yard bounds,
  To lay thy weary head.

Come, thou shalt have a home like ours,
  A low and narrow cell;
With a gray stone to mark the spot,
  For thee the turf shall swell.

Cold are its walls—but not for thee;
  And dark—but thou shalt sleep;   10
Unfelt, the enclosing clods above
  Their endless guard shall keep.

'Mid scenes from nature's solitude
  Won by assiduous toil,
Thy bones shall find a pleasant grave,
  And sleep in virgin soil.

Yes—o'er thee where thy first strains rose,
  Thine earliest haunts to hail,
Shall the tall crow-foot's yellow gems
  Bend in the mountain gale.   20

There, as he seeks his tardy kine,
  When flames the evening sky
With thoughtful look, the cottage boy
  Shall pass thy dwelling by.

Why shudder at that breathless sleep,
  That night of solid gloom?
We heard thee pray for rest and peace—
  Thou'lt find them in the tomb.

Come, we will close thy glazing eye,
    Compose thy dying head;   30
And gently from its house of clay
    Thy struggling spirit lead.

1814   1826

From "THIS GRASSY SLOPE, THIS ANCIENT TREE"

This grassy slope, this ancient tree,
From infancy were dear to me:
Here, when the summer sun rides high,
Beneath these boughs I love to lie:—
The turf is cool—the shade is deep,—
And freshly here the breezes creep,
And, at the foot of this green hill,
The murmuring river welters still—
Look round—how lovely spreads the scene—
Gay meads and cottages between   10
And many a field where Zephyr strays
Among the rustling rows of maize—
Scarce forty years have passed away
Since waste and wild the prospect lay—
Here never had the hand of toil
Dared violate the virgin soil,
Nor echoing ax had ever here
Startled in deep brown dell the deer—
But Nature unreclaimed and rude
Reigned in this sylvan solitude   20
And listened midst her reverend groves
To the wild birds that told their loves—
The roar of winds—the solemn sound
Of water dashed from rocks around.
No beasts of prey within it dwelt,
No fear its harmless tenants felt,
Save when the tawny hunter came
In these broad hills to trace his game—
Here many a *maple of the rock*

That Time and Tempest seemed to mock   30
As proudly raised its branching brow
As this which knows no rival now ✳ ✳ ✳

1814-15

"FAREWELL—THE BITTER WORD IS SAID"

Farewell—the bitter word is said—
    And thou to distant scenes must go
Where wide the western lakes are spread
    And deep the western rivers flow.

Yet shalt thou there with pensive eye,
    When softly beams the twilight star,
Look sometimes on the eastern sky
    And think on all thy friends afar.

The memory of thine earliest home,
    With feelings which no words can speak,   10
Like a soft spell shall o'er thee come
    And tears shall gem thy rosy cheek.

Oh, often may those thoughts return;
    And oft thy moist and glistening eye,
While sunset's fading splendours burn,
    Be turned upon the eastern sky.

1817–19?

"THEY TAUGHT ME, AND IT WAS A FEARFUL CREED"

They taught me, and it was a fearful creed
That God forgets his creatures in the grave
And to the eternity of darkness leaves
Thought and its organs. Fearfully upon my heart
Fastened the terrible doubt—and the strong fear
Of death o'ermastered me and visions came—

Horrible visions such as I pray God
I may not see again. Methought I died
And I was laid beneath the thick green grass
Of my own native mountains.—There were tears,   10
Warm tears, shed over me—such tears as fall
On many a humble grave, and dear hands wrung
In agony to think that I should die.
And all that I had learnt of virtue here
In the world's suffering—all that studious toil
Had taught me—all that from the book
Of Nature I had striven to transcribe
Into my mind—and from the laid-up thoughts
Of men of other days had now no place—
Parted—blotted out forever. . . .   20

Ca. 1818

HOUSATONIC

The mist, above no lovelier stream,
   Is melted by the early sun,
Than that whose quiet waters gleam
   Along the vales of Barrington.

With boughs the rippling edge is dark,
   The middle current bright with day;
And from the winding margin,—mark,
   How softly stretch the lawns away.

Above, the craggy mountains frown,
   And sunny dells the slope divide,   10
And many a charming rill comes down,
   To mingle with the stiller tide.

Oh, I shall love, till life depart,
   That stream so sweet, that scene so wild;—
For the dear maid, who stole my heart,
   There listened to my vows and smiled.

Bright river! thy fresh banks may fade,—
    The axe may lop the tree and vine,
The winding avenue of shade,
    Through which thy waters steal and shine!   20

The arid blast thy wave may drink,
    The summer sun his heats may shed,
And gaze upon thee till thou shrink
    Among the pebbles of thy bed.

Yet with me shall thy image stay,
    And wear undimmed its living hues;
While Love's warm pencil, every day,
    The tints retouches and renews.

As green thy bowers shall flourish there,
    As bright thy glimmering current run,   30
And thy wild banks shall bloom as fair
    As when my blushing maid was won.

1818–20?

THE EARLY ANEMONE

    Not idly do I stray
At prime, where far the mountain ranges run,
    And note, along my way,
Each flower that opens in the early sun,
Or gather blossoms by the valley's spring,
Where the sun stoops and dancing insects sing.

    Each has her moral rede—
Each of the gentle family of flowers;
    And I with patient heed,
Oft spell their lessons in my graver hours.   10
The faintest streak that on a floweret lies
May speak instruction to initiate eyes.

Ca. 1822

THE ROBBER

Beside a lonely mountain path,
    Within a mossy wood,
That crowned the wild, wind-beaten cliffs,
    A lurking robber stood.
His foreign garb, his gloomy eye,
    His cheek of swarthy stain,
Bespoke him one who might have been
    A pirate on the main,
Or bandit on the far-off hills
    Of Cuba or of Spain.   10

His ready pistol in his hand,
    A shadowing bough he raised,
Glared forth as crouching tiger glares,
    And muttered as he gazed—
"Sure he must sleep upon his steed—
    I dreamed the laggard near;
I'll give him for the gold he wears,
    A sounder slumber here:
His charger, when I press his flank,
    Shall leap like mountain deer."   20

Long, long he watched, and listened long,
    There came no traveler by.
The ruffian growled a harsher curse,
    And gloomier grew his eye;
While o'er the sultry heaven began
    A leaden haze to spread,
And past his noon, the summer sun
    A dimmer beam to shed;
And on that mountain summit fell
    A silence deep and dread.   30

Then ceased the bristling pine to sigh,
    Still hung the birchen spray;

The air that wrapped those massy cliffs
  Was motionless as they;
Mute was the cricket in his cleft—
  But mountain torrents round,
Sent hollow murmurs from their glens,
  Like voices under ground.
A change came o'er the robber's cheek,
  He shuddered at the sound.   40

'Twere vain to ask what painful thought
  Convulsed his brow with pain;
"The dead talk not," he said at length,
  And turned to watch again.
Skyward he looked—a lurid cloud,
  Hung low and blackening there,
And through its skirts the sunshine came,
  A strange, malignant glare;
His ample chest drew in with toil
  The hot and stifling air.   50

His ear had caught a distant sound—
  But not the tramp of steed—
A roar, as of a torrent stream
  Swollen into sudden speed.
The gathered vapors in the west,
  Before a rushing blast,
Like living monsters of the air,
  Black, serpent-like, and vast,
Writhe, roll, and sweeping o'er the sun,
  A frightful shadow cast.   60

Hark, to that nearer, mightier crash!
  As if a giant crowd,
Trampling the oaks with iron feet,
  Has issued from the cloud;
While fragments of dissevered rock
  Go thundering from on high,

And eastward, from their eyrie cliffs,
   The shrieking eagles fly;
And lo! the expected traveler comes,
   Spurring his charger by.   70

To that wild warning of the air
   The assassin lends no heed;
He lifts the pistol to his eye,
   He notes the horseman's speed:
Firm in his hand and sure his aim—
   But ere the flash is given,
Its eddies filled with woods uptorn,
   And spray from torrents driven,
The whirlwind sweeps the crashing wood—
   The giant firs are riven.   80

Riven, and wrenched up from splintering cliffs
   They rise like down in air;
At once the forest's rocky floor
   Lies to the tempest bare.
Rider and steed and robber whirled
   O'er precipices vast,
'Mong trunks, and boughs, and shattered crags,
   Mangled and crushed are cast.
The catamount and eagle made,
   At morn, a grim repast.   90

1833   1833

APPENDIX II. A LIST OF LITERARY ARTICLES AND ADDRESSES BY BRYANT

Review of Solyman Brown, *An Essay on American Poetry*, in *North American Review*, VII, 198–211 (July, 1818), collected in part as "Early American Verse" in *Prose Writings*, I, 45–56. (For extract, see p. 165 above.)

On the Use of Trisyllabic Feet in Iambic Verse, in *North American Review*, IX, 426–31 (Sept., 1819), collected with new material in *Prose Writings*, I, 57–67. (For the original text, see p. 158 above; for new material, see p. 409 below.)

Review of James A. Hillhouse, *Percy's Masque*, in *North American Review*, XI, 364–93 (Oct., 1820), collected in part as "On Writing Tragedy" in *Prose Writings*, II, 349–51.

Review of Richard Henry Dana, Sr., *The Idle Man*, Vol. II, No. 1, in *Columbian Centinel*, Nov. 27, 1822.

Review of Catherine M. Sedgwick, *Redwood*, in *North American Review*, XX, 245–72 (April, 1825), collected in part as "American Society as a Field for Fiction" in *Prose Writings*, II, 351–60. (For extracts, see p. 176 above and p. 413 below.)

Review of Henry Pickering, *The Ruins of Pæstum and Athens, and Other Poems*, in *North American Review*, XIX, 42–9 (July, 1824).

Review of James A. Hillhouse, *Hadad*, in *New-York Review*, I, 1–13 (June, 1825), collected in part as "On the Dramatic Use of Scripture Characters" in *Prose Writings*, II, 361–4.

Review of Jehan de Nostre Dame, *Vies des Plus Célèbres et Anciens Poètes Provençaux*, in *idem*, I, 104–25 (July, 1825), collected as "Nostradamus's Provençal Poets" in *Prose Writings*, I, 68–92.

Review of Francis Wayland, *The Duties of an American Citizen*, in *New-York Review*, I, 142–3 (July, 1825).

Review of Daniel Webster, *Address Delivered at the Laying of the Corner Stone of the Bunker Hill Monument*, in *idem*, I, 214–9 (August, 1825).

Review of *United States Literary Gazette*, Nos. 1–8, in *idem*, I, 219–21 (August, 1825).

Review of *Memoirs and Recollections of Count Segur*, in *idem*, I, 291–300 (Sept., 1825).

Review of Walter Scott, *Lives of the Novelists*, in *idem*, I, 413–28 (Nov., 1825).

Review of Rammohun Roy, *The Precepts of Jesus*, in *idem*, I, 442–55 (Nov., 1825).

Review of Richard H. Lee, *Memoir of the Life of Richard Henry Lee*, in *idem*, II, 23–32 (Dec., 1825).

Review of Thomas Moore, *Memoirs of the Life of the Rt. Hon. Richard Brinsley Sheridan*, in *idem*, II, 165–81 (Feb., 1826), collected in part as "The Character of Sheridan" in *Prose Writings*, II, 365–69.

Review of James G. Percival, *Poem: Delivered before the Connecticut Alpha of Phi Beta Kappa*, in *New-York Review*, II, 245–52 (March, 1826).

Lectures on Poetry (delivered in April, 1826), in *Prose Writings*, I, 3–56. (For full text, see pp. 184–223 above.)

Review of Robert Benson, *Sketches of Corsica*, in *New-York Review*, II, 348–63 (April, 1826), collected in part as "Bonaparte's Corsican Traits" in *Prose Writings*, II, 370–3.

Review of Henry Wheaton, *Some Account of the Life, Writings, and Speeches of William Pinkney*, in *New-York Review*, II, 435–44 (May, 1826).

Review of Grenville Mellen, *The Rest of the Nations: A Poem*, in *United States Review and Literary Gazette*, IV, 461–2 (Sept., 1826).

Review of Richard Henry Dana, Sr., *Poems*, in *North American Review*, XXVI, 239–47 (Jan., 1828).

Recollections of the South of Spain, in *The Talisman for 1829*. New York: 1828, pp. 43–51, collected with "Early Spanish Poetry" (see below) under the title "Moriscan Romances" in *Prose Writings*, I, 92–102. (For full text, see pp. 240 ff. above.)

Early Spanish Poetry, in *The Talisman for 1830*, New York: 1829, pp. 227–37, collected with "Recollections of the South of Spain" under the title "Moriscan Romances" in *Prose Writings*, I, 92–102.

Phanettes des Gantelmes, in *The Talisman for 1830*, pp. 238–54, collected as "Female Troubadours" in *Prose Writings*, I, 103–114.

The Writings of Fitz-Greene Halleck, in *New-York Mirror*, XIV, 97 (Sept. 24, 1836), quoted in *Some Notices of the Life and Writings of Fitz-Greene Halleck* (see below).

To the Reader, in *Selections from the American Poets* (ed. Bryant). New York: 1840, pp. iii–iv.

Discourse on the Life and Genius of Cooper (delivered Feb. 25, 1852), in *Memorial of James Fenimore Cooper*. New York: [1852], pp. 39–74, and collected in *Prose Writings*, I, 299–331. (For extracts, see p. 273 above.)

William Gilmore Simms, in *Homes of American Authors*. New York: 1853, pp. 257–62, reprinted in *Little Journeys to the Homes of American Authors*. New York: 1896, pp. 157–66.

Robert Burns (extracts from addresses delivered Jan. 25, 1859, Jan. 25, 1871, and Jan. 25, 1876), in *Prose Writings*, II, 314–23.

Frederick Schiller (delivered Nov. 11, 1859), in *idem*, II, 215–20.

A Discourse on the Life, Character and Genius of Washington Irving (delivered April 3, 1860). New York: 1860, collected in *Prose Writings*, I, 332–68. (For extracts, see p. 289 above.)

Some Notices of the Life and Writings of Fitz-Greene Halleck (delivered Feb. 2, 1869). New York: 1869, collected in *Prose Writings*, I, 369–93.

Translators of Homer (delivered Feb. 22, 1870), in *idem*, II, 267–9.

Preface, *The Iliad of Homer*. Boston: 1870, pp. iii–xiii.

Shakespeare (delivered April 23, 1870, and May 22, 1872), in *Prose Writings*, II, 300–9.

A Discourse on the Life, Character, and Writings of Gulian Crommelin Verplanck (delivered May 17, 1870). New York: 1870, collected in *Prose Writings*, I, 394–431.

Introduction, *A Library of Poetry and Song* (ed. Bryant). New York: 1871, pp. xxi–xxxi, collected as "Poets and Poetry

of the English Language" in *Prose Writings*, I, 147–160.
(For an extract, see p. 301 above.)

The Mercantile Library (delivered Nov. 6, 1870), in *Prose
Writings*, II, 270–3.

German Literature (delivered May 17, 1871), in *idem*, II, 287–
90.

Literary Missionaries (delivered in 1872), in *idem*, II, 298–9.

Oldham's Poems, in *Old and New*, VI, 329–35 (Sept., 1872),
collected in *Prose Writings*, I, 114–28.

Sir Walter Scott (delivered Nov. 4, 1872), in *idem*, II, 310–13.

Preface, *The Odyssey of Homer* (second edition). Boston:
1873, pp. iii–vi.

Franklin as a Poet (delivered Jan. 17, 1874), in *Prose Writings*,
II, 329–31.

Abraham Cowley, in *North American Review*, CXXIV, 368–82
(May, 1877), and collected in *Prose Writings*, I, 129–46.

A considerable number of reviews and literary notes which
Bryant is known to have contributed to various periodicals
have not been identified. Mr. C. I. Glicksberg has recently
attributed to Bryant (*New England Quarterly*, VII, 696–9,
Dec., 1934) two literary notices in the *United States Review and
Literary Gazette*, of which he was joint editor in 1826–27; but
it is certain that additional items in that journal must be from his
pen. Again, only a few of the notes on contemporary books
which, for many years, he wrote for the *New York Evening
Post* have been identified (see Nevins, *The Evening Post*, pp.
216–23). However, the reviews and notes published in these
two periodicals are usually hack work, and are in the main so
mediocre that definite attribution of them to Bryant would not
better his reputation as a critic.

APPENDIX III. CONTEMPORARY CRITICISM OF BRYANT

REVIEW OF *THE EMBARGO, OR SKETCHES OF THE TIMES; A SATIRE* (Boston: 1808)

Monthly Anthology, V, 339–40 (June, 1808)

[By A. H. EVERETT]

If this poem be really written by a youth of thirteen, it must be acknowledged an extraordinary performance. We have never met with a boy at that age, who had attained to such command of language and to so much poetick phraseology. Though the poem is unequal, and there are some flat and prosaick passages, yet is there no small portion of fire and some excellent lines. ＊ ＊ ＊

We regret that the young poet has dared to aim the satirick shaft against the breast of our most excellent President. But, as the lines are a good specimen of the author's powers, we cannot resist the temptation of quoting them, conscious that the first magistrate of this country, secure in the impenetrable armour of moral rectitude, "smiles at the drawn dagger, and defies its point."

[Ll. 73-100 are quoted.]

If the young bard has met with no assistance in the composition of this poem, he certainly bids fair, should he continue to cultivate his talent, to gain a respectable station on the Parnassian mount, and to reflect credit on the literature of his country.

REVIEW OF *POEMS* (Cambridge: 1821)

North American Review, XII, 380–1 (Oct., 1821)

[By WILLARD PHILLIPS]

Of what school is this writer? The Lake, the Pope, or the Cockney; or some other? Does he imitate Byron or Scott, or

Campbell? These are the standing interrogatories in all tribunals having the jurisdiction of poetry, and it behoves us to see that they are administered. He is then of the school of nature, and of Cowper; if we may answer for him; of the school which aims to express fine thoughts, in true and obvious English, without attempting or fearing to write like any one in particular, and without being distinguished for using or avoiding any set of words or phrases. It does not, therefore, bring any system into jeopardy to admire him, and his readers may yield themselves to their spontaneous impressions, without an apprehension of deserting their party.

There is running through the whole of this little collection, a strain of pure and high sentiment, that expands and lifts up the soul and brings it nearer to the source of moral beauty. This is not indefinitely and obscurely shadowed out, but it animates bright images and clear thoughts. There is everywhere a simple and delicate portraiture of the subtle and ever vanishing beauties of nature, which she seems willing to conceal as her choicest things, and which none but minds the most susceptible can seize, and no other than a writer of great genius, can body forth in words. There is in this poetry something more than mere painting. It does not merely offer in rich colours what the eye may see or the heart feel, or what may fill the imagination with a religious grandeur. It does not merely rise to sublime heights of thought, with the forms and allusions that obey none but master spirits. Besides these, there are wrought into the composition a luminous philosophy and deep reflection, that make the subjects as sensible to the understanding, as they are splendid to the imagination. There are no slender lines and unmeaning epithets, or words loosely used to fill out the measure. The whole is of rich materials, skilfully compacted. A throng of ideas crowds every part, and the reader's mind is continually and intensely occupied with 'the thick coming fancies.'

The first poem is in the majestic and flexible stanza of Spenser; the last is in the common heroic blank verse; and in both there is a powerful sway of versification, and a sure and ready style of execution. The others are shorter than these. They have great freedom and propriety of language, and are abundantly rich in sentiment, and marked by the utmost fineness and delicacy of perception. We are not endeavoring to speak favorably of this poetry, we wish only to speak of it justly, and those who read it and apprehend its beauties will say, that we do it no more than justice. * * *

Perhaps some may wish us to mention that the sense is not invariably suspended at the conclusion of the lines, and in two instances, we think there are two, does not conclude with the stanza. There are some instances of trisyllabic feet, such as are found in Spenser and Byron and others, who have written in the same stanza. Whether these are beauties or defects is hardly worth the inquiry in such a production, where they are buried and lost in so much that is great and superlatively beautiful.

AMERICAN WRITERS

Blackwood's Edinburgh Magazine, XVI, 304–11 (Sept., 1824)

[By JOHN NEAL]

BRYANT, WILLIAM CULLEN.—This gentleman's poetry has found its way, piecemeal, into England, and having met with a little of our newspaper praise, which has been repeated with great emphasis in America, is now set among his associates for a poet of extraordinary promise, on the ground of having produced, within the course of several years, about fifty duodecimo pages of poetry, such as we shall give a specimen of. Mr B. is not, and never will be, a great poet. He wants fire—he wants the very rashness of a poet—the prodigality and fervour of those, who are overflowing with inspiration. Mr B., in fact, is a sensible young man, of a thrifty disposition, who knows how to manage a few plain ideas in a very handsome way. It is a bad thing for a poet, or for one whom his friends believe to be a poet, ever to spend a long time about the manufacture of musical prose, in imitation of anybody,—as Mr Bryant and Mr Percival both do of Milman, who has quite set the fashion in America for blank verse. Some lines, (about fifteen or twenty,) to a "WATER-FOWL," which are very beautiful, to be sure, but with no more poetry in them than there is in the Sermon on the Mount, are supposed, by his countrymen, "to be well known in Europe." * * *

REVIEW OF *MISCELLANEOUS POEMS SELECTED FROM THE UNITED STATES LITERARY GAZETTE*
(Boston: 1826)

North American Review, XXII, 432–43 (April, 1826)

[By ALVAN LAMSON]

* * * Mr. Bryant, who has contributed the largest number of pieces to the volume before us, has been for several years a favorite with the American public. * * * As a poet, he possesses rare gifts. His poetry has truth, delicacy, and correctness, as well as uncommon vigor and richness; he is always faithful to nature; his delineations are accurate, vivid, and forcible; he selects his groups and images with judgment, and sketches with spirit and exactness. He writes as one, 'who, in the love of nature, holds communion with her visible forms.' Nothing is borrowed, nothing artificial; his pictures have an air of freshness and originality, which could come from the student of nature alone. He is alive to the beautiful forms of the outward world. These forms hold a language to his heart. Nature to him is not an inert mass, mere dead matter; it is almost a feeling, and a sentiment. His poetry is always refreshing; the scenes of stillness and repose, into which he introduces us, seem fitted to exclude care and sorrow; he draws us from haunts of men, where we become familiar with loathsome forms of vice and misery, where our hearts are torn with anxiety, or wounded by neglect and ingratitude, and makes us 'partake of the deep contentment,' which the mute scenes of earth breathe. He is less the poet of artificial life, than of nature, and the feelings. There is something for the heart, as well as for the understanding and fancy, in all he writes; something, which touches our sensibility, and awakens deep toned, sacred reflections.

Again, Mr. Bryant charms us by his simplicity. Like all true lovers of nature, he is fond of those chaste beauties, which strike on the heart at once, and are incapable of being heightened by any extraneous ornament. His pictures are never overcharged. Nothing is turgid or meretricious, strange or fantastic. His heart is open to the healthful influences of nature; he muses among her gay and beautiful forms, and throws out upon the world his visions and feelings in a garb of attractive simplicity and grace. His strains, moreover, are exquisitely finished. He leaves nothing crude and imperfect; he throws off no hasty sketches, no vague, shadowy, and ill assorted images. His portraits have a picturesque distinctness; the outlines are accurately traced, and the colors laid on with delicacy and skill. We are never disgusted with grossness; nothing appears overstrained or feeble, deformed, misshapen, or out of place.

To write such poetry at any time would be no trifling distinction. Mr. Bryant deserves the greater praise, as he has exhibited a pure and classical standard in an age, the tendency of which is, in some respects, towards lawless fanaticism and wildness. There is a fashion in literature, as in everything else. The popular style is now the rapid, the hasty, the abrupt, and unfinished. The age is certainly not a superficial one. It is distinguished beyond any former period for habits of deep, earnest thought. But one of its characteristics seems to be an impatience of restraint. It is fond of strong excitement, however produced. Whatever excites the mind into a state of fervor, whatever powerfully awakens the feelings, is listened to and applauded. It may be vague, fantastic, and shapeless, produced by a sort of extemporaneous effort, and sent abroad without the labor of revision. It will not have the less chance of becoming, for a time at least, popular. The press was never more prolific than at present. A great deal is written, and, as might be naturally supposed, much is written in haste. The mass of popular literature is swelling to an overgrown bulk; but much of it is crude, coarse, and immature. Mr. Bryant has not been seduced by the temptations to slovenliness and negligence, which the age holds out to view; but, on the contrary, he affords

a happy specimen of genuine, classical English. We are gratified to meet with such examples, especially among the distinguished and favored poets of our own country. It augurs
well for the interests of taste and letters.

We cannot express in too strong terms our approbation of
the moral and devotional spirit, that breathes from all, which
Mr. Bryant writes. Poetry, which is conversant with the
deeper feelings of the heart, as well as the beautiful forms of
outward nature, has, we conceive, certain affinities with devotion. It is connected with all our higher and holier emotions,
and should send out an exalting, a healing, and sustaining
influence. We are pleased to find such an influence pervading
every strain, uttered by a poet of so much richness of fancy, of
so much power and sweetness, as Mr. Bryant. No sentiment
or expression ever drops from him, which the most rigid
moralist would wish to blot. His works we may put into the
hands of youth, confident, that in proportion as they become
familiar with them, the best sympathies of their nature will be
strengthened, and the moral taste be rendered more refined and
delicate. Much of his poetry is description; but his descriptions
are fitted to 'instruct our piety,' and impart a warmth and glow
of moral feeling. * * *

REVIEW OF *POEMS* (New York: 1832)

Southern Review, VIII, 443–62 (Feb., 1832)

[By Hugh Swinton Legaré]

It seems from the very modest preface of the author, that
most of the following Poems have been already printed as
occasional pieces. But for this information we should not have
been aware of the fact, for although we have often heard Mr.
Bryant advantageously spoken of, it has so happened that we
have never, until the publication of this little volume, read any
thing of his in verse. All that we know of him even now is, that
he is an editor of one of the most respectable daily journals in the
country, and the author of this pretty collection of poesy—the
most faultless, and we think, upon the whole, the best collec-

tion of American poetry which we have ever seen. We beg leave to assure him, therefore, that we are extremely desirous to become better acquainted with him. To know more of his past history is within our own power—but it depends upon him whether we shall see as much of him hereafter, as it is undoubtedly his interest that we should. A writer who is capable of what he has done, is capable of a great deal more. The elements of poetical talent—in a certain department of the art—he unquestionably possesses in a high degree. Let him refine them by elaborate cultivation—let him combine them in a work, calculated to display the higher attributes of genius, by sustained invention and unity of purpose, and we predict, with confidence, that he will entwine his name with his land's language and go down to posterity as one of the first, both in time and excellence, of American poets—and that, without the sinister assistance of such an auxiliary as Mr. Kettell. * * *

The diction of these poems is unobjectionable—and that is saying a great deal. It is simple and natural—there is no straining after effect, no meretricious glare, no affected point and brilliancy. It is clear and precise—Mr. Bryant does not seem to think mysticism any element of the true sublime, or the finest poetry at all inconsistent with common sense. It is idiomatic and racy—the language of people of this world such as they use when they utter home-bred feelings in conversation with one another around the fireside or the festive board, not the fastidious, diluted, unexpressive jargon used no where but in second-rate books, and called elegant only by critics of the Della Cruscan School. These are negative merits, it is true, but not the less solid and important on that account. To say of a writer that his language is simple, natural, precise, idiomatic—and to add of what he writes that it is poetical, is to pronounce him one whom the gods have made a poet and who can make himself what he pleases. This is to us the charm of Mr. Bryant's verses. They flow spontaneously from a heart softened by the most touching sensibilities, and they clothe themselves in the very language which nature has adapted, and as it were consecrated to the expression of those sensibilities. * * *

REVIEW OF *POEMS* (New York: 1832)

North American Review, XXXIV, 502-4 (March, 1832)

[By William J. Snelling]

* * * Bryant is not a first-rate poet; but he has great power, and is original in his way. In saying this, we do not mean to be understood, that he has struck out an entirely new path. Others before him have sung the beauties of creation, and the greatness of God; but no one ever observed external things more closely, or transferred his impressions to paper in more vivid colors. A violet becomes, in his hands, a gem fit to be placed in an imperial diadem; a mountain leads his eyes to the canopy above it. The woods, the hills, the flowers,—whatever, in short, is his subject, is brought before our eyes with a fidelity of delineation, and a brightness of coloring, which the actual pencil cannot rival. The picture is always finished to the minutest particular. * * *

To equal, if not excel Thomson, in his own department of literature, would be distinction enough for any one man; but his excellence in descriptive poetry is not Mr. Bryant's chief merit. The bent of his mind is essentially contemplative. He loves to muse in solitude, in the depths of the forest, and on the high places of the hills. Whatever is great, whatever is fair, is felt by him as soon as seen. His thoughts go beyond external appearances, to dwell upon things not visible to common mortals. To him, the streams are subjects for meditation; the fruits of the soil teach him a lesson of gratitude to their Giver; the great things of the earth suggest to him the immensity of the whole, of which they are parts; the starry heavens tell him of the power and magnificence of their Creator. * * * He is too much of a philosopher to entertain visions of gloom. The evil experience of the past leads him to hope and expect better for the future. When the good and wise take their final departure, the thought that they leave the heirs of their wisdom and virtue behind them, consoles him. Death is, in his eyes, a deliverer, sent by God to relieve the wretched and to strike down the arm of the oppressor. The 'Hymn to Death' is one of the noblest sermons that were ever written. There is as much poetry in 'The Old Man's Funeral,' as in any poem of equal length, which we remember to have read, and a great deal more practical wisdom.

There have been greater poets than Mr. Bryant. He cannot crowd so many brilliant thoughts into the same compass, as Shakespeare could. He cannot harrow up the soul or appeal to the darker feelings like Byron. He cannot change from grave to gay. He had no versatility of talent; but he knows the exact extent of his powers, and never attempts any thing for which he is not qualified. He never strains after effect, like some we could mention, or fails as they do. The fact is highly honorable to him. 'Know thyself,' is a lesson too hard for most minds. Mr. Bryant has learned it. * * * We do not believe that he will ever be the favorite of the multitude. His spirit delights not in broils and bloodshed. His lines are never mysterious or horrible. He is an honest man, and will have nothing to say to corsairs or moss-troopers. He has not blazed upon the literary atmosphere, like a comet; every man cannot be a Shakspeare or a Byron. He has brought forward no hero or heroine, with whom the reader may sympathize or identify himself. He cannot lay claim to fertility of invention. He tells no story; he lays no plot, which may sustain his thoughts, as the wooden skeleton does the sculptor's clay model. The reader will find in his verses, no jingling of spurs or splintering of lances; on the other hand, he has taste and feeling; but these, we fear, are not the qualities, in which the vulgar take most pleasure. The mighty, but placid stream does not strike the imagination like the roaring cataract. Marco Bozzaris, the ballad of Chevy Chase, and the like, will delight all men, because they appeal to feelings, which nature has implanted in all men's bosoms; but we contemplate the immensity of the universe, and the attributes of the spiritual world, with effort. Bryant does not address the feelings or sympathies of common readers. He communes not with others, but himself. His poetry is entirely spiritual. Hence it will not be esteemed by the unthinking; but it will charm those for whom it was written,—men of sound judgment and cultivated taste.

AMERICAN LAKE POETRY

American Quarterly Review, XI, 154–74 (March, 1832)

[By JAMES McHENRY]

* * * We come now to the volume of Bryant, another author who has abundantly experienced the favour of the periodical press, without receiving that of the public. The faults of this poet—we mean the obstructions to his popularity, for his admirers will not consider them faults—are the same in kind, but not in degree, with those of Willis. He belongs to the same school, though he does not carry its peculiarities to such a fanatical extent. His versification is formed upon the same quaint and sluggish model; but he oftener deviates from it, and infuses into it a degree of spirit, which renders many of his productions not unpleasing to those who are fond of poring over sentimental stanzas or fragments in prosing blank verse. * * *

But we wish not to prejudice our readers against Mr. Bryant's poetry. Throughout the principal part of the effusions before us, he exhibits a manliness of thought, and a facility of expression, which, after the perusal of Willis's rhapsodies, we found a real relief to our jaded faculties. Mr. Bryant, although he generally uses the prosaic diction of the Lake School, keeps tolerably clear of its abstruse manner of thinking; and but seldom indulges in the conceits and occult meanings so prevalent in the poetry of that school, particularly as it is written by Shelley, Keats, Willis, and Percival. He also avoids the contemptible affectation of infantile simplicity with which Wordsworth so often degrades his pages; but he has none of this amiable but heavy poet's original vein of philosophical reflection on the dispositions of man, and but little of his graphical power in depicting the appearances of nature. * * *

We shall make no extracts from Bryant's volume, for the

sole reason that it contains but little that we can severely condemn, and less, perhaps, that we can warmly praise. Its chief blemishes are of a negative description. It possesses little that can excite the reader, either by awakening his curiosity, or interesting his heart. Page after page may be perused, if the reader has sufficient patience, with dull placidity, or rather perfect unconcern, so that the book shall be laid aside without any single passage having been impressed on the mind as worthy of recollection. A vague remembrance may be left of many passages abounding in good sense, and correct in their moral tendency; but on the whole, rather common-place, and encumbered with verbosity. The positive faults are principally in the diction. But as they are common to the writings of all the disciples of the Lake School, we shall not here enlarge upon them, especially as this article is already extended beyond the bounds we had prescribed for it. We cannot, however, avoid taking notice of a very awkward offence against prosody, of frequent occurrence in the pages of Bryant—we mean the compressing into two syllables such words as *beautiful, delicate, prodigal, merciful, innocent, horrible*, &c., which no ear accustomed to pronounce English words accurately, can tolerate. No poet who studies harmony of composition—and harmony of composition, let the Lake Poets say what they please, will always be preferred by the great majority of poetical readers, to ruggedness—will ever write such verses as the following, which we find in the first poem of Mr. Bryant's volume.

"Does *prodigal* autumn to our age deny—"

* * * Many may think this blemish in versification of too little importance for serious reprehension. Where it occurs seldom, and in poetry of a stirring and animated nature, such as Paradise Lost, in which it is sometimes, although rarely, met with, it may be overlooked. But its excessive and affected use in poetry possessed of but few redeeming qualities, is a proper object of rebuke; and in despite of the sneers of Anacreon Moore, we maintain that Fadladeen was guilty of no hypercriticism when he censured the harsh and unmetrical practice in question. None of our really eminent poets indulge in it; for the few examples of it in Paradise Lost, are to be considered inadvertencies, which, with the other acknowledged blemishes in that great work, will always obtain indulgence, on account of the high order of the beauties with which they are surrounded.

Since the time that Wordsworth published his preface to the dull and drawling *Excursion*, a work which not one reader of English poetry in a hundred has had the patience to read through, his followers, who there found excellence in metrical numbers and poetical diction very erroneously undervalued, have availed themselves of the license his doctrine admitted, and his practice sanctioned, to write slovenly and rugged verses. Smooth poetry has been called effeminate, and harmonious numbers are said to be written for the ear and not the understanding of the reader. These reasoners forget that smoothness and harmony, in themselves sources of pleasure, and perhaps the only ones in which prose cannot pretend to rival poetry, do not imply the exclusion of any other excellence of composition; and that vigour of idea and fervour of expression are as compatible with them as with rude phraseology and negligent metre. Indeed, it is manifest, that, if measure be at all used in poetical writing, and the Lake Poets have never entirely discarded it, the more accurately it is used, the poetry must, in that respect at least, be the better. But the Lake Poets have amply tried the experiment of careless versification, and they have signally failed to render it popular. They now know that no editorial praise can attract the public suffrage towards their works. They feel it, they complain of it. They rail against the public for want of taste; forgetting that the taste of the public, whatever it may be, is the taste of mankind springing from the impulses of nature, to understand and gratify which is the true business of the poet who would gain a station among the illustrious masters of his art.

PREFACE TO *POEMS* (London: 1832)

By WASHINGTON IRVING

To Samuel Rogers, Esq.

MY DEAR SIR,

During an intimacy of some years standing, I have uniformly remarked a liberal interest on your part in the rising character and fortunes of my country, and a kind disposition to promote the success of American talent, whether engaged in literature or the arts. I am induced, therefore, as a tribute of gratitude, as well as a general testimonial of respect and friendship, to lay before you the present volume, in which, for the first time, are collected together the fugitive productions of one of our living poets, whose writings are deservedly popular throughout the United States.

Many of these poems have appeared at various times in periodical publications; and some of them, I am aware, have met your eye, and received the stamp of your approbation. They could scarcely fail to do so, characterised as they are by a purity of moral, an elevation and refinement of thought, and a terseness and elegance of diction, congenial to the bent of your own genius and to your cultivated taste. They appear to me to belong to the best school of English poetry, and to be entitled to rank among the highest of their class.

The British public has already expressed its delight at the graphic descriptions of American scenery and wild woodland characters, contained in the works of our national novelist, Cooper. The same keen eye and fresh feeling for nature, the same indigenous style of thinking and local peculiarity of imagery, which give such novelty and interest to the pages of that gifted writer, will be found to characterise this volume, condensed into a narrower compass and sublimated into poetry.

The descriptive writings of Mr. Bryant are essentially American. They transport us into the depths of the solemn primeval forest—to the shores of the lonely lake—the banks of the wild nameless stream, or the brow of the rocky upland rising like a promontory from amidst a wide ocean of foliage; while they shed around us the glories of a climate fierce in its extremes, but splendid in all its vicissitudes. His close observation of the phenomena of nature, and the graphic felicity of his details, prevent his descriptions from ever becoming general and common-place; while he has the gift of shedding over them a pensive grace that blends them all into harmony, and of clothing them with moral associations that make them speak to the heart. Neither, I am convinced, will it be the least of his merits in your eyes, that his writings are imbued with the independent spirit, and the buoyant aspirations incident to a youthful, a free, and a rising country.

It is not my intention, however, to enter into any critical comments on these poems, but merely to introduce them, through your sanction, to the British public. They must then depend for success on their own merits; though I cannot help flattering myself that they will be received as pure gems, which, though produced in a foreign clime, are worthy of being carefully preserved in the common treasury of the language.

I am, my dear Sir,

Ever most faithfully yours,

WASHINGTON IRVING.

London, March 1832.

AMERICAN POETRY. WILLIAM CULLEN BRYANT

Blackwood's Edinburgh Magazine, XXXI, 646–64 (April, 1832)

[By JOHN WILSON]

* * * We turn our attention to the productions of Bryant, who has for a good many years been one of their most admired poets. Many of them have appeared at various times in periodical publications; and now collected together for the first time by Washington Irving, (it is delightful to see such service done by one man of genius to another,) they make a most interesting volume. "They appear to me," says the amiable editor, "to belong to the best school of English poetry, and to be entitled to rank among the highest of their class. The British public has already expressed its delight at the graphic descriptions of American scenery and wild woodland characters, contained in the works of our national novelist, Cooper. The same keen eye and just feeling for nature, the same indigenous style of thinking, and local peculiarity of imagery, which give such novelty and interest to the pages of that gifted writer, will be found to characterise this volume, condensed into a narrower compass, and sublimated into poetry."

To the American scenery and woodland characters, then, let us first of all turn; and while here we find much to please, we must strongly express our dissent from Mr. Irving's opinion, that in such delineations Bryant is equal to Cooper. He may be as true to nature, as far as he goes; but Cooper's pictures are infinitely richer "in local peculiarity of imagery;" and in "indigenous style of thinking," too, the advantage lies with the novelist. But Bryant is never extravagant, which Cooper often is, who too frequently mars by gross exaggeration the effect of his pictures of external nature. The poet appears to be "a man of milder mood" than the romancer; and of finer taste. But there is nothing in the whole volume comparable in original power to many descriptions in the Prairie and the Spy. Neither do we approve the unconsidered praise implied in the somewhat pedantic expressions, "condensed into a narrower compass, and sublimated into poetry." None of these poems are long; but condensation is not by any means their distinguishing merit, especially of the descriptive passages; we see much simplicity, but no sublimation; and to us the chief charm of Bryant's genius consists in a tender pensiveness, a moral melancholy, breathing over all his contemplations, dreams, and reveries, even such as in the main are glad, and giving assurance of a pure spirit, benevolent to all living creatures, and habitually pious in the felt omnipresence of the Creator. His poetry overflows with natural religion—with what Wordsworth calls the "religion of the woods." * * *

It is indeed in the beautiful that the genius of Bryant finds its prime delight. He ensouls all dead insensate things, in that deep and delicate sense of their seeming life, in which they breathe and smile before the eyes "that love all they look upon," and thus there is animation and enjoyment in the heart of the solitude. Here are some lines breathing a woodland and (you will understand us) a Wordsworthian feeling: while we read them, as Burns says, "our hearts rejoice in nature's joy," and in our serene sympathy we love the poet.

["Inscription for the Entrance to a Wood" is quoted entire.]

There are three other pieces in blank verse (which Mr. Bryant writes well—better, as far as we know, than any other American poet), "Monument Mountain," "A Winter Piece," and the "Conjunction of Jupiter and Venus." The "Winter Piece" we think the best—and it reminds us—though 'tis no imitation— of Cowper. * * *

But there is much poetry in this volume of a kind that, to many minds, will be more affecting than any thing we have yet quoted—for it relates to the sons of the soil, whose race are now so sadly thinned, and as civilisation keeps hewing its way towards the shores of other seas, will at last be entirely extinct —the Red Men of the Woods. Fine mention is made of them in the "Ages," the largest, but by no means the best, poem in the collection. * * *

Mr. Bryant has painted some beautiful pictures of the Indian female character. In "Mountain Monument [*sic*]" he tells the story of a young girl pining away in passion for a youth within the forbidden though not close degrees of consanguinity, and in settled sadness and remorse throwing herself from a rock. It is a tradition, and very touchingly is it narrated. But the "Indian Girl's Lament" will inspire more universal sympathy. Into her lips he puts language at once simple and eloquent, such as the true poet fears not to breathe from his own heart, when in mournful imagination personating a sufferer, knowing that no words expressive of tenderest, and purest, and saddest emotions, can ever be otherwise than true to nature, when passionate in the fidelity of its innocence, nor yet unconsoled in its bereavement by a belief that pictures a life of love beyond the grave.

["The Indian Girl's Lament" is quoted entire.]

Many of the most delightful poems in this volume have been
inspired by a profound sense of the sanctity of the affections.
That love, which is the support and the solace of the heart in
all the duties and distresses of this life, is sometimes painted by
Mr. Bryant in its purest form and brightest colours, as it beauti-
fies and blesses the solitary wilderness. The delight that has
filled his own being, from the faces of his own family, he
transfuses into the hearts of the creatures of his imagination, as
they wander through the woods, or sit singing in front of their
forest-bowers. Remote as some of these creatures are from
the haunts and habits of our common civilized life, they rise
before us at once with the strange beauty of visionary phantoms, and with a human loveliness, that touch with a mingled
charm our fancy and our heart. Our poetic and our human
sensibilities are awakened together, and we feel towards them
the emotions with which we listen to sweet voices from unknown beings smiling or singing to us in dreams.

* * * That [Mr. Bryant's] * * * writings "are imbued with
the independent spirit and the buoyant aspirations incident to
a youthful, a free, and a rising country," will not, says Mr.
Irving, be the "least of his merits" in the eyes of Mr. Rogers,
to whom the volume is inscribed; and in ours it is one of the
greatest; for we, too, belong to a country who, though not
young—God bless her, *auld* Scotland!—hath yet an independent spirit and buoyant aspirations, which she is not loath to
breathe into the bosom of one of her aged children—CHRISTO-
PHER NORTH.

REVIEW OF *POEMS* (London: 1832)

Foreign Quarterly Review, X, 121–38 (August, 1832)

* * * Mr. Bryant is not a writer of marked originality, but
neither is he a copyist. It is true we are often reminded by him
of other writers—of Thomson, of Young, of Akenside, of
Cowper, not unfrequently of Wordsworth, and sometimes of

Campbell and of Rogers. We are reminded of them by discovering passages which we feel they might have written, and which partake of the spirit which breathes in their works; but we perceive no traces of direct imitation, no resemblance which does not seem to arise rather from the congeniality of our author's mind than from his study of their productions. He cannot be truly called the follower of any one of them. Like each of them, he has, though unmarked by strong peculiarities, a manner of his own, and is, like them, original. This may not be very evident on the first hasty glance at his writings; for his is an unpretending, unconspicuous originality, not that which results from eager straining after novelty of effect, but such as will be naturally unfolded in the works of him who, drawing little from books, records the impressions of his own mind, the fruits of his own observation. * * *

The turn of his mind is contemplative and pensive, disposed to serious themes, such as are associated with solemnity and awe. He is a Jaques without his moroseness. The mutability, the uncertainty of all around us, and even Death itself, are to him welcome themes. Yet he is not a gloomy poet. There is nothing misanthropic, nothing discontented, nothing desponding in his tone. On the contrary, there is in it a calm and philosophic spirit, which disposes rather to tranquil cheerfulness; and he treats subjects which in other hands might be food for melancholy, in the happy consciousness of being able to extract from them that germ of comfort which, if rightly considered, they are calculated to afford. * * *

In poetry descriptive of the aspects of nature Mr. Bryant principally excels. He has evidently observed accurately, and with the eye of a genuine lover of natural scenery, and he describes eloquently and unaffectedly what he has seen—selecting happily, using no tumid exaggeration and vain pomp of words, not perplexing us with vague redundancies, but laying before us with graceful simplicity the best features of the individual scene which has been presented to his eye. Nor is he limited in his sphere. Nature, under aspects the most different, seems alike congenial to his pen. Winter and summer—storm and sunshine—the hurricane and the zephyr—the rivulet and the mighty Hudson—a humble flower and the solemn magnificence of boundless forests—are alike depicted, and with equal beauty. He has much of the descriptive power of Thomson, divested of the mannerism which pervaded that period of our poetry—much of the picturesqueness of touch which shines in the verse of Sir Walter Scott, but ennobled by associations which that great writer did not equally summon to his aid—much of the fidelity of Wordsworth, but without his minuteness and occasional overstrained and puerile simplicity, yet closely following him in that better characteristic, his power of elevating the humblest objects by connection with some moral truth. In this Mr. Bryant eminently shines. His descriptions of nature are never mere barren descriptions, undignified by association, unproductive of pure and generous feelings, unaccompanied by some great lesson. He fulfils better than many of his predecessors the character imagined by Shakspeare, who find "books in the running brooks, sermons in stones, and good in everything." He is singularly happy in touching the relations of inanimate objects to man and his lot, and of all to their Creator. To him the aspect of nature seems ever associated with grateful and religious feelings, and he renders it a means of praise and worship. He treats it, however, not like the sceptic, who deifies nature, that he may exclude revelation and make religion as vague as possible. The view which Mr. Bryant takes of it suggests to us no such idea. This great use to which he applies the aspects of the external world is finely exhibited in his "Forest Hymn," and in many others which we might select. * * *

His want of metrical polish is rendered very evident by comparison whenever he has adopted the measure of Moore. His blank verse is good, and more satisfactory to the ear than his other poetry. This may be thought minute criticism, but, if Mr. Bryant's faults had not been few, we should not have stopped to notice such as these. We cannot advise him to prosecute the sportive style. He does not trifle lightly and gracefully. He has rarely attempted it, and with little success.

* * * Mr. Bryant is in the main a very unaffected writer, but there is a little occasional tendency to *prettiness*—to the namby-pamby Rosa-Matildaism of modern album poetry, against which we would warn him. We have no flagrant instances to adduce; but whoever will look at his "Song of the Stars" will see plainly what we mean. These flaunting tags of garish embroidery consort ill with the correct and simple garb in which his thoughts are usually clothed.

We need add little to the preceding observations to express our sense of Mr. Bryant's merits. It will be seen that approbation predominates greatly over censure. We do not consider him a first-rate poet, but we would assign him an honourable station in the second class, and regard him as eminently entitled to that respect which both in this and in his native land his poetical labours will, we trust, never fail to receive.

REVIEW OF *POEMS* (New York: 1836)

Southern Literary Messenger, III, 41–9 (Jan., 1837)

[By EDGAR ALLAN POE]

Mr. Bryant's poetical reputation, both at home and abroad, is greater, we presume, than that of any other American. British critics have frequently awarded him high praise; and here, the public press have been unanimous in approbation. We can call to mind no dissenting voice. Yet the nature, and, most especially the manner, of the expressed opinions in this case, should be considered as somewhat equivocal, and but too frequently must have borne to the mind of the poet doubts and dissatisfaction. * * *

In all the rhapsodies of Mr. Bryant, which have reference to the beauty or the majesty of nature, is a most audible and thrilling tone of love and exultation. As far as he appreciates her loveliness or her augustness, no appreciation can be more ardent, more full of heart, more replete with the glowing soul of adoration. Nor, either in the moral or physical universe coming within the periphery of his vision, does he at any time fail to perceive and designate, at once, the legitimate items of the beautiful. Therefore, could we consider (as some have considered) the mere enjoyment of the beautiful when perceived, or even this enjoyment when combined with the readiest and truest perception and discrimination in regard to beauty presented, as a sufficient test of the poetical sentiment, we could have no hesitation in according to Mr. Bryant the very highest poetical rank. But something more, we have elsewhere presumed to say, is demanded. Just above, we spoke of "objects in the moral or physical universe coming within the periphery of his vision." We now mean to say, that the relative extent of these peripheries of poetical vision must ever be a primary consideration in our classification of poets. Judging Mr. B. in this manner, and by a *general* estimate of the volume before us, we should, of course, pause long before assigning him a place with the spiritual Shelleys, or Coleridges, or Wordsworths, or with Keats, or even Tennyson, or Wilson, or with some other burning lights of our own day, to be valued in a day to come. Yet if his poems, as a whole, will not warrant us in assigning him this grade, one such poem as the last upon which we have commented ["Oh Fairest of the Rural Maids"], is enough to assure us that he may attain it.

The writings of our author, as we find them *here*, are characterized by an air of calm and elevated contemplation more than by any other individual feature. In their mere didactics, however, they err essentially and primitively, inasmuch as such things are the province rather of Minerva than of the Camenae. Of imagination, we discover much—but more of its rich and certain evidences, than of its ripened fruit. In all the minor merits Mr. Bryant is pre-eminent. His *ars celare artem* is most efficient. Of his "completeness," unity, and finish of style we have already spoken. As a versifier, we know of no writer, living or dead, who can be said greatly to surpass him. A Frenchman would assuredly call him "*un poète des plus corrects.*"

Between Cowper and Young, perhaps, (with both of whom he has many points of analogy,) would be the post assigned him by an examination at once general and superficial. Even in this view, however, he has a juster appreciation of the beautiful than the one, of the sublime than the other—a finer taste than Cowper—an equally vigorous, and far more delicate imagination than Young. In regard to his proper rank among American poets there should be no question whatever. Few— at least few who are fairly before the public, have more than very shallow claims to a rivalry with the author of *Thanatopsis*.

REVIEW OF *COMPLETE POETICAL WORKS* (New York: 1846)

Godey's Magazine and Lady's Book, XXXII, 182–6 (April, 1846)

[By EDGAR ALLAN POE]

* * * But although it may be said, in general, that Mr. Bryant's position is *comparatively* well settled, still for some time past there has been a growing tendency to under-estimate him. The new licentious "schools" of poetry—I do not now speak of the transcendentalists, who are the merest nobodies, fatiguing even themselves—but the Tennysonian and Barrettian schools, having, in their rashness of spirit, much in accordance with the whole spirit of the age, thrown into the shade necessarily all that seems akin to the conservatism of half a century ago. The conventionalities, even the most justifiable *decora* of composition, are regarded, *per se*, with a suspicious eye. When I say *per se*, I mean that, from finding them so long in connexion with conservatism of thought, we have come at last to dislike them, not merely as the outward visible signs of that conservatism, but as things evil in themselves. It is very clear that those accuracies and elegancies of style, and of general manner, which in the time of Pope were considered as *prima facie* and indispensable indications of genius, are now conversely regarded. How few are willing to admit the possibility of reconciling genius with artistic skill! Yet this reconciliation is not only possible, but an absolute necessity. It is a mere prejudice which has hitherto prevented the union, by studiously insisting upon a natural repulsion which not only does not exist, but

which is at war with all the analogies of nature. The greatest poems will not be written until this prejudice is annihilated; and I mean to express a very exalted opinion of Mr. Bryant when I say that his works in time to come will do much towards the annihilation.

I have never disbelieved in the perfect consistency, and even congeniality, of the highest genius and the profoundest art; but in the case of the author of "The Ages," I *have* fallen into the general error of undervaluing his poetic ability on account of the mere "elegancies and accuracies" to which allusion has already been made. I confess that, with an absolute abstraction from all personal feelings, and with the most sincere intention to do justice, I was at one period beguiled into this popular error; there can be no difficulty, therefore, on my part, in excusing the inadvertence in others.

It will never do to claim for Bryant a genius of the loftiest order, but there has been latterly, since the days of Mr. Longfellow and Mr. Lowell, a growing disposition to deny him *genius* in *any* respect. He is now commonly spoken of as "a man of high poetical *talent*, very 'correct,' with a warm appreciation of the beauty of nature and great descriptive powers, but rather too much of the old-school manner of Cowper, Goldsmith and Young." This is the truth, but not the whole truth. Mr. Bryant has genius, and that of a marked character, but it has been overlooked by modern schools, because deficient in those externals which have become in a measure symbolical of those schools.

Dr. Griswold, in summing up his comments on Bryant, has the following significant objections. "His genius is not versatile; he has related no history; he has not sung of the passion of love; he has not described artificial life. Still the tenderness and feeling in 'The Death of the Flowers,' 'Rizpah,' 'The Indian Girl's Lament,' and other pieces, show that he might have excelled in delineations of the gentler passions had he made them his study."

Now, in describing *no* artificial life, in relating *no* history, in *not* singing the passion of love, the poet has merely shown himself the profound artist, has merely evinced a proper consciousness that such are not the legitimate themes of poetry. That they are not, I have repeatedly shown, or attempted to show, and to go over the demonstration now would be foreign to the gossiping and desultory nature of the present article. What Dr. Griswold means by "the gentler passions" is, I presume, not very clear to himself, but it is possible that he employs the phrase in consequence of the gentle, unpassionate emotion induced by the poems of which he quotes the titles. It is precisely this "unpassionate emotion" which is the limit of the true poetical art. Passion proper and poesy are discordant. Poetry, in elevating, tranquilizes the *soul*. With *the heart* it has nothing to do. * * *

REVIEW OF *THIRTY POEMS* (New York: 1864)

Independent, XVI, 2 (Jan. 21, 1864)

* * * [Mr. Bryant] is now in his seventieth year, and after a life of almost incessant intellectual labor, in one of the most exacting and laborious of professions, he comes before us— the patriarch of our literature—in an aspect quite as extraordinary as that in which he originally presented himself to the world. With eye undimmed—with faculties unworn—with heart still eager and hopeful—at a period of life when, to most men, if the golden bowl be not yet broken at the fountain, or the silver chord be loosed, the grasshopper at least has become a burden; he flings into our laps "Thirty Poems," mostly new and all excellent. The long interval which has elapsed between his earliest and his latest publication has been filled with the evidences of an unflagging poetic activity. Not a year has passed in which we have not been delighted, and made better by some product of his genius, always fresh and always riper and richer. No great poem—using the word "great" in the sense of size—has illustrated his career—no mighty epic flight, no grand dramatic masterpiece, no long narrative of heroic deeds, or of crime and sorrow and woe—and yet that career is wreathed and festooned along its entire path by poems

which are great in the sense of surpassing loveliness and perfection. It has been the singular felicity of Mr. Bryant that he
has done whatever he has done with consummate finish and
completeness. If he has not, as the critics often tell us, the
comprehensiveness or philosophic insight of Wordsworth,
the weird fancy of Coleridge, the gorgeous diction of Keats,
the exquisite subtlety of Tennyson, he is, nevertheless, the one
among all our contemporaries who has written the fewest
things carelessly, and the most things well. His wastes of arid
sand do not threaten to swallow up his oases of verdure and
bloom. He is all parterre or meadow, where there are few
weeds and innumerable flowers. * * *

Yet we cannot close this rapid reference to the volume
without adding, that it is a great consolation to us to know
that he who is the first poet of his country is also to be regarded,
on many accounts, as its first citizen. Those who worship
Genius are often obliged to qualify that worship by many a
sad regret, and many a heavy sob; but in this case, the sentiment
of admiration and love may go forth almost unstinted. The
life and character of the artist are as pure and transparent as his
writings, which is but saying, indeed, that his poems are but
the honest expression of his inmost soul. The sweet, tender,
thoughtful, and majestic spirit which breathes throughout his
verse is the spirit which inspires the man. In all his personal
relations—we are told—his friends revere always the same
truthfulness, earnestness, hopefulness, and large, many-sided
charity, chastened by a rigid sense of justice. If he does not
always "sing, as the birds sing among the leafy branches,"
spontaneously and joyfully, he sings what the Lord of nature
puts it into his heart to sing—what he feels and knows to be
the inmost truth of every reflective and loving human existence.
He is accused of coldness—and to a limited extent the accusa-
tion is well brought; yet, not to speak of the mild and genial
human associations which he weaves into all the soft changes
and successions of internal nature, who shall say that the
writer of "The Future Life," "The Conqueror's Grave,"
"The Old Man's Funeral," "The Return of Youth," and "The

Battle-field," is not warm and glowing with the deepest human sympathies? With the more violent human passions—with pride and ambition and even love—with the action of man in the turbulence and turmoil of our stormy, social battle—he exhibits no fellow-feeling; we almost deplore the want of it as we read his faultless periods, full of admiration; but we should remember that the function of the poet of Nature is not to describe her in her angry and desolating aspects, but to reveal her infinite loveliness and beneficence; to invoke the sweet influences by which she ministers to the healing of our perturbed and diseased minds, and to lift our souls, through the loving meditation of her outward splendors and beauties, to the perception of those inward splendors and beauties in which we shall see her, as the "visible garment of God," the glorious symbol of that spiritual realm, more effulgent, more lovely, more gentle, more majestic, where all the true and noble and just shall breathe

"An ampler ether, a diviner air."

NOTES

The text of all poems, unless otherwise indicated, is that of the last edition prepared by Bryant himself, the *Poetical Works* of 1876. The number following each title below indicates the page on which the selection begins.

THANATOPSIS (3)

Bryant in an autobiographical fragment (Godwin, I, 37) left the following account of his reading prior to the composition of "Thanatopsis": "About this time my father brought home, I think from one of his visits to Boston, the 'Remains of Henry Kirke White,' which had been republished in this country. I read the poems with great eagerness, and so often that I had committed several of them to memory, particularly the ode to the Rosemary. The melancholy tone which prevails in them deepened the interest with which I read them, for about that time I had, as young poets are apt to have, a liking for poetry of a querulous caste. I remember reading, at this time, that remarkable poem Blair's 'Grave,' and dwelling with great satisfaction upon its finer passages. I had the opportunity of comparing it with a poem on a kindred subject, also in blank verse, that of Bishop Porteus on 'Death,' and of observing how much the verse of the obscure Scottish minister excelled in originality of thought and vigor of expression that of the English prelate. In my father's library I found a small, thin volume of the miscellaneous poems of Southey, to which he had not called my attention, containing some of the finest of Southey's shorter poems. I read it greedily. Cowper's poems had been in my hands from an early age, and I now passed from his shorter poems, which are generally mere rhymed prose, to his 'Task,' the finer passages of which supplied a form of blank verse that captivated my admiration." "Thanatopsis" was the youthful Bryant's answer to the questions concerning death raised by these poets.

The exact date of the first draft of the poem is much disputed. In 1855, Bryant stated that it was written when he was seventeen or eighteen (letter to S. H. Holliday, quoted in *Poetical Works*, I, 329); in 1869, he placed it tentatively in his eighteenth year (letter to James Grant Wilson, quoted in *Bryant and His Friends*, p. 36, footnote). But in the letter of 1869, Bryant went on to say: "I was not a college student at the time, though I was pursuing college studies with a view of entering Yale College." Since he left Williams in May, 1811, and gave up all thought of Yale in the following autumn, it follows that "Thanatopsis" was written between those two dates. More definite is Godwin's statement that Bryant wrote the poem "about a month after his last visit to the college to attend the Commencement" (I, 89, footnote). Since in 1811 commencement was held on September 4, the first draft of "Thanatopsis" was apparently written late in September or early in October of that year—when the poet was still sixteen or, as he would have phrased it, in his seventeenth year.

How frequently or how extensively Bryant revised the poem before it was printed six years later, no one can say. However, an early manuscript version, evidently dating between 1811 and 1817, survives. Here is found an unpublished introductory section, demonstrating that "Thanatopsis" was originally composed as a personal lyric, the utterance of Bryant's own "better genius."

When the poem was ready for other eyes, young Bryant left it in his father's desk. The latter copied it with a second poem on death ("Not That from Life, and All Its Woes," p. 350 above) and submitted them to the *North American Review*. Its editors mistook the two poems for one, named them "Thanatopsis," and published them in September, 1817. (For additional details, see "Bryant and *The North American Review*," *American Literature*, I, 14–26, March, 1929.) The first published version of the poem reads as follows:

> ————Yet a few days, and thee,
> The all-beholding sun, shall see no more,
> In all his course; nor yet in the cold ground,
> Where thy pale form was laid, with many tears,
> Nor in th' embrace of ocean shall exist
> Thy image. Earth, that nourished thee, shall claim
> Thy growth, to be resolv'd to earth again;
> And, lost each human trace, surrend'ring up
> Thine individual being, shalt thou go
> To mix forever with the elements,
> To be a brother to th' insensible rock
> And to the sluggish clod, which the rude swain
> Turns with his share, and treads upon. The oak
> Shall send his roots abroad and pierce thy mould.
> Yet not to thy eternal resting place
> Shalt thou retire alone—nor couldst thou wish
> Couch more magnificent. Thou shalt lie down
> With patriarchs of the infant world—with kings
> The powerful of the earth—the wise, the good,
> Fair forms, and hoary seers of ages past,
> All in one mighty sepulchre.—The hills,
> Rock-ribb'd and ancient as the sun,—the vales
> Stretching in pensive quietness between;
> The venerable woods—the floods that move
> In majesty,—and the complaining brooks,
> That wind among the meads, and make them green,
> Are but the solemn decorations all,
> Of the great tomb of man.—The golden sun,

The planets, all the infinite host of heaven
Are glowing on the sad abodes of death,
Through the still lapse of ages. All that tread
The globe are but a handful to the tribes
That slumber in its bosom.—Take the wings
Of morning—and the Borean desert pierce—
Or lose thyself in the continuous woods
That veil Oregan, where he hears no sound
Save his own dashings—yet—the dead are there,
And millions in those solitudes, since first
The flight of years began, have laid them down
In their last sleep—the dead reign there alone.—
So shalt thou rest—and what if thou shalt fall
Unnoticed by the living—and no friend
Take note of thy departure? Thousands more
Will share thy destiny.—The tittering world
Dance to the grave. The busy brood of care
Plod on, and each one chases as before
His favourite phantom.—Yet all these shall leave
Their mirth and their employments, and shall come
And make their bed with thee!———

Bryant occasionally revised "Thanatopsis" after 1817, the most important change being the addition of an introduction and a conclusion in 1821.

The remarkable liberalism of Bryant's religious position in "Thanatopsis" and the importance of the poem in his spiritual development are discussed on pp. xxv ff. above.

1–17. This familiar introduction was hastily composed in Cambridge,
while Bryant was arranging for the publication of his *Poems* in 1821, in
which volume it first appeared. In these lines the poet attributes the discussion of death which forms the body of the poem, not to his own "better
genius" (as in an early manuscript), but to nature. Bryant had now read
Wordsworth; and echoes of that poet are heard in the introduction.

7. *healing:* before 1836, "gentle."

31. *thine:* before 1836, "thy."

51. *pierce the Barcan wilderness:* in 1817, "the Borean desert pierce"; in
1821, "the Barcan desert pierce"; in 1855, "traverse Barca's desert sands";
in 1871, the present reading. The Barcan desert is found in northern Africa.

53. *Oregon:* before 1871, "Oregan." The river is now named the Columbia.

58. *withdraw:* before 1836, "shalt fall."

59. *In silence from:* in 1817, "Unnoticed by"; in 1832, "Unheeded by";
in 1855, the present reading.

66–81. The conclusion grew out of various drafts made prior to 1821,
when it was first published. It will be observed that nothing in the com-

pleted poem is contradictory to the thought of the fragment published in 1817.

70. *The speechless babe, and the gray-headed man:* in 1821,

> The bowed with age, the infant in the smiles
> And beauty of its innocent age cut off;

in 1832, "And the sweet babe, and the gray-headed man"; in 1871, the present reading.

75. *that mysterious realm:* in 1821, "the pale realms of death."

THE YELLOW VIOLET (5)

Written in 1814 during a holiday at Cummington, in the midst of Bryant's study of the law, "The Yellow Violet" was later rejected by the editors of the *North American Review*, who decided to print no more poetry in that journal, and was not published until 1821.

Cf. Wordsworth's first poem "To a Daisy" and the lines of Burns on the same flower.

INSCRIPTION FOR THE ENTRANCE TO A WOOD (6)

Composed among the trees which still stand near the Bryant homestead, this poem was published with "Thanatopsis" in the *North American Review*, Sept., 1817, as "A Fragment." The original text reads as follows:

> Stranger, if thou hast learnt a truth which needs
> Experience more than reason, that the world
> Is full of guilt and misery; and hast known
> Enough of all its sorrows, crimes and cares
> To tire thee of it—enter this wild wood,
> And view the haunts of Nature. The calm shade
> Shall bring a kinder calm, and the sweet breeze
> That makes the green leaves dance, shall waft a balm
> To thy sick heart. Here thou wilt nothing find
> Of all that pain'd thee in the haunts of man,
> And made thee loathe thy life. The primal curse
> Fell, it is true, upon the unsinning earth,
> But not in vengeance. Misery is wed
> To guilt. Hence in these shades we still behold
> The abodes of gladness, here from tree to tree
> And through the rustling branches flit the birds
> In wantonness of spirit;—theirs are strains
> Of no dissembled rapture—while below
> The squirrel with rais'd paws and form erect
> Chirps merrily. In the warm glade the throngs
> Of dancing insects sport in the mild beam
> That wak'd them into life. Even the green trees

Partake the deep contentment; as they bend
To the soft winds the sun from the blue sky
Peeps in and sheds a blessing on the scene.
Scarce less the cleft-born wild-flower seems to enjoy
Existence, than the winged plunderer
That sucks its sweets. The massy rocks themselves
And the old and ponderous trunks of prostrate trees
That lead from knoll to knoll a causeway rude
Or bridge the sunken stream, and their dark roots
With all their earth upon them, twisting high
Breathe fix'd tranquillity. The rivulet
Sends forth glad sounds, and tripping o'er its bed
Of pebbly sands or leaping down the rocks,
Seems with continuous laughter to rejoice
In its own being. Softly tread the marge,
Lest from her midway perch thou scare the wren
That dips its bill in water.

Bryant, who was familiar with Southey's shorter poems, was perhaps encouraged to write these lines by the English poet's "Inscriptions," particularly "For a Tablet on the Banks of a Stream" and "In a Forest."

6–10. Cf. Wordsworth's "Lines Composed a Few Miles above Tintern Abbey," especially ll. 22–30.

26–28. Cf. Wordsworth's "Lines Written in Early Spring," ll. 11–12.

I CANNOT FORGET WITH WHAT FERVID DEVOTION (7)

Stanzas 1–5 of this text were in 1832 condensed from stanzas 1–7 of the original version, which was more personal and revelatory than the later revision. As first published in the *New-York Review*, Feb., 1826, these seven stanzas read as follows:

I cannot forget the high spell that enchanted,
    Nor the visions that brightened my earlier days,
When verse was a passion, and warmly I panted
    To wreath my young brows with unwithering bays.

And I bowed to the impulse with fervid devotion,
    And gave my whole soul to the love of the lyre;
Each gaze at the glories of earth, sky, and ocean,
    To my kindled emotions was wind over fire.

And deep were my musings in life's opening blossom,
    Midst the twilight of mountain groves wandering long;
How thrilled my full veins, and how beat my young bosom,
    When over me came the wild spirit of song.

'Mong the high and hoar fells that for ages have listened
  To the rush of the pebble-paved river between,
Where the king-fisher screamed, and gray precipice glistened,
  All breathless with awe have I gazed on the scene;

Till I felt the dark power o'er my reveries stealing,
  From his throne in the depth of that stern solitude,
And he breathed through my lips, in that tempest of feeling,
  Strains full of his spirit, though artless and rude.

Yet, beautiful day dreams! ye shone as a warning
  Of glooms that should frown, when your glory should
    fade;
Your halos were bright in the beams of my morning,
  How quickly they vanish in storm and in shade!

I have mixed with the world, and its follies have stained me,
  No longer your pure rural worshipper now;
And even in those haunts where your spells once enchained me,
  Ye shrink from the signet of care on my brow.

The youthful disillusionment and the momentary alienation from nature, clearly evident here and suggested in "Inscription for the Entrance
to a Wood," are discussed on pp. xxxiii and xli–xlii above.

THE HUNTER OF THE WEST. A SONG (8)

Godwin states (*Poetical Works*, I, 332) that this song is probably a section from a projected Indian poem, begun in 1814–15 but never completed.
Bryant did not include the poem in the edition of 1876; this text therefore
follows Godwin's edition of 1883.

For Bryant's treatment of frontiersmen and the frontier, see pp. xlvii ff.
above.

TO A WATERFOWL (9)

On Dec. 15, 1815, Bryant went from Cummington to Plainfield, where
he was establishing himself as a lawyer. He later recalled (Godwin, I,
143–4) that as he walked over the hills, he felt "very forlorn and desolate
indeed, not knowing what was to become of him in the big world, which
grew bigger as he ascended, and yet darker with the coming on of night.
The sun had already set, leaving behind it one of those brilliant seas of
chrysolite and opal which often flood the New England skies; and, while
he was looking upon the rosy splendor with rapt admiration, a solitary
bird made wing along the illuminated horizon. He watched the lone wanderer until it was lost in the distance, asking himself whither it had come
and to what far home it was flying. When he went to the house where he
was to stop for the night, his mind was still full of what he had seen and

felt, and he wrote these lines." In an early manuscript, the poem is entitled "On seeing a waterfowl fly over a little after Sunset."

Hartley Coleridge declared and Matthew Arnold agreed that "To a Waterfowl" is the finest short poem in the English language.

For a discussion of the place of this poem in Bryant's spiritual development, see p. xxvi above.

7. *As, darkly seen against the crimson sky:* originally, "darkly painted on"; next, "limned upon"; then, "shadowed on." When Richard Henry Dana, Sr., begged Bryant to restore the first reading, he agreed to do so, but made the change only in *A Library of Poetry and Song.*

THE BURIAL-PLACE (10)

"The first half of this fragment may seem to the reader borrowed from the essay on Rural Funerals in the fourth number of 'The Sketch-Book.' The lines were, however, written more than a year before that number appeared. The poem, unfinished as it is, would hardly have been admitted into this collection, had not the author been unwilling to lose what had the honor of resembling so beautiful a composition." [*Bryant's note.*]

GREEN RIVER (12)

Bryant frequently escaped from Great Barrington and the law to the banks of Green River. This poem he "picked out of his waste-basket" for Richard Henry Dana, Sr., and his *Idle Man.*

23–24. Originally these lines read:

> And the swimmer comes in the season of heat
> To bathe in these waters so pure and sweet.

OH FAIREST OF THE RURAL MAIDS (14)

Of several poems recording Bryant's love for Frances Fairchild, he published only this. Godwin printed a second (I, 167–8, footnote); and two additional examples are published for the first time on pp. 353 and 354 above.

Edgar Allan Poe in 1837 characterized "Oh Fairest of the Rural Maids" as "a gem, of which we cannot sufficiently express our admiration." Most of all, he praised its "rich simplicity . . . of design and execution." "This is strikingly perceptible in the opening and concluding lines, and in *expression* of thought. But there is a far higher and more strictly *ideal* beauty, which it is less easy to analyse. The original conception is of the very loftiest order of Poesy." In 1840 and 1846, Poe continued to rhapsodize over "the truest poem written by Bryant."

For Wordsworthian aspects of the poem, see p. xliv above and, particularly, Wordsworth's "Three Years She Grew in Sun and Shower."

13–14. *Thine eyes are springs.* Poe declared: "the image . . . is one which,

for appropriateness, completeness, and every perfect beauty of which imagery is susceptible, has never been surpassed."

16. *The brook:* Bryant perhaps alludes to a tributary of his beloved Green
River, the Seekonk, near which Frances Fairchild spent her early years.

OH GOD, WHOSE DREAD AND DAZZLING BROW (15)

This hymn is one of five (not six, as stated by Godwin) written at the
suggestion of the novelist, Catherine Maria Sedgwick of Stockbridge, for a
collection prepared for Unitarian congregations by Henry D. Sewall in
1820. It is here printed as it appeared in that volume.

In 1864, Bryant revised the hymn, changing stanzas 2–4. In stanza two,
he paid this tribute to Christ:

> Aid our weak steps and eyesight dim
>   The paths of peace to find,
> And lead us all to learn of Him
>   Who died to save mankind.

Bryant's Unitarian hymns and their revision are discussed on pp. xxvii
and lxvi–lxvii above.

HYMN TO DEATH (15)

Here Bryant, happy in Great Barrington with Frances Fairchild, momentarily shook off his persistent fear of death and briefly attained serenity,
only to fall back into his customary gloom when he received news of his
father's death in Cummington. The last lines of the poem (134–168) were
then added, in repudiation of the preceding "desultory numbers" where,
in "an idle revery," Bryant rashly praised death.

A WINTER PIECE (20)

The poem was originally entitled "Winter Scenes." Its Wordsworthian
tone should blind no one to its rich autobiographical content. This tribute
to the joys of winter in New England antedates Whittier's "Snow-Bound"
by forty-five years.

THE WEST WIND (24)

In an early manuscript draft of this poem, there appears an additional
stanza:

> Then Zephyr! Why that pensive sound
>   Ah thou art like our wayward race.
> When all is glad and bright around
>   Thou lovest to sigh and murmur still.

A WALK AT SUNSET (25)

59. In the edition of 1876, this line reads "But never shall . . ." It is
here corrected to correspond with l. 55.

SPAIN (27)

Perhaps out of this early concern for Spanish independence grew Bryant's lifelong interest in Spanish life and literature (see Bryant's essays, "Recollections of the South of Spain," p. 240 above, and "Burgos—The Cartuja—A Bull Fight," p. 284 above).

"Spain," first published in 1823, was never included by Bryant among his collected works; this text therefore follows Godwin's edition of 1883.

THE INDIAN GIRL'S LAMENT (28)

For Bryant's treatment of the noble savage, see p. xlv above.

THE RIVULET (29)

The rivulet flows past the Bryant homestead, through the grove commemorated in "Inscription for the Entrance to a Wood."
13–14. In 1824, these lines read thus:

> To crop the violet on its brim,
> And listen to the throstle's hymn.

23. In 1824:

> High visions then, and lofty schemes
> Glorious and bright as fairy dreams,
> And daring hopes, that now to speak.

29. In 1824:

> Yet tell in proud and grand decay.

33–34. In 1824:

> But thou, gay, merry rivulet,
> Dost dimple, play, and prattle yet.

43–44. In 1824:

> As fresh the herbs that crowd to drink
> The moisture of thy oozy brink.

68. In 1824:

> A few brief years shall pass away.

THE MASSACRE AT SCIO (32)

"This poem, written about the time of the horrible butchery of the Sciotes by the Turks, in 1824, has been more fortunate than most poetical predictions. The independence of the Greek nation which it foretold, has come to pass, and the massacre, by inspiring a deeper detestation of their oppressors, did much to promote that event." [*Bryant's note.*]

CONSUMPTION (34)

Entitled "Sonnet" in the original manuscript, this poem appears in some editions as "To —————" and as "To Consumption." The sonnet is addressed to Bryant's favorite sister, Mrs. Sarah Bryant Shaw, who died of consumption a few months after the publication of these lines. She is also referred to in "The Past" and "The Death of the Flowers."

This poem to a dying woman naturally appealed to Poe, who called it Bryant's best sonnet. "With the exception of a harshness in the last line but one," Poe said, "it is perfect."

SUMMER WIND (34)

Poe in 1837 pointed out that Bryant in this poem repeatedly succeeded in making "the sound the echo of the sense." On the sensuous nature of Bryant's treatment of nature, particularly the wind, see p. xxxvii above.

LOVE'S SEASONS. A SONG (35)

This highly romantic poem of love was written three years after the marriage of Frances Fairchild and Bryant, when the poet had outgrown his adolescent Byronism.

I BROKE THE SPELL THAT HELD ME LONG (37)

For several years after Bryant's arrival in Great Barrington, he devoted himself to the profession of law, writing little poetry until 1824, when nature and the *United States Literary Gazette* recalled him "to the love of song" (see pp. liv ff. above).

HYMN OF THE WALDENSES (37)

During the 1820's, much interest was shown by Protestant countries in these ancient Protestants of the Alps, who had long been persecuted by both Italian and French Catholics.

Bryant's devotion to Protestantism did not blind him to the merits of Catholicism and Catholics. In 1825, he declared (*New-York Review*, I, 143, July, 1825): "It is not always among the Protestants that the conscience is left free, nor is the enlightened Catholic the necessary enemy of toleration. No particular set of doctrines is certain to protect a people against civil or religious despotism. The tyranny which oppresses the Catholics of Ireland is as wicked and inexcusable, as that which crushes the liberals of Spain."

MONUMENT MOUNTAIN (38)

"The mountain called by this name is a remarkable precipice in Great Barrington, overlooking the rich and picturesque valley of the Housatonic, in the western part of Massachusetts. At the southern extremity is, or was a few years since, a conical pile of small stones, erected, according to the tradition of the surrounding country, by the Indians, in memory of a woman of the Stockbridge tribe who killed herself by leaping from the edge of the precipice. Until within a few years past, small parties of that tribe used to arrive from their settlement in the western part of the State of New York, on visits to Stockbridge, the place of their nativity and former residence. A young woman belonging to one of these parties related, to a friend of the author, the story on which the poem of Monument Mountain is founded. An Indian girl had formed an attachment for her cousin, which, according to the customs of the tribe, was unlawful. She was, in consequence, seized with a deep melancholy, and resolved to destroy herself. In company with a female friend, she repaired to the mountain, decked out for the occasion in all her ornaments, and, after passing the day on the summit in singing with her companion the traditional songs of her nation, she threw herself headlong from the rock, and was killed." [*Bryant's note.*]

AFTER A TEMPEST (42)

This landscape is a generalized painting of the Berkshires about Great Barrington.

1–2. In 1824:

> The day had been a day of wind and storm;—
> The wind was laid, the storm was overpast.

33–34. In 1824:

> And happy living things that trod the bright
> And beauteous scene; while, far beyond them all.

AUTUMN WOODS (44)

Such poems as "Autumn Woods," "November," and "October" refute the charge occasionally made by literary critics that Bryant ignored the true splendors of the American autumn, to write only of the gloom of the "conventional *literary* Autumn" of Europe.

NOVEMBER (46)

In a note on his original sonnets, Bryant remarked that none "is framed according to the legitimate Italian model, which, in the author's opinion, possesses no peculiar beauty for an ear accustomed only to the metrical forms of our own language. The sonnets in this collection are rather poems in fourteen lines than sonnets." Bryant therefore cannot be severely condemned for the irregularity of his sonnets.

A FOREST HYMN (49)

This poem was the last written by Bryant in Great Barrington, before removing to New York. When he later attempted to revise certain lines, he discovered that he had "marred the unity and effect of the passage." He then declared: "The truth is, that an alteration ought never to be made without the mind being filled with the subject. In mending a faulty passage in cold blood, we often do more mischief, by attending to particulars and neglecting the entire construction and sequence of ideas, than we do good" (Godwin, I, 297).

Poe in 1837 justly praised the poem for its "great rhythmical beauty," of which he believed it was scarcely possible to speak too highly, and which evinced in Bryant "the greatest delicacy of ear."

34–36. In 1825:

> Here are seen
> No traces of man's pomp or pride;—no silks
> Rustle, no jewels shine, nor envious eyes
> Encounter.

In 1832, John Wilson protested that these lines "have no business there." "Such sarcastic suggestions jar and grate; and it would please us much to see that they were omitted in a new edition." Impressed by this criticism, Bryant revised the passage.

38–47. Cf. Wordsworth's "Lines Composed a Few Miles above Tintern Abbey," ll. 93–102.

50. In 1825:

> Wells softly forth and visits the strong roots.

66–68. Cf. Shelley's "Adonais," ll. 478–82.
86. In 1825:

> Upon the sepulchre, and blooms and smiles.

97–101. Cf. "Tintern Abbey," ll. 107–11.

JUNE (53)

"June" was written during a visit to Great Barrington, after Bryant had taken up his residence in New York. "Fifty-two years later," remarks Godwin (*Poetical Works*, I, 343), "when his death occurred in the month of June, it was generally remarked how its tender wishes had turned into prophecy. He was buried in a rural cemetery in Roslyn, amid the sights and sounds, . . . for which he supposes his soul would yearn even after death."

"Sweet," "perfectly modulated," and "inexpressibly pathetic" were the adjectives applied to the poem by Poe in 1846. Here, he continued, "there is, very properly, nothing of the *passion* of grief; but the subdued sorrow which comes up, as if perforce, to the surface of the poet's gay sayings about his grave, we find thrilling us to the soul, while there is yet a spiritual *elevation* in the thrill."

LINES ON REVISITING THE COUNTRY (54)

The poem was composed among the Berkshires during the summer in which Bryant wrote "June."

7–18. This daughter was Frances, born in Great Barrington. Her introduction to external nature, although recorded in Wordsworthian terms, was actuated by Bryant's own devotion to the Berkshires.

THE AFRICAN CHIEF (56)

On this glorification of the noble savage, Bryant left the following note: "The story of the African chief, related in this ballad, may be found in the 'African Repository' for April, 1825. The subject of it was a warrior of majestic stature, the brother of Yarradee, king of the Solima nation. He had been taken in battle, and was brought in chains for sale to the Rio Pongas, where he was exhibited in the market-place, his ankles still adorned with massy rings of gold which he wore when captured. The refusal of his captors to listen to his offers of ransom drove him mad, and he died a maniac."

TO A MOSQUITO (58)

Bryant's humor, never acute, was more pervasive than has been commonly recognized; and his intimate friends knew that throughout his life he possessed a touch of Yankee wit. This humor was most frequently evident during Bryant's early years in New York, where he was active with Sands and Verplanck in "literary pranks" (Godwin, I, 236–40) and where he composed "To a Mosquito" and "A Meditation on Rhode Island Coal." In later years, Bryant's dry wit occasionally found outlet in anonymous political satires, published in the *Post* but never collected (Nevins, pp. 126–7). However, he eventually came to agree with his reviewers that humor was not his field, and in his acknowledged writings, confined himself to playfulness and sober whimsicality.

"To a Mosquito" is in the mood of the amiably satirical verse of Halleck, to whom, indeed, one of Bryant's "literary pranks" was popularly attributed (Godwin, I, 239).

THE DEATH OF THE FLOWERS (60)

This poem was written in memory of Bryant's favorite sister, Mrs. Sarah Bryant Shaw, who died in 1824. Conventionally sentimental as are these lines, the grief which they express was profound. Godwin even suggests (I, 192) that the death of this sister perhaps "inclined" Bryant "more willingly" to leave Massachusetts.

3. In 1825:

> the summer leaves lie dead.

7. In 1825:

Where are the flowers, the bright young flowers, that smiled beneath the feet,
With hues so passing beautiful, and breath so passing sweet?

11. In 1825:

> The rain is falling on their graves, but the cold November rain.

18. In 1825:

And the blossoms never smiled again by upland, glade or glen.

THE GLADNESS OF NATURE (61)

Although critics of Bryant frequently ignore the joyous elements in his pictures of nature and discuss only the dark and the somber, he in reality emphasized the joyousness of nature from his early poems, as "Inscription for the Entrance to a Wood" of 1815, to his latest, as "Among the Trees" of 1868 (see p. 142 above).

A SUMMER RAMBLE (62)

Bryant frequently announced, but never more clearly than here, his belief that the idealist, "heart-sick with the wrongs of men," can find rest and joy only among "the sinless, peaceful works of God."

Cf. Wordsworth's poem, "To My Sister."

29-30. The poet's companion is his wife.

THE HURRICANE (64)

"This poem," Bryant stated, "is nearly a translation from one by José Maria de Heredia, a native of the island of Cuba, who published in New York, about the year 1825, a volume of poems in the Spanish language."

For similar treatment of storm and tempest by Bryant himself, see his prose tale, "The Hurricane," and the poems, "A Hymn of the Sea" (p. 102 above) and "The Winds" (p. 95 above).

THE PAST (66)

"Mr. Bryant, I infer from passages in his private letters, regarded this as the best poem he had written up to that time [1828], in which opinion the late Mr. Gulian C. Verplanck agreed with him." [*Godwin's note.*]

16. *The venerable form* is that of Doctor Peter Bryant.

56. *The beautiful and young* is Mrs. Sarah Bryant Shaw (cf. "Consumption" and "The Death of the Flowers").

THE EVENING WIND (68)

At the suggestion of John Keese, Bryant inserted a new stanza after stanza three of the original poem. These additional lines appeared in Keese's anthology, *The Poets of America*, and in Bryant's anthology, *A Library of Poetry and Song*, but in no edition of Bryant's poems:

Stoop o'er the place of graves, and softly sway
The sighing herbage by the gleaming stone
That they who near the churchyard willows stray,
And listen in the deepening gloom, alone,

> May think of gentle souls that passed away,
> Like thy pure breath, into the vast unknown,
> Sent forth from heaven among the sons of men,
> And gone into the boundless heaven again.

THE SIESTA (69)

For a discussion of Bryant's use of Spanish material, see p. liii above.

TO COLE, THE PAINTER, DEPARTING FOR EUROPE (70)

Thomas Cole and Bryant frequently rambled together among the Catskills. This plea that in Europe his friend should not forget American scenes is in accordance with Bryant's sane nationalism (see p. lxi above).

TO THE FRINGED GENTIAN (70)

John Burroughs insisted (*Pepacton*, pp. 92–3) that the fringed gentian does not come late and alone "when woods are bare," but early in autumn and accompanied by other flowers. In reality, the fringed gentian appears among the hills and mountains of western Massachusetts exactly as Bryant describes it (see pp. xxxiv f. above).

HYMN OF THE CITY (71)

It was inevitable that Bryant the poet should experience difficulty in interpreting the American city and that, on those rare occasions when he found glimpses of beauty in New York, those glimpses should remind him of external nature.

SONG OF MARION'S MEN (72)

"The exploits of General Francis Marion, the famous partisan warrior of South Carolina, form an interesting chapter in the annals of the American Revolution. The British troops were so harassed by the irregular and successful warfare which he kept up at the head of a few daring followers, that they sent an officer to remonstrate with him for not coming into the open field and fighting 'like a gentleman and a Christian.' " [*Bryant's note.*]

3. *The British soldier trembles.* When Bryant's poems were issued in England in 1832, the publisher asked Washington Irving, who sponsored the volume, to make this line less offensive to English readers. It was therefore altered to read: "The foeman trembles in his camp." Bryant, who knew nothing of the change, and Irving, who believed that he was acting for the best interests of author and publisher, were severely attacked for "cowardly subservience" to British opinion. (As recently as 1932, a prejudiced historian characterized the incident as an "outrageous" case of "kow-towing to English influence.") Although Bryant disapproved of the change and was momentarily irritated, no lasting ill-feeling resulted between Irving and the poet. (For a full account of the episode, see Pierre Irving, *The Life and Letters of Washington Irving.* New York: 1862, II, 472–9; III, 102–11.)

THE PRAIRIES (74)

This poem records Bryant's emotions at first seeing the prairies, on a visit to his brothers in Illinois in 1832. He also recorded his impressions in prose—see "A Letter from Illinois" (p. 258 above), and "An Excursion to Rock River" (p. 267 above). For Bryant's general conception of the plains, see p. xlix above.

13. "The prairies of the West, with an undulating surface, *rolling prairies*, as they are called, present to the unaccustomed eye a singular spectacle when the shadows of the clouds are passing rapidly over them. The face of the ground seems to fluctuate and toss like billows of the sea." [*Bryant's note.*]

20. The edition of 1876 reads: "the limited brooks."

EARTH (77)

"Earth" was written in Pisa in 1834. For a preliminary draft of this poem, in six-line stanzas, see *Poetical Works*, II, 351–2.

TO THE APENNINES (80)

The poem was written during Bryant's first visit to Italy (1834). It is obvious that the history of Europe was to this American democrat a depressing commentary on human frailty.

LIFE (82)

"Life" was written in Munich in 1835.

11–12. "Close to the city of Munich, in Bavaria, lies the spacious and beautiful pleasure-ground, called the English Garden, in which these lines were written, originally projected and laid out by our countryman, Count Rumford, under the auspices of one of the sovereigns of the country. Winding walks, of great extent, pass through close thickets and groves interspersed with lawns; and streams, diverted from the river Isar, traverse the grounds swiftly in various directions, the water of which, stained with the clay of the soil it has corroded in its descent from the upper country, is frequently of a turbid-white color." [*Bryant's note.*]

CATTERSKILL FALLS (84)

The material for the background of this poem is drawn from Bryant's excursions among the Catskill Mountains. The narrative is designed to exemplify "the popular belief that they who perish by cold enjoy in their last moments singularly splendid and fantastic visions of life" (Godwin, I, 384).

THE BATTLE-FIELD (87)

"The Battle-field" reveals Bryant's ideals for himself and the *Post* in the midst of the abuse showered upon him as an extreme Democrat and

"Locofoco," by opposing newspapers (Godwin, I, 336–7). In actual practice, Bryant the editor was independent and fearless, but not always urbane and even-tempered.

THE FUTURE LIFE (90)

This poem was addressed to the poet's wife, who remarked to a friend concerning it: "Oh, my dear, I am always sorry for anyone who sees me after reading those lines, he must be so disappointed!" (Godwin, II, 247, footnote.) Cf. "The Life That Is."

1. *How shall I know thee.* Bryant, although he never in maturity questioned immortality, apparently retained something of his youthful uncertainty concerning the exact conditions of the future life (cf. ll. 49–52 of "Life").

27. *And wrath has left its scar.* Here Bryant frankly acknowledges that he possessed a "torrid temper"—a temper which, because it was held rigidly in check, has not generally been recognized by literary historians.

THE FOUNTAIN (91)

"This poem, 'The Evening Revery,' 'Noon,' and several others in blank verse, were originally printed as parts of 'an unfinished poem,' which, however, is not to be found among the poet's papers; nor is it possible to tell now in what way they were to be joined in a longer composition. Having travelled a great deal in all parts of our country, he was familiar with the experiences of settlers in different regions, and it may be conjectured that he contemplated a poem in which the aspects of American nature and life as they are seen from the shores of Massachusetts to the prairies of the great West should be presented in a series of pictures connected by a narrative of personal adventures, as Wordsworth has connected the principal parts of his 'Excursion' by the story of his pedler. He never, however, disclosed his plan to any one, and even this suggestion is mere guess-work." [*Godwin's note.*]

34. "The *Sanguinaria Canadensis*, or bloodroot, as it is commonly called, bears a delicate white flower of a musky scent, the stem of which breaks easily, and distills a juice of bright-red color." [*Bryant's note.*]

57. In 1842:

> Gashed horribly by tomahawks. The woods.

92. In 1842:

> Swelled loud and clear the voice of chanticleer.

THE OLD MAN'S COUNSEL (97)

The old man who speaks here is Deacon Ebenezer Snell of Cummington, Bryant's grandfather. Contemporary accounts, including Bryant's, indicate that Deacon Snell was not often "merry" or "genial" (ll. 13–14).

THE ANTIQUITY OF FREEDOM (100)

This portrait of the spirit of freedom, visualized in simple yet militant and optimistic terms, reveals Bryant's mature faith in the immortal spirit of democracy.

49. The edition of 1876 reads: ". . . into a feeble age"—an obvious typographical error.

A HYMN OF THE SEA (102)

The "Hymn" was inspired by a visit to the summer home of Richard Henry Dana, Sr., at Cape Ann, on the Massachusetts coast.

52–53. In 1842:

> The long wave rolling from the Arctic pole
> To break upon Japan.

This, Bryant declared as soon as the poem was in print, "was not what I meant; it does not give space enough for my wave, nor does it place my new continent or new islands in the widest and loneliest part of the ocean. I meant the Southern or Antarctic pole, and by what strange inattention to the meaning of the word I came to write Arctic I am sure I cannot tell" (Godwin, I, 391, footnote).

OH MOTHER OF A MIGHTY RACE (104)

Bryant wrote this extravagant glorification of the New World at the expense of the Old shortly after his second voyage to Europe and after a visit to his brothers in Illinois. It will be observed that Bryant finds the American spirit at its best on the western frontier (ll. 25–30).

THE PLANTING OF THE APPLE-TREE (106)

Long before this poem was composed, the boy William Cullen Bryant and his brothers under their mother's direction had planted near the Bryant homestead, apple trees which survived for several decades. Some forty years later, Bryant himself was planting trees on his estate at Roslyn and meditating: "Hereafter, men, whose existence is at present merely possible, will gather pears from the trees which I have set in the ground, and wonder what old *covey*. . .of past ages planted them" (Godwin, II, 28). Out of such experiences came "The Planting of the Apple-Tree."

THE MAY SUN SHEDS AN AMBER LIGHT (108)

The poet here commemorates his mother, Mrs. Sarah Snell Bryant, who died in 1847 in her eightieth year.

ROBERT OF LINCOLN (109)

The bobolink was from Bryant's youth in Massachusetts to his death, one of his favorite birds. John Burroughs protested (*Pepacton*, p. 91) that the bobolink never feeds "seeds" (l. 49) to its young.

AN INVITATION TO THE COUNTRY (111)

These lines, addressed to Bryant's second daughter, Julia, propose that they leave their town house in "gloomy" New York for their summer home on Long Island. It was among the "sweet sounds" and "fair sights" of Roslyn, here described, that Bryant composed the majority of his poems after 1843.

THE SONG OF THE SOWER (113)

In his own manner, Bryant here suggests something of the vastness and the variety of America, its rich opportunities and its novel problems— themes on which Walt Whitman was then writing in his very different fashion.

THE CLOUD ON THE WAY (119)

The death of several friends in 1859 concentrated Bryant's thought once more on the familiar question, "How shall a man face the grave?" "The Cloud on the Way" is the poet's reply at sixty-five.

THE TIDES (121)

"The Tides" was written, Bryant declared, "in the mood in which I produce what seem to me to be my best verses" (Godwin, II, 267).

ITALY (122)

The progress of liberty in Italy always interested Bryant. On his eightieth birthday, he said: "The union of the Italian principalities under one head, and the breaking up of that anomaly in politics, the possession of political power by a priesthood, seemed, during the greater part of the fourscore years . . . an event belonging to a distant and uncertain future, yet it was drawing near by steps not apparent to the common eyes, and it came in our own day" (Godwin, II, 348). Cf. Bryant's address, "Italian Unity" (1871) in *Prose Writings*, II, 274–7, and his last public address, "Mazzini" (p. 337 above).

OUR COUNTRY'S CALL (124)

This poem and Bryant's second patriotic utterance at the outbreak of the Civil War, "Not Yet," were widely quoted and reprinted. "Our Country's Call," according to Godwin (II, 157), "helped to fill the ranks of the army and to inspire them with fortitude, trust, and endurance."

CASTLES IN THE AIR (126)

During the Civil War, the pen of the aging poet was busy with fantasies and fairy tales: "Castles in the Air," "A Tale of Cloudland," "Sella," and "The Little People of the Snow."

As this poem was not included in the edition of 1876, it is here printed from Godwin's edition of 1883.

THE POET (129)

Commonly heeding his own advice to write only when emotion moved (ll. 7–24), Bryant produced very little poetry (on an average, less than three poems per year) from 1830 onward, when public affairs and the *Post* consumed his energy. He likewise heeded his advice concerning revision (ll. 25–30), altering his poems less and less frequently as editorial duties came more and more to command his best powers.

This impassioned plea for emotional intensity in the poet is supplemented by Bryant's last important prose utterance on poetry, in the introduction to *A Library of Poetry and Song* (p. 301 above).

THE FIFTH BOOK OF HOMER'S ODYSSEY (131)

During 1863 Bryant published in the *Atlantic Monthly* extracts from a verse translation of the Fifth Book of the *Odyssey*, and in 1864 he included the entire Fifth Book in *Thirty Poems*. In 1865 he took up the *Iliad*, after the death of his wife in 1866 he occupied himself more persistently with the task, and in 1870 he published a complete translation. Meanwhile, he had returned to the *Odyssey*, and in 1871–2 he published a translation of the entire poem, in which was incorporated the earlier version of Book Five.

Bryant modestly described the project as "the most suitable literary occupation for an old man like me, who feels the necessity of being busy about something, and yet does not like hard work" (Godwin, II, 287). Perfunctory as much of the translation is, the volumes brought Bryant high praise from critics and rich financial returns from the public.

THE DEATH OF LINCOLN (139)

"Written, at the request of the Committee of Arrangements, when the body of the murdered President was carried in funeral procession through the city of New York, April, 1865." [*Godwin's note.*]

Cf. Bryant's editorials in support of Lincoln: "The Election of Lincoln" (p. 325 above) and "A Certain and an Uncertain Policy" (p. 333 above).

THE DEATH OF SLAVERY (139)

Although Bryant was able to clothe with emotion the abstract aspects of peace, liberty, and patriotism, he naturally found it difficult to write impassioned verse concerning concrete issues of the market place which he daily discussed in the *Post*—currency, free trade, abolition. Critics therefore need have expressed no surprise that his courageous attack on negro slavery was conducted almost wholly in prose. "The African Chief" (p. 56 above) is an early exception; and "The Death of Slavery," a more memorable one.

AMONG THE TREES (142)

Although Godwin is correct in stating (*Poetical Works*, II, 366) that Bryant here expresses the findings of that "philosophical speculation which, beginning with Leibnitz and ending with Lotze, ascribes consciousness to all the existences of the natural world," the poet appears to voice an old man's fancy rather than a reasoned philosophical conclusion.

92. In the edition of 1876, the word "his" is inadvertently omitted.

TREE-BURIAL (146)

In both of his final poems on the Indian, "Tree-Burial" and "Legend of the Delawares," Bryant characteristically employs the red man to exemplify the mutability of mankind.

"Tree-Burial" was originally published under an incongruous Greek title, "Dendrotaphia," probably with Browne's "Hydriotaphia" in memory.

A LIFETIME (148)

Although these stanzas at times descend to the level of doggerel, their autobiographical significance is obvious.

THE FLOOD OF YEARS (153)

Bryant's uncertainty of mind concerning the future life disappeared in his last years. Asked whether this poem expressed his own belief concerning immortality, Bryant in 1876 replied: "Certainly I believe all that is said in the lines you have quoted: otherwise I could not have written them. I believe in the everlasting life of the soul; and it seems to me that immortality would be but an imperfect gift without the recognition in the life to come of those who are dear to us" (*Poetical Works*, II, 367).

ON THE USE OF TRISYLLABIC FEET IN IAMBIC VERSE (158)

Bryant began writing this plea for freedom in versification as early as 1811, according to Godwin (*Prose Writings*, I, 56, footnote). It appeared in the *North American Review* for Sept., 1819 (IX, 426–31). Because the chief importance of this essay is historical, it is here reprinted from the original text of 1819, rather than from a revised text included in Bryant's *Prose Writings*. It has not been determined exactly when this revision was made, but it was evidently written several years after the first version. In the undated later text, the following paragraphs are inserted by way of introduction:

"Rhymed heroic verse, though one of the noblest kinds of verse in our language, has never attained its full perfection. Our ears have become so habituated to what are called smooth verses, that is, to the unvaried iambic (or as little varied as the genius of our tongue will permit), and to the sense concluding with the couplet, so as to make every two correspondent rhyming lines throughout a poem a perfect stanza, and this taste has been so long established and so often confirmed by the judgments of critics, that a very considerable literary revolution must yet take place before any improvement in the fabric of this species of verse will meet with general reception and approval. The precepts of Lord Kames and other writers, who framed their rules of versification chiefly from the writings of Pope, as the ancient critics gathered their rules for the composition of an epic poem from an analysis of the Iliad, are still in vogue; and the dogmas of Johnson on this subject are regarded with reverence, though his ear, delighted as it was with monotony, and insensible as it was to music, was wearied, as he somewhat reluctantly confessed, with the practices to which Pope so invariably adhered.

"I am aware that of late much has been done in England toward effecting an improvement in this respect; yet it has not always been done skilfully, and those who have attempted it have sometimes exhibited an odd mixture of the old manner with the new. The versification of Crabbe is least exceptionable whenever he forgets to imitate the rhythm of his predecessors. Byron seems hardly to have formed any system of versification, nor has he sufficiently studied variety; Leigh Hunt has erred in the contrary extreme, for in his story of 'Rimini,' he labors violently to be harsh; and sometimes his lines are as rugged as those of old Donne, in whom many passages are absolutely unreadable. I do not know whether those who are best qualified to judge on this subject will agree with me when I prefer the versification of Moore in his 'Veiled Prophet of Khorassan' to that of any other poet of the present day. It is true that it wants compression; it is true that many of his insufferably long periods, running through couplet after couplet, beget a suspicion that some of the fine images of which they are made up were introduced more because they were necessary to the rhyme than to the sense; but it is true likewise that there are passages free from these faults—passages which for vigorous and varied harmony are not surpassed by any in our language.

"Against the innovations proposed, however, there is still a strong party, both in England and in our own country, which numbers in its ranks men of taste and learning, elegant writers, acute and accomplished critics, against whom one would not willingly enter the lists of combat. These, although they may perhaps allow that there is a little too much monotony in the structure of Pope's lines, would yet approve a versification modelled in general upon his style. It will not, I hope, be deemed indecorous to suggest to them that the example of men, whose genius and learning we have been taught to admire almost from our cradles, is apt to mould our opinions and tastes on such subjects before we have had time to examine the reasons on which they are founded, and that to the ear which is accustomed to a certain rhythm or measured succession of sounds every other must at first seem harsh and unpleasing. No man whose poetical reading has been confined to rhyme ever comprehended at first the beauty and sweetness of blank verse; no man accustomed to one particular kind of measure will on the instant perceive all the melody of another; and it is the same with different styles of the same kind of verse. We grow attached to the manner with which we have long been familiar, and it fastens itself on our taste by a thousand pleasing associations. Where the ear is inured to the regular iambic, and to pauses at the end of every couplet, and, wherever it is possible, at the end of every line, it perceives nothing but harshness and irregularity in more varied pauses and a greater license of prosody.

"Few readers of verse can admire more than I do the acknowledged excellences of the writings of Pope—the compression which gives so much force to his precepts and so much point to his wit, and the dexterity and felicity of his satire, and I speak of his merits or his faults here only as they relate to his versification. He must be regarded as in a great measure the founder and perfector of that style of versification which prevailed as well among his contemporaries as among those who wrote after him till a very few years since, and for the adoption of which, by the poet and his admirers, it is not difficult to account. Everybody who has heard children or illiterate persons read poetry must have remarked their peculiar notion of quantity. In reading verses of six, eight, or ten syllables, they make an iambic of every foot, placing a marked stress upon every other syllable, in defiance of accent and emphasis, and pausing at the end of every line, to the utter destruction of the sense, in order to preserve the jingle of the rhyme. This puerile habit is not apt to be corrected until we become sick of the chime and the see-saw, from a wider acquaintance with poetical examples, and begin to perceive a beauty in variety. In some instances, in fact, it continues during life, as those can attest who have heard the devotional poetry of Dr. Watts from the lips of many of our reverend clergy. This habit is acquired at first from observing the general structure of verse; as, for example, that an iambic is the basis of lines of ten syllables, and the trochee of lines of seven syllables, and as general rules pass always before exceptions, the introduction of any other feet into these kinds of verse, except of the iambic in the one and of the trochee in the other, seems to the unpracticed and inexperienced ear irregular, unpleasing, and a manifest trasgression of the laws of metre.

"We are not, therefore, to wonder that Pope—who wrote his pastorals (which his admirers call his most perfect specimen of melodious numbers) at an age when he could hardly be supposed to have divested himself of childish taste—should have adhered, when he acquired a greater command of language, as uniformly as possible to the iambic, and should have contrived pauses in the sense at the end of every couplet, and often at the end of every line, so that the rhyme might be readily perceived without violence to the meaning. Nor is it any more a matter of surprise that this way of versification should have been so favorably received. It was novel, it was uniform in the quantity beyond all former example, and the pauses were balanced with singular regularity. The multitudes who read poetry like children found the manner in some measure reconciled with the meaning. And all this was brought about with such rare ease and so little embarrassment in the diction that, on the whole, the effect was extremely imposing, and well calculated to attract admiration, were it merely as a specimen of ingenuity. It was, moreover, natural that Pope, seeing the applause which this style of versification had gained him, should have gone on writing verses in the same way to the end of his life, and it was equally natural that his success should have led those who wrote in his own time and after him to imitate so pleasing a model.

"But to the more immediate purpose of this paper, which is to show, particularly by citations from the older poets, that there may be departures from the accepted rules without marring the beauty of the structure."

In revising the essay, Bryant identified one of "our latest modern poets," from whom he quoted on p. 163, as Thomas Moore, and the poem as "The Veiled Prophet."

That the use of trisyllabic feet in iambic measure required defence in America was demonstrated as late as 1832, when Bryant was rebuked for introducing trisyllabics among his own iambics (see extract from *American Quarterly Review*, March, 1832, pp. 373 f. above).

REVIEW OF SOLYMAN BROWN, *AN ESSAY ON AMERICAN POETRY* (165)

At the request of Willard Phillips, Bryant reviewed Solyman Brown, *An Essay on American Poetry, with Several Miscellaneous Pieces* . . . (New Haven: 1818), for the *North American Review* in July, 1818. The "Essay," a versified survey of classical and modern poetry, Bryant riddled with unsparing sarcasm; and the fugitive poems and notes which followed, he damned by quoting ridiculous excerpts. Finally, he disposed of the unfortunate author in two sentences: "Mr. Brown has fallen into a great mistake in thinking himself qualified to write a book. In the present instance, with talents of a very humble order, he has assumed a very pompous tone, and made a great parade of small acquisitions."

Bryant's own discussion of American poetry which prefaced this criticism of Brown is here reprinted from the *North American Review* (VII, 198–207). Godwin published the essay from what he described as "a corrected copy" (*Prose Writings*, I, 45, footnote), but he does not state when or by whom the corrections were made.

REVIEW OF CATHERINE M. SEDGWICK, *REDWOOD* (176)

During his years as a lawyer in Great Barrington, Bryant became closely acquainted with the distinguished Sedgwick family of Stockbridge, Mass., including Catherine Maria Sedgwick, the novelist. In the *North American Review* for April, 1825, he reviewed her novel *Redwood* (New York: 1824). His comments on *Redwood* are prefaced by the vigorous defence of American themes in prose fiction which is reprinted in the present volume. (Cf. Bryant's exposition of the resources of America for the poet in the lecture, "On Poetry in Its Relation to Our Age and Country," p. 203 above.) The review concludes with the following plea for patriotism in the treatment of native characters:

"The peculiarities in the manners and character of our countrymen, have too long been connected with ideas merely low and ludicrous. We complain of our English neighbors for holding them up as objects simply ridiculous and laughable, but it is by no means certain that we have not encouraged them by our example. It is time, however, that they were redeemed from these gross and degrading associations. It is time that they should be mentioned, as they deserve to be, with something else than a sneer, and that a feeling of respect should mingle with the smile they occasion. We are happy to see the author of this work connecting them, as we find them connected in real life, with much that is ennobling and elevated, with traits of sagacity, benevolence, moral courage and magnanimity. These are qualities, which by no means impair any comic effect those peculiarities may have; they rather relieve and heighten it. They transform it from mere buffoonery to the finest humor. When this is done, something is done to exalt our national reputation abroad, and to improve our national character at home. It is also a sort of public benefit, to show what copious and valuable materials the private lives and daily habits of our countrymen offer to the writer of genius. It is as if one were to discover to us rich ores and gems lying in the common earth about us."

The text of these extracts follows the *North American Review*, XX, 246-56. The passage entitled "Romance" has not hitherto been reprinted.

LECTURES ON POETRY (184)

Newly arrived in New York where he sought to establish himself as a man of letters, Bryant in 1825 was invited to speak on poetry before the Athenæum Society. The result was a series of four lectures, delivered in April, 1826, but not published until 1884, when they were included in the *Prose Writings* edited by Godwin. Godwin's text is here followed.

For comment on these lectures, see pp. lviii ff. above.

A BORDER TRADITION (224)

This tale was published anonymously in the *United States Review and Literary Gazette* in Oct., 1826 (I, 40-52). In the library of the late Charles Taylor of Great Barrington, Mass., there is a copy of the tale with a memorandum naming Bryant as the author. This attribution has recently been substantiated by Mr. C. I. Glicksberg (*New England Quarterly*, VII, 687-701, Dec., 1934).

The surroundings of Great Barrington correspond with the setting of "A Border Tradition"; and Great Barrington was settled by both Dutch and Yankees, as is the village here described. It may be assumed, there-fore, that "A Border Tradition" was inspired not only by the American sketches of Washington Irving, whose influence on "A Border Tradition" is obvious, but also by Bryant's own interest in New England scenes and characters.

RECOLLECTIONS OF THE SOUTH OF SPAIN (240)

"Recollections of the South of Spain" was published in *The Talisman for 1829* (New York: 1828), pp. 43–51. It appears with slight editorial changes in *Prose Writings*, where it is combined with a second essay, "Early Spanish Poetry," under the title, "Moriscan Romances." "Recol-lections of the South of Spain" is here reprinted from Bryant's original text in *The Talisman*.

Since Bryant had not visited Europe when he wrote this essay, his allusions to experiences in Spain are of course fictitious. For his treatment of Spanish literature, see p. liii above.

THE INDIAN SPRING (245)

Although the success of Cooper's novels of the frontier undoubtedly encouraged Bryant to write this tale, he here portrays Indian character and handles the problems of narration in his own fashion. Cf. his poems on Indian life, discussed on pp. xlv ff. above.

"The Indian Spring" was published in *The Talisman for 1830* (New York: 1829), pp. 7–26, and was collected after his death in *Prose Writings*. It is here reprinted from the original text of *The Talisman*.

A LETTER FROM ILLINOIS (258)

This letter, written in 1832 by Bryant to his wife, during his first visit to his brothers on the Illinois frontier, was published in 1884 as part of "Illinois Fifty Years Ago" in *Prose Writings* and is here reprinted from that text.

Compare the enthusiastic poems written in the same year, "The Prairies" (p. 74 above) and "The Hunter of the Prairies" (p. xlviii above), with this realistic letter and "An Excursion to Rock River," written in 1841 (p. 267 above).

LETTERS OF A TRAVELLER (264)

Bryant was an active traveller not only in the Western states, but in the South, the West Indies, Europe, and the Near East. His surprisingly uncritical records of things seen were first printed in the *Post* and then collected as *Letters of a Traveller* (1850), *Letters of a Traveller, Second Series* (1859), and *Letters from the East* (1869). In these extracts, the text is that of the first collected editions.

DISCOURSE ON THE LIFE AND GENIUS OF COOPER (273)

When Bryant first met Cooper in 1824, the quiet New Englander was disconcerted by the novelist's vigor: "Mr. Cooper engrossed the whole conversation, and seems a little giddy with the great success his books have met with" (Godwin, I, 189). Later, Bryant was impressed by Cooper's evident sensitiveness: "He seems to think his own works his own property, instead of being the property of the public, to whom he has given them" (*idem*, I, 221). Meanwhile, the two met in friendly fashion at dinners and literary gatherings; each came to respect the other; but it was impossible that they should become intimate.

On Feb. 25, 1852, Bryant delivered his discourse on Cooper before the New York Historical Society, with Daniel Webster in the chair and Irving among the audience. Although Cooper was still widely unpopular because of his keen strictures on American society and his battle with the press, Bryant courageously praised his honesty and right-mindedness. Particularly creditable to Bryant is his appreciation of Cooper's services as a social critic—services which, until recent years, literary historians have been slow to recognize.

This text is that of the first printing of the "Discourse," in *Memorial to James Fenimore Cooper*. New York: [1852].

A DISCOURSE ON THE LIFE, CHARACTER AND GENIUS OF WASHINGTON IRVING (289)

Bryant and Irving did not meet until after the latter's return in 1832 from England, where he had generously found a publisher for Bryant's poems. (For Irving's opinion of his countryman's poetry, see the former's preface to the London edition of 1832, p. 375 above.) The controversy which later arose because Irving as editor had allowed a line in "The Song of Marion's Men" to be altered to avoid offending British readers (see p. 375 above) caused no permanent ill will between the two; and their later contacts, while not frequent, were always pleasant.

On April 3, 1860, Bryant delivered this memorial address on Irving, before the New York Historical Society. His boyish delight in Knickerbocker's *History of New York*, his critical appreciation of Irving's contribution to native letters, and his personal knowledge of Irving's amiability of character combined to make the *Discourse* unvaryingly sympathetic and appreciative.

The original text of 1860 is followed in the present volume.

INTRODUCTION TO *A LIBRARY OF POETRY AND SONG* (301)

These remarks on the luminous style are preceded in the "Introduction" by a brief historical résumé of English poetry. Here Bryant touches on

Chaucer, Spenser, Milton, Dryden, Pope, Wordsworth (p. xlv, footnote, above), Byron (p. xlii, footnote, above), and others.

As early as 1824, Bryant had defended simplicity of style: "An inverted style, by occupying the reader with the search of a meaning, and a diffuse style, by wasting his attention on epithets and expletives, which add nothing to the progress of the story, tend of course to distract the attention and impair the general effect. An elaborate magnificence of diction, overlaying the merely narrative parts of a poem, is like a load of costly drapery about the limbs of a competitor in a foot race" (review of Henry Pikering, *The Ruins of Pæstum*, in *North American Review*, XIX, 427, July, 1824).

EDITORIALS IN THE *NEW YORK EVENING POST* (303)

Bryant's honesty and courage as editor of the *Post* from 1827 to 1878 made him one of the most influential journalists in nineteenth-century America. Because he was always vigorous and because his temper occasionally slipped the leash, he was also known among his contemporaries as an aggressive, not to say a violent, editor. Thus sympathetic reviewers of his poetry found it surprising that serene and elevated verse could come from the pen which wrote ironical and caustic editorials for the *Post*. And Bryant's political opponents described him, with partisan bias, as "virulent" and "malignant." (For an excellent narrative of Bryant's career as editor, see Allan Nevins, *The Evening Post*.)

The editorials in the present collection are reprinted from the original texts in the *Post*. Four items ("Freedom of Speech," "Mr. Webster's Wit," "The Corn-Law Controversy," and "Friar Tuck Legislation") appear in revised form in Bryant's *Prose Writings*, altered, it appears, by Godwin.

THE REMOVAL OF THE DEPOSITS (303)

As an advocate of sound currency, Bryant supported President Andrew Jackson in the latter's campaign against the Bank of the United States. This satirical comment on the defeat of the Bank is more bookish in style than Bryant's later editorials. It was published Sept. 23, 1833.

THE RIGHT OF WORKMEN TO STRIKE (305)

For many years, the *Post* suffered financially because New York business men withheld advertising from its columns on the ground that Bryant was a champion of the laboring man. Typical was his defense of a group of tailors who were fined in New York City for organizing a union and refusing to work at unjust wages. This sane editorial on the right to strike was considered inflammatory when it appeared on June 13, 1836.

FREEDOM OF SPEECH (308)

Bryant's sincere devotion to the cause of human liberty was here reinforced by his equally sincere professional concern for the freedom of the press. The editorial was published August 8, 1836.

THE DEATH OF LOVEJOY (310)

Bryant's sternness in condemning the killing of Lovejoy may be attributed to his devotion both to abolition and to free speech. The editorial appeared on Nov. 18, 1837.

MR. WEBSTER'S WIT (312)

On occasion, Bryant was even more severe in his strictures on Daniel Webster than in this heavily ironical editorial, published Nov. 20, 1837. (For Bryant's attitude toward Webster, see p. xx above.)

THE CORN LAW CONTROVERSY (314)

Ever an advocate of free trade, Bryant missed no opportunity of arguing the question before the American public (cf. "Freedom of Exchange," *Prose Writings*, II, 242–56). "The Corn-Law Controversy" was published August 24, 1843.

FRIAR TUCK LEGISLATION (317)

Bryant as a free trader believed that Americans who profited by high tariffs were little better than highway robbers. This somewhat circuitous statement of that belief was published April 26, 1844.

A NEW PUBLIC PARK (319)

Bryant was apparently the first to campaign for an adequate public park for New York; and to him goes much of the credit for the opening of Central Park in that city. This plea for such a park was published July 3, 1844.

A SHORT METHOD WITH DISUNIONISTS (320)

Bryant had long since abandoned the youthful faith in states' rights which had made him defend the possible secession of New England during the second war with England (see p. xvi above) when he published this editorial on Sept. 26, 1855.

THE NEW FEDERAL CONSTITUTION (322)

Here Bryant vehemently refuses to accept as constitutional the Dred Scott decision, contending that this ruling of the Supreme Court, if allowed to stand, abrogates the federal constitution. The editorial was published March 9, 1857.

THE ELECTION OF LINCOLN (325)

Bryant's opinion of Lincoln is discussed on p. xxii above. See also "A Certain and an Uncertain Policy," p. 333 above. These paragraphs are taken from an editorial entitled "The Result of Yesterday's Election," published Nov. 7, 1860.

PEACEABLE SECESSION AN ABSURDITY (327)

The *Post* was a determined foe of the "monstrous and absurd doctrine" of nullification. This editorial appeared on Nov. 12, 1860.

WHAT THE "CONSERVATIVES" WANT (332)

This editorial of July 3, 1862, is typical of the vigorous assaults on greed and corruption made by Bryant for a half-century in the columns of the *Post*.

A CERTAIN AND AN UNCERTAIN POLICY (333)

Here Bryant, convinced at last that Lincoln was conducting the war wisely, eulogizes the President's policy in a plea for his re-election. The editorial was published on Sept. 20, 1864.

MAZZINI (337)

On May 29, 1878, Bryant made his last public appearance, delivering this brief address at the unveiling of a bust of Mazzini in Central Park, New York. For earlier evidence of Bryant's interest in the cause of Italian freedom and unity, see "Italy," p. 122 above.

This address is reprinted from the *Prose Writings* of 1884.

THE EMBARGO (341)

Dr. Peter Bryant took this poem by his son, aged thirteen, to Boston where it was printed in a small edition in 1808. (For a contemporary review of the poem, see p. 363 above.) A year later, a revision, with additional poems, appeared. (For a discussion of the poem and its revision, see "The Juvenile Verse of William Cullen Bryant," *Studies in Philology*, XXVI, 103–11.) Bryant did not include "The Embargo" among his collected poems, and during his late years was irritated when it was mentioned. The poem is here collected for the first time, the text being that of the rare first edition.

TO A FRIEND ON HIS MARRIAGE (348)

This poem was written in 1813 when Bryant was studying law at Worthington, Mass. (not at Bridgewater, as stated by Godwin), and was addressed to a friend who may now be identified as Jacob Porter of Plainfield. "To a Friend on His Marriage" was published at Cambridge in 1813 in a pamphlet prepared by Porter: *To the Memory of Mrs. Betsey Porter*. Heretofore the reprinting of the poem in the *North American Review*, VI, 384–5 (March, 1818), has been accepted as its first appearance. This text is that of the pamphlet of 1813.

NOT THAT FROM LIFE, AND ALL ITS WOES (350)

Written in 1814, during Bryant's period of Byronic despair, this poem was copied with "Thanatopsis" by Dr. Peter Bryant and submitted by him to the *North American Review*, where the two poems were published as one. It has occasionally been suggested that Bryant himself, like the editors of the *Review*, considered "Not That from Life" an integral part of "Thanatopsis." Among his own manuscripts, however, the poems appear separately; and the first draft of "Thanatopsis" is there prefaced, not by these quatrains, but by a blank verse introduction.

"Not That from Life" is here reprinted from the *North American Review*, Sept., 1817.

A CHORUS OF GHOSTS (351)

These melancholy lines, written in 1814 and published in 1826, were not included among Bryant's collected poems. They are here reprinted from the *New-York Review*, March, 1826.

In an early manuscript, stanza four is omitted and the following lines appear as stanza seven:

> There is no tie that binds to life,
> No charm that wins thy stay;
> Tomorrow none will recollect
> That thou didst live today.

THIS GRASSY SLOPE, THIS ANCIENT TREE (352)

These lines, part of an unfinished poem on nature in New England, are here published for the first time, from the original manuscript in the possession of the Minna G. Goddard Estate.

FAREWELL—THE BITTER WORD IS SAID (353)

In 1817 and again in 1819, Frances Fairchild visited her sister in East Bloomfield, New York, then a primitive settlement in the wilderness. These lines express Bryant's grief over his separation (probably in 1819) from the young woman who was to become his wife. The poem is now published for the first time, from the original manuscript in the possession of the Minna G. Goddard Estate.

THEY TAUGHT ME, AND IT WAS A FEARFUL CREED (353)

This fragment, clearly revealing Bryant's fear of death, is here published for the first time, from the original manuscript in the possession of the Minna G. Goddard Estate.

HOUSATONIC (354)

"Housatonic" is one of several poems recording Bryant's love for Frances Fairchild. Cf. the vastly superior lines, "Oh Fairest of the Rural Maids," p. 14 above. "Housatonic" is here published for the first time, from the original manuscript in the possession of the Minna G. Goddard Estate.

The Housatonic River flows through Great Barrington, Mass.

THE EARLY ANEMONE (355)

Possibly Bryant refrained from publishing "The Early Anemone" because of its evident resemblance to Wordsworth's utterances on nature. It is here published for the first time, from the original manuscript in the possession of the Minna G. Goddard Estate.

THE ROBBER (356)

"The Robber" was well received by the American public: Nathaniel Parker Willis praised the poem, and it was reprinted in the *Atlantic Club-Room* (New York: 1834) and the *Chaplet of Roses* (New York: 1851). Bryant planned to include it among his collected poems but was dissuaded by his close friend and constant critic, Richard Henry Dana, Sr. (Godwin, I, 299). As an example of Bryant's ill-advised excursions in the grotesque, it is here reprinted from the *New-York Mirror*, XI, 4 (July 6, 1833).

INDEX

421